SOURCES FOR EUROPE IN THE MODERN WORLD

WITH GUIDED WRITING EXERCISES

Edited by Allison Scardino Belzer
GEORGIA SOUTHERN UNIVERSITY

and

Edited by Jonathan S. Perry
UNIVERSITY OF SOUTH FLORIDA—SARASOTA-MANATEE

Writing Exercises by Catherine Johnson and Katharine Beals

NEW YORK   OXFORD
OXFORD UNIVERSITY PRESS

Oxford University Press is a department of the University of Oxford.
It furthers the University's objective of excellence in research, scholarship,
and education by publishing worldwide. Oxford is a registered trade mark
of Oxford University Press in the UK and certain other countries.

Published in the United States of America by Oxford University Press
198 Madison Avenue, New York, NY 10016, United States of America.

Library of Congress Cataloging-in-Publication Data

Names: Belzer, Allison Scardino, editor. | Berenson, Edward, 1949- Europe
  in the modern world.
Title: Sources and writing exercises for Europe in the modern world /
  edited by Allison Scardino Belzer, Georgia Southern University and Jonathan S. Perry, University
of South Florida, Sarasota-Manatee; with Catherine
  Johnson, Katharine Beals.
Description: Second edition. | New York : Oxford University Press, [2021] |
  Includes bibliographical references. | Summary: "A higher education
  history primary source textbook to accompany Edward Berenson's Europe in
  the Modern World, Second Edition"— Provided by publisher.
Identifiers: LCCN 2020005790 (print) | LCCN 2020005791 (ebook) | ISBN
  9780190078898 (paperback) | ISBN 9780190085896 (epub) | ISBN
  9780190084974
Subjects: LCSH: Europe—History—1492—Sources.
Classification: LCC D208 .S5748 2021 (print) | LCC D208 (ebook) | DDC
  940.2—dc23
LC record available at https://lccn.loc.gov/2020005790
LC ebook record available at https://lccn.loc.gov/2020005791

9 8 7 6 5 4 3 2 1

Printed by Sheridan Books, Inc., United States of America

CONTENTS

HOW TO READ A PRIMARY SOURCE

This sourcebook is composed of 105 primary sources. A primary source is any text, image, or other source of information that gives us a firsthand account of the past created by someone who witnessed or participated in the historical event in question. While such sources can provide significant and fascinating insight into the past, they must also be read carefully to limit modern assumptions about historical modes of thought. Here are a few elements to keep in mind when approaching a primary source.

AUTHORSHIP

Who produced this source of information? A man or a woman? A member of the elite or of the lower class? An outsider looking in at an event or an insider looking out? What profession or lifestyle did the author pursue which might influence how he or she recorded the information?

GENRE

What type of source are you examining? Different genres—categories of material—have different goals and stylistic elements. For example, a personal letter meant exclusively for the eyes of a distant relative might include unveiled opinions and relatively trivial pieces of information, like the writer's vacation plans. On the other hand, a political speech intended to convince a nation of a leader's point of view might subdue personal opinions beneath artful rhetoric and focus on large issues like national welfare or war. "Reading" a visual source such as a painting or an object requires observing details that go beyond a first impression.

AUDIENCE

Who is reading, listening to, or observing the source? Is it a public or private audience? National or international? Religious or nonreligious? The source may be geared toward the expectations of a particular group; it may be recorded in a language that is specific to a particular group. Identifying audience can help us understand why the author chose a certain tone or why he or she included certain types of information.

HISTORICAL CONTEXT

When and why was this source produced? On what date? For what purposes? What historical moment does the source address? It is paramount that we approach primary sources in context to avoid anachronism (attributing an idea or habit to a past era where it does not belong) and faulty judgment. For example, when considering a medieval record, we must take account of the fact that in the Middle Ages the widespread understanding was that God created the world and could still interfere in the activity of mankind—such as sending a terrible storm when a community had sinned. Knowing the context helps us to avoid importing modern assumptions—like the fact that storms are caused by atmospheric pressure—into historical texts. In this way we can read the source more faithfully, carefully, and generously.

BIAS AND FRAMING

Is there an overt argument being made by the source? Did the author have a particular agenda? Did any political or social motives underlie the reasons for writing the document? Does the document exhibit any qualities that offer clues about the author's intentions?

STYLISTIC ELEMENTS

Stylistic features such as tone, vocabulary, word choice, and the manner in which the material is organized and presented should also be considered when examining a source. They can provide insight into the creator's perspective and offer additional context for considering a source in its entirety.

NEW AND EXPANDED FOR THIS EDITION

CHAPTER 1

- 1.4 The Council of Trent, *Canons on the Sacraments*, 1547 and *Tridentine Index of Books*, 1564
- 1.5 The Account of Walpurga Hausmännin, Midwife Accused of Witchcraft, 1587
- 1.6 VISUAL SOURCE: François Dubois, *The Saint Bartholomew's Day Massacre in Paris*, 1572–1584

CHAPTER 2

- 2.1 Ogier Ghiselin de Busbecq on Roxelana in *The Turkish Letters*, 1555
- 2.4 Mbemba A Nzinga (Afonso I) of Kongo, Correspondence with Joao III of Portugal, 1526
- 2.6 VISUAL SOURCE: Spanish Piece of Eight Coin, 1768

CHAPTER 3

- 3.2 Robert Baillie, Letter to William Spang, August 23, 1648
- 3.3 Otto von Guericke, *The Destruction of Magdeburg in the Thirty Years' War*, 1631
- 3.4 Henry IV of France, *The Edict of Nantes*, 1598 & Louis XIV, *The Edict of Fontainebleau*, 1685
- 3.6 VISUAL SOURCE: *The Resolution of the Women of London to the Parliament*, 1642

CHAPTER 4

- 4.2 John Locke, *Second Treatise on Government*, 1689
- 4.3 Immanuel Kant, *What Is Enlightenment?* 1784
- 4.6 Mary Wollstonecraft, *A Vindication of the Rights of Woman*, 1791
- 4.7 VISUAL SOURCE: Jacques-Louis David, *Portrait of Antoine-Laurent Lavoisier and his Wife (Marie-Anne Pierette Paulze)*, 1788

CHAPTER 5

- 5.2 *Declaration of the Rights of Man and Citizen*, August 26, 1789
- 5.3 Olympe de Gouges, *The Declaration of the Rights of Woman and Citizen*, September 1791

ABOUT THE EDITORS

Allison Scardino Belzer, PhD, is a professor of History at Georgia Southern University where she teaches modern European and world history. She double majored in History and Italian at Vassar College and earned her master's and doctorate degrees at Emory University. Her book *Women and the Great War: Femininity under Fire in Italy* (Palgrave, 2010) investigates how the war affected women living at home and near the fighting front. Belzer recently authored "Literature and the Great War," a module for Oxford University Press's *Uncovering History* series. Her current research focuses on a family of British supporters of the Italian Risorgimento. The best part of her job is being in the classroom with students and sharing with them sources that make history come alive. She lives with her family in Savannah, Georgia.

Jonathan S. Perry, PhD, is an Associate Professor of History at the University of South Florida Sarasota-Manatee. He earned degrees at Ohio University (double B.A.s in History and Latin) and at the University of North Carolina at Chapel Hill (M.A. and Ph.D in History), and he has taught at a number of American and Canadian colleges, including Chapel Hill, Brevard College (N. Carolina), the University of Central Florida (Orlando), York University (Toronto), and USF-SM. He has published a series of articles on, among other topics, classical scholarship in Fascist Italy, Latin epigraphy (the study of inscriptions), sport terminology in the ancient world, and women and Greek athletics. His first book, *The Roman Collegia: The Modern Evolution of an Ancient Concept* (Brill, 2006), traces the development of a Roman concept from 1843 through the present.

ABOUT THE WRITING HISTORY EXERCISES

The discipline of history cannot be separated from the written word. And writing a paper for a history class is vastly less difficult when you are fluent in the fundamentals. That is the rationale for embedding Writing History exercises in this book. The exercises provided here and on our website will give you enough practice to write smooth and cohesive prose and do so fluently. At the same time, because all of the exercises are drawn from sentences and paragraphs in the text, they reinforce your knowledge of the material.

In the Writing History sections, we begin at the sentence level and build from there. Good writing entails, first, writing sentences, and, second, connecting those sentences into larger units of thought: into paragraphs and papers whose arguments and analyses would be impossible to create without written language.

After introducing the paper, we move on to the sophisticated elements that great writers have always used but that are rarely, if ever, explicitly taught. Here we show how the structure of the sentence allows writers to develop, and especially to refine, their thought and style. We also demonstrate how to avoid the common stylistic mistakes that can obscure the meaning of texts and conclude with a new section on sentences that use double focus to emphasize the most important material.

WRITING HISTORY TOPICS

PART I. THE SENTENCE

1. COORDINATION

Practice coordination (joining two or more independent clauses) by solving jumbled sentence puzzles and combining sentences.

2. SUBORDINATION

Practice subordination (joining dependent clauses with independent clauses) by solving jumbled sentence puzzles and combining sentences.

PART II. THE THESIS STATEMENT AND THE TOPIC SENTENCE

3. THESIS STATEMENTS

Create thesis statements using coordination and subordination.

4. THESIS ASSEMBLY

Build a thesis statement from a series of factual statements or claims.

5. THE THESIS STATEMENT AND ITS SUPPORTING IDEAS

Use the principle of parallelism to build a set of one-sentence supporting ideas (topic sentences) on the base of the thesis sentence.

PART III. THE PARAGRAPH

6. COHESION ACROSS SENTENCES

Revise incoherent paragraphs to create cohesive "known-new" links between each sentence.

7. PARAGRAPH FLOW

Revise incoherent paragraphs for cohesion.

8. TEXT RECONSTRUCTION

Restore a paragraph's jumbled sentences to original order using text reconstruction.

9. TEXT RECONSTRUCTION AND COMPOSITION

Continue the techniques of text reconstruction by first arranging sentences and then, after some time has elapsed, producing your own version of the paragraphs.

PART IV. THE PAPER

10. PAPER RECONSTRUCTION

Restore a paper's jumbled paragraphs to the original order using text reconstruction.

11. ANALYZING AND SORTING MATERIAL INTO MAIN IDEAS

Divide a list of phrases or sentences into thesis statement, supporting ideas (topic sentences), and evidence.

PART V. TOOLS FOR REFINING MEANING AND CORRECTING STYLISTIC MISTAKES

12. CREATING THE COMPLEX NOUN PHRASES OF ACADEMIC WRITING

Learn to write more efficiently by using noun phrases to reduce the number of words in a sentence.

13. USING PASSIVE VOICE, *IT*-SHIFTS, AND *WHAT*-SHIFTS TO TELL YOUR READER WHAT MATTERS MOST

Learn techniques for adding emphasis.

14. USING PARALLELISM TO SIMPLIFY COMPLEX IDEAS

Use techniques to revise mediocre paragraphs into stylish and coherent texts.

15. USING COORDINATION AND SUBORDINATION TO FIND AND FIX COMMON PUNCTUATION MISTAKES

Identify and correct classic coordination mistakes, such as run-on sentences and comma splices, and subordination mistakes, such as sentence fragments and dangling modifiers.

EPILOGUE. DOUBLE FOCUS

Use the technique of "double focus" to emphasize the most important ideas in a sentence.

ABOUT THE WRITING HISTORY CONTRIBUTORS

Catherine Johnson, PhD, is the coauthor, with John Ratey, of Shadow Syndromes (1997) and, with Temple Grandin, of Animals in Translation (2005) and Animals Make Us Human (2010). She teaches writing at the college level and was trained in precision teaching at Morningside Academy's Summer School Institute. Catherine and her husband, Ed Berenson, live in Westchester County outside New York City and have three sons.

Katharine Beals, PhD, is an adjunct professor at the Drexel University School of Education and a lecturer at the University of Pennsylvania Graduate School of Education. She holds a doctorate in linguistics from the University of Chicago, and her specialties include English syntax and pragmatics. She is a coauthor of Speech and Language Technologies for Language Disorders (2015) and the author of Raising a Left-Brain Child in a Right-Brain World (2009).

CHAPTER 1

THE AGE OF RELIGIOUS REFORM, 1490–1648

1.1 MARTIN LUTHER, *95 THESES*, 1517

While he was dutifully preparing lectures for his students at the University of Wittenberg, Martin Luther (1483–1546) was confronted with a real-world problem that seemed to call on his particular expertise: the theological implications of the sale of "indulgences"—papal letters designed to smooth a sinner's route to heaven. As Luther knew, indulgences had become little more than a means to empty the pockets of believers into the coffers of the Church.

In 1515, Pope Leo X authorized the selling of new indulgences to inhabitants of the Holy Roman Empire. He did so to enable Prince Albert of Hohenzollern, the Archbishop of Magdeburg, to pay the large fee that Leo had imposed in exchange for allowing the prince—against all precedent—to become archbishop of two cities at once, Magdeburg and now Mainz. Albert then enlisted the prodigiously wealthy Fugger banking family to advance Leo the agreed-upon amount and also to oversee the sale of indulgences. The pope, who owed part of his personal wealth as a Medici to loans to papal candidates before him, used half of the sum raised by Albert's agents to fund the rebuilding of St. Peter's Basilica in Rome.

Luther took particular exception to the cleric Johann Tetzel, who sold indulgences with a sales pitch that had made him famous: "As soon as the coin in the coffer rings, the soul into Heaven springs." He responded to Tetzel with a series of debating propositions that constituted a thoroughgoing attack on the selling of indulgences and other abuses he believed the Church was inflicting on uninformed Christians. Luther's propositions took the form of 95 "theses" written in sophisticated Latin and nailed, on October 31, 1517, to the door of Wittenberg's cathedral. There has long been a scholarly debate over whether Luther actually posted his theses on the church door, but recent scholarship strongly suggest that he did just that. His theses were translated into German and disseminated throughout the German-speaking lands of the Holy Roman Empire. Notice in the excerpts below how Luther turns the tables on the indulgence sellers and their supposed rationales, especially in Theses 28, 50, and 75.

From Kurt Aland, ed., *Martin Luther's 95 Theses* (St. Louis, MO: Concordia Publishing House, 1967), pp. 50–52, 54, and 56–57.

Out of love and zeal for truth and the desire to bring it to light, the following theses will be publicly discussed at Wittenberg under the chairmanship of the reverend father Martin Luther, Master of Arts and Sacred Theology and regularly appointed Lecturer on these subjects at that place. He requests that those who cannot be present to debate orally with us will do so by letter.

In the Name of Our Lord Jesus Christ. Amen.

1. When our Lord and Master Jesus Christ said, "Repent" [Matt. 4:17], he willed the entire life of believers to be one of repentance.
2. This word cannot be understood as referring to the sacrament of penance, that is, confession and satisfaction, as administered by the clergy.
3. Yet it does not mean solely inner repentance; such inner repentance is worthless unless it produces various outward mortifications of the flesh.
4. The penalty of sin remains as long as the hatred of self, that is, true inner repentance, until our entrance into the kingdom of heaven.
5. The pope neither desires nor is able to remit any penalties except those imposed by his own authority or that of the canons.
6. The pope cannot remit any guilt, except by declaring and showing that it has been remitted by God; or, to be sure, by remitting guilt in cases reserved to his judgment. If his right to grant remission in these cases were disregarded, the guilt would certainly remain unforgiven.

. . .

18. Furthermore, it does not seem proved, either by reason or Scripture, that souls in purgatory are outside the state of merit, that is, unable to grow in love.
19. Nor does it seem proved that souls in purgatory, at least not all of them, are certain and assured of their own salvation, even if we ourselves may be entirely certain of it.
20. Therefore the pope, when he uses the words "plenary remission of all penalties," does not actually mean "all penalties," but only those imposed by himself.

21. Thus those indulgence preachers are in error who say that a man is absolved from every penalty and saved by papal indulgences.
22. As a matter of fact, the pope remits to souls in purgatory no penalty which, according to canon law, they should have paid in this life.
23. If remission of all penalties whatsoever could be granted to anyone at all, certainly it would be granted only to the most perfect, that is, to very few.
24. For this reason most people are necessarily deceived by that indiscriminate and high-sounding promise of release from penalty.
25. That power which the pope has in general over purgatory corresponds to the power which any bishop or curate has in a particular way in his own diocese or parish.
26. The pope does very well when he grants remission to souls in purgatory, not by the power of the keys, which he does not have, but by way of intercession for them.
27. They preach only human doctrines who say that as soon as the money clinks into the money chest, the soul flies out of purgatory.
28. It is certain that when money clinks in the money chest, greed and avarice can be increased; but when the church intercedes, the result is in the hands of God alone.

. . .

49. Christians are to be taught that papal indulgences are useful only if they do not put their trust in them, but very harmful if they lose their fear of God because of them.
50. Christians are to be taught that if the pope knew the exactions of the indulgence preachers, he would rather that the basilica of St. Peter were burned to ashes than built up with the skin, flesh, and bones of his sheep.

. . .

71. Let him who speaks against the truth concerning papal indulgences be anathema and accursed;

72. But let him who guards against the lust and license of the indulgence preachers be blessed;

73. Just as the pope justly thunders against those who by any means whatsoever contrive harm to the sale of indulgences.

74. But much more does he intend to thunder against those who use indulgences as a pretext to contrive harm to holy love and truth.

75. To consider papal indulgences so great that they could absolve a man even if he had done the impossible and had violated the mother of God is madness.

STUDY QUESTIONS

1. How do these individual "theses" build upon each other logically? Is Luther using logic and reason in the debate more often than the literal words of the Bible?

2. How do the theses combine practical matters and specific instances with a generally theological approach? Why might Luther have employed this technique?

1.2 THOMAS MÜNTZER, *A HIGHLY PROVOKED DEFENSE*, 1524

Thomas Müntzer (c. 1490–1525), an early supporter of Luther's innovations, took control of a group of Protestant reformers at Allstedt (Holy Roman Empire) in 1523 and quickly created a theocratic government based on the literal words of the Bible. He became incensed with what he considered Luther's betrayal of Protestant principle, especially in Luther's 1523 *Letter to the Princes of Saxony*, which sided with the princes against the peasantry. Müntzer believed that Luther was nothing more than a *"Gaistloße Sanfft lebende fleysch"* ("a [Holy] Spirit-less, soft-living Flesh") who had traded the best interests of the Saxon peasants for a comfortable living at the side of the Saxon nobility. Müntzer styled himself as the spiritual advisor of peasants whose radical understanding of the Bible, made possible by Luther's accessible German translation, convinced them to shake off the bonds with which their lords had shackled them.

So devoted was Müntzer to the peasants' cause that put his life on the line, participating on May 15, 1525 in an armed rebellion at Frankenhausen that was quickly put down by soldiers of the Holy Roman Empire. Müntzer was captured, tortured until he recanted his "heresies," and executed. Luther was so hostile to this rebellion and to the Peasants' War (1524–1526) overall that he vigorously denounced them in what became one of his most famous pamphlets, *Against the Robbing and Murdering Hordes of Peasants*. In that document, Luther compared the peasant rebels to rabid dogs and advised the German lords to "stab, smite, and slay" them. In siding with the German nobility, Luther made clear how much he differed from Müntzer, who had denounced him along with the lords.

Tryntje Helfferich, ed. and trans., *On the Freedom of a Christian, with Related Texts* (Indianapolis: Hackett, 2013), pp. 105–115. Reprinted by permission of Hackett Publishing Company, Inc. All rights reserved.

Highly Provoked Defense and Answer against the Spiritless, Soft-Living Flesh at Wittenberg Who, in a Perverse Manner and through the Theft of the Holy Scripture, Has Most Miserably Defiled Wretched Christendom. Thomas Müntzer of Allstedt.

. . .

For this reason, it is no great wonder that the most ambitious scribe, Doctor Liar [Müntzer here makes a pun on Luther's name, since the word "*Lügner*" means "Liar" in German], becomes a more haughty fool every day, cloaking himself with Your Holy Scripture and availing himself of it in the most deceptive manner, without any mortal injury to his own fame and comfort. First and foremost, and as if he had gained Your judgment (through You, the gates of truth), he will have nothing to do with You (Isa. 58:2–3), and so is bold to Your face and fundamentally despises Your true Spirit. He declares himself here clearly and irrevocably in that, out of a raging envy and through the most bitter hate, and without any honest, truthful cause, he makes me—who is Your vested member and within You—a laughingstock in front of his derisive, mocking, and most ferocious associates. And, as an irreparable offense against me, he vilifies me as a Satan or devil before the simple people, and, with his perverse, blasphemous judgment, reviles and mocks me.

But in You I am delighted, and I am fully satisfied through Your mild consolation, for as You stated most pleasantly to Your dear friends in Matthew 10:24: "The disciple is not above the master." Since they have blasphemously called You Beelzebub—who are an innocent duke and comforting Savior—how much more will they attack me, Your undaunted foot soldier, after I have followed Your voice (John 10:3–5) and spoken out against that flattering scoundrel at Wittenberg? Indeed, things must happen in this way, if one will not allow the soft-living know-it-alls, with their contrived faith and Pharisaical deceits, to be seen as right, but will ensure that their fame and grandeur collapse. You too were unable to gain the respect of those of Your time. They let themselves think that they were more learned than You and Your disciples. Indeed, with their literalistic presumption, they were surely more learned than Doctor Mockery [another pun on Luther's name, this time in Latin, since "*Ludibrii*" means "Of Mockery"] could ever be. . . .

Shame on you, Luther, you arch-knave! Will you insinuate yourself with an erring world (Luke 9:25), and will you justify all mankind? You know well, however, whom you shall malign: the poor monks and priests and merchants; they cannot defend themselves, thus you can easily vilify them. But you say no one should judge the godless rulers, even if they tread Christ underfoot. To satisfy the peasants, you wrote that the princes will be shattered through the word of God. And you say in your commentary on the recent imperial mandate: "The princes will be toppled from their thrones." Yet you still esteem them as greater than merchants. You should tweak the noses of your princes too. They have deserved it much more perhaps than the others. Which of their rents, extortions, etc., have they given up? Although you have chastised the princes, you can easily give them renewed courage, you new pope, by giving them monasteries and churches. Then they will be satisfied with you. This is what I would advise you! Otherwise the peasants may chime in! . . .

O Doctor Liar, you treacherous fox, through your lies you have saddened the heart of the righteous, whom God has not afflicted. Thereby you have strengthened the power of the godless evildoers, so that they remain set on their old paths. Thus you will suffer the same fate as a captured fox. The people will be free, and God alone will be lord over them!

STUDY QUESTIONS

1. What did Müntzer take to be Luther's true motive in undertaking reform? What evidence did he have for this conclusion?
2. How does Müntzer threaten Luther and his supporters with the force of the "peasants"? Why?

1.3 RECORDS FROM JOHN CALVIN'S GENEVA, 1542–1547

When John Calvin (1509–1564) returned in 1541 to Geneva, Switzerland, after visiting several Reformed European cities, he established a theocratic municipal government, hoping to regulate souls as well as the rhythms of civic life. The center of his system was a body composed of twelve "Elders," a term borrowed from the Greek New Testament's word for officials. The Elders met once each week, together with the Company of Pastors, to form the "Consistory," whose records have been preserved in 20 volumes. The documents are extraordinarily revealing for their insights into the continued attractions of Catholicism—as well as of what the Consistory called "sinful living" more generally. Specific sinful behaviors included a widow's saying, *Requiescat in pace* (Latin for "Rest in peace") over her husband's grave, a goldsmith's making a Catholic chalice, a barber who had tonsured a priest (shaved his scalp to signal religious devotion), and someone who said the pope was, actually, a fine man. The Consistory punished such errant language and behavior through penalties established by a series of "ordinances" endorsed, it was said, by the entire populace of Geneva. These fines, Calvin believed, would curtail such behavior in the future—redounding to the glory of the individual soul and the city to which he belonged.

[On November 2, 1542, Jehan Mouri of Peissy appeared before the Consistory] because he fornicated in this city and he is married, and other reasons. [Mouri] answers that he did not fornicate and that someone puts this crime on him because he is examining the rights of the Council. Although he was found in a tavern with this girl with a pot of wine and a *quart* loaf [a portion of a loaf of bread], he did not fornicate with her, because he is married, and he takes God to witness that it is not so. Admittedly he was behind this house and told the host to take him up to another room in order, he said, that the watch would not make him pay for a pot of wine. And the host took him up and he drank the said pot of wine with the said girl and the *quart* loaf and had a tart made, which he says he had made for the girl's mother, who was ill. The Consistory advises and is of the opinion that he be remanded to Monday before the Council. [Court records indicate that he was sentenced for the crime on December 18, 1542; the nature of the sentence is unknown.]

[On January 10, 1544, the wife of Loys Piaget appeared before the Consistory.] [Piaget] answers that she received Communion in the morning, and Monsieur Amied Gervays gave her to drink, and she received it for the honor of Jesus and did not let it fall and would not want to receive it thus. And she no longer prays to saints, and she formerly prayed for the dead, and she has frequented the sermons as much as she could. And she says she still says the Ave Maria and does not think this is idolatry, and it does not seem to her she does wrong to pray to the Virgin Mary, and she has no faith in saints but in God and in the Virgin Mary. And one may do what one wants with her. She believes the Virgin Mary is a creature, the mother of Our Lord, her son she bore. She answers that she wants to believe only in the Word of God and does not believe she does wrong by invoking the Virgin Mary. And she does not know whether any other than Our Lord should be adored. And says that if she has adored the Virgin Mary may the Consistory pardon her. The opinion of the Consistory is that since she is possessed by the devil, that for the present she be commanded to go to the sermon three times a week for six weeks, and catechism, and that she be given strict remonstrances, or remanded

From Denis R. Janz, *A Reformation Reader: Primary Texts with Introductions*, 2nd ed. (Minneapolis: Fortress, 2008), pp. 256–260.

before the Council, and that here in a week the confession of her faith be examined, and she be admonished more thoroughly to frequent the sermons. And that she cease to carry or say her rosary and her knotted cords, and every day for a week, and appear here next Thursday and be given strict remonstrances. Ordered to go to the sermon every day for a week.

From the *Geneva Ordinances* (1547):

Blasphemies

1. Those who have blasphemed, swearing by the body or by the blood of our Lord, or such-like, ought to do reverence for the first time; for the second a penalty of five sous [a unit of coinage, derived ultimately from the *"solidus"* of the Roman Empire, equivalent to 1/20th of a pound (*livre*) of silver]; for the third ten sous; and for the last time put in the pillory for an hour.
2. Anyone who abjures or renounces God or his baptism is for the first time to be put for ten days on bread and water; for the second and third time he is to be punished with some more rigorous corporal punishment, at the discretion of their lordships.

. . .

Drunkenness

1. There is to be no treating of one another to drinks, under penalty of three sous.
2. The taverns are to be closed during service, under penalty that the taverner pay three sous and anyone entering them the same.
3. If anyone be found drunk, he is to pay for the first time three sous and be brought before the consistory; the second time he must pay the sum of five sous; and the third ten sous and be put in prison.
4. There are to be no carousings, under penalty of ten sous.

Songs and Dances

If anyone sing songs that are unworthy, dissolute or outrageous, or spin wildly round in the dance, or the like, he is to be imprisoned for three days, and then sent on to the consistory.

Usury

No one is to lend at interest or for profit greater than 5 percent, on pain of confiscation of the capital sum and of being required to make appropriate amends according to the needs of the case.

STUDY QUESTIONS

1. What do the protests of the man and woman being examined reveal about daily life in Calvin's Geneva? What lines of reasoning do they seem to have employed in their defense, and why?
2. How did the state authorities regulate "sin" in Geneva? Was it an "authoritarian" state as a result?

1.4 THE COUNCIL OF TRENT, *CANONS ON THE SACRAMENTS*, 1547 AND *TRIDENTINE INDEX OF BOOKS*, 1564

In the 1520s, Charles V, the Holy Roman Emperor, called for a General Council of the Church to heal the theological divide between the Catholics and Protestants in his realm. When the Council finally assembled at the small Alpine town of Trent in 1545, no Protestants were in attendance. Not

From Rev. H. J. Schroeder, O.P., ed. and trans., *Canons and Decrees of the Council of Trent* (Rockford, IL: TAN Books and Publishers, 1978) [reprint of 1941 edition by B. Herder Book Co.], pp. 51–56 and J. Barry Colman, ed., *Readings in Church History*, rev. ed., vol. 2 (Westminster, MD: Christian Classics, 1985), pp. 109–112.

surprisingly, the Council's first significant decree contradicted Protestantism's belief in the truth of scripture alone and its second rejected the Protestant maxim of justification by faith alone. The Council maintained that human beings have free will and can merit God's grace through the good works they perform, especially by participating in the Church's seven sacraments. The Council of Trent met periodically until 1563, and in those meetings, it addressed practical aspects of Church governance, as well as specific matters of Church doctrine.

In a typical session in March 1547, the Council recorded its pronouncements on several matters, portions of which appear in the first excerpt below, the *Canons on the Sacraments*. The original document is in Latin, and each "error" it identifies ends with the pronouncement *"Anathema sit"* ("Let him be anathema"). This condemnation is taken from a Greek word used six times in the New Testament, meaning something like "Let him be laid up" (i.e., as a sacrifice on the altar). In the context of Catholic doctrine, it means, "Let him be given up to special judgment by God" because he has committed a grave infraction against the teachings of the Church.

After the Council of Trent concluded its work, Pope Pius IV issued his committee's report concerning banned books, creating what is called the *Tridentine Index* (referring to the Latin name for Trent, Tridentum, and Index for "list"). Excerpted in the second document below are some of the "Ten Rules Concerning Prohibited Books," explaining which books and authors were forbidden for Catholics and spelling out the penalties for selling or possessing them. Note how the Church fathers perceived the ideas of non-Catholics.

CANONS ON THE SACRAMENTS IN GENERAL

Canon 1. If anyone says that the sacraments of the New Law were not at all instituted by our Lord Jesus Christ, or that there are more or less than seven, namely, baptism, confirmation, Eucharist, penance, extreme unction, order and matrimony, or that any one of these seven is not truly and intrinsically a sacrament, let him be anathema.

Can. 2. If anyone says that these sacraments of the New Law do not differ from the sacraments of the Old Law, except that the ceremonies are different and the external rites are different, let him be anathema.

Can. 3. If anyone says that these seven sacraments are so equal to each other that one is not for any reason more excellent than the other, let him be anathema.

Can. 4. If anyone says that the sacraments of the New Law are not necessary for salvation but are superfluous, and that without them or without the desire of them men obtain from God through faith alone the grace of justification, though all are not necessary for each one, let him be anathema.

Can. 5. If anyone says that these sacraments have been instituted for the nourishment of faith alone, let him be anathema.

Can. 10. If anyone says that all Christians have the power to administer the word and all the sacraments, let him be anathema.

Can. 13. If anyone says that the received and approved rites of the Catholic Church, accustomed to be used in the administration of the sacraments, may be despised or omitted by the ministers without sin and at their pleasure, or may be changed by any pastor of the churches to other new ones, let him be anathema.

CANONS ON BAPTISM

Canon 1. If anyone says that the baptism of John had the same effect as the baptism of Christ, let him be anathema.

Can. 2. If anyone says that true and natural water is not necessary for baptism and thus twists into some metaphor the words of our Lord Jesus Christ: *Unless a man be born again of water and the Holy Ghost*, let him be anathema.

Can. 3. If anyone says that in the Roman Church, which is the mother and mistress of all churches, there is not the true doctrine concerning the sacrament of baptism, let him be anathema.

Can. 4. If anyone says that the baptism which is given by heretics in the name of the Father, and of the Son, and of the Holy Ghost, with the intention of doing what the Church does, is not true baptism, let him be anathema.

Can. 12. If anyone says that no one is to be baptized except at that age at which Christ was baptized, or when on the point of death, let him be anathema.

Can. 13. If anyone says that children, because they have not the act of believing, are not after having received baptism to be numbered among the faithful, and that for this reason are to be rebaptized when they have reached the years of discretion; or that it is better that the baptism of such be omitted than that, while not believing by their own act, they should be baptized in the faith of the Church alone, let him be anathema.

Can. 14. If anyone says that those who have been thus baptized when children, are, when they have grown up, to be questioned whether they will ratify what their sponsors promised in their name when they were baptized, and in case they answer in the negative, are to be left to their own will; neither are they to be compelled in the meantime to a Christian life by any penalty other than exclusion from the reception of the Eucharist and the other sacraments, until they repent, let him be anathema.

TRIDENTINE INDEX OF BOOKS, 1564

Ten Rules Concerning Prohibited Books Drawn up by the Fathers Chosen by the Council of Trent and Approved by Pope Pius IV

1. All books which have been condemned either by the supreme pontiffs or by ecumenical councils before the year 1515 and are not contained in this list, shall be considered condemned in the same manner as they were formerly condemned.

2. The books of those heresiarchs, who after the aforesaid year originated or revived heresies, as well as of those who are or have been the heads or leaders of heretics, as Luther, Zwingli, Calvin, Balthasar Friedberg, Schwenkfeld, and others like these, whatever may be their name, title or nature of their heresy, are absolutely forbidden. . . .

3. The translations of writers, also ecclesiastical, which have till now been edited by condemned authors, are permitted provided they contain nothing contrary to sound doctrine. Translations of the books of the Old Testament may in the judgment of the bishop be permitted to learned and pious men only, provided such translations are used only as elucidations of the Vulgate Edition for the understanding of the holy Scriptures and not as the sound text. Translations of the New Testament made by authors of the first class of this list shall be permitted to no one, since great danger and little usefulness usually results to readers from their perusal. . . .

4. . . . Book dealers who sell or in any other way supply Bibles written in the vernacular to anyone who has not this permission, shall lose the price of the books, which is to be applied by the bishop to pious purposes, and in keeping with the nature of the crime they shall be subject to other penalties which are left to the judgment of the same bishop. . . .

7. Books which professedly deal with, narrate or teach things lascivious or obscene are absolutely prohibited, since not only the matter of faith but also that of morals, which are usually easily corrupted through the reading of such books, must be taken into consideration, and those who possess them are to be severely punished by the bishops. Ancient books written by heathens may by reason of their elegance and quality of style be permitted, but may by no means be read to children.

9. All books and writings dealing with [divinations from earth, water, air, fire, dreams, bones], or with [card reading], mixing of poisons, augury, auspices, sorcery, or magic arts, are absolutely repudiated. The bishops shall diligently see to it that books, treatises, catalogues determining destiny by astrology, which in the matter of future events, consequences, or fortuitous occurrences, or of actions that depend on the human will, attempt to affirm something as certain to take place, are not read or possessed. Permitted, on the other hand, are the opinions and natural observations which have been written in the interest of navigation, agriculture, or the medical art.

Finally, all the faithful are commanded not to presume to read or possess any books contrary to the prescriptions of these rules or the prohibition of this list. And if anyone should read or possess books by heretics or writings by any author condemned and prohibited by reason of heresy or suspicion of false teaching, he incurs immediately the sentence of excommunication. He, on the other hand, who reads or possesses books prohibited under another name shall, besides incurring the guilt of mortal sin, be severely punished according to the judgment of the bishops.

STUDY QUESTIONS

1. In what ways do these canons and rules attack specific Protestant practices and beliefs?
2. How do these selections epitomize the Council of Trent's response to the threat of the Protestant Reformation?

1.5 THE ACCOUNT OF WALPURGA HAUSMÄNNIN, MIDWIFE ACCUSED OF WITCHCRAFT, 1587

Most of the roughly 100,000 people accused of being witches between the early sixteenth and the early eighteenth centuries were female and of lower social standing. The case of Walpurga Hausmännin stands out because she was accused of killing 43 children, although the details of the accusations against her are fairly typical. Hausmännin was a widowed midwife who came under suspicion of witchcraft in 1587 in Dillingen, Germany. In this era, child mortality rates were high, about 15% of newborns died within a few months. An elderly midwife like Hausmännin would have had ample opportunities to deliver unhealthy or stillborn babies over the years. A midwife was rarely accused after one death, but numerous deaths, perhaps combined with the personality of an outsider, might heighten her neighbors' scrutiny. Also, as a single woman, Hausmännin lacked the protection and social standing of marriage. Over half of the European women accused of witchcraft were unmarried, suggesting that communities targeted their most vulnerable women. The account of her crimes highlights patterns in the accusations against women: she had sexual relations outside of marriage (in this case with a servant who was allegedly the Devil in disguise), she attended witches' gatherings, she preyed on innocent children, and she manufactured destructive weather.

Confessions of Walpurga Hausmännin, formerly licensed midwife at Dillingen, who, for almost thirty years, practiced witchcraft and was in league with the Evil One. She was burnt at the stake at Dillingen on the 20th day of September anno Domini 1587.

The herein mentioned, malefic and miserable woman, Walpurga Hausmännin, now imprisoned and in chains, has, upon kindly questioning and also torture, following on persistent and fully justified accusations, confessed her witchcraft and admitted the

From E. William Monter, *European Witchcraft* (New York: John Wiley & Sons, Inc), pp. 75–81, taken from *News and Rumor in Renaissance Europe* (The Fugger Newsletters), selected and edited by George T. Mathews (New York: G. P. Putnam's Sons, 1959), pp. 137–143.

following. When one-and-thirty years ago, she had become a widow, she cut corn for Hans Schlumperger of this place, together with his former servant, Bis im Pfarrhof, by name. Him she enticed with lewd speeches and gestures and they convened that they should, on an appointed night, meet in her, Walpurga's, dwelling, there to indulge in lustful intercourse. So when Walpurga in expectation of this, sat awaiting him at night in her chamber, meditating upon evil and fleshly thoughts, it was not the said bondsman who appeared unto her, but the Evil One in the latter's guise and raiment and indulged in fornication with her. . . . After the act of fornication she saw and felt the cloven foot of her whoremonger, and that his hand was not natural, but as if made of wood. She was greatly affrighted thereat and called upon the name of Jesus, whereupon the Devil left her and vanished.

On the ensuing night, the Evil Spirit visited her again in the same shape and whored with her. He made her many promises to help her in her poverty and need, wherefore she surrendered herself to him body and soul. Thereafter the Evil One inflicted upon her a scratch below the left shoulder, demanding that she should sell her soul to him with the blood that had flown therefrom. To this end he gave her a quill and, whereas she could not write, the Evil One guided her hand. She believes that nothing offensive was written, for the Evil One only swept with her hand across the paper. This script the Devil took with him and whenever she piously thought of God Almighty, or wished to go to church, the Devil reminded her of it.

Further, the above-mentioned Walpurga confesses that she oft and much rode on a pitchfork by night with her paramour, but not far, on account of her duties. At such devilish trysts she met a big man with a grey beard, who sat in a chair, like a great prince and was richly attired. That was the Great Devil to whom she had once more dedicated and promised herself body and soul. Him she worshipped and before him she knelt, and unto him she rendered other such-like honours. But she pretends not to know with what words and in which fashion she prayed. She only knows that once she heedlessly pronounced the name of Jesus. Then the above-mentioned Great Devil struck her in the face and Walpurga

had to disown (which is terrible to relate) God in heaven, the Christian name and belief, the blessed Saints and the Holy Sacraments, also to renounce the heavenly hosts and the whole of Christendom. Thereupon the Great Devil baptized her afresh, naming her Höfelin, and her paramour-devil, Federlin.

At those devilish meetings, she ate, drank and fornicated with her paramour. Because she would not allow him to drag her along everywhere he had beaten her harshly and cruelly. For food she often had a good roast or an innocent child, which was also roasted, or a suckling pig, and red and white wine, but no salt. . . .

At the command and threat of her whoremonger she had oft dishonored the consecrated font, emptied it before her house or even destroyed the same. . . . She had also been obliged sorely to dishonor the blessed Mother of God, the Holy Virgin Mary, to spit out in front of her and say: "Shame, thou ugly hussy!" Her paramour, Federlin, came to her in many diverse places in order to fornicate with her, even in the street by night and while she lay in durance. She confesses, also, that her paramour gave her a salve in a little box with which to injure people and animals, and even the precious fruit of the field.

He also compelled her to do away with and to kill young infants at birth, even before they had been taken to Holy Baptism. This she did, whenever possible. These as follows:

[A list of 43 specific infant deaths follows, including these examples:]

1 and 2. About ten years ago, she had rubbed Anna Hämännin, who dwelt not far from Durstigel, with her salve on the occasion of her first childbirth and also otherwise damaged her so that mother and child remained together and died.

3. Dorothea, the stepdaughter of Christian Wachter, bore her first child ten years before; at its birth she made press on its little brain so that it died. The Devil had specially bidden her destroy the first-born.

5. When, four years ago, the organist's wife was awaiting her confinement, she touched her naked body with her salve whereby the child promptly died and came stillborn.

8. Three years ago when she was called to a mill to the miller's wife there she had let the child fall into the water and drown.

11. When six years ago, she partook of food with Magdalena Seilerin, . . . she had put a salve in her drink, so that she was delivered prematurely. This child she, Walpurga, secretly buried under the doorway of the said wife of the scribe on the pretext that then she would have no other miscarriage. The same she also did with many others. When she was questioned under torture for the reasons of this burial, she admitted that it was done in order to cause disunion between two spouses. This her Devil-Paramour had taught her.

15. She had also rubbed a salve on a beautiful son of the late Chancellor, Jacob by name: this child had lovely fair hair and she had given him a hobby-horse so that he might ride on it till he lost his senses. He died likewise.

16. Eight years ago she gave the rightfully wedded wife of Otto Vischer, when she was big with child, a drink, whereafter the child was born dead.

25. A child of the Governor here, Wilhelm Schenk von Stauffenberg, named Werner, she had so infected with her salve that he died within three days.

30. Three years ago she had sucked out the blood of publican Kunz's child, a twin, so that it died.

She confesses likewise, that the blood which she sucked from the child, she had to spit out again before the devil, as he had need of it to concoct a salve. She could work the children no harm if they were protected by holy water. But if she herself gave the child holy water, she was able to do it damage, as she had previously passed water into it.

. . .

When eight years ago she was helping Michel Klingler to push a cart, and Klingler wanted to lift the shafts with his head, she touched it with her salve. Since then, Klingler is fading away and death is the only thing before him.

. . .

She rubbed with her salve and brought about the death of Lienhart Geilen's three cows, of Bruchbauer's horse, two years ago of Max Petzcl's cow, three years ago of Duri Striegel's cow, two years ago of Hans Striegel's cow, of the cow of the Governor's wife, of a cow of Frau Schotterin, and two years ago of a cow of Michel Klingler, on the village green. In short, she confesses that she destroyed a large number of cattle over and above this. A year ago she found bleached linen on the common and rubbed it with her salve, so that the pigs and geese ran over it and perished shortly thereafter. Walpurga confesses further that every year since she has sold herself to the Devil, she has on St. Leonard's Day exhumed at least one or two innocent children. With her Devil-Paramour and other play-fellows she has eaten these and used their hair and their little bones for witchcraft.

She was unable to exhume the other children she had slain at birth, although she attempted it, because they had been baptized before God.

She had used the said little bones to manufacture hail; this she was wont to do once or twice a year. . . . She likewise manufactured hail last Whitsun, and when she and others were accused of having held a witches' revel, she had actually held one near the upper gate by the garden of Peter Schmidt. At that time her play-fellows began to quarrel and struck one another, because some wanted to cause it to hail over Dillingen Meadows, others below it. At last the hail was sent over the marsh towards Weissingen, doing great damage. She admits that she would have caused still more and greater evils and damage if the Almighty had not graciously prevented and turned them away.

After all this, the Judges and Jury of the Court of this Town of Dillingen, by virtue of the Imperial and Royal Prerogative and Rights of His Right Reverence, Herr Marquard, Bishop of Augsburg, and Provost of the Cathedral, our most gracious Prince and Lord, at last unanimously gave the verdict that the aforesaid Walpurga Hausmännin be punished and dispatched from life to death by burning at the stake as being a maleficent and well-known witch and sorceress, convicted according to the context of Common Law and the Criminal Code of the Emperor Charles V and the Holy Roman Empire. All her goods and chattels and estate left after her to go to the Treasury of our Most High Prince and Lord. The aforesaid Walpurga to be led, seated on a cart, to which she is tied, to the place of her execution, and her body first to be torn five times with red-hot irons. The first time outside the town hall in the left breast and the right arm, the second time at the lower gate in the right breast, the third time at the mill brook outside the hospital gate in the left arm, the fourth time at the place of execution in the left hand. But since for nineteen years she was a licensed and pledged midwife of the city of Dillingen, yet has acted so vilely, her right hand with which she did such knavish tricks is to be cut off at the place of execution. Neither are her ashes after the burning to remain lying on the ground, but are thereafter to be carried to the nearest flowing water and thrown thereinto. Thus a venerable jury have entrusted the executioner of this city with the actual execution and all connected therewith.

STUDY QUESTIONS

1. What were the specific crimes that Walpurga Hausmännin confessed and how did they impact her community?
2. What do the accusations against her indicate about popular perceptions of what witches actually did?

1.6 VISUAL SOURCE: FRANÇOIS DUBOIS, *THE SAINT BARTHOLOMEW'S DAY MASSACRE IN PARIS*, 1572–1584

Beginning on August 24, 1572, French royal troops attacked the Huguenot elite who had come to Paris to witness the wedding of their leader, Henry of Navarre, to King Charles's sister Margaret. The attacks against Protestants quickly spread to other French towns, leaving over 5,000 people dead. This painting, the earliest known depiction of the massacre, provides a contemporary view of events, allowing historians to see how people experienced and remembered the Saint Bartholomew's Day Massacre. François Dubois, the artist, was a Protestant who fled France for safe haven in Geneva where he worked on this image; nothing else by him survives, and we do not know whether he witnessed the violence directly. The massacre met with mixed international reactions. Pope Gregory XIII celebrated the event and commissioned commemorative frescoes and a medal. Venetians joined the pope by organizing a procession to give thanks to God for what they saw as Charles' staunch defense of Catholicism. Meanwhile, Dubois and his fellow Protestants saw the massacre as an unfair preemptive strike against them and interpreted it as further proof that Catholics monarchs did not deserve their subjects' obedience.

One way to understand the action Dubois portrayed is to look at the painting as if it were a comic book combined into one image. At the center is the townhouse where Catholic allies of the royal family threw the Protestant leader Admiral de Coligny out of a window and then decapitated him. The leaders of the Catholic faction stand around his corpse. On the hill on the right is the gallows where Coligny's body was hung by its feet. The geography is truncated to make it easier for viewers to follow the narrative. On the left, the Louvre (now a museum, then the royal palace) looms in the background. The female figure in black towering over a pile of bodies is Catherine de Medici, the Queen Mother.

FIGURE 1.6   Saint Bartholomew's Day Massacre

STUDY QUESTIONS

1. Describe the range of atrocities the Catholics are shown committing. Who is being targeted?
2. What does this artifact reveal about the Huguenots' view of this event? Whom did they blame for the attack?

COORDINATION

Coordination means joining two or more grammatical "equals" into a longer unit: nouns with nouns, verbs with verbs, sentences with sentences, and so on. Often, coordinated units are joined by a *coordinator: for, and, nor, but, or, yet, so.* (FANBOYS)

Writers use coordination to link ideas logically (clarity), reduce word count (efficiency), and create flow (style).

When using coordination, novice writers make two mistakes (both covered in Chapter 14): *comma splices* and *faulty parallelism.* See the website for additional examples.

The following sentences are examples of effective coordination:

- Augustinian monks endured the torments of **hunger, thirst, cold, and sleeplessness.** (coordinated adjectives)
- Martin's father **married up** and **achieved** a modest success in business. (coordinated verbs or "verb phrases")
- They worried that women who **left** the convent or **received** visitors there opened themselves to sexual temptation. (coordinated verbs)
- Becoming a monk required a **vow of poverty** and **the surrender of all worldly possessions.** (coordinated direct objects)
- **A violent thunderstorm burst over him**, and a **bolt of lightning knocked him to the ground.** (coordinated sentences)

EXERCISE: UNSCRAMBLE SENTENCES

Instructions

1. Unscramble the sentences below.

2. Next, *writing from memory*, transcribe each sentence onto a separate piece of paper, including all punctuation, or adding punctuation as necessary. You should be able to remember sentences up to 10 words long. If the sentence is longer, transcribe it in chunks of 5 to 10 words at a time.

3. Check your version against the original.

Be sure not to skip the transcription step. Transcribing from memory forces you to focus on sentence *structure*, which is surprisingly difficult to "see." We do not notice sentence structure when we read because our conscious brain focuses on meaning, not grammar. *Transcribing sophisticated sentences from memory brings structure to the fore and is a shortcut to writing sophisticated sentences yourself.*
So don't skip Step 2!

EXAMPLE

Arrange the phrases below to create a sentence by A. E. Housman on the subject of writing history.
    The sentence begins with the word "accuracy."

_____	not
___1___	accuracy
_____	a virtue
_____	a duty
_____	is

ANSWER

___4___	not
___1___	accuracy
___5___	a virtue
___3___	a duty
___2___	is

Accuracy is a duty, not a virtue. —A. E. Housman

---

1. Martin Luther is said to have spoken the sentence below. Unscramble the sentence, keeping the punctuation as is, and transcribe it from memory on a separate piece of paper.

_____	I stand;
_____	I can do
___1___	Here
_____	no other.

---

2. The phrases below can be combined into two different sentences. Create the two possibilities, inserting commas as necessary to make your meaning clear.

Transcribe one or both from memory.

_____	_____	and he could not help but admire
_____	_____	Hans Luther believed in God and Jesus
_____	_____	like essentially everyone in sixteenth-century Europe
_____	_____	those who devoted their lives
_____	_____	to serving the Lord

3. Unscramble the sentence below and transcribe it from memory. Original punctuation included.

___7___	where they worked
_____	deliberately sent
_____	the Catholic population.
_____	to places like Ireland,
___5___	of religious civil wars and
_____	Jesuit generals
___3___	their top soldiers
_____	to shore up
_____	into the middle

EXERCISE: COMBINE SENTENCES USING COORDINATION

Sample Exercise

Combine the two sentences below using a comma and the word "*and.*"

Martin recounted the thunderstorm story to his father.
That story has become part of Luther lore.

Combined

Martin recounted the thunderstorm story to his father, and that story has become part of Luther lore.

4. Combine the sentences into one using a FANBOYS (*for, and, nor, but, or, yet, so*) and a comma.

The era's warfare was expensive and logistically complex.
To finance and organize it required expanded bureaucracies and centralized governments.

5. Now combine the sentences into one using a semicolon.

The era's warfare was expensive and logistically complex.
To finance and organize it required expanded bureaucracies and centralized governments.

6. Combine the sentences below using a FANBOYS and the words "*Calvin*" and "*he.*"

Calvin wrote relatively little.
Calvin spoke a great deal.

7. Now combine the sentences using the words "*Calvin*" but not "*he.*"

Calvin wrote relatively little.
Calvin spoke a great deal.

8. Combine the sentences below using one semicolon.

Calvin composed his sermons in bed.
Calvin delivered his sermons without notes.
Luther depended on ink.
Luther depended on paper.

STRUCTURING SENTENCES FOR EMPHASIS USING COORDINATION

End focus: The most important information in a sentence typically appears toward the end.

End weight: The longest word or phrase in a sentence usually appears at the end.

EXERCISE: USE COORDINATION TO STRUCTURE SENTENCES FOR EMPHASIS

Instructions

Order the phrases to emphasize the most important information. Write your sentence on a separate piece of paper, adding punctuation as necessary.

9. Luther [phrase], [phrase], and [phrase].

A. Phrase: moved into a "cell" barely large enough for a bed
B. Phrase: shaved his head
C. Phrase: donned jet-black robes

10. Select the version that illustrates the principle of *end weight*.

A. Becoming a monk required the surrender of all worldly possessions and a vow of poverty.
B. Becoming a monk required a vow of poverty and the surrender of all worldly possessions.

You will find suggested answers to the exercises in the back of this book. For more Writing History exercises, as well as study resources for this chapter, visit oup.com/us/berenson.

CHAPTER 2

STATES AND EMPIRES, 1450–1700

2.1 OGIER GHISELIN DE BUSBECQ ON ROXELANA IN *THE TURKISH LETTERS*, 1555

Ogier Ghiselin de Busbecq (1522–1590) was born in Flanders but secured a place in history while serving for six years in the Ottoman Empire as an ambassador for the Austrian Hapsburgs. He wrote four letters to a friend, Nicholas Michault, describing events inside the court of Suleiman the Magnificent (also known as Süleyman I), the powerful Ottoman sultan. Although not intended for an audience beyond the Hapsburgs, the letters nevertheless were published in Paris in 1589. They reflect how Europeans viewed the Ottomans and provide details about their customs and politics. These excerpts come from his first letter (1555) and focus on the status of women in the Ottoman Empire and especially on Roxelana, Suleiman's beloved wife. Her independence perplexed Busbecq (and certainly many others). He saw her as far more powerful than was customary for women both in Christian Europe and the Ottoman Empire. That she was a foreigner, hailing from Russia-Ukraine, added to her mystique. Because she left nothing written in her own hand, historians have to rely on contemporaries' accounts about her, knowing that enemies might skew their discussions of her.

Passing on to other topics, I will tell you about Turkish women and the manner in which they are guarded. The Turks are the most careful people in the world of the modesty of their wives, and therefore keep them shut up at home and hide them away, so that they scarce see the light of day. But if they have to go into the streets, they are sent out so covered and wrapped up in veils that they seem to those who meet them mere gliding ghosts. They have the means of seeing men through their linen or silken veils, while no part of their own body is exposed to men's view. For it is a received opinion among them, that no woman who is distinguished in the very smallest degree by her figure or youth, can be seen by a man without his desiring her, and therefore without her receiving some contamination; and so it is the universal practice to confine the women to the harem. Their brothers

From Ogier Ghiselin de Busbecq, *The Life and Letters of Ogier Ghiselin de Busbecq*, Vol. I, translated by Charles Thornton Forster and F. H. Blackburne Daniell (London: Kegan Paul, 1881), pp. 228–231, 112–121.

are allowed to see them, but not their brothers-in-law. Men of the richer classes, or of higher rank, make it a condition when they marry, that their wives shall never set foot outside the threshold, and that no man or woman shall be admitted to see them for any reason whatever, not even their nearest relations, except their fathers and mothers, who are allowed to pay a visit to their daughters at the Turkish Easter.

On the other hand, if the wife has a father of high rank, or has brought a larger dowry than usual, the husband promises on his part that he will take no concubine, but will keep to her alone. Otherwise, the Turks are not forbidden by any law to have as many concubines as they please in addition to their lawful wives. Between the children of wives and those of concubines there is no distinction, and they are considered to have equal rights. As for concubines they either buy them for themselves or win them in war; when they are tired of them there is nothing to prevent their bringing them to market and selling them; but they are entitled to their freedom if they have borne children to their master. This privilege Roxelana, Suleiman's wife, turned to her own advantage, when she had borne him a son while still a slave. Having thus obtained her freedom, and become her own mistress, she refused to submit any longer to his will, unless, contrary to the custom of the Ottoman Sultans, she was made his lawful wife. The only distinction between the lawful wife and the concubine is that the former has a dowry while the slaves have none. A wife who has a portion settled on her is mistress of her husband's house, and all the other women have to obey her orders. The husband, however, may choose which of them shall spend the night with him. He makes known his wishes to the wife, and she sends to him the slave he has selected. Hardly a pleasant task, one would fancy, for a wife, whatever the feelings of the other might be! Only Friday night, which is their Sabbath, is supposed to belong to the wife; and she grumbles if her husband deprives her of it. On all the other nights he may do as he pleases. . . .

People of consideration with large harems appoint eunuchs to guard them. They also have baths at home, in which they and their women perform their [washings], while people of smaller means patronize the public baths. They consider cleanliness of the body as even of more importance in a religious point of view than purity of the soul, which is the reason of their frequent [washings]. The great mass of women use the public baths for females and assemble there in large numbers. Among them are found many girls of exquisite beauty, who have been brought together from different quarters of the globe by various chances of fortune; so cases occur of women falling in love with one another at these baths, in much the same fashion as young men fall in love with maidens in our own country. Thus you see a Turk's precautions are sometimes of no avail, and when he has succeeded in keeping his wives from a male lover, he is still in danger from a female rival! The women become deeply attached to each other, and the baths supply them with opportunities of meeting. Some therefore keep their women away from them as much as possible, but they cannot do so altogether, as the law allows them to go there. This evil affects only the common people; the richer classes bathe at home, as I mentioned.

————

Now that I am speaking of Roostem [the grand vizier, something like a prime minister], I may as well tell you how he came to be deprived of his high office. Suleiman had a son by a concubine, who came from the Crimea, if I remember rightly. His name was Mustapha, and at the time of which I am speaking he was young, vigorous, and of high repute as a soldier. But Suleiman had also several other children by a Russian woman [Roxelana]. To the latter he was so much attached that he placed her in the position of a wife, and assigned her a dowry, the giving and receiving of which constitutes a marriage amongst the Turks. In taking her as his wife, he broke through the custom of his later predecessors on the throne, none of whom . . . had a lawful wife. . . .

Up to the time of Suleiman, [sultans] abstained from contracting a legal marriage with any woman, by way of insuring themselves, under all circumstances, against . . . misfortune. The mothers of their children were women in the position of slaves, the idea being that, if they were insulted, the disgrace to the Sultan would not be so great as in the case of a lawful wife. You must not be surprised at this, for the Turks do not consider the position of the children of concubines and mistresses inferior to that of the offspring of wives; both have precisely the same rights of inheritance to their father's property.

Thus, then, matters stood. Mustapha's high qualities and matured years marked him out, to the soldiers who loved, and the people who supported him, as the successor of his father, who was now in the decline of life. On the other hand, his step-mother [Roxelana], by throwing the claim of a lawful wife into the scale, was doing her utmost to counterbalance his personal merits and his rights as eldest son, with a view to obtaining the throne for her own children. In this intrigue she received the advice and assistance of Roostem, whose fortunes were inseparably linked with hers by his marriage with a daughter she had had by Suleiman. Of all the Pashas at Suleiman's court none had such influence and weight as Roostem. . . .

Well, inasmuch as Roostem was chief Vizier, and as such had the whole of the Turkish administration in his hands, he had no difficulty, seeing that he was the Sultan's adviser in everything, in influencing his master's mind. The Turks, accordingly, are convinced that it was by the calumnies of Roostem and the spells of Roxelana, who was in ill repute as a practiser of witchcraft, that the Sultan was so estranged from his son as to entertain the design of getting rid of him. A few believe that Mustapha, being aware of the plans of Roostem and the practices of his stepmother, determined to anticipate them, and thus engaged in designs against his father's throne and person. The sons of Turkish Sultans are in the most wretched position in the world, for, as soon as one of them succeeds his father, the rest are doomed to certain death. The Turk can endure no rival to the throne, and, indeed, the conduct of the Janissaries [elite military troops] renders it impossible for the new Sultan to spare his brothers; for if one of them survives, the Janissaries are forever asking largesses. If these are refused, forthwith the cry is heard, "Long live the brother!" "God preserve the brother!"—a tolerably broad hint that they intend to place him on the throne. So that the Turkish Sultans are compelled to celebrate their succession by imbruing their hands in

the blood of their nearest relatives. Now whether the fault lay with Mustapha, who feared this fate for himself, or with Roxelana, who endeavored to save her children at the expense of Mustapha, this much at any rate is certain—the suspicions of the Sultan were excited, and the fate of his son was sealed. . . .

[Mustafa] left Amasia, the seat of his government, and went to his father's camp, which lay at no great distance, either trusting in his innocence, or feeling confident that no evil would happen to him in the presence of the army. However that may be, he fell into a trap from which there was no escape. . . .

There was great uneasiness among the soldiers, when Mustapha arrived in the camp. He was brought to his father's tent, and there everything betokened peace. There was not a soldier on guard, no aide-de-camp, no policeman, nothing that could possibly alarm him and make him suspect treachery. But there were in the tent certain mutes—a favorite kind of servant among the Turks—strong and sturdy fellows, who had been appointed as his executioners. As soon as he entered the inner tent, they threw themselves upon him, and endeavored to put the fatal noose around his neck. Mustapha, being a man of considerable strength, made a stout defense, and fought—not only for his life, but also for the throne; there being no doubt that if he escaped from his executioners, and threw himself among the Janissaries, the news of this outrage on their beloved prince would cause such pity and indignation, that they would not only protect him, but also proclaim him Sultan. Suleiman felt how critical the matter was, being only separated by the linen hangings of his tent from the stage, on which this tragedy was being enacted. . . . Hereon the mutes, gaining fresh strength . . . , threw Mustapha down, got the bowstring round his neck, and strangled him. Shortly afterwards they laid his body on a rug in front of the tent, that the Janissaries might see the man they had desired as their Sultan. When this was noised through the camp, the whole army was filled with pity and grief; nor did one of them fail to come and gaze on that sad sight. Foremost of all were the Janissaries, so astounded and indignant that, had there been anyone to lead them, they would have flinched from nothing. But they saw their chosen leader lying lifeless on the ground. . . . First they declared that Suleiman was a dotard and a madman. They then expressed their abhorrence of the cruel treachery of the stepmother [Roxelana], and the wickedness of Roostem, who, between them, had extinguished the brightest light of the house of Othman. Thus they passed that day fasting, nor did they even touch water; indeed, there were some of them who remained without food for a still longer time.

For several days there was a general mourning throughout the camp, and there seemed no prospect of any abatement of the soldiers' sorrow, unless Roostem were removed from office. This step Suleiman accordingly took, at the suggestion (as it is generally believed) of Roostem himself. He dismissed him from office, and sent him back to Constantinople in disgrace. . . .

Meanwhile, Roxelana, not contented with removing Mustapha from her path, was compassing the death of the only son he had left, who was still a child; for she did not consider that she and her children were free from danger, so long as his offspring survived. Some pretext, however, she thought necessary, in order to furnish a reason for the murder, but this was not hard to find. . . . For the sake, therefore, of the family, the empire, and religion itself, a stop must be put to domestic feuds; no price could be too great for the accomplishment of such an end, even though a father's hands had to be dipped in his children's blood; nay, the sacrifice of one's children's lives was not to be esteemed of any great account, if the safety of the faith was thereby assured. . . .

Suleiman was easily induced by these arguments to sign the death-warrant of his grandson. He commissioned Ibrahim Pasha to go to Ghemlik with all speed, and put the innocent child to death.

STUDY QUESTIONS

1. What strikes Busbecq as noteworthy about Roxelana and the position of women in the Ottoman Empire? In what ways did she trespass across traditional boundaries set up for women?
2. What do the stories about the death of his eldest son and grandson reveal about Suleiman's power and the position of the sultan in the Ottoman Empire at this time?

2.2 HERNÁN CORTÉS, *SECOND LETTER FROM MEXICO TO EMPEROR CHARLES V,* 1522

With a handful of untrained and poorly equipped soldiers, the Spanish conquistador Hernán Cortés (1485-1547) overthrew the powerful Aztec civilization in Mexico between 1519 and 1520. Cortés decided to inform Charles V, the King of Spain and Holy Roman Emperor, of his achievements in a series of written updates, or *"cartas de relación"* ("letters of relation"). Despite their ostensible purpose, these "letters" were designed for more than the edification and delight of the Emperor. Like Julius Caesar's dispatches from the Gallic Wars of the 50s BCE, these accounts were

From *Hernán Cortés: Letters from Mexico,* edited and translated by Anthony Pagden (New Haven, CT: Yale University Press, 1986), pp. 72–74.

designed for broad public consumption. Cortés sent each *Letter* to Spain as soon as it was ready, and it seems likely that his father Martín arranged for their immediate publication. Through the five *Letters* ultimately published, Cortés developed a persona for himself as a conquering hero and agent of imperial power—but he also exposed the ruthlessness and brutality of his "conquest" of Mexico.

From henceforth they offered themselves as vassals of Your Sacred Majesty and swore to remain so always and to serve and assist in all things that Your Highness commanded them. A notary set all this down through the interpreters which I had. Still I determined to go with them; on the one hand, so as not to show weakness and, on the other, because I hoped to conduct my business with Mutezuma from that city because it bordered on his territory, as I have said, and on the road between the two there is free travel and no frontier restrictions.

When the people of Tascalteca saw my determination it distressed them considerably, and they told me many times that I was mistaken, but since they were vassals of Your Sacred Majesty and my friends they would go with me to assist me in whatever might happen. Although I opposed this and asked them not to come, as it was unnecessary, they followed me with some 100,000 men, all well armed for war, and came within two leagues of the city. After much persuasion on my part they returned, though there remained in my company some five or six thousand of them. That night I slept in a ditch, hoping to divest myself of these people in case they caused trouble in the city, and because it was already late enough and I did not want to enter too late. The following morning, they came out of the city to greet me with many trumpets and drums, including many persons whom they regard as priests in their temples, dressed in traditional vestments and singing after their fashion, as they do in the temples. With such ceremony they led us into the city and gave us very good quarters, where all those in my company were most comfortable. There they brought us food, though not sufficient. . . .

During the three days I remained in that city they fed us worse each day, and the lords and principal persons of the city came only rarely to see and speak with me. And being somewhat disturbed by this, my interpreter, who is an Indian woman from Putunchan, which is the great river of which I spoke to Your Majesty in the first letter, was told by another Indian woman and a native of this city that very close by many of Mutezuma's men were gathered, and that the people of the city had sent away their women and children and all their belongings, and were about to fall on us and kill us all; and that if she wished to escape she should go with her and she would shelter her. All this she told to Gerónimo de Aguilar, an interpreter whom I acquired in Yucatán, of whom I have also written to Your Highness; and he informed me. I then seized one of the natives of this city who was passing by and took him aside secretly and questioned him; and he confirmed what the woman and the natives of Tascalteca had told me. Because of this and because of the signs I had observed, I decided to forestall an attack, and I sent for some of the chiefs of the city, saying that I wished to speak with them. I put them in a room and meanwhile warned our men to be prepared, when a harquebus was fired, to fall on the many Indians who were outside our quarters and on those who were inside. And so it was done, that after I had put the chiefs in the room, I left them bound up and rode away and had the harquebus fired, and we fought so hard that in two hours more than three thousand men were killed. . . .

After fifteen or twenty days which I remained there the city and the land were so pacified and full of people that it seemed as if no one were missing from it, and their markets and trade were carried on as before. I then restored the friendly relations between this city of Curultecal and Tascalteca, which had existed in the recent past, before Mutezuma had attracted them to his friendship with gifts and made them enemies of the others.

STUDY QUESTIONS

1. Does Cortés offer a justification for his treatment of the people of Tascalteca? Why or why not?
2. What were the risks associated with Cortés' reliance on translators as he conquered the natives of Mexico?

2.3 THE POLITICAL TESTAMENT OF FREDERICK WILLIAM ("THE GREAT ELECTOR"), MAY 19, 1667

Combining armed force and strategic marriages, Frederick William of Brandenburg (ruled 1640–1688) rapidly expanded the territorial dimensions of his medium-sized state in northeastern Germany. To maintain his grip on these lands in the face of potential Swedish and Polish designs, the "Great Elector" needed as strong an army as possible, but this required substantial tax revenue. To obtain it, Frederick William extracted considerable sums from his Estates (representative assemblies), essentially by exempting the members of these groups while making everyone else pay. He also promised to support the nobles in their efforts to force peasants to work for minimal compensation on their lands.

These efforts enabled Frederick William to accrue increasing power for himself, much of it at the nobles' expense, and he hoped to pass this power along to his son and heir. In this remarkable document, composed in the midpoint of his reign, he reveals to his son the secrets of his power—but he also justifies the accumulation of power and alerts his successor to potential threats against it. Pay particular attention to the speaker's advice about how to maintain the appearance of control without unduly antagonizing those who resent strong rulers.

The fatherly love that I, as a father, bear for my son and future successor has compelled me to leave for him some useful lessons born of long experience, and to put these briefly into writing. [I do this] in consideration that it will be beneficial and necessary for him to know how he should lead his entire government, and how he should act, first and foremost regarding God, also regarding his peers, as well as his subjects, granted and entrusted to him by God, in religious and secular matters. . . .

Now, the first proper virtue of a righteous ruler is that he properly and sincerely fear, love, and keep God in mind, God who created him and made him lord and ruler of so many lands and people. Let His word, which alone leads to salvation, be the only true guideline of your entire reign and life, because therein lies the proper God-pleasing art of ruling and high politics. At the same time, diligently call to God daily—morning, noon, and night—with an ardent prayer, first for wisdom and understanding, also for gracious support with the heavy burden of reigning

From Mbemba a Nanzinga/King Alfonso I of Kongo, Correspondence with King Joao III of Portugal, 1526. Translated by Basil Davidson.

in His almighty name's honor and for the best of the entrusted land and people, and act so that you may answer to God, temporally in this world and eternally in the next. . . .

Now regarding religion and the building of churches in your lands, and in what form you could best lead, it is primarily to be seen, and to be considered, that the Reformed [Calvinist] religion, which is founded solely on the true word of God and on the works of the Apostles without any human additions, should be spread further in your lands. This should happen in such a way so that it is not with force, or prohibition of the Lutheran churches, or withdrawal of their incomes or revenues, but rather from your own means that you promote the building of Reformed churches in your lands. . . . To promote this work, primarily you have to see that when there are subjects of the Reformed religion in your lands who are qualified and talented, that they are accepted and appointed before others as your officials and officers, at court and in the country. Yes, because in Brandenburg there are none available, accept foreigners and favor them over the Lutherans. Give the Reformed children the ordinary benefices and stipends, so that they learn something and thereby can serve you better. At the same time, appoint preachers in Stettin and in the countryside who are not argumentative, and who do not brand your religion heretical or damn it, but rather who are peaceful people. So, then seek to promote religious peace, and bring back to life my edicts. In any case fill the schools and academies with teachers and professors who are moderate, and not argumentative. Those who do not want this, order them to leave the country. . . .

In the council listen diligently, note all of the councilors' opinions well and also have a protocol diligently kept. Decide nothing important in the presence of the councilors, out of the necessity of discretion. Instead, take such to consider privately, have one or another privy councilor come to you, ponder all the opinions that were presented and resolved, and be like the bee who sucks the best nectar from the flowers. If it is a difficult matter, then pray to God that He tells you in your heart what you should do or have done, first of all for the honor of His name, for the best and prosperity of the territory, people, and

subjects, and also for you and your house. Then promptly carry out the work that you have planned. So that it will go well and felicitously. Have all the letters that come in the mail or otherwise brought to you yourself. Open and read them, and then divide the work among the councilors, or have someone else do the division. When you have the councilors vote, then see to it that you start from the bottom, and not from the top, since the great authority of the senior councilors may prevent the junior ones from expressing their ideas or speaking freely, because they are often put through the wringer or interrupted by the more senior ones. . . .

Though I hope it will not happen, if the emperor, Spain, and the House of Austria go too far and violate the peace treaty concluded at Münster and Osnabrück, or if they would like to try to introduce new religious or worldly things in the empire that run contrary to German freedom and lead to the oppression of the ancient customs and structure, then normally you have to use the foreign crowns against them. At the same time, if Sweden or France want to go too far, then you have to hold to the emperor and the House of Austria, so that you can maintain the proper balance between them. The Italian princes handle this in such a way. When they see that one or the other is gaining and becoming great and powerful and that the one side is superior to the other, then they hold to the weaker and set themselves opposite the other. . . . The changing of the times will provide opportunities to make alliances with others. One must always orient oneself, and aim, and do that which is useful and beneficial to one's state: alliances are good, indeed, but one's own force is still better. One can rely more surely on it [one's own force], and a lord is of no consideration if he does not have his own means and soldiers. For that is what made me considerable once I followed this principle, and I always deplore that at the beginning of my reign, to my great disadvantage, I let myself be distracted from that and against my will followed other advice. . . .

Your own proper subjects in the districts must buy the salt and the herring from those you have assigned, and not from merchants or officials, as happens now. One will want to object that this is something new, but the previous Dukes of Prussia also did it, and the old receipts prove such adequately, and what was right for one's predecessors must be right for you. Let yourself in no way be distracted from this, because this can bring in many thousands annually for you. You must, however, arrange for loyal people who understand this work and perform it loyally. The officials themselves now use one who was already drawn in, and they will try to hinder this necessary work through their clients, and thereby spare no effort and toil. Take good care that you do not keep a much too extensive court, but instead reduce it on occasion. Always regulate the expenditures according to the revenues, and have officials diligently render receipts every year. When the finances are in a good state again, then you will have enough means, and you will not have to request money from the estates or address them. Then it is also not necessary to hold the many and expensive parliaments, because the more parliaments you hold, the more authority is taken from you, because the estates always try something that is detrimental to the majesty of the ruler.

STUDY QUESTIONS

1. To what extent is the role of king a matter of appearance rather than substance?
2. Was Frederick William paranoid about possible assaults on his power or of the king's potential to be undermined by others?

2.4 MBEMBA A NZINGA (AFONSO I) OF KONGO, CORRESPONDENCE WITH JOAO III OF PORTUGAL, 1526

Despite presiding over the most powerful state in the region, Kongolese royals had to negotiate with the Portuguese, who had landed in their territory in 1483 and wanted to impose their own rules. In 1491, the Kongolese king, Nzinga a Nkuwu, converted to Christianity, as did his son and heir, Mbemba a Nzinga, and vowed to spread Catholicism throughout west-central Africa. As new converts, the king and prince adopted Western royal names, João I and Afonso I respectively. In 1526, twenty years into his reign, Afonso wrote to his counterpart in Portugal, King Joao III, seeking help with Portuguese traders he felt were damaging his economy. Afonso's correspondence with the European monarch leaves historians a record of how an African ruler responded to the arrival of outsiders. In this letter, Afonso made clear his frustration that the Portuguese were expanding the slave trade beyond the boundaries he had set. Although he was unsuccessful in his entreaties with the Portuguese king, Afonso did create a new administrative system to regulate the slave trade.

From Mbemba a Nanzinga/King Alfonso I of Kongo, Correspondence with King Joao III of Portugal, 1526. Translated by Basil Davidson.

Sir, Your Highness should know how our Kingdom is being lost in so many ways that it is convenient to provide for the necessary remedy, since this is caused by the excessive freedom given by your agents and officials to the men and merchants who are allowed to come to this Kingdom to set up shops with goods and many things which have been prohibited by us, and which they spread throughout our Kingdoms and Domains in such an abundance that many of our vassals, whom we had in obedience, do not comply because they have the things in greater abundance than we ourselves; and it was with these things that we had them content and subjected under our vassalage and jurisdiction, so it is doing a great harm not only to the service of God, but the security and peace of our Kingdoms and State as well.

And we cannot reckon how great the damage is, since the mentioned merchants are taking every day our natives, sons of the land and the sons of our noblemen and vassals and our relatives, because the thieves and men of bad conscience grab them wishing to have the things and wares of this Kingdom which they are ambitious of; they grab them and get them to be sold; and so great, Sir, is the corruption and licentiousness that our country is being completely depopulated, and Your Highness should not agree with this nor accept it as in your service. And to avoid it we need from your Kingdoms no more than some priests and a few people to teach in schools, and no other goods except wine and flour for the holy sacrament. That is why we beg of Your Highness to help and assist us in this matter, commanding your factors [agents] that they should not send here either merchants or wares, because it our will that in these Kingdoms there should not be any trade of slaves nor outlet for them. Concerning what is referred [to] above, again we beg of Your Highness to agree with it, since otherwise we cannot remedy such an obvious damage. Pray Our Lord in his mercy to have Your

Highness under His guard and let you do forever the things of His service. . . .

Moreover, Sir, in our Kingdoms there is another great inconvenience which is of little service to God, and this is that many of our people, keenly desirous as they are of the wares and things of your Kingdoms, which are brought here by your people, and in order to satisfy their voracious appetite, seize many of our people, freed and exempt men, and very often it happens that they kidnap even noblemen and the sons of noblemen, and our relatives, and take a them to be sold to the white men who are in our Kingdoms; and for this purpose they have concealed them; and others are brought during the night so that they might not be recognized.

And as soon as they are taken by the white men they are immediately ironed and branded with fire, and when they are carried to be embarked, if they are caught by our guards' men the whites allege that they have bought them but they cannot say from whom, so that it is our duty to do justice and to restore to the freemen their freedom, but it cannot be done if your subjects feel offended, as they claim to be.

And to avoid such a great evil we passed a law so that any white man living in our Kingdoms and wanting to purchase goods in any way should first inform three of our noblemen and officials of our court whom we rely upon in this matter, and these are Dom Pedro Manipanza and Dom Manuel Manissaba, our chief usher, and Gocalo Pires our chief freighter, who should investigate if the mentioned goods are captives or free men, and if cleared by them there will be no further doubt nor embargo for them to be taken and embarked. But if the white men do not comply with it they will lose the aforementioned goods. And if we do them this favor and concession it is for the part Your Highness has in it, since we know that it is in your service too that these goods are taken from our Kingdom, otherwise we should not consent to this.

STUDY QUESTIONS

1. What actions by the Portuguese most bothered King Afonso?
2. What does this letter reveal about strengths and weaknesses of Kongo's alliance with Portugal? Who seemed to have the upper hand?

2.5 LOUIS XIV, *LE CODE NOIR*, MARCH 1685

The French Empire of the seventeenth and eighteenth centuries derived its most significant revenues from the sugar plantations established on the Caribbean islands of Martinique, Guadeloupe, and Saint-Domingue (the future Haiti). On these islands, the treatment of black slaves was so harsh that the French government developed a set of regulations known as *Le Code Noir* ("the Black Code") that was designed, in part, to make their treatment more humane. The code forbade plantation owners to torture, mutilate, or execute their slaves—at least without reasonable "cause"—and it required them to provide enslaved people with adequate food and shelter, as well as Catholic instruction. It should be remembered that 1685 was also the year in which Louis XIV revoked the *Edict of Nantes* issued by his predecessor King Henry IV in 1598 (see document 3.4). By this act, Louis erased the privileges accorded to France's Protestant communities in the attempt to end the violence of the French Wars of Religion. Notice particularly how Louis understood a Catholic monarch's duties toward all of his subjects, both white and black, but also the reality of their varying privileges.

Louis, by the grace of God, King of France and Navarre: to all those here present and to those to come, GREETINGS. In that we must care equally for all the peoples that Divine Providence has put under our tutelage, we have agreed to have the reports of the officers we have sent to our American islands studied in our presence. These reports inform us of their need for our authority and our justice in order to maintain the discipline of the Roman, Catholic, and Apostolic Faith in the islands. Our authority is also required to settle issues dealing with the condition and quality of the slaves in said islands. We desire to settle these issues and inform them that, even though they reside in climes infinitely far from our normal abode, we are always present for them, not only through the reach of our power but also by the promptness of our help toward their needs. For these reasons, and on the advice of our council and of our certain knowledge, absolute power and royal authority, we have declared, ruled, and ordered, and declare, rule, and order, that the following pleases us:

Article I. We desire and we expect that the Edict of 23 April 1615 of the late King, our most honored lord and father who remains glorious in our memory, be executed in our islands. This accomplished, we enjoin all of our officers to chase from our islands all the Jews who have established residence there. As with all declared enemies of Christianity, we command them to be gone within three months of the day of issuance of this present [order], at the risk of confiscation of their persons and their goods.

Article II. All slaves that shall be in our islands shall be baptized and instructed in the Roman, Catholic, and Apostolic Faith. We enjoin the inhabitants who shall purchase newly-arrived Negroes to inform the Governor and Intendant of said islands of this fact within no more than eight days, or risk being fined an arbitrary amount. They shall give the necessary orders to have them instructed and baptized within a suitable amount of time. . . .

Article VI. We enjoin all our subjects, of whatever religion and social status they may be, to observe

Adapted from https://thelouvertureproject.org/index.php?title=Le_Code_Noir, http://www.axl.cefan.ulaval.ca/amsudant/guyanefr1685.htm (French text).

Sundays and the holidays that are observed by our subjects of the Roman, Catholic, and Apostolic Faith. We forbid them to work, nor make their slaves work, on said days, from midnight until the following midnight. They shall neither cultivate the earth, manufacture sugar, nor perform any other work, at the risk of a fine and an arbitrary punishment against the masters, and of confiscation by our officers of as much sugar worked by said slaves before being caught.

Article VII. We forbid them also to hold slave markets or any other market on said days at the risk of similar punishments and of confiscation of the merchandise that shall be discovered at the market, and an arbitrary fine against the sellers . . .

Article XI. We forbid priests from conducting weddings between slaves if it appears that they do not have their masters' permission. We also forbid masters from using any constraints on their slaves to marry them without their wishes.

Article XII. Children born from marriages between slaves shall be slaves, and if the husband and wife have different masters, they shall belong to the masters of the female slave, not to the master of her husband.

Article XIII. We desire that if a male slave has married a free woman, their children, either male or female, shall follow the status of the mother and be free as is their mother, regardless of their father's condition of slavery. And if the father is free and the mother a slave, the children shall also be slaves. . . .

Article XV. We forbid slaves from carrying any offensive weapons or large sticks, at the risk of being whipped and having the weapons confiscated. The weapons shall then belong to him who confiscated them. The sole exception shall be made for those who have been sent by their masters to hunt and who are carrying either a letter from their masters or his known mark.

Article XVI. We also forbid slaves who belong to different masters from gathering, either during the

day or at night, under the pretext of a wedding or other excuse, either at one of the master's houses or elsewhere, and especially not in major roads or isolated locations. They shall risk corporal punishment that shall not be less than the whip and the fleur de lys [the royal symbol would be branded on the body], and for frequent recidivists and in other aggravating circumstances, they may be punished with death, a decision we leave to their judges. We enjoin all our subjects, even if they are not officers, to rush to the offenders, arrest them, and take them to prison, and that there be no decree against them. . . .

Article XXXIII. The slave who has struck his master in the face or has drawn blood, or has similarly struck the wife of his master, his mistress, or their children, shall be punished by death. . . .

Article XXXVIII. The fugitive slave who has been on the run for one month from the day his master reported him to the police, shall have his ears cut off and shall be branded with a fleur de lys on one shoulder. If he commits the same infraction for another month, again counting from the day he is reported, he shall have his hamstring cut and be branded with a fleur de lys on the other shoulder. The third time, he shall be put to death. . . .

Article LIX. We grant to freed slaves the same rights, privileges and immunities that are enjoyed by freeborn persons. We desire that they are deserving of this acquired freedom, and that this freedom gives them, as much for their person as for their property, the same happiness that natural liberty has on our other subjects.

Versailles, March 1685, the forty second year of our reign.

Signed LOUIS,
and below the King.
Colbert, visa, Le Tellier.
Read, posted and recorded at the sovereign council of
  the coast of Saint Domingue, kept at Petit Gouave,
  6 May 1687, Signed Moriceau.

STUDY QUESTIONS

1. What is the best example in this code of the contradictions between benevolent concern and the reinforcement of enslaved status?
2. How does the "Black Code" develop the concept that good order and discipline benefit all of a king's subjects?

2.6 VISUAL SOURCE: SPANISH PIECE OF EIGHT COIN, 1768

The conquest of the New World gave Spain access to precious metals, especially gold and silver deposits. Worked mostly by indigenous people in unhealthy and dangerous conditions, the mines yielded unprecedented wealth. One of the most productive sites was the Potosí mine in Bolivia, nicknamed Silver Mountain, which is still active today. Potosí was also a site for minting the "piece of eight," probably the most famous coin of all time. Its name comes from the value of the coin— one ounce of silver was worth eight Spanish *reales*. An inch and a half in diameter, the piece of eight could be divided, when necessary, into smaller pieces (halves and quarters). The example here shows the number 8 on the right of the crowned coat of arms of Charles III, King of Spain, whose name appears in Latin around the border. On the other side, the date 1768 appears at the bottom, flanked by the logo of the Potosí mine (PTS letters on top of one another) and an image of the crown atop maps of the Earth's hemispheres. The banners circling the columns display the words "Plus" and "Ultra," which in Latin both mean "more." These images represent the expanse of the Spanish empire and the great value of its South American silver.

After being minted in Bolivia, the pieces of eight travelled by llama across the Andes mountains to the Pacific coast, where waiting Spanish ships transported them to Panama for the journey across the isthmus and then onto vessels bound for Spain. By the 1590s, some six million pounds of silver a year flowed out of Spanish America. Only twenty percent of the silver remained in the Western hemisphere; the rest was sent east and west, with ten percent landing in China.

Although most of these coins headed for Spanish ports, only a small fraction of them remained in Spain; the rest circulated across the globe. Spain used the funds to finance costly wars in the Netherlands, Germany, and Eastern Europe. The piece of eight thus became an international currency. Europeans used the coins to purchase goods available only in Indian and Pacific Ocean markets, especially in China, where merchants exchanged silver for silk, spices, ivory, and porcelain. The Chinese, for their part, needed the silver to pay their taxes. In North America, where there were no silver mines, British colonists obtained pieces of eight through their Caribbean trade and used them as their currency. Other countries also adapted the coins for their own ends. The British Museum has examples of coins counterstamped by local authorities from Indonesia, Belgium, Scotland, and Australia. Ironically, the flood of silver hurt the Spanish economy by causing massive inflation that made it increasingly difficult for locals to afford the high taxes demanded by the government.

CNG/Wikipedia
https://commons.wikimedia.org/wiki/File:Potosì_8_reales_1768_131206.jpg.

FIGURE 2.6   Spanish Piece of Eight Coin

STUDY QUESTIONS

1. How did the expansion of the supply of silver affect the early modern global economy in general and the economy of Europe in particular?
2. What kinds of information can historians learn from studying coins that they might not otherwise be able to find?

SUBORDINATION

In this chapter we will be working with *subordination*. Where *coordination* joins grammatical "equals," *subordination* joins "nonequals": subordination joins an *independent clause* with a *subordinate clause*, also called a *dependent clause*.

REVIEW:

A clause has a **subject** and a **verb** or **verb phrase**. The subject may or may not be stated.

Examples:

The dog sat.	The subject is "the dog." The verb is "sat."
Sit!	The verb is *sit*. The subject—you—is implied.

An **independent clause** can "stand on its own" as a complete sentence.

Example:

Rex barked.	The subject is *Rex*, the verb is *barked*, and the sentence is complete.

A **subordinate clause** also has a subject and a verb, but it cannot stand on its own.

Example:

as Rex barked	The subject is *Rex*; the verb is *barked*. The word *as* is a subordinator, which means that "*as Rex barked*" is not a complete sentence.

The addition of "*as*" to the beginning of "*Rex barked*" makes the clause subordinate. In a complete sentence, a subordinate clause must be attached to an independent clause, which the subordinate clause is said to "depend on."

The cat hissed *as Rex barked.*
NOT:
The cat hissed. As Rex barked.

"*The cat hissed*" is independent. It can stand on its own as a complete sentence. "*As Rex barked*" is subordinate or dependent. It cannot stand on its own as a complete sentence.

Subordinate clauses usually begin with a *subordinator*. Among the most common: *that, whether, if, after, before, since, till, until, although, because, provided, though, unless, if*. Relative pronouns that often begin dependent clauses: *who, that, which, where, when, whose*.

For self-timed discrimination exercises, see the website—which we strongly recommend you do if you have ever seen the words "incomplete sentence" or "fragment" on a paper. Your goal is to know instantly, without having to think about it, whether you have written an independent or a subordinate clause. Good writers are fluent in grammar, syntax, and punctuation; timed exercises will help you become fluent too.

Writers use subordination to achieve economy and flow: to eliminate unnecessary words and to create smoother sentences and smoother connections *between* sentences. Subordination can also tell readers which idea is most important (usually the idea in the main clause) and which idea(s) are less important (usually, those in the subordinate clause).

EXERCISES: JUMBLED-SENTENCE PUZZLES USING SUBORDINATE CLAUSES

1.

Unscramble the sentence below and transcribe it from memory onto a separate piece of paper. Original punctuation included.

_____ All of these empires

___3___ although no other empire

___2___ contained a variety of different peoples,

_____ matched the diversity

_____ of the Ottomans

2.

Unscramble the sentence below and transcribe it from memory onto a separate piece of paper. Original punctuation included.

___2___ and financially devastated

_____ whose king

_____ to venal officeholders, financiers, and other private interests.

_____ much of his once-substantial power

_____ Spain was exhausted

___3___ by constant warfare

_____ had mortgaged

_____ and saddled with a state

3.

Unscramble the sentence below and transcribe it from memory onto a separate piece of paper. Original punctuation included.

_____ was

_____ positioned

___4___ because

_____ to dominate Europe

_____ for the next century and a half.

_____ Great Britain

___7___ it

___3___ the most successful country

_____ its constitutional government and efficient state

4.

Unscramble the sentence below and transcribe it from memory onto a separate piece of paper. Original punctuation included.

_____ by God and king to fight.

__7___ as in the past,

_____ military commanders were those

_____ Fearing armed competition from the nobles,

__3___ and increasingly,

__5___ who purchased their commissions

_____ kings discouraged their military activity,

_____ rather than being called,

5.

Unscramble the sentence below and transcribe it from memory onto a separate piece of paper. Original punctuation included.

__3___ at the dawn of the fifteenth century,

__6___ which they launched in early 1453.

_____ Osman's heirs built a powerful navy

_____ After failing to capture

__2___ the Byzantine capital, Constantinople,

_____ to prepare for a second attack,

EXERCISES: SENTENCE COMBINING USING SUBORDINATE CLAUSES

6.

Combine the sentences by replacing the underlined words with "that."

Roxelana demonstrated women's ability to participate in the affairs of state.

Women's ability to participate in the affairs of state was beneficial to the Ottoman empire.

_____

_____

_____

7.

Combine the sentences by placing the word "because" before "They."

Ottoman rulers ceased to marry.

They did not want to elevate another family to an elite status.

_____

_____

_____

8.

Now combine the sentences in the opposite order. You will need a comma after the subordinate clause because it opens the sentence.

They did not want to elevate another family to an elite status.

Ottoman rulers ceased to marry.

_____

_____

_____

9.

Combine the sentences by placing "although" in front of "No empire" and inserting a comma after "peoples."

All empires contained a variety of different peoples.

No empire matched the diversity of the Ottomans.

_____

_____

_____

10.

Now combine the sentences in the opposite order, inserting "although" after "the Ottomans."

No empire matched the diversity of the Ottomans.

All empires contained a variety of different peoples.

_____

_____

_____

11.

Combine the sentences by placing "although" before the first sentence and inserting a comma after "1700."

France and Spain stood apart as mortal enemies during much of the period from 1500 to 1700.

Their political systems had much in common.

_____

_____

_____

12.

Combine the sentences by placing "although" before the first sentence and a comma after "slaves."

They were brought into the sultan's harem as slaves.

The mothers of royal sons sometimes became powerful figures.

_____

_____

_____

13.

Combine the sentences by replacing the second "Hernando Cortés" with "who."

Hernando Cortés was a conqueror.

Hernando Cortés claimed territory in Mexico in April 1519.

_____

_____

_____

14.

Replace the second "Treaty of Tordesillas" with "which." You will need to add a comma after "Tordesillas."

In 1494, the pope announced the Treaty of Tordesillas.

The Treaty of Tordesillas purported to divide the New World between Portugal and Spain.

_____

_____

_____

15.

Combine the three sentences below by replacing the underlined words with "that" and "who." Add a comma after "the Spanish people."

The influx of silver from the New World produced a Europe-wide price inflation.

The Europe-wide price inflation impoverished the Spanish people.

The Spanish people were already suffering from highly regressive taxation.

_____

_____

_____

EXERCISES: STRUCTURING SENTENCES FOR EMPHASIS USING SUBORDINATION

Some subordinate clauses can be placed in multiple positions within a sentence. More specifically, clauses that begin with subordinators are usually moveable:

Ottoman rulers ceased to marry *because they did not want to elevate another family to an elite status.*

Because they did not want to elevate another family to an elite status, Ottoman rulers ceased to marry.

Ottoman rulers, *because they did not want to elevate another family to an elite status,* ceased to marry.

In contrast, clauses that begin with relative pronouns tend to have only one correct position in a sentence:

Ottoman sultans were monarchs *who fathered children with concubines rather than wives.*

NOT ALLOWED: *Who fathered children with concubines rather than wives,* Ottoman sultans were monarchs.

Proficient writers often place less important information within a subordinate clause and, to achieve *sentence end focus,* position the subordinate clause at the beginning or middle of the sentence, if possible.

Instructions

In the sentence pairs below, choose the version that emphasizes the most important information. The relevant subordinate clauses are underlined.

16.

A.   Since concubines came from all over the empire, they brought new gene pools into the royal line.

B.   Concubines brought new gene pools into the royal line since they came from all over the empire.

17.

A.   Since each state was relatively small, they had to manage themselves as efficiently as possible.

B.   States had to manage themselves as efficiently as possible since each was relatively small.

18.

A.   Most political and economic power resided in regional assemblies led by merchant and landed elites, <u>although the Dutch created a monarchy</u>.

B.   <u>Although the Dutch created a monarchy</u>, most political and economic power resided in regional assemblies led by merchant and landed elites.

19.

A.   The Habsburg kings presided more completely over Austria and Bohemia <u>although they ruled German-speaking Central Europe indirectly</u>.

B.   <u>Although the Habsburg kings ruled German-speaking Central Europe indirectly</u>, they presided more completely over Austria and Bohemia.

20.

A.   <u>Although a business enterprise</u>, the Dutch East India Company acted like an aggressive, imperial state.

B.   The Dutch East India Company acted like an aggressive, imperial state, <u>although a business enterprise</u>.

You will find suggested answers to the exercises in the back of this book. For more Writing History exercises, as well as study resources for this chapter, visit oup.com/us/berenson.

CHAPTER 3

CRISES OF THE SEVENTEENTH CENTURY

3.1 DUC DE SAINT-SIMON, THE DAILY HABITS OF LOUIS XIV AT VERSAILLES, C. 1715

Louis de Rouvroy, the Duc de Saint-Simon (1675–1755), a minor noble at King Louis XIV's court at Versailles, would achieve lasting fame with the posthumous publication of his copious, frank, and witty observations of the court. While resident at Versailles for brief periods after 1702 until the king's death in 1715, Saint-Simon paid particular attention to the maneuverings of his fellow aristocrats, in the process garnering the resentment of many of them, especially the king's illegitimate children ("the Bastards"), who occupied a prominent place at court.

At eight o'clock the chief *valet de chambre* on duty, who alone had slept in the royal chamber, and who had dressed himself, awoke the King. The chief physician, the chief surgeon, and the nurse (as long as she lived), entered at the same time. The latter kissed the King; the others rubbed and often changed his shirt, because he was in the habit of sweating a great deal. At the quarter [hour], the grand chamberlain was called (or, in his absence, the first gentleman of the chamber), and those who had, what was called the *grandes entrées*. The chamberlain (or chief gentleman) drew back the curtains which had been closed again, and presented the holy water from the vase, at the head of the bed. These gentlemen stayed but a moment, and that was the time to speak to the King, if any one

had anything to ask of him; in which case the rest stood aside. When, contrary to custom, nobody had aught to say, they were there but for a few moments. He who had opened the curtains and presented the holy water, presented also a prayer-book. Then all passed into the cabinet of the council. A very short religious service being over, the King called, they re-entered. The same officer gave him his dressing-gown; immediately after, other privileged courtiers entered, and then everybody, in time to find the King putting on his shoes and stockings, for he did almost everything himself and with address and grace. Every other day we saw him shave himself; and he had a little short wig in which he always appeared, even in bed, and on medicine days. He often spoke of the chase, and

From *Memoirs of the Duc de Saint-Simon*, translated by Bayle St. John and edited by W. H. Lewis (New York: Macmillan, 1964), pp. 140–141, 144–145.

sometimes said a word to somebody. No toilette table was near him; he had simply a mirror held before him.

As soon as he was dressed, he prayed to God, at the side of his bed, where all the clergy present knelt, the cardinals without cushions, all the laity remaining standing; and the captain of the guards came to the balustrade during the prayer, after which the King passed into his cabinet.

He found there, or was followed by all who had the entrée, a very numerous company, for it included everybody in any office. He gave orders to each for the day; thus within half a quarter of an hour it was known what he meant to do; and then all this crowd left directly. The bastards, a few favourites, and the valets alone were left. It was then a good opportunity for talking with the King; for example, about plans of gardens and buildings; and conversation lasted more or less according to the person engaged in it.

. . .

At ten o'clock his supper was served. The captain of the guard announced this to him. A quarter of an hour after the King came to supper, and from the ante-chamber of Madame de Maintenon [his principal mistress] to the table again, any one spoke to him who wished. This supper was always on a grand scale, the royal household (that is, the sons and daughters of France), at table, and a large number of courtiers and ladies present, sitting or standing, and on the evening before the journey to Marly all those ladies who wished to take part in it. That was called presenting yourself for Marly. Men asked in the morning, simply saying to the King, "Sire, Marly." In later years, the King grew tired of this, and a valet wrote up in the gallery the names of those who asked. The ladies continued to present themselves.

The King, wishing to retire, went and fed his dogs; then said good night, passed into his chamber to the *ruelle* [the "little path" between a bed and the wall] of his bed, where he said his prayers, as in the morning, then undressed. He said good night with an inclination of the head, and whilst everybody was leaving the room stood at the corner of the mantelpiece, where he gave the order to the colonel of the guards alone. Then commenced what was called the *petit coucher*, at which only the specially privileged remained. That was short. They did not leave until he got into bed. It was a moment to speak to him.

STUDY QUESTIONS

1. Why does Saint-Simon pay particular attention to moments of the day during which a courtier could speak directly with the King?
2. How could Louis XIV's daily habits be described as a mixture of religious and more "secular" pursuits?

3.2 ROBERT BAILLIE, LETTER TO WILLIAM SPANG, AUGUST 23, 1648

Robert Baillie (1602–1662) was a Presbyterian minister from Glasgow whose letters and journals are invaluable sources for historians studying the tumultuous seventeenth century. Excerpted here is a letter Baillie wrote to his cousin William Spang in 1648 about the goings on of the

From Robert Baillie, *The Letters and Journals of Robert Baillie, A.M. Principal of the University of Glasgow*, Volume Third, edited by David Laing (Edinburgh: Robert Ogle, 1842), pp. 50–66.

General Assembly, the governing body of the Scottish Presbyterian Church, held in Edinburgh. Spang lived in the Netherlands where he served a local Presbyterian congregation. It was a fraught time, with political tensions running high in the wake of the English Civil War. The Scots had fiercely resisted the Church of England's efforts to dominate their lands, and Baillie, although generally a moderate in political and religious matters, had been part of the Scottish movement to keep their own Presbyterian ministers separate from the Anglican hierarchy and to reject the Anglican *Book of Common Prayer*.

Meanwhile, Scotland was suffering the effects of the Little Ice Age. Baillie describes the unusual weather and the rise in disease as the plague spread through Scotland's cities. Perhaps not coincidentally in such strained circumstances, the leaders in the assembly called for strict conformity to their ideology, casting about for ways to discipline wayward members of society and codify lessons taught in schools.

Note that Baillie wrote in Elizabethan English, the language of Shakespeare; his spelling and punctuation have been modernized.

For MR. WILLIAM SPANG. AUGUST 23rd 1648.

Reverend and dear cousin,

What is become of you since your journey to Danzig? I long much to hear, desiring earnestly to know your safe return, and understand how affairs go in these bounds. How things go here since my last, I give you this account. . . . Our condition for the time is sad: The pestilence in Glasgow, Aberdeen, and Edinburgh also; the continuance of very intemperate rain upon the corns; the irreconcilable differences of Church and State, looking towards a very great persecution of them who have been the best instruments both of Church and State, are great signs of the wrath of God; especially the hearts of the body of people being evidently hardened, and the minds likewise of the ministry diverted from pressing that humiliation and mourning, which the times call for above all things else.

But leaving the State, our General Assembly sat down on Wednesday July 12th.

. . .

At this time I was grieved for the state of Glasgow. The pest did increase. My brother son's house was infected; my brother's house enclosed many in danger: one night near a dozen died of the sickness. Some good, but unadvised people, were not much grieved for the calamity of that Town; and if it had fallen only upon their opposites, their insulting had been grievous, yet the Lord has been marvelously gracious to my brother and his son: no harm at all has come to them; and the danger of the Town, blessed be God, is much diminished. The long great rains for many weeks did prognosticate famine; but these three days bypassed there is also a great change of weather; the Lord continue it.

Our Assembly drew over to the end of the fifth week: many, dwelling far off and superexpended [overtired], fled away. I suspected the Moderator drew long of purpose, waiting for a letter from the Parliament of England, which came not. We hear now the House of Commons passed a declaration to us; but the Lords consented not to it. I did not love to have any correspondence with them now, but others loved it too well. . . . Many good overtures against the sins of the time did likewise pass. One of them I was feared for; it was first, that all Ministers conversing with Malignants should be censured by Presbyteries. This would have snared many; for the notion of the Malignants now by the Engagement, is extended to very many: I got it some way qualified, but not so as it will be found needful.

That which some days in the end of the Assembly troubled us was Mr. Andrew Ramsay and Mr. William Colvill's process. Mr. Andrew had, in preaching, often fallen out into diverse impertinencies and contradictions to his brethren; he had been often admonished; but the man's weakness and age, and diverse who resorted to him, permitted him not much to amend. Not only he had spoken for the En-gagement; but in prejudice of our proceedings and Presbyterial government itself. Much he denied which was proven. . . . One or two of your friends in our Presbytery had been, for their silence and ambiguity about the Engagement, referred to the Assembly, had I not diverted and gotten that evil kept off them; for had they come before us, readily they had never come off.

We appointed visitations for Universities and hospitals, and put on them the sharpest men we had. Likely Edinburgh will not submit to have either University or hospitals visited, though they have most need; and I pressed their visitation before any other; since, as yet, they have ever declined it. . . .

The matter of this unhappy Engagement I hope will not last, and so the ground of our difference with the State shall be removed: but new grounds of division may possibly arise, which may make our contentions greater. This much I have written to yow, to oblige you to write oftener and larger; so much the more as our intercourse with London is stopped, and we know not what is doing either there or abroad. What you learn weekly by your Gazettes, I pray, once in the month at least, let us have its sum, as you shall have occasion to send it. So I rest,

Your Cousin, to serve you,
August 23d [1648] Robert Baillie.

STUDY QUESTIONS

1. What effects of the Little Ice Age did Baillie describe? How did he account for the changes in weather and their consequences?
2. How did Baillie respond to the assembly's desire to punish those who were seen as not loyal enough to orthodox Presbyterian beliefs?

3.3 OTTO VON GUERICKE, *THE DESTRUCTION OF MAGDEBURG IN THE THIRTY YEARS' WAR, 1631*

Otto von Guericke (1602–1686) served as the mayor of Magdeburg, a town held by German Protestants that was well situated to serve as a military base for the Catholic forces of the Holy Roman Empire to defend their newly acquired territory from invading Swedes. After the Swedish king Gustavus Adolphus attacked German territory, the Empire's forces laid siege to Magdeburg and a year later breached its walls. As Guericke's account shows, the invaders committed atrocious acts of violence against the civilian population, burning down the town and causing about 25,000 deaths. The sack of Magdeburg, like the Saint Bartholomew's Day Massacre (see document 1.6), became a rallying cry for Protestants during the Thirty Years' War and moved them to show no mercy toward their Catholic opponents. The sack had political consequences as well because it pushed the Elector of Brandenburg to ally with Sweden.

From James Harvey Robinson, *Readings in Modern European History*, Volume 2 (Boston: Ginn and Co., 1906), pp. 211–212.

So then General Pappenheim [the commander of the Holy Roman Empire's forces] collected a number of his people on the ramparts by the New Town, and brought them from there into the streets of the city. Von Falckenberg [the Swedish commander of the defense forces] was shot, and fires were kindled in different quarters; then indeed it was all over with the city, and further resistance was useless. Nevertheless some of the soldiers and citizens did try to make a stand here and there, but the imperial troops kept bringing on more and more forces—cavalry, too—to help them, and finally they got the Kröckenthor open and let in the whole imperial army and the forces of the Catholic League,—Hungarians, Croats, Poles, Walloons, Italians, Spaniards, French, North and South Germans.

Thus it came about that the city and all its inhabitants fell into the hands of the enemy, whose violence and cruelty were due in part to their common hatred of the adherents of the Augsburg Confession [i.e., Protestants], and in part to their being imbittered by the chain shot which had been fired at them and by the derision and insults that the Magdeburgers had heaped upon them from the ramparts.

Then was there naught but beating and burning, plundering, torture, and murder. Most especially was every one of the enemy bent on securing much booty. When a marauding party entered a house, if its master had anything to give he might thereby purchase respite and protection for himself and his family till the next man, who also wanted something, should come along. It was only when everything had been brought forth and there was nothing left to give that the real trouble commenced. Then, what with blows and threats of shooting, stabbing, and hanging, the poor people were so terrified that if they had had anything left they would have brought it forth if it had been buried in the earth or hidden away in a thousand castles. In this frenzied rage, the great and splendid city that had stood like a fair princess in the land was now, in its hour of direst need and unutterable distress and woe, given over to the flames, and thousands of innocent men, women, and children, in the midst of a horrible din of heartrending shrieks and cries, were tortured and put to death in so cruel and shameful a manner that no words would suffice to describe, nor no tears to bewail it. . . .

Thus in a single day this noble and famous city, the pride of the whole country, went up in fire and smoke; and the remnant of its citizens, with their wives and children, were taken prisoners and driven away by the enemy with a noise of weeping and wailing that could be heard from afar, while the cinders and ashes from the town were carried by the wind to Wanzleben, Egeln, and still more distant places.

In addition to all this, quantities of sumptuous and irreplaceable house furnishings and movable property of all kinds, such as books, manuscripts, paintings, memorials of all sorts, . . . which money could not buy, were either burned or carried away by the soldiers as booty. The most magnificent garments, hangings, silk stuffs, gold and silver lace, linen of all sorts, and other household goods were bought by the army sutlers [civilian merchants buying and selling provisions to the military in the field] for a mere song and peddled about by the cart load all through the archbishopric of Magdeburg and in Anhalt and Brunswick. Gold chains and rings, jewels, and every kind of gold and silver utensils were to be bought from the common soldiers for a tenth of their real value.

STUDY QUESTIONS

1. What does this account of the sack of Magdeburg reveal about who fought in the Thirty Years' War and who was affected?
2. What shocked Otto von Guericke the most about the actions of the invading troops? How did he account for their violence?

3.4 HENRY IV OF FRANCE, *THE EDICT OF NANTES*, 1598 & LOUIS XIV, *THE EDICT OF FONTAINEBLEAU*, 1685

Henry of Navarre (1553–1610) was a vocal and prominent Huguenot whose marriage to Margaret, the younger sister of the French monarch, helped trigger the Saint Bartholomew's Day Massacre (see document 1.6) in 1572. He converted to Catholicism in 1593, after becoming King Henry IV of France. However, he did not forget the Protestants whose cause he had championed earlier in life. He wanted Protestants to be able to live in peace with France's Catholic majority. To secure the peaceful coexistence of his kingdom's rival religious groups, he issued the *Edict of Nantes* (1598), which allowed Protestants to practice their religion unmolested in certain parts of the country while maintaining Catholicism as the country's dominant faith.

Catholic extremists opposed Henry's edict. One of them, François Ravaillac, assassinated him in 1610, but not before Henry had established a new French ruling family, the Bourbons. His progeny did not, however, maintain his religious toleration. His son, Louis XIII, withdrew certain Protestant rights and protections, and his grandson, Louis XIV, revoked the *Edict of Nantes* altogether with the *Edict of Fontainebleau* in 1685. One hundred and fifty thousand French Protestants then fled to England and the Netherlands, draining the country of some its wealthiest and most educated citizens.

THE EDICT OF NANTES

Henry, by the grace of God king of France and of Navarre, to all to whom these Presents come, greeting:

Among the infinite benefits which it has pleased God to heap upon us, the most signal and precious is his granting us the strength and ability to withstand the fearful disorders and troubles which prevailed on our advent in this kingdom. The realm was so torn by innumerable factions and sects that the most legitimate of all the parties was fewest in numbers. God has given us strength to stand out against this storm; we have finally surmounted the waves and made our port of safety,—peace for our state. For which his be the glory all in all, and ours a free recognition of his grace in making use of our instrumentality in the good work. . . . We implore and await from the Divine Goodness the same protection and favor which he has ever granted to this kingdom from the beginning. . . .

We have, by this perpetual and irrevocable edict, established and proclaimed and do establish and proclaim:

I. First, that the recollection of everything done by one party or the other between March, 1585, and our accession the crown, and during all the preceding period of troubles, remain obliterated and forgotten, as if no such things had ever happened.

III. We ordain that the Catholic Apostolic and Roman religion shall be restored and

From James Harvey Robinson, *Readings in Modern European History,* Volume 2 (Boston: Ginn and Co., 1906), pp. 183–185, 287-291.

reestablished in all places and localities of this our kingdom and countries subject to our sway, where the exercise of the same has been interrupted, in order that it may be peaceably and freely exercised, without any trouble or hindrance; forbidding very expressly all persons, of whatsoever estate, quality, or condition, from troubling, molesting, or disturbing ecclesiastics in the celebration of divine service, in the enjoyment or collection of tithes, fruits, or revenues of their benefices, and all other rights and dues belonging to them; and that all those who during the troubles have taken possession of churches, houses, goods or revenues, belonging to the said ecclesiastics, shall surrender to them entire possession and peaceable enjoyment of such rights, liberties, and sureties as they had before they were deprived of them.

VI.   And in order to leave no occasion for troubles or differences between our subjects, we have permitted, and herewith permit, those of the said religion called Reformed to live and abide in all the cities and places in our kingdom and countries of our sway without being annoyed, molested, or compelled to do anything in the matter of religion contrary to their consciences, . . . upon condition that they comport themselves in other respects according to that which is contained in the present edict.

VII.   It is permitted to all lords, gentlemen, and other persons making profession of the said religion called Reformed, holding the right of high justice [or a certain feudal tenure], to exercise the said religion in their houses.

IX.   We also permit those of the said religion to make and continue the exercise of the same in all villages and places of our dominion where it was established by them and publicly enjoyed several and divers[e] times in the year 1597, up to the end of the month of August, notwithstanding all decrees and judgments to the contrary.

XIII.   We very expressly forbid to all those of the said religion its exercise, either in respect to ministry, regulation, discipline, or the public instruction of children, or otherwise, in this our kingdom and lands of our dominion, otherwise than in the places permitted and granted by the present edict.

XIV.   It is forbidden as well to perform any function of said religion in our court or retinue, or in our lands and territories beyond the mountains, or in our city of Paris, or within five leagues of the said city.

XVIII.   We also forbid all our subjects, of whatever quality and condition, from carrying off by force or persuasion, against the will of their parents, the children of the said religion, in order to cause them to be baptized or confirmed in the Catholic Apostolic and Roman Church; and the same is forbidden to those of the said religion called Reformed, upon penalty of being punished with especial severity.

XXI.   Books concerning the said religion called Reformed may not be printed and publicly sold, except in cities and places where the public exercise of the said religion is permitted.

XXII.   We ordain that there shall be no difference or distinction made in respect to the said religion, in receiving pupils to be instructed in universities, colleges, and schools; nor in receiving the sick and poor into hospitals, retreats, and public charities.

XXIII.   Those of the said religion called Reformed shall be obliged to respect the laws of the Catholic Apostolic and Roman Church, recognized in this our kingdom, for the consummation of marriages contracted, or to be contracted, as regards the degrees of consanguinity and kinship.

THE EDICT OF FONTAINEBLEAU

Louis, by the grace of God king of France and Navarre, to all present and to come, greeting:

I. Be it known that for these causes and others us hereunto moving, and of our certain knowledge, full power, and royal authority, we have, by this present perpetual and irrevocable edict, suppressed and revoked, and do suppress and revoke, the edict of our said grandfather [Henry IV], given at Nantes in April, 1598, in its whole extent, together with the particular articles agreed upon in the month of May following, and the letters patent issued upon the same date; and also the edict given at Nimes in July, 1629; we declare them null and void, together with all concessions, of whatever nature they may be, made by them as well as by other edicts, declarations, and orders, in favor of the said persons of the R.P.R. [Religion prétendue réformée, "the religion called the Reformed"], the which shall remain in like manner as if they had never been granted ; and in consequence we desire, and it is our pleasure, that all the temples of those of the said R.P.R. situate in our kingdom, countries, territories, and the lordships under our crown, shall be demolished without delay.

II. We forbid our subjects of the R.P.R. to meet any more for the exercise of the said religion in any place or private house, under any pretext whatever, . . .

III. We likewise forbid all noblemen, of what condition soever, to hold such religious exercises in their houses or fiefs, under penalty to be inflicted upon all our said subjects who shall engage in the said exercises, of imprisonment and confiscation.

IV. We enjoin all ministers of the said R.P.R., who do not choose to become converts and to embrace the Catholic, apostolic, and Roman religion, to leave our kingdom and the territories subject to us within a fortnight of the publication of our present edict, without leave to reside therein beyond that period, or, during the said fortnight, to engage in any preaching, exhortation, or any other function, on pain of being sent to the galleys. . . .

VII. We forbid private schools for the instruction of children of the said R.P.R., and in general all things whatever which can be regarded as a concession of any kind in favor of the said religion.

VIII. As for children who may be born of persons of the said R.P.R., we desire that from henceforth they be baptized by the parish priests. We enjoin parents to send them to the churches for that purpose, under penalty of five hundred livres fine, to be increased as circumstances may demand; and thereafter the children shall be brought up in the Catholic, apostolic, and Roman religion, which we expressly enjoin the local magistrates to see done.

IX. And in the exercise of our clemency towards our subjects of the said R.P.R. who have emigrated from our kingdom, lands, and territories subject to us, previous to the publication of our present edict, it is our will and pleasure that in case of their returning within the period of four months from the day of the said publication, they may, and it shall be lawful for them to, again take possession of their property, and to enjoy the same as if they had all along remained there: on the contrary, the property abandoned by those who, during the specified period of four months, shall not have returned into our kingdom, lands, and territories subject to us, shall remain and be confiscated in consequence of our declaration of the 20th of August last.

X. We repeat our most express prohibition to all our subjects of the said R.P.R., together with their wives and children, against leaving our kingdom, lands, and territories subject to us, or transporting their goods and effects therefrom under penalty, as respects the men, of being sent to the galleys, and as respects the women, of imprisonment and confiscation.

XI.   It is our will and intention that the declarations rendered against the relapsed shall be executed according to their form and tenor.

XII.   As for the rest, liberty is granted to the said persons of the R.P.R., pending the time when it shall please God to enlighten them as well as others, to remain in the cities and places of our kingdom, lands, and territories subject to us, and there to continue their commerce, and to enjoy their possessions, without being subjected to molestation or hindrance on account of the said R.P.R., on condition of not engaging in the exercise of the said religion, or of meeting under pretext of prayers or religious services, of whatever nature these may be, under the penalties above mentioned of imprisonment and confiscation. This do we give in charge to our trusty and well-beloved counselors, etc.

STUDY QUESTIONS

1. What Reformed actions did Henry IV's edict limit and which did it allow? Why is the Edict of Nantes considered an important statement of religious tolerance in Europe?
2. Why did King Louis XIV's revocation of the edict in 1685 send thousands of French protestants abroad? What specific freedoms would they have lost if they stayed in France?

3.5 GERRARD WINSTANLEY, *THE TRUE LEVELLERS STANDARD ADVANCED*, 1649

Gerrard Winstanley (1609–1676) was a failed clothing-maker who became an impoverished agricultural laborer. Around 1649, saying he had had a vision from God, Winstanley took it upon himself to communicate his revelations in a series of religious pamphlets. In these writings, Winstanley maintained that the entire earth was "the common treasury" of all men: it belonged to everyone.

Fueled by this conviction, Winstanley and a group of laborers dug up and planted crops on private lands. Their contemporaries called them "Diggers," although the group called itself "true levellers," a reference to the "Levellers" of the English Revolution who had advocated political democratization but not dramatic social change. The Diggers wished to "level" the ground between the wealthy and the poor in England during the Cromwellian "Commonwealth" (1642–1660). They believed Levellers and other English revolutionaries had not gone far enough in their efforts to reform religion and society because they had allowed landlords to reassert their invalid claims to the "common wealth" of English land. Leveller communities sprung up in various pockets of England throughout the Commonwealth period, and Winstanley's pamphlets remained influential for future generations of radical reformers.

From Gerrard Winstanley Archive, *The True Levellers Standard Advanced: Or The State of Community Opened, and Presented to the Sons of Men,* at: https://www.marxists.org/reference/archive/winstanley/1649/levellers-standard.htm and http://www.kingston.ac.uk/cusp/Lectures/Hill.htm

A Declaration to the Powers of England, and to all the Powers of the World, shewing the Cause why the Common People of England have begun, and gives Consent to Digge up, Manure, and Sowe Corn upon George-Hill in Surrey; by those that have Subscribed, and thousands more that gives Consent.

In the beginning of Time, the great Creator Reason made the Earth to be a Common Treasury, to preserve Beasts, Birds, Fishes, and Man, the lord that was to govern this Creation; for Man had Domination given to him, over the Beasts, Birds, and Fishes; but not one word was spoken in the beginning, That one branch of mankind should rule over another.

And the Reason is this, Every single man, Male and Female, is a perfect Creature of himself; and the same Spirit that made the Globe, dwels in man to govern the Globe; so that the flesh of man being subject to Reason, his Maker, hath him to be his Teacher and Ruler within himself, therefore needs not run abroad after any Teacher and Ruler without him, for he needs not that any man should teach him, for the same Anoynting that ruled in the Son of man, teacheth him all things.

But since humane flesh (that king of Beasts) began to delight himself in the objects of the Creation, more than in the Spirit of Reason and Righteousness, who manifests himself to be the indweller in the Five Sences, of Hearing, Seeing, Tasting, Smelling, Feeling; then he fell into blindness of mind and weakness of heart, and runs abroad for a Teacher and Ruler: And so selfish imaginations taking possession of the Five Sences, and ruling as King in the room of Reason therein, and working with Covetousnesse, did set up one man to teach and rule over another; and thereby the Spirit was killed, and man was brought into bondage, and became a greater Slave to such of his own kind, than the Beasts of the field were to him.

And hereupon, The Earth (which was made to be a Common Treasury of relief for all, both Beasts and Men) was hedged in to In-closures by the teachers and rulers, and the others were made Servants and Slaves: And that Earth that is within this Creation made a Common Store-house for all, is bought and sold, and kept in the hands of a few, whereby the great Creator is mightily dishonoured, as if he were a respector of persons, delighting in the comfortable Livelihoods of some, and rejoycing in the miserable povertie and straits of others. From the beginning it was not so.

But this coming in of Bondage, is called "A-dam," because this ruling and teaching power without, doth "dam" up the Spirit of Peace and Liberty; First within the heart, by filling it with slavish fears of others. Secondly without, by giving the bodies of one to be imprisoned, punished and oppressed by the outward power of another. And this evil was brought upon us through his own Covetousnesse, whereby he is blinded and made weak, and sees not the Law of Righteousnesse in his heart, which is the pure light of Reason, but looks abroad for it, and thereby the Creation is cast under bondage and curse, and the Creator is sleighted. . . .

But when once the Earth becomes a Common Treasury again, as it must, for all the Prophesies of Scriptures and Reason are Circled here in this Community, and mankind must have the Law of Righteousness once more writ in his heart, and all must be made of one heart, and one mind.

Then this Enmity in all Lands will cease, for none shall dare to seek a Dominion over others, neither shall any dare to kill another, nor desire more of the Earth than another; for he that will rule over, imprison, oppresse, and kill his fellow Creatures, under what pretence soever, is a destroyer of the Creation, and an actor of the Curse, and walks contrary to the rule of righteousnesse: (*Do, as you would have others do to you; and love your Enemies, not in words, but in actions*).

Therefore you powers of the Earth, or Lord Esau, the Elder brother, because you have appeared to rule the Creation, first take notice, That the power that sets you to work, is selvish Covetousness, and an aspiring Pride, to live in glory and ease over Jacob, the meek Spirit; that is, the Seed that lies hid, in & among the poor Common People, or younger Brother, out of whom the blessing of Deliverance is to rise and spring up to all Nations.

And Reason, the living king of righteousnesse, doth only look on, and lets thee alone, That whereas thou counts thy self an Angel of Light, thou shalt appear in the light of the Sun, to be a Devil, A-dam, and the Curse that the Creation groans under; and the time is now come for thy downfal, and Jacob must rise, who is the universal Spirit of love and righteousnesse, that fils, and will fill all the Earth. . . .

Secondly, In that we begin to Digge upon George-Hill, to eate our Bread together by righteous labour, and sweat of our browes, It was shewed us by Vision in Dreams, and out of Dreams, That that should be the Place we should begin upon; And though that Earth in view of Flesh, be very barren, yet we should trust the Spirit for a blessing. And that not only this Common, or Heath should be taken in and Manured by the People, but all the Commons and waste Ground in England, and in the whole World, shall be taken in by the People in righteousness, not owning any Propriety; but taking the Earth to be a Common Treasury, as it was first made for all. . . .

Thus we have discharged our Souls in declaring the Cause of our Digging upon George-Hill in Surrey, that the Great Councel and Army of the Land may take notice of it, That there is no intent of Tumult or Fighting, but only to get Bread to eat, with the sweat of our brows; working together in righteousness, and eating the blessings of the Earth in peace.

And if any of you that are the great Ones of the Earth, that have been bred tenderly, and cannot work, do bring in your Stock into this Common Treasury, as an Offering to the work of Righteousness; we will work for you, and you shall receive as we receive. But if you will not, but Pharaoh like, cry, *Who is the Lord that we should obey him?* and endeavour to Oppose, then know, That he that delivered Israel from Pharaoh of old, is the same Power still, in whom we trust, and whom we serve; for this Conquest over thee shall be got, *not by Sword or Weapon, but by my Spirit saith the Lord of Hosts.*

STUDY QUESTIONS

1. Why does Winstanley describe the earth as a "common treasury" for mankind? What is his evidence for "God's plan" in this regard?
2. How do the Diggers' communal living arrangements prove that they are worthy of "possessing" the land?

3.6 VISUAL SOURCE: *THE RESOLUTION OF THE WOMEN OF LONDON TO THE PARLIAMENT, 1642*

The English Civil War broke out in August 1642 with royalist forces loyal to King Charles squaring off against Parliaments' supporters. Both sides called for men to join the fight, which lasted until 1651. Brutal campaigns in England, Ireland, and Scotland affected civilians as well, many of whom were weakened by the effects of the Little Ice Age. Studies suggest that about 7% of the population died from fighting and disease. Although they did not serve as soldiers, women experienced the violence of war firsthand, and some performed wartime activities. And as mothers, wives, and sisters, almost all women would have felt they had a personal stake in the war. Even though women were not recruited as soldiers or taken seriously as political actors, they did have a role as constituents.

From The British Library, *Women and the English Civil Wars,* https://www.nationalarchives.gov.uk/education/resources/women-english-civil-wars/.

This image comes from the front page of a 1642 pamphlet discussing the resolve of the "Women of London." The pamphlet's author hoped to take advantage of the printing press, whose use expanded dramatically during the English Civil War. Although no author is listed, we can speculate what side in the conflict this individual would have supported and who the pamphlet's intended audience would have been.

Note that the "s" character in old English looks like a modern "f."

FIGURE 3.6   The Resolution of the Women

STUDY QUESTIONS

1. Given the limited roles women could play in early modern European society, what responsibilities did this pamphlet assign them? How could women participate in the war?
2. In addition to gleaning insights about the political situation in England in 1642, what can this pamphlet cover reveal about daily life in this era and about how women's experiences differed from men's?

THESIS STATEMENTS

To write a good thesis statement, you must know what a good thesis statement is. Recent research tells us that the most effective way of learning to identify a good thesis statement is to practice *discriminating* between real thesis statements and non–thesis statements—and, even more importantly, between real thesis statements and near misses, which can look good at first glance but on further inspection fall short.

"Discrimination training" is essential because all composition is a process of writing and revising, and writing and revising again, until you are satisfied with the results. If you cannot *readily* tell the difference between a good thesis statement and even a close approximation, you will stop work too soon.

DISCRIMINATION TRAINING

These exercises develop your ability to discriminate a genuine thesis statement from a non-thesis, or a stronger thesis from a weaker one, *in your own work*—to know whether you have arrived at a good thesis statement or whether you need to keep working.

To help you discriminate, consider what distinguishes a **non-thesis**, a **near-miss**, and a genuine **thesis statement**.

1. A **non-thesis** is a statement of fact that no reasonable person could deny.

   Example: The French Revolution was a major political phenomenon.

   Explanation: People can argue over what caused the French Revolution, or over whether its outcomes made things better or worse, but it is undeniable that the Revolution constituted a major political phenomenon.

2. A **near-miss** is often a statement showing a relationship or correlation between two things, without explaining **how** and why the connection exists.

   Example: The French Revolution led to a series of wars.

   Explanation: Here, the writer claims that the revolution and war are connected but does not explain how and why one led to the other.

3. A **thesis statement** makes a claim and also says why the claim is true. Often, a thesis statement will include the word "because."

   Example: The French Revolution led to a series of wars because its republican ideology threatened Europe's monarchs, who wanted to restore the old regime.

   It might help to think of thesis statements in terms of "who," "what," "when," "where," "why," and "how." Both a non-thesis and a near-miss will include who, what, when, and/or where, but they lack the all-important why or how. In general, a good thesis statement will answer the questions why or how.

Example

Non-thesis:

During the seventeenth century, Europe experienced both a mini ice age and a large number of political eruptions.

This is a statement of fact. There is no **claim** that can be justified or disputed.

Near miss:

During the seventeenth century, Europe experienced a mini ice age that was one of many reasons for the period's large number of political eruptions.

This statement makes a **claim** (the mini ice age was related to political eruptions) but fails to explain **why** the claim is being made. Why was the mini ice age one of the reasons for the large number of political eruptions, and how did the extreme weather patterns shape political developments?

Thesis statement

Although many other factors were involved, a key reason Europe experienced a large number of political eruptions during the seventeenth century was a mini ice age that caused massive hardship and, with it, widespread discontent.

Here, there is a distinct **claim** about the relationship between the mini ice age and the large number of political eruptions, and there is also an **explanation of why and how** the two are related—namely because the mini ice age caused unprecedented hardship, which manifested itself as political strife. A reader who disagreed with this thesis could try to show that hardship and political eruptions were unrelated.

EXERCISE: IDENTIFY THE THESIS

Identify the thesis statements in the exercises below:

1.

a. The Thirty Years' War was the deadliest war in seventeenth-century Europe, resulting in the loss of two million soldiers, mostly German, and of another three million noncombatants, also mostly German.

b. The Thirty Years' War was the deadliest war in seventeenth-century Europe because it mobilized an unprecedented number of soldiers, coincided with dramatic climate change, caused massive damage to crops and housing, and stoked murderous religious passions.

c. The Thirty Years' War was the deadliest war in seventeenth-century Europe.

2.

a. The experience of the Fronde convinced Louis XIV to establish control over France's leading nobles, the only group with the potential to dilute his power, by luring them to Versailles and making them dependent on him.

b. Louis XIV established control over France's leading nobles, the only group with the potential to dilute his power, by luring them to Versailles and making them dependent on him.

c. The Fronde convinced Louis XIV to establish control over France's leading nobles, the only group with the potential to dilute his power.

3.

a. Throughout the seventeenth century, many rulers shored up their powers by oppressing peasants and currying the favor of nobles.

b. Throughout the seventeenth century, peasants suffered the most of all social groups because they worked harder for less compensation, had to pay higher taxes and serve in the military, and, in some cases, were treated as virtual slaves.

c. Throughout the seventeenth century, peasants rose up in rebellion, avoided military service, and refused to pay their taxes.

4.

a. Louis XIV went to war with Spain, the Netherlands, the German States, and England, culminating in the War of Spanish Succession, which involved numerous European countries and also the Caribbean Islands and parts of India and North America.

b. Louis XIV went to war so often that he undermined his own power and also the power of France.

c. Had Louis XIV gone to war less often—or not at all—his reign would have been more successful than was actually the case, because constant warfare left his treasury depleted and his rival powers, especially England and the Netherlands, relatively strong.

5.

a. The English Revolution was both a religious and political contest, pitting Anglicans against Puritans and the monarchy against parliament.

b. While the English Revolution was partly a political struggle, pitting the monarchy against parliament, it was more fundamentally a religious one, the result of a deep schism within English Protestantism.

c. The English Revolution led to the execution of a king, the rise of a dictator, and the invasion of Ireland.

You will find suggested answers to the exercises in the back of this book. For more Writing History exercises, as well as study resources for this chapter, visit oup.com/us/berenson.

CHAPTER 4

SCIENCE AND ENLIGHTENMENT, 1600–1789

4.1 GALILEO GALILEI, LETTER TO THE GRAND DUCHESS CHRISTINA DE' MEDICI, 1615

In this famous letter to the dowager Grand Duchess Christina de' Medici, Galileo Galilei (1564–1642) defends himself against accusations that supporting the Copernican theory of planetary motion was heretical. Historians often cite the letter as a sign of his growing conflict with Church and to demonstrate the theory's theological and scientific ramifications. Galileo's embrace of heliocentrism elicited sharp responses from Church officials—and, in the spring of 1615, the Grand Duchess, mother of Galileo's patron Cosimo II, expressed her own reservations about the implications of Copernican theory because of a passage in the Old Testament in which Joshua, one of Moses's lieutenants, makes the sun stop in the sky. In this letter, Galileo attempts to reconcile experimental science and received religion. Seventeen years later, in 1632, Galileo would be found guilty of heresy by the Inquisition, condemned to house arrest, and forced to issue a public repudiation of the heliocentric theory first advanced by Copernicus nearly 100 years earlier.

Thus let these people apply themselves to refuting the arguments of Copernicus and of the others, and let them leave its condemnation as erroneous and heretical to the proper authorities; but let them not hope that the very cautious and very wise Fathers and the Infallible One with his absolute wisdom are about to make rash decisions like those into which they would be rushed by their special interests and feelings. For in regard to these and other similar propositions which do not directly involve the faith, no one can doubt that the Supreme Pontiff always has the absolute power of permitting or condemning them; however, no creature has the power of making them be true or false, contrary to what they happen to be by nature and de facto. So it seems more advisable to first become sure about the necessary and

From Galileo Galilei, Letter to the Grand Duchess Christina de' Medici, 1615, Maurice A. Finocchiaro, trans. and ed., *The Galileo Affair: A Documentary History*, (University of California Press 1989).

immutable truth of the matter, over which no one has control, than to condemn one side when such certainty is lacking; this would imply a loss of freedom of decision and of choice insofar as it would give necessity to things which are presently indifferent, free, and dependent on the will of the supreme authority. In short, if it is inconceivable that a proposition should be declared heretical when one thinks that it may be true, it should be futile for someone to try to bring about the condemnation of the earth's motion and sun's rest unless he first shows it to be impossible and false.

There remains one last thing for us to examine: to what extent it is true that the Joshua passage [Joshua 10: 12–13] can be taken without altering the literal meaning of the words, and how it can be that, when the sun obeyed Joshua's order to stop, from this it followed that the day was prolonged by a large amount.

. . .

I think therefore, if I am not mistaken, that one can clearly see that, given the Ptolemaic system, it is necessary to interpret the words in a way different from their literal meaning. Guided by St. Augustine's very useful prescriptions, I should say that the best nonliteral interpretation is not necessarily this, if anyone can find another which is perhaps better and more suitable. So now I want to examine whether the same miracle could be understood in a way more in accordance with what we read in Joshua, if to the Copernican system we add another discovery which I recently made about the solar body. However, I continue to speak with the same reservations—to the effect that I am not so enamored with my own opinions as to want to place them ahead of those of others; nor do I believe it is impossible to put forth interpretations which are better and more in accordance with the Holy Writ.

Let us first assume in accordance with the opinion of the above-mentioned authors, that in the Joshua miracle the whole system of heavenly motions was stopped, so that the stopping of only one would not introduce unnecessarily universal confusion and great turmoil in the whole order of nature. . . .

Furthermore, what deserves special appreciation, if I am not mistaken, is that with the Copernican system one can very clearly and very easily give a literal meaning to another detail which one reads about the same miracle; that is, that the sun stopped in the middle of heaven. Serious theologians have raised a difficulty about this passage: it seems very probable that, when Joshua asked for the prolongation of the day, the sun was close to setting and not at the meridian; for it was then about the time of the summer solstice, and consequently the days were very long, so that if the sun had been at the meridian then it does not seem likely that it would have been necessary to pray for a lengthening of the day in order to win a battle, since the still remaining time of seven hours or more could very well have been sufficient. . . .

We can remove this and every other implausibility, if I am not mistaken, by placing the sun, as the Copernican system does and as it is most necessary to do, in the middle, namely, at the center of the heavenly orbs and of the planetary revolutions; for at any hour of the day, whether at noon or in the afternoon, the day would not have been lengthened and all heavenly turnings stopped by the sun stopping in the middle of the heavens, namely, at the center of the heavens, where it is located. Furthermore, this interpretation agrees all the more with the literal meaning inasmuch as, if one wanted to claim that the sun's stopping occurred at the noon hour, then the proper expression to use would have been to say that it "stood still at the meridian point," or "at the meridian circle," and not "in the middle of the heaven"; in fact, for a spherical body such as heaven, the middle is really and only the center.

STUDY QUESTIONS

1. How is Galileo dealing with the apparently irreconcilable conclusions of science and the Bible?
2. What tone does Galileo take in confronting his critics, for example in his analysis of the Joshua passage?

4.2 JOHN LOCKE, *SECOND TREATISE ON GOVERNMENT*, 1689

Having witnessed firsthand the political turnover in England in the seventeenth century, John Locke (1632–1704) thought deeply about the nature of politics. His *Second Treatise on Government*, which responded to England's Glorious Revolution and influenced the subsequent American Revolution, provided a description of political liberalism: religious tolerance, equality under the law, freedom of expression, and a limit on the arbitrary power of government. Like Thomas Hobbes before him and Jean-Jacques Rousseau afterwards, Locke looked at government as the result of a social contract whereby people voluntarily joined together to form a government to protect their natural rights, rights they enjoyed by virtue of being human. For Locke these rights included life, liberty, and the preservation of property. In this excerpt, Locke explains his view of what life was like in the "state of nature" before there were governments, and he contrasts power dynamics inside the home with those inside the state. Notice also his discussion of the reasons why absolute monarchy cannot adequately support civil society.

CHAPTER II: OF THE STATE OF NATURE

Sect. 4. To understand political power right, and derive it from its original, we must consider, what state all men are naturally in, and that is, a state of perfect freedom to order their actions, and dispose of their possessions and persons, as they think fit, within the bounds of the law of nature, without asking leave, or depending upon the will of any other man.

A state also of equality, wherein all the power and jurisdiction is reciprocal, no one having more than another; there being nothing more evident, than that creatures of the same species and rank, promiscuously born to all the same advantages of nature, and the use of the same faculties, should also be equal one amongst another without subordination or subjection, unless the lord and master of them all should, by any manifest declaration of his will, set one above another, and confer on him, by an evident and clear appointment, an undoubted right to dominion and sovereignty.

Sect. 6. But though this be a state of liberty, yet it is not a state of license: though man in that state have an uncontrollable liberty to dispose of his person or possessions, yet he has not liberty to destroy himself, or so much as any creature in his possession, but where some nobler use than its bare preservation calls for it. The state of nature has a law of nature to govern it, which obliges every one: and reason, which is that law, teaches all mankind, who will but consult it, that being all equal and independent, no one ought to harm another in his life, health, liberty, or possessions: for men being all the workmanship of one omnipotent, and infinitely wise maker; all the servants of one sovereign master, sent into the world by his order, and about his business; they are his property, whose workmanship they are, made to last during his, not one another's pleasure: and being furnished with like faculties, sharing all in one community of nature, there cannot be supposed any such subordination among us, that may authorize us to destroy one another, as if we were made for one

From John Locke, *Two Treatises on Government*, 1764 edition with modernized English spelling and grammar, https://source-books.fordham.edu/mod/1690locke-sel.asp.

another's uses, as the inferior ranks of creatures are for ours. Every one, as he is bound to preserve himself, and not to quit his station willfully, so by the like reason, when his own preservation comes not in competition, ought he, as much as he can, to preserve the rest of mankind, and may not, unless it be to do justice on an offender, take away, or impair the life, or what tends to the preservation of the life, the liberty, health, limb, or goods of another.

Sect. 8. And thus, in the state of nature, one man comes by a power over another; but yet no absolute or arbitrary power, to use a criminal, when he has got him in his hands, according to the passionate heats, or boundless extravagancy of his own will; but only to retribute to him, so far as calm reason and conscience dictate, what is proportionate to his transgression, which is so much as may serve for reparation and restraint: for these two are the only reasons, why one man may lawfully do harm to another, which is that we call punishment. In transgressing the law of nature, the offender declares himself to live by another rule than that of reason and common equity, which is that measure God has set to the actions of men, for their mutual security; and so he becomes dangerous to mankind, the tie, which is to secure them from injury and violence, being slighted and broken by him. Which being a trespass against the whole species, and the peace and safety of it, provided for by the law of nature, every man upon this score, by the right he has to preserve mankind in general, may restrain, or where it is necessary, destroy things noxious to them, and so may bring such evil on any one, who has transgressed that law, as may make him repent the doing of it, and thereby deter him, and by his example others, from doing the like mischief. And in the case, and upon this ground, EVERY MAN HAS A RIGHT TO PUNISH THE OFFENDER, AND BE EXECUTIONER OF THE LAW OF NATURE.

CHAPTER VII: OF POLITICAL OF CIVIL SOCIETY

Sec. 85. Master and servant are names as old as history, but given to those of far different condition; for a freeman makes himself a servant to another, by selling him, for a certain time, the service he undertakes to do, in exchange for wages he is to receive: and though this commonly puts him into the family of his master, and under the ordinary discipline thereof; yet it gives the master but a temporary power over him, and no greater than what is contained in the contract between them. But there is another sort of servants, which by a peculiar name we call slaves, who being captives taken in a just war, are by the right of nature subjected to the absolute dominion and arbitrary power of their masters. These men having, as I say, forfeited their lives, and with it their liberties, and lost their estates; and being in the state of slavery, not capable of any property, cannot in that state be considered as any part of civil society; the chief end whereof is the preservation of property.

Sec. 86. Let us therefore consider a master of a family with all these subordinate relations of wife, children, servants, and slaves, united under the domestic rule of a family; which, what resemblance soever it may have in its order, offices, and number too, with a little commonwealth, yet is very far from it, both in its constitution, power and end: or if it must be thought a monarchy, and the paterfamilias the absolute monarch in it, absolute monarchy will have but a very shattered and short power, when it is plain, by what has been said before, that the master of the family has a very distinct and differently limited power, both as to time and extent, over those several persons that are in it; for excepting the slave (and the family is as much a family, and his power as paterfamilias as great, whether there be any slaves in his family or no) he has no legislative power of life and death over any of them, and none too but what a mistress of a family may have as well as he. And he certainly can have no absolute power over the whole family, who has but a very limited one over every individual in it. But how a family, or any other society of men, differ from that which is properly political society, we shall best see, by considering wherein political society itself consists.

Sec. 87. Man being born, as has been proved, with a title to perfect freedom, and an uncontrolled enjoyment of all the rights and privileges of the law of nature, equally with any other man, or number of men in the world, has by nature a power, not only to preserve his property, that is, his life, liberty and estate, against the injuries and attempts of other men; but to judge of, and punish the breaches of that law in others, as he is persuaded the offense deserves, even with death itself, in crimes where the heinousness of the fact, in his opinion, requires it. But because no political society can be, nor subsist, without having in itself the power to preserve the property, and in order thereunto, punish the offences of all those of that society; there, and there only is political society, where every one of the members has quitted this natural power, resigned it up into the hands of the community in all cases that exclude him not from appealing for protection to the law established by it. And thus all private judgment of every particular member being excluded, the community comes to be umpire, by settled standing rules, indifferent, and the same to all parties; and by men having authority from the community, for the execution of those rules, decides all the differences that may happen between any members of that society concerning any matter of right; and punishes those offences which any member has committed against the society, with such penalties as the law has established: whereby it is easy to discern, who are, and who are not, in political society together. Those who are united into one body, and have a common established law and judicature to appeal to, with authority to decide controversies between them, and punish offenders, are in civil society one with another: but those who have no such common appeal, I mean on earth, are still in the state of nature, each being, where there is no other, judge for himself, and executioner; which is, as I have before shewed it, the perfect state of nature.

Sec. 90. Hence it is evident, that absolute monarchy, which by some men is counted the only government in the world, is indeed inconsistent with civil society, and so can be no form of civil-government at all: for the end of civil society, being to avoid, and remedy those inconveniencies of the state of nature, which necessarily follow from every man's being judge in his own case, by setting up a known authority, to which every one of that society may appeal upon any injury received, or controversy that may arise, and which every one of the society ought to obey; wherever any persons are, who have not such an authority to appeal to, for the decision of any difference between them, there those persons are still in the state of nature; and so is every absolute prince, in respect of those who are under his dominion.

Sec. 91. For he being supposed to have all, both legislative and executive power in himself alone, there is no judge to be found, no appeal lies open to any one, who may fairly, and indifferently, and with authority decide, and from whose decision relief and redress may be expected of any injury or inconviency, that may be suffered from the prince, or by his order: so that such a man, however intitled, Czar, or Grand Seignior, or how you please, is as much in the state of nature, with all under his dominion, as he is with the rest of mankind: for wherever any two men are, who have no standing rule, and common judge to appeal to on earth, for the determination of controversies of right betwixt them, there they are still in the state of nature, and under all the inconveniencies of it, with only this woeful difference to the subject, or rather slave of an absolute prince: that whereas, in the ordinary state of nature, he has a liberty to judge of his right, and according to the best of his power, to maintain it; now, whenever his property is invaded by the will and order of his monarch, he has not only no appeal, as those in society ought to have, but as if he were degraded from the common state of rational creatures, is denied a liberty to judge of, or to defend his right; and so is exposed to all the misery and inconveniencies, that a man can fear from one, who being in the unrestrained state of nature, is yet corrupted with flattery, and armed with power.

STUDY QUESTIONS

1. According to Locke, what is the function of government? In other words, when people form a government, what should they expect from their sovereign?
2. What powers does a paterfamilias have over his family? How does his role differ from a monarch's?

4.3 IMMANUEL KANT, *WHAT IS ENLIGHTENMENT?* 1784

The most celebrated definition of enlightenment comes from the German philosopher Immanuel Kant (1724–1804). Enlightenment, he wrote, was "man's release from his self-incurred tutelage." In Kant's view, people became stuck in a childlike state by failing to think for themselves. They could release themselves only by following their own reason rather than the dictates of someone else.

Radical as Kant's views appear, they did not move him to take a public stance against organized religion or against political authorities, as his support for his sovereign, the Prussian ruler Frederick the Great, reveals. As strongly as Kant believed in the necessity of following one's own reason in theory, in reality, he thought enlightenment should develop gradually and with the least disruption possible to existing social relations.

Enlightenment is man's release from his self-incurred tutelage. Tutelage is man's inability to make use of his understanding without direction from another. Self-incurred is this tutelage when its cause lies not in lack of reason but in lack of resolution and courage to use it without direction from another. *Sapere aude!* [Dare to Know!] Have courage to use your own reason!—that is the motto of enlightenment.

Laziness and cowardice are the reasons why so great a portion of mankind, after nature has long since discharged them from external direction, nevertheless remains under lifelong tutelage, and why it is so easy for others to set themselves up as their guardians. It is so easy not to be of age. If I have a book which understands for me, a pastor who has a conscience for me, a physician who decides my diet, and so forth, I need not trouble myself. I need not think, if I can only pay—others will readily undertake the irksome work for me.

That the step to competence is held to be very dangerous by the far greater portion of mankind (and by the entire fair sex)—quite apart from its being arduous—is seen to by those guardians who have so kindly assumed superintendence over them. After the guardians have first made their domestic cattle dumb and have made sure that these placid creatures will not dare take a single step without the harness of the cart to which they are confined, the guardians then show them the danger which threatens if they try to go alone. Actually, however, this danger is not

From Immanuel Kant, *Foundations of the Metaphysics of Morals,* trans. by Lewis White Beck (Indianapolis: The Liberal Arts Press, 1959), 85-91.

so great, for by falling a few times they would finally learn to walk alone. But an example of this failure makes them timid and ordinarily frightens them away from all further trials.

For any single individual to work himself out of the life under tutelage which has become almost his nature is very difficult. He has come to be fond of this state, and he is for the present really incapable of making use of his reason, for no one has ever let him try it out. Statutes and formulas, those mechanical tools of the rational employment or rather misemployment of his natural gifts, are the fetters of an everlasting tutelage. Whoever throws them off makes only an uncertain leap over the narrowest ditch because he is not accustomed to that kind of free motion. Therefore, there are only few who have succeeded by their own exercise of mind both in freeing themselves from incompetence and in achieving a steady pace.

But that the public should enlighten itself is more possible; indeed, if only freedom is granted, enlightenment is almost sure to follow. For there will always be some independent thinkers, even among the established guardians of the great masses, who, after throwing off the yoke of tutelage from their own shoulders, will disseminate the spirit of the rational appreciation of both their own worth and every man's vocation for thinking for himself. . . .

For this enlightenment, however, nothing is required but freedom, and indeed the most harmless among all the things to which this term can properly be applied. It is the freedom to make public use of one's reason at every point. But I hear on all sides, "Do not argue!" The officer says: "Do not argue but drill!" The tax collector: "Do not argue but pay!" The cleric: "Do not argue but believe!" Only one prince in the world [Frederick the Great of Prussia] says, "Argue as much as you will, and about what you will, but obey!" Everywhere there is restriction on freedom.

Which restriction is an obstacle to enlightenment, and which is not an obstacle but a promoter of it? I answer: The public's use of one's reason must always be free, and it alone can bring about enlightenment among men. The private use of reason, on the other hand, may often be very narrowly restricted without particularly hindering the progress of enlightenment. By the public use of one's reason I understand the use which a person makes of it as a scholar before the reading public. Private use I call that which one may make of it in a particular civil post or office which is entrusted to him. . . . Thus it would be ruinous for an officer in service to debate about the suitability or utility of a command given to him by his superior; he must obey. But the right to make remarks on errors in the military service and to lay them before the public for judgment cannot equitably be refused him as a scholar. The citizen cannot refuse to pay the taxes imposed on him; indeed an impudent complaint at those levied on him can be punished as a scandal (as it could occasion general refractoriness). But the same person nevertheless does not act contrary to his duty as a citizen when, as a scholar, he publicly expresses his thoughts on the inappropriateness or even the injustice of those levies. . . .

If we are asked, "Do we now live in an enlightened age?" the answer is, "No," but we do live in an age of enlightenment. As things now stand, much is lacking which prevents men from being, or easily becoming, capable of correctly using their own reason in religious matters with assurance and free from outside direction. But, on the other hand, we have clear indications that the field has now been opened wherein men may freely deal with these things and that the obstacles to general enlightenment or the release from self-imposed tutelage are gradually being reduced. In this respect, this is the age of enlightenment, or the century of Frederick.

STUDY QUESTIONS

1. Why does Kant believe one must "dare" to know? Why is it easier simply to follow the orders and opinions of others?
2. Considering that all Enlightenment thinkers advocated for increased freedom, what specific kinds of "freedom" does Kant prioritize?

4.4 JEAN-JACQUES ROUSSEAU, *DISCOURSE ON INEQUALITY*, 1754

Jean-Jacques Rousseau (1712–1778), originally of Geneva, differed sharply from other leading figures of the Enlightenment in his view of the inherent and "original" nature of human societies. Rousseau posited a presocial state of nature in which the first humans lived in isolation from one another, with each individual depending on no one but him- or herself to survive. Because original humans had no sustained interactions with other people, he reasoned, they felt no need to dominate others, or to distinguish themselves from other human beings in any way.

Rousseau outlined these ideas in his famous *Discourse on Inequality* (also called his *Second Discourse*), which argued that human beings were better off in their original, primitive state than in their contemporary social arrangements. Other writers believed that humans had progressed from savagery to civilization, but Rousseau portrayed "civilization" in largely negative terms. He preferred the "noble savage": a human alone in the state of nature, living apart from the corrupting influences of the civilized world.

It appears, at first view, that men in a state of nature, having no moral relations or determinate obligations one with another, could not be either good or bad, virtuous or vicious; unless we take these terms in a physical sense, and call, in an individual, those qualities vices which may be injurious to his preservation, and those virtues which contribute to it; in which case, he would have to be accounted most virtuous, who put least check on the pure impulses of nature. But without deviating from the ordinary sense of the words, it will be proper to suspend the judgment we might be led to form on such a state, and be on our guard against our prejudices, till we have weighed the matter in the scales of impartiality, and seen whether virtues or vices preponderate among civilized men; and whether their virtues do them more good than their vices do harm; till we have discovered, whether the progress of the sciences sufficiently indemnifies them for the mischiefs they do one another, in proportion as they are better informed of the good they ought to do; or whether they would not be, on the whole, in a much happier condition if they had nothing to fear or to hope from any one, than as they are, subjected to universal dependence, and obliged to take everything from those who engage to give them nothing in return.

Above all, let us not conclude, with Hobbes, that because man has no idea of goodness, he must be naturally wicked; that he is vicious because he does not know virtue; that he always refuses to do his fellow-creatures services which he does not think they have a right to demand; or that by virtue of the right he truly claims to everything he needs, he foolishly imagines himself the sole proprietor of the whole universe. Hobbes had seen clearly the defects of all the modern definitions of natural right: but the consequences which he deduces from his own show that he understands it in an equally false sense. In reasoning on the principles he lays down, he ought to have said that the state of nature, being that in which the care for our own preservation is the least prejudicial to that of others, was consequently the best

From Jean-Jacques Rousseau, *Discourse on the Origin and Basis of Inequality among Men*, 1754.

calculated to promote peace, and the most suitable for mankind. He does say the exact opposite, in consequence of having improperly admitted, as a part of savage man's care for self-preservation, the gratification of a multitude of passions which are the work of society, and have made laws necessary. A bad man, he says, is a robust child. But it remains to be proved whether man in a state of nature is this robust child: and, should we grant that he is, what would he infer? Why truly, that if this man, when robust and strong, were dependent on others as he is when feeble, there is no extravagance he would not be guilty of; that he would beat his mother when she was too slow in giving him her breast; that he would strangle one of his younger brothers, if he should be troublesome to him, or bite the arm of another, if he put him to any inconvenience. But that man in the state of nature is both strong and dependent involves two contrary suppositions. Man is weak when he is dependent, and is his own master before he comes to be strong. Hobbes did not reflect that the same cause, which prevents a savage from making use of his reason, as our jurists hold, prevents him also from abusing his faculties, as Hobbes himself allows: so that it may be justly said that savages are not bad merely because they do not know what it is to be good: for it is neither the development of the understanding nor the restraint of law that hinders them from doing ill . . .

We find, with pleasure, the author of the *Fable of the Bees* [Bernard de Mandeville] obliged to own that man is a compassionate and sensible being, and laying aside his cold subtlety of style, in the example he gives, to present us with the pathetic description of a man who, from a place of confinement, is compelled to behold a wild beast tear a child from the arms of its mother, grinding its tender limbs with its murderous teeth, and tearing its palpitating entrails with its claws. What horrid agitation must not the eyewitness of such a scene experience, although he would not be personally concerned! What anxiety would he not suffer at not being able to give any assistance to the fainting mother and the dying infant!

Such is the pure emotion of nature, prior to all kinds of reflection! Such is the force of natural compassion, which the greatest depravity of morals has as yet hardly been able to destroy! for we daily find at our theatres men affected, nay shedding tears at the sufferings of a wretch who, were he in the tyrant's place, would probably even add to the torments of his enemies; like the bloodthirsty Sulla, who was so sensitive to ills he had not caused, or that Alexander of Pheros who did not dare to go and see any tragedy acted, for fear of being seen weeping with Andromache and Priam, though he could listen without emotion to the cries of all the citizens who were daily strangled at his command. . . .

Mandeville well knew that, in spite of all their morality, men would have never been better than monsters, had not nature bestowed on them a sense of compassion, to aid their reason: but he did not see that from this quality alone flow all those social virtues, of which he denied man the possession. But what is generosity, clemency or humanity but compassion applied to the weak, to the guilty, or to mankind in general? Even benevolence and friendship are, if we judge rightly, only the effects of compassion, constantly set upon a particular object: for how is it different to wish that another person may not suffer pain and uneasiness and to wish him happy? Were it even true that pity is no more than a feeling, which puts us in the place of the sufferer, a feeling, obscure yet lively in a savage, developed yet feeble in civilised man; this truth would have no other consequence than to confirm my argument. Compassion must, in fact, be the stronger, the more the animal beholding any kind of distress identifies himself with the animal that suffers . . .

It is then certain that compassion is a natural feeling, which, by moderating the violence of love of self in each individual, contributes to the preservation of the whole species. It is this compassion that hurries us without reflection to the relief of those who are in distress: it is this which in a state of nature supplies the place of laws, morals and virtues, with the advantage that none are tempted to disobey its gentle voice: it is this which will always prevent a sturdy savage from robbing a weak child or a feeble old man of the sustenance they may have with pain and difficulty acquired, if he sees a possibility of providing for himself by other means: it is this which, instead of inculcating that sublime maxim of rational justice. Do to others as you would have them do unto you, inspires all men with that other maxim of natural goodness, much less perfect indeed, but perhaps more useful; Do good to yourself with as little evil as possible to others. In a word, it is rather in this natural feeling than in any subtle arguments that we must look for the cause of that repugnance, which every man would experience in doing evil, even independently of the maxims of education. Although it might belong to Socrates and other minds of the like craft to acquire virtue by reason, the human race would long since have ceased to be, had its preservation depended only on the reasonings of the individuals composing it.

STUDY QUESTIONS

1. How does Rousseau contrast his own opinions with those of Hobbes, especially in respect to human's essential "depravity"?
2. What does Rousseau consider to be the *limits* of cooperation among human beings? Does his conception of the state of nature allow for a state of pure reason?

4.5 VOLTAIRE, "TOLERATION" AND "TORTURE" FROM THE *PHILOSOPHICAL DICTIONARY*, 1769

Voltaire (the pen-name of François-Marie Arouet, 1694–1778) epitomized the Enlightenment. His *Dictionnaire philosophique* (*Philosophical Dictionary*), the first edition of which appeared in 1764, distilled his thought on philosophical matters in what he self-deprecatingly called an "alphabetical abomination." In this "dictionary," arranged alphabetically, Voltaire tackled matters like "Atheism," "Fanaticism," the "Soul," and "Superstition," always with a light touch, despite the weightiness of (and the violence often associated with) the subject matter. Voltaire invariably found ways to deploy humor in the pursuit of serious moral, religious, and ethical truths, as the popularity of his *"contes philosophiques"* (philosophical tales), including *Candide*, *Zadig*, and *Micromégas*, attests. Voltaire's humorous, light-hearted approach could not have come easily, especially when he added to the 1769 version of the *Dictionary* a brilliant essay on the use of torture as a legal instrument. This essay was inspired by court cases and interrogation methods of the time.

TOLÉRANCE: TOLERATION

What is toleration? It is the prerogative of humanity. We are all steeped in weaknesses and errors: let us forgive one another's follies, it is the first law of nature . . .

Of all religions the Christian is undoubtedly that which should instill the greatest toleration, although so far the Christians have been the most intolerant of all men . . .

If we look at the matter at all closely we see that the catholic, apostolic and Roman religion is the

From Voltaire, *Philosophical Dictionary*, edited and translated by Theodore Besterman (London: Penguin, 1972), pp. 387–396.

opposite of the religion of Jesus in all its ceremonies and in all its dogmas.

But then must we all judaize because Jesus judaized all his life?

If it were permissible to reason consistently in matters of religion, it would be clear that we should all become Jews because our savior Jesus Christ was born a Jew, lived a Jew, and died a Jew, and because he said expressly that he accomplished, that he fulfilled the Jewish religion. But it is even clearer that we should tolerate each other because we are all weak, inconsistent, subject to mutability and to error. Would a reed laid into the mud by the wind say to a neighbouring reed bent in the opposite direction: "Creep in my fashion, wretch, or I shall petition to have you torn up and burned"?

TORTURE

Although there are few articles on jurisprudence in these respectable alphabetical reflections, a word must nevertheless be said about torture, otherwise named the question. It is a strange way to question one. Yet it was not invented by the merely curious. It would appear that this part of our legislation owes its first origin to a highwayman. Most of these gentlemen are still in the habit of squeezing thumbs, burning the feet of those who refuse to tell them where they have put their money, and questioning them by means of other torments.

The conquerors, having succeeded these thieves, found this invention of the greatest utility. They put it into practice when they suspected that some vile plot was being hatched against them, as, for instance, that of being free, a crime of divine and human *lèse-majesté* [insulting the king (i.e., treason, something of which Voltaire was often accused himself)]. The accomplices had to be known; and to arrive at this knowledge those who were suspected were made to suffer a thousand deaths, because according to the jurisprudence of these first heroes anyone suspected of having had

so much as a disrespectful thought about them was worthy of death. And once a man has thus deserved death it matters little whether appalling torments are added for a few days or even several weeks. All this even had something of the divine about it. Providence sometimes tortures us by means of the stone, gravel, gout, scurvy, leprosy, pox great and small, griping of the bowels, nervous convulsions, and other executants of the vengeance of providence.

Now since the first despots were images of divinity, as all their courtiers freely admitted, they imitated it so far as they could.

. . .

The grave magistrate who has bought for a little money the right to conduct these experiments on his fellow creatures tells his wife at dinner what happened during the morning. The first time her ladyship is revolted, the second time she acquires a taste for it, for after all women are curious, and then the first thing she says to him when he comes home in his robes is: "My angel, did you give anyone the question today?"

The French, who are considered to be a very humane people, I do not know why, are astonished that the English, who have had the inhumanity to take the whole of Canada from us [in 1760 and ratified in 1763, as a result of the Seven Years' War], have renounced the pleasure of applying the question.

. . .

In 1700 the Russians were regarded as barbarians. We are now only in 1769, and an empress [Catherine the Great] has just given this vast state laws that would have done honour to Minos, to Numa, and to Solon if they had had enough intelligence to compose them. The most remarkable of them is universal toleration, the second is the abolition of torture. Justice and humanity guided her pen, she has reformed everything. Woe to a nation which, long civilized, is still led by atrocious ancient practices! "Why should we change our jurisprudence?" it asks. "Europe uses our cooks, our tailors, our wig-makers; therefore our laws are good."

STUDY QUESTIONS

1. Does Voltaire make a convincing case that the use of torture results from excessive curiosity and a warped desire to inflict suffering?
2. How does he ridicule the continuation of "ancient" practices into modern times, and how do these essays reflect the values of the philosophical Enlightenment?

4.6 MARY WOLLSTONECRAFT, *A VINDICATION OF THE RIGHTS OF WOMAN*, 1791

Mary Wollstonecraft (1759–1797) was a pioneer for women's rights. Her book *A Vindication of the Rights of Woman* was a trailblazing call to increase women's participation in society. Born on a farm in England, Wollstonecraft worked as a schoolteacher and governess as young woman. She traveled to Paris during the French Revolution and later spent time in Scandinavia. She was deeply concerned with the kind of education offered to middle- and upper-class girls in Europe, which she considered inferior to what boys were learning. Jean-Jacques Rousseau, who believed women were intellectually inferior to men, endorsed the practice of separate education for the sexes. In her *Vindication*, Wollstonecraft argued with this popular idea, explaining that it was the second-rate education provided women, not an inferior ability, that made them appear intellectually unequal to men.

In her own life Wollstonecraft refused to abide by traditional expectations of women. She had a child out of wedlock with her lover, Gilbert Imlay. When Imlay abandoned them, she attempted suicide, then recovered her strength during her travels. Her next relationship was with the famous English radical William Godwin, whom she married after discovering that she was pregnant. Wollstonecraft died days after the birth of their child, Mary, who would grow up to publish *Frankenstein* under her married name, Mary Shelley. Wollstonecraft's books were well received in her lifetime, but after her death revelations concerning her personal life tarnished her image. Today she is regarded as an important early feminist who influenced generations of women's rights advocates.

INTRODUCTION

After considering the historic page, and viewing the living world with anxious solicitude, the most melancholy emotions of sorrowful indignation have depressed my spirits, and I have sighed when obliged to confess that either Nature has made a great difference between man and man, or that the civilisation which has hitherto taken place in the world has been very partial. I have turned over various books written on the subject of education, and patiently observed the conduct of parents and the management of schools; but what has been the result?—a profound conviction that the neglected education of my fellow-creatures is the grand source of the misery I deplore, and that women, in particular, are rendered weak and wretched by a variety of concurring causes. . . .

My own sex, I hope, will excuse me, if I treat them like rational creatures, instead of flattering their fascinating graces, and viewing them as if they were in a state of perpetual childhood, unable to stand alone. I earnestly wish to point out in what true dignity and human happiness consists. I wish to persuade women to endeavour to acquire strength, both of mind and body, and to convince them that the soft phrases, susceptibility of heart, delicacy of sentiment, and refinement of taste, are almost synonymous with epithets of weakness, and that those beings who are only the objects of pity, and that kind of love which

From Mary Wollstonecraft, *A Vindication of the Rights of Woman* (1792), Introduction and Ch. IX, from text available at https://sourcebooks.fordham.edu/mod/MW-VIND.asp

has been termed its sister, will soon become objects of contempt.

Dismissing, then, those pretty feminine phrases, which the men condescendingly use to soften our slavish dependence, and despising that weak elegancy of mind, exquisite sensibility, and sweet docility of manners, supposed to be the sexual characteristics of the weaker vessel, I wish to show that elegance is inferior to virtue, that the first object of laudable ambition is to obtain a character as a human being, regardless of the distinction of sex, and that secondary views should be brought to this simple touchstone.

The education of women has of late been more attended to than formerly; yet they are still reckoned a frivolous sex, and ridiculed or pitied by the writers who endeavour by satire or instruction to improve them. It is acknowledged that they spend many of the first years of their lives in acquiring a smattering of accomplishments; meanwhile strength of body and mind are sacrificed to libertine notions of beauty, to the desire of establishing themselves—the only way women can rise in the world,—by marriage. And this desire making mere animals of them, when they marry they act as such children may be expected to act:—they dress, they paint, and nickname God's creatures. . . . Can they be expected to govern a family with judgment, or take care of the poor babes whom they bring into the world?

. . .

Women are, in fact, so much degraded by mistaken notions of female excellence, that I do not mean to add a paradox when I assert that this artificial weakness produces a propensity to tyrannise, and gives birth to cunning, the natural opponent of strength, which leads them to play off those contemptible infantile airs that undermine esteem even whilst they excite desire. Let men become more chaste and modest, and if women do not grow wiser in the same ratio, it will be clear that they have weaker understandings. It seems scarcely necessary to say that I now speak of the sex in general. Many individuals have more sense than their male relatives; and, as nothing preponderates where there is a

constant struggle for an equilibrium without it has naturally more gravity, some women govern their husbands without degrading themselves, because intellect will always govern.

CHAPTER IX. OF THE PERNICIOUS EFFECTS WHICH ARISE FROM THE UNNATURAL DISTINCTIONS ESTABLISHED IN SOCIETY

It is vain to expect virtue from women till they are in some degree independent of men; nay, it is vain to expect that strength of natural affection which would make them good wives and mothers. Whilst they are absolutely dependent on their husbands they will be cunning, mean, and selfish; and the men who can be gratified by the fawning fondness of spaniel-like affection have not much delicacy, for love is not to be bought; in any sense of the words, its silken wings are instantly shrivelled up when anything beside a return in kind is sought. Yet whilst wealth enervates men, and women live, as it were, by their personal charms, how can we expect them to discharge those ennobling duties which equally require exertion and self-denial? . . .

But what have women to do in society? . . . Women might certainly study the art of healing, and be physicians as well as nurses. . . .

They might also study politics, and settle their benevolence on the broadest basis; for the reading of history will scarcely be more useful than the perusal of romances, if read as mere biography; if the character of the times, the political improvements, arts, etc., be not observed. . . .

Business of various kinds, they might likewise pursue, if they were educated in a more orderly manner, which might save many from common and legal prostitution. Women would not then marry for a support, as men accept of places under Government, and neglect the implied duties; nor would an attempt to earn their own subsistence, a most laudable one! sink them almost to the level of those poor abandoned creatures who live by prostitution. . . . The few employments open to women, so far from being liberal, are menial; and when a superior education enables them to take charge of the education of children as governesses, they are not treated like the tutors of sons, though even clerical tutors are not always treated in a manner calculated to render them respectable in the eyes of their pupils, to say nothing of the private comfort of the individual. . . .

Some of these women might be restrained from marrying by a proper spirit of delicacy, and others may not have had it in their power to escape in this pitiful way from servitude; is not that Government then very defective, and very unmindful of the happiness of one-half of its members, that does not provide for honest, independent women, by encouraging them to fill respectable stations? . . .

It is a melancholy truth; yet such is the blessed effect of civilisation! the most respectable women are the most oppressed; and, unless they have understandings far superior to the common run of understandings, taking in both sexes, they must, from being treated like contemptible beings, become contemptible. How many women thus waste life away the prey of discontent, who might have practised as physicians, regulated a farm, managed a shop, and stood erect, supported by their own industry, instead of hanging their heads surcharged with the dew of sensibility, that consumes the beauty to which it at first gave lustre; nay, I doubt whether pity and love are so near akin as poets feign, for I have seldom seen much compassion excited by the helplessness of females, unless they were fair; then, perhaps, pity was the soft handmaid of love, or the harbinger of lust.

How much more respectable is the woman who earns her own bread by fulfilling any duty, than the most accomplished beauty!—beauty did I say!—so sensible am I of the beauty of moral-loveliness, or the harmonious propriety that attunes the passions of a well-regulated mind, that I blush at making the comparison; yet I sigh to think how few women aim at attaining this respectability by withdrawing from the giddy whirl of pleasure, or the indolent calm that stupefies the good sort of women it sucks in.

Proud of their weakness, however, they must always be protected, guarded from care, and all the rough toils that dignify the mind. If this be the fiat of fate, if they will make themselves insignificant and contemptible, sweetly to waste "life away," let them not expect to be valued when their beauty fades, for it is the fate of the fairest flowers to be admired and pulled to pieces by the careless hand that plucked them. In how many ways do I wish, from the purest benevolence, to impress this truth on my sex; yet I fear that they will not listen to a truth that dear bought experience has brought home to many an agitated bosom, nor willingly resign the privileges of rank and sex for the privileges of humanity, to which those have no claim who do not discharge its duties.

. . .

Would men but generously snap our chains, and be content with rational fellowship instead of slavish obedience, they would find us more observant daughters, more affectionate sisters, more faithful wives, more reasonable mothers—in a word, better citizens. We should then love them with true affection, because we should learn to respect ourselves; and the peace of mind of a worthy man would not be interrupted by the idle vanity of his wife, nor the babes sent to nestle in a strange bosom, having never found a home in their mother's.

STUDY QUESTIONS

1. How does Wollstonecraft account for women's secondary status in European society? How would offering more opportunities for women benefit society?
2. In what ways do Wollstonecraft's views reflect the ideas of the Enlightenment?

4.7 VISUAL SOURCE: JACQUES-LOUIS DAVID, ANTOINE LAURENT LAVOISIER AND HIS WIFE (MARIE ANNE PIERRETTE PAULZE), 1788

In this painting, the most famous French artist of the day depicts the most renowned French scientist of the eighteenth century. A pioneer in the Neoclassical style, Jacques-Louis David navigated the different phases of the French Revolution to become the favorite of Emperor Napoleon Bonaparte. This iconic portrait, which predates the Revolution, portrays the chemist Antoine Laurent Lavoisier (1743-1794) and his wife, the former Marie Anne Pierrette Paulze (1758-1836), and offers insights about the role of science in early modern European society. David depicts them together in their home, with their living room transformed into a chemistry lab. Note how meticulously David portrays the equipment, probably chosen for aesthetic value as much as for scientific import. Although the husband sits at the desk, ostensibly doing scientific work, the wife stands next to a folio, signaling to the viewer that she works as an artist. In fact, she trained under David, and it is likely she commissioned this double portrait.

While it was not unusual for a couple to appear together in a commissioned portrait, here the wife's presence indicates more than the companionship she provided for her important husband. Antoine Lavoisier performed groundbreaking chemical studies, but he collaborated with his wife Marie Anne. She worked in his laboratory, translated foreign-language papers whose findings he needed, and drew illustrations of his equipment and observations. 170 of her drawings appear in his landmark publication, the two-volume *Elements of Chemistry*, which outlined the scientific principles that provided the foundations for modern chemistry.

The harmony portrayed here did not last. When the French Revolution turned more destructive during the Terror, the artist and his subject found themselves on opposite sides. David supported the radical Jacobins and voted in favor of executing Louis XVI for treason. Antoine Lavoisier, like many scientists of the day, had benefitted from his affiliation with the royal government, for which he supervised the manufacture of gunpowder and collected taxes. A few months after the death of the king, revolutionaries sent Lavoisier to the guillotine. His wife later published his papers and spent her life promoting his discoveries.

FIGURE 4.7 Antoine Laurent Lavoisier and His Wife

STUDY QUESTIONS

1. What does this portrait reveal about where science happened in this era and who was involved in creating new scientific knowledge?
2. How does this image express the intellectual values promoted in Europe during the Enlightenment?

THESIS ASSEMBLY

As we saw in the previous chapter, a good thesis involves putting ideas together to a) make a claim and b) explain how and why the claim is true. In some cases, especially in the intellectual history we have studied in this chapter, a good thesis can offer a comparison, evaluation, or interpretation of competing ideas or phenomena.

EXAMPLE

In the exercises below, you will build a thesis statement from a series of factual statements or claims.

Factual Statement:

Seventeenth-century natural philosophers challenged Aristotelian philosophy.

Factual statement:

Seventeenth-century natural philosophers rejected the Aristotelian idea that natural phenomena possessed human qualities.

Factual statement:

Seventeenth-century natural philosophers rejected the Aristotelian idea that everything was already known.

Thesis statement involving an evaluation:

In challenging Aristotelian philosophy, and in rejecting the ideas that everything was already known and that natural phenomena possessed human qualities, *seventeenth-century natural philosophers gave better explanations of natural phenomena.*

The italicized clause evaluates seventeenth-century natural philosophy in relation to Aristotelian philosophy.

EXERCISE: CREATING THESIS STATEMENTS

Directions: Using the sentence combining techniques you practiced in Chapters 1 and 2, combine the sentences below into a thesis statement.

1.

The Scottish Enlightenment generally did not reject religion.

The French Enlightenment generally rejected religion.

The French Enlightenment was more radical than the Scottish Enlightenment.

2.

Hobbes had a pessimistic view of human nature.

As a result of his pessimistic view of human nature, Hobbes believed in the need for absolutist government.

The Scottish Enlightenment had an optimistic view of human nature.

The Scottish Enlightenment's optimistic view of human nature opened the way to political liberty.

3.

Changes in thought in the seventeenth century did not amount to a "scientific revolution."

Changes in thought in the seventeenth century occurred gradually.

New forms of thought and practice in the seventeenth century often co-existed with older ones.

4.

Galileo epitomized the new scientific methods of the seventeenth century.

Galileo especially epitomized empiricism and experimentation.

Empiricism and experimentation involved the effort to understand the natural world through direct human observation.

Empiricism and experimentation challenged existing religious and philosophical dogmas, which were based on unverified beliefs.

5.

The most prominent philosophers of the eighteenth century focused on reason, religion, and morality.

The most prominent philosophers of the eighteenth century also focused on what it meant to be a human being.

The most prominent philosophers of the eighteenth century made a major departure from existing forms of explanation and understanding.

6.

Smith is well known for his arguments in favor of the division of labor.

Smith's ideas about sympathy also made him sensitive to the negative aspects of the division of labor.

Smith's sensitivity to the negative aspects of the division of labor often remains unacknowledged.

7.

Female Enlightenment thinkers did not gain as much recognition as their male counterparts.

Women writers contributed to the Enlightenment in important ways.

Some women managed to have their works published.

Other women hosted salons and decided whom to invite and what to discuss.

8.

Different Enlightenment thinkers challenged religion in different ways.

Those who challenged religion included Mandeville, the Scottish philosophers, and Kant.

No one was more critical of religion than Voltaire, who denounced most aspects of religious practice and belief.

You will find suggested answers to the exercises in the back of this book. For more Writing History exercises, as well as study resources for this chapter, visit oup.com/us/berenson.

CHAPTER 5

THE ERA OF THE FRENCH REVOLUTION, 1750–1815

5.1 TOUSSAINT LOUVERTURE, "DICTATORIAL PROCLAMATION," NOVEMBER 25, 1801

François-Dominique Toussaint Louverture (c. 1743–1803), a black man born into slavery, played a commanding role in Saint-Domingue's slave revolt of 1791–1793. By 1798, he had made himself the military governor and de facto ruler of what had been France's most lucrative colonial possession. After the revolt he led the effort to throw off what remained of colonial rule and to create a new country called Ayiti (Haïti in French) or "land of high mountains," the name used by the island's original inhabitants.

Toussaint now confronted an economy devastated by seven years of bloody fighting, many of Haiti's sugar fields and once-opulent mansions having been burned to the ground. He decided to restore plantation sugar production—which he considered the only efficient means of producing the tropical products so highly valued in Europe—and forced all ex-slaves not serving in the army to work on plantations, often for their former masters. In the process, Toussaint became a virtual dictator. As "ruler for life" according to the new constitution of 1801, he presided over a parliament devoid of power and a population with no meaningful political or civil rights. To many ex-slaves and French revolutionaries, Toussaint's leadership looked like a betrayal of the revolution and a return to the Old Regime.

Cap Français, 4 Frimmaire [Frimaire], Year X [November 25, 1801]

Since the revolution, I have done all that depended upon me to return happiness to my country and to ensure liberty for my fellow citizens. Forced to combat internal and external enemies of the French Republic, I made war with courage, honor and loyalty. I have never strayed from the rules of justice with my enemies; as much as was in my power I sought to soften the horrors of war, to spare the blood of men . . . Often after victory I received as brothers those who, the day before, were under enemy flags.

Schoelcher, Victor (1889). Vie de Toussaint Louverture. Paris: Paul Ollendorf.

Through the overlooking of errors and faults I wanted to make even its most ardent enemies love the legitimate and sacred cause of liberty.

I constantly reminded my brothers in arms, general and officers, that the ranks to which they had been raised were nothing but the reward for honor, bravery and irreproachable conduct. That the higher they were above their fellow citizens, the more irreproachable all their actions and words must be; that scandals caused by public men had consequences even more dire for society than those of simple citizens; that the ranks and functions they bore had not been given to them to serve only their ambition, but had as cause and goal the general good. . . .

It is up to officers to give their soldiers with good lessons good examples. Every captain should have the noble goal of having his company the best disciplined, the most cleanly attired, the best trained. He should think that the lapses of his soldiers reflect on him and believe himself lowered by the faults of those he commands. . . .

The same reproaches equally apply to cultivators on the habitations. Since the revolution perverse men have told them that freedom is the right to remain idle and to follow only their whims. Such a doctrine could not help but be accepted by all the evil subjects, thieves and assassins. It is time to hit out at the hardened men who persist in such ideas.

As soon as a child can walk he should be employed on the habitations according to his strength in some useful work, instead of being sent into the cities where, under the pretext of an education that he does not receive, he goes to learn vice, to add to the horde of vagabonds and women of evil lives, to trouble by his existence the repose of good citizens, and to terminate it with the final punishment. Military commanders and magistrates must be inexorable with this class of men. Despite this, they must be forced to be useful to society upon which, without the most severe vigilance, they will be a plague. . . .

Idleness is the source of all disorders, and if it is allowed with one individual I shall hold the military commanders responsible, persuaded that those who tolerate the lazy and vagabonds are secret enemies of the government. . . .

Consequently, I decree the following:

I. Any commander who during the late conspiracy had knowledge of the troubles which were to break out and who tolerated pillage and murder or who, able to prevent or block the revolt allowed the law that declares that "life, property and the asylum of every citizen are sacred and inviolable"; to be broken, will be brought before a special tribunal and punished in conformity with the law of August 10, 1801. Any military commander who, by lack of foresight or negligence, has not stopped the disorders that have been committed, will be discharged and punished with one year in prison. In consequence of this a rigorous inquest will be carried out, according to which the government will pronounce on his destiny.

II. All generals and commanders of *arrondissements* and quarters who in the future will neglect to take all necessary measures to prevent or block sedition will be brought before a special tribunal and punished in conformity with the law of August 10, 1801.

III. In case of troubles, or upon indication that such will break out, the national guard of a quarter or *arrondissement* shall be at the orders of the military commanders upon their simple requisition. Any military commander who shall not have taken all the measures necessary to prevent troubles in his quarter, or the spreading of trouble from a quarter neighboring to that which he commands, and any military man, be he of the line or the national guard, who shall refuse to obey legal orders shall be punished with death.

IV. Any individual, man or woman, whatever his or her color, who shall be convicted of having pronounced serious statements tending to incite sedition shall be brought before a court martial and punished in conformity with the law.

V. Any Creole individual, man or woman, convicted of making statements tending to alter public tranquility but who shall not be worthy of death shall be sent to the fields to work with a chain on one foot for six months. . . .

XIX. Any person convicted of having disturbed or attempted to disturb a married couple shall be denounced to the civil and military authorities, who shall render an account to the governor, who shall pronounce on their fate in accordance with the needs of the case.

XX. My regulations on cultivation, given at Port-Républicain the 20th of Vendémiaire of the year IX [1800], shall be executed exactly as stated. All military commanders are enjoined to execute it rigorously and literally in all that is not contrary to the present proclamation.

The present proclamation shall be printed, transcribed on the registers of administrative and judiciary bodies, read, published and posted wherever needed, and also inserted in the *Bulletin Officiel de Saint-Domingue*. A copy shall be sent to all ministers of religion for it to be read to all parishioners after mass.

All generals, military commanders and all civil authorities in all departments are enjoined to maintain a firm hand in ensuring the full and complete execution of all of these dispositions on their personal responsibility and under penalty of disobedience.

STUDY QUESTIONS

1. Why did Toussaint consider "idleness" particularly deleterious to the future of an independent Haiti?
2. Were his pronouncements "authoritarian" in nature? Why was he particularly concerned about "sedition"?

5.2 *DECLARATION OF THE RIGHTS OF MAN AND CITIZEN, AUGUST 26, 1789*

In June 1789, when the "Third Estate" reconstituted itself as the "National Assembly," among the first measures it considered was a universal declaration of the rights and duties of individual French citizens. A proposal to this effect was made in July by the Marquis de Lafayette, but swift-moving events in Paris, such as the fall of the Bastille on July 14, pushed the Revolution in new directions. Nevertheless, a subcommittee continued to debate the document, and a draft proposal of 24 articles was edited down to 17. Like the Declaration of Independence in the American colonies (1776), this document was a compromise statement, drawn up and edited by committees. It nonetheless offered a stirring statement of Enlightened principles concerning both men's role in a state and popular sovereignty as the foundation of legitimate government.

The representatives of the French people, organized in National Assembly, considering that ignorance, forgetfulness or contempt of the rights of man, are the sole causes of public miseries and of the corruption of governments, have resolved to set forth, in a solemn declaration the natural,

Frank Malloy Anderson, *The Constitutions and Other Select Documents Illustrative of the History of France, 1789-1907*, 2ed. Minneapolis, MN: PW Wilson Company, 1908, 59-61.

inalienable and sacred rights of man, in order that this declaration, being ever present to all the members of the social body, may unceasingly remind them of their rights and their duties; in order that the acts of the legislative power and those of the executive power may be at each moment compared with the aim of every political institution, and thereby may be more upon simple and incontestible principles, may always take the direction of maintaining the constitution and the happiness of all.

In consequence, the National Assembly recognizes and declares, in the presence and under the auspices of the Supreme Being, the following rights of man and of the citizen:

1. Men are born and remain free and equal in rights. Social distinctions can be based only upon public utility.
2. The aim of any political association is the preservation of the natural and imprescriptible rights of man. These rights are liberty, property, security, and resistance to oppression.
3. The source of all sovereignty is essentially in the nation; no body, no individual can exercise authority that does not directly proceed from it.
4. Liberty consists in the power to do anything that does not injure others; accordingly, the exercise of the natural rights of each man has no limits except those that secure to the other members of society the enjoyment of these same rights. These limits can be determined only by law.
5. The law has the right to forbid only such actions as are injurious to society. Nothing can be forbidden that is not prohibited by the law, and no one can be constrained to do that which the law does not require.
6. The law is the expression of the general will. All the citizens have the right to take part personally, or by their representatives, in its formation. It must be the same for all, whether it protects or punishes. All the citizens being equal in its eyes, are equally eligible to all public dignities, places, and employments, according to their capacities and without other distinction than that of their virtues and their talents.

7. No man can be accused, arrested, or detained, except in the cases determined by the law and according to the forms that it has prescribed. Those who procure, expedite, execute, or cause to be executed arbitrary orders ought to be punished: but every citizen summoned or seized in virtue of the law ought to render instant obedience; he makes himself guilty by resistance.
8. The law ought to establish only penalties that are strictly and obviously necessary, and no one can be punished except in virtue of a law established and promulgated prior to the offense and legally applied.
9. Every man being presumed innocent until he has been pronounced guilty, if it is thought indispensable to arrest him, any severity that may not be necessary to secure his person ought to be strictly suppressed by law.
10. No one should be disturbed on account of his opinions, even religious, provided their manifestation does not trouble the public order established by law.
11. The free communication of ideas and opinions is one of the most precious of the rights of man: every citizen then can freely speak, write, and print, subject to responsibility for the abuse of this freedom in the cases determined by law.
12. The protection of the rights of man and citizen requires a public force; this force then is instituted for the advantage of all and not for the personal benefit of those to whom it is entrusted.
13. For the maintenance of the public force and for the expenses of administration a general tax is indispensable; it ought to be equally apportioned among all the citizens according to their means.
14. All citizens have the right to ascertain, by themselves or by their representatives, the necessity of the public tax, to consent to it freely, to follow the employment of it, and to determine the quota, the assessment, the collection, and the duration of it.
15. Society has the right to make accountable every public agent of the administration.

16. Any society in which the guarantee of rights is not secured, or the separation of powers not determined, has no constitution at all.
17. Property being a sacred and inviolable right, no one can be deprived of it, unless a legally established public necessity evidently demands it, under the condition of a just and prior compensation.

STUDY QUESTIONS

1. To what extent does the Declaration of the Rights of Man mix specific provisions and general principles of human rights?
2. Which provisions and ideas reflect the values of the Enlightenment?

5.3 OLYMPE DE GOUGES, *THE DECLARATION OF THE RIGHTS OF WOMAN AND CITIZEN*, SEPTEMBER 1791

Women were not included among the new office-holders of Revolutionary France, nor were they members of the National Assembly, which in theory represented all members of the country's Third Estate. The extent to which the benefits of the Revolution should be extended to females and to the slaves controlled by masters in France's global empire sparked immediate debate. Some men advocated the extension of rights and privileges to women and slaves, but women also took action on their own behalf. They did so in organizations such as the *"Cercle Social"* (Social Circle), which brought together female activists who sought to pursue their own goals in the developing Revolution.

One of the leaders of this group was Marie Gouze Aubry (1748–1793), a playwright, pamphleteer, and political activist, who, under the pen-name Olympe de Gouges, attacked the institution of slavery and the oppression of women. In 1791 de Gouges published this thoughtful meditation on what the National Assembly should declare concerning "the rights of woman," as opposed merely to "the rights of man." Other members of the Social Circle were arrested as the Revolution entered its radical phase, and Olympe de Gouges was executed by guillotine in November 1793.

To be decreed by the National Assembly in its last sessions or by the next legislature.

PREAMBLE

The mothers, daughters, sisters, representatives of the nation, ask to constitute a National Assembly.

Translated and reprinted in Eleanor S. Riemer and John C. Fout, eds., *European Women: A Documentary History 1789-1945*. New York: Schocken Books, 63-67.

Considering that ignorance, forgetfulness or contempt of the rights of woman are the sole causes of public miseries, and of corruption of governments, they have resolved to set forth in a solemn declaration, the natural, unalterable and sacred rights of woman, so that this declaration, being ever present to all members of the social body, may unceasingly remind them of their rights and their duties; in order that the acts of women's power, as well as those of men, may be judged constantly against the aim of all political institutions, and thereby be more respected for it, in order that the complaints of women citizens, based henceforth on simple and indisputable principles, may always take the direction of maintaining the Constitution, good morals and the welfare of all.

In consequence, the sex superior in beauty and in courage, in maternal suffering recognizes and declares, in the presence of and under the auspices of the Supreme Being, the following rights of woman and of the woman citizen:

1. Woman is born free and remains equal to man in rights. Social distinctions may be based only on common utility.
2. The aim of every political association is the preservation of the natural and imprescriptible rights of man and woman. These rights are liberty, prosperity, security, and above all resistance to oppression.
3. The source of all sovereignty rests essentially in the Nation, which is nothing but the joining together of Man and Woman; no body, no individual can exercise authority that does not emanate expressly from the it.
4. Liberty and justice consist in giving back to others all that belongs to them; thus the only limits on the exercise of woman's natural rights are the perpetual tyranny by which man opposes her; these limits must be reformed by the laws of nature and of reason.
5. The laws of nature and reason forbid all actions that are harmful to society; all that is not forbidden by these wise and divine laws cannot be prevented, and no one can be constrained to do what they do not prescribe.

6. Law must be the expression of the general will: all citizens, men and women alike, must personally or through their representatives concur in its formation; it must be the same for all, all citizens, men and women alike, being equal it, must be equally eligible for all high offices, positions and public employments, according to their virtues and talents.
7. No woman can be an exception; she will be accused, apprehended, and detained in cases determined by law; women, like men, will obey this rigorous rule.
8. The law must establish only those penalties which are strictly and clearly necessary, and no woman can be punished by virtue of a law established and promulgated prior to the offense, and legally applied to women.
9. When a woman is declared guilty, full severity is exercised by the law.
10. No one ought to be disturbed for one's fundamental opinions; however fundamental they are; since a woman has the right to mount the scaffold, she must also have the right to address the House, provided her interventions do not disturb the public order as it has been established by law.
11. The free communication of ideas and opinions is one of the most precious rights of woman, since this freedom ensures the legitimacy of fathers toward their children. Every woman citizen can therefore say freely: I am the mother of a child that belongs to you, without being force her to conceal the truth because of a barbaric prejudice; except to be answerable for abuses of this liberty as determined by law.
12. The safeguard of the rights of woman and of the woman citizen is a necessary benefit; this guarantee must be instituted for the advantage of all, and not for the personal benefit of those to whom it is entrusted.
13. For the upkeep of public forces and for administrative expenses, the contributions of woman and man are equal; a woman shares in all the labors required by law, in the painful tasks; she must therefore have an equal share in the

distribution of offices, employments, trusts, dignities and work.

14. Women and men citizens have the right to ascertain by themselves of through their representatives the necessity of public taxes. Women citizens will not only assume an equal part in providing the wealth but also in the public administration and in determining the quota, the assessment, the collection and the duration of the impost.

15. The mass of women, joined together to contribute their taxes with those of men, have the right to demand from every public official an accounting of his administration.

16. Any society in which the guarantee of rights is not assured, nor the separation of powers determined, has no Constitution; the Constitution is null if the majority of the individuals of whom the nation is compromised have not participated in its drafting.

17. Ownership of property is for both sexes, mutually and separately; it is for each a sacred and inviolable right; no one can be deprived of it as a true patrimony of nature, unless a public necessity, legally established, evidently requires it, and with the condition of a just and prior indemnity.

Postscript

Woman wake up! The alarm bell of reason is making itself heard throughout the universe; recognize your rights. The powerful empire of nature is no longer beset by prejudices, fanaticism, superstition and lies. The torch of truth has dispelled all the clouds of stupidity and usurpation. The enslaved man multiplied his forces but has had to resort to yours to break his chains. Once free he became unjust to his female companion. O women! women, when will you stop being blind? What advantages have you received from the Revolution? A more pronounced scorn, a more marked contempt? During the centuries of corruption, your only power was over the weakness of men. Your empire is destroyed, what then is left to you? The conviction that men are unjust. The claiming of your patrimony based on the wise laws of nature. The good word of the Lawgiver of the Marriage of Cana? Are you afraid that our French lawmakers, correctors of this morality, so long tied up with the politics which is no longer in style will say to you: "Women, what is there in common between you and us?" – Everything, you would have to reply. If they persisted in their weakness, in putting forth this inconsistency which is a contradiction of their principles, you should courageously oppose these hale pretentions of superiority with the force of reason; unite under a banner of philosophy, unfold all the energy of your character and you will soon see these proud men, your servile adorers, crawling at your feet, but proud to share with you the treasures of the Supreme Being. Whatever the obstacles that you oppose us may be, it is in your power to free us, you only to will it. . . .

Since it is now a question of national education, let us see if our wise lawmakers will think wisely about the education of women.

STUDY QUESTIONS

1. What does de Gouges consider woman's "natural and reasonable" share in the "common" life of a society?
2. What arguments does de Gouges anticipate will be used by revolutionary men to keep women unequal?

5.4 SOCIETY OF THE FRIENDS OF THE BLACKS, *ADDRESS TO THE NATIONAL ASSEMBLY IN FAVOR OF THE ABOLITION OF THE SLAVE TRADE,* FEBRUARY 5, 1790

In addition to inspiring Olympe de Gouges, the Declaration of the Rights of Man and Citizen encouraged the Society of the Friends of the Blacks to call publicly for an end to the slave trade. Modelled after the London Committee for the Abolition of the Slave Trade, the Society, founded in 1788, brought together some of the most prominent French intellectuals and politicians of the day, including Lafayette, Rouchefoucault, Condorcet, and Lavoisier (see document 4.7). Under pressure from supporters of slavery, who appreciated the immense wealth flowing into France from the colonies, the Society was keen to defend itself against the charge that it advocated conferring full political rights on French blacks. Nevertheless, the warnings of Society members about slave revolts soon came to pass when blacks in Saint-Domingue, the most prosperous economy in the Caribbean, rose up against their masters in 1791 under the leadership of Toussaint Louverture.

The humanity, justice, and magnanimity that have guided you in the reform of the most profoundly rooted abuses gives hope to the Society of the Friends of Blacks that you will receive with benevolence its demand in favor of that numerous portion of humankind, so cruelly oppressed for two centuries.

This Society, slandered in such cowardly and unjust fashion, only derives its mission from the humanity that induced it to defend the blacks even under the past despotism. Oh! Can there be a more respectable title in the eyes of this august Assembly which has so often avenged the rights of man in its decrees?

You have declared them, these rights; you have engraved on an immortal monument that all men are born and remain free and equal in rights; you have restored to the French people these rights that despotism had for so long despoiled; . . . you have broken the chains of feudalism that still degraded a good number of our fellow citizens; you have announced the destruction of all the stigmatizing distinctions that religious or political prejudices introduced into the great family of humankind. . . .

We are not asking you to restore to French blacks those political rights which alone, nevertheless, attest to and maintain the dignity of man; we are not even asking for their liberty. No; slander, bought no doubt with the greed of the shipowners, ascribes that scheme to us and spreads it everywhere; they want to stir up everyone against us, provoke the planters and their numerous creditors, who take alarm even at gradual emancipation. They want to alarm all the French, to whom they depict the prosperity of the colonies as inseparable from the slave trade and the perpetuity of slavery.

No, never has such an idea entered into our minds; we have said it, printed it since the beginning of our Society, and we repeat it in order to reduce to

From *Liberty, Equality, Fraternity,* https://chnm.gmu.edu/revolution/d/290/.

nothing this grounds of argument, blindly adopted by all the coastal cities, the grounds on which rest almost all their addresses [to the National Assembly]. The immediate emancipation of the blacks would not only be a fatal operation for the colonies; it would even be a deadly gift for the blacks, in the state of abjection and incompetence to which cupidity has reduced them. It would be to abandon to themselves and without assistance children in the cradle or mutilated and impotent beings.

It is therefore not yet time to demand that liberty; we ask only that one cease butchering thousands of blacks regularly every year in order to take hundreds of captives; we ask that henceforth cease the prostitution, the profaning of the French name, used to authorize these thefts, these atrocious murders; we demand in a word the abolition of the slave trade. . . .

In regard to the colonists, we will demonstrate to you that if they need to recruit blacks in Africa to sustain the population of the colonies at the same level, it is because they wear out the blacks with work, whippings, and starvation; that, if they treated them with kindness and as good fathers of families, these blacks would multiply and that this population, always growing, would increase cultivation and prosperity. . . .

Have no doubt, the time when this commerce will be abolished, even in England, is not far off. It is condemned there in public opinion, even in the opinion of the ministers. . . .

If some motive might on the contrary push them [the blacks] to insurrection, might it not be the indifference of the National Assembly about their lot? Might it not be the insistence on weighing them down with chains, when one consecrates everywhere this eternal axiom: that all men are born free and equal in rights. So then therefore there would only be fetters and gallows for the blacks while good fortune glimmers only for the whites? Have no doubt, our happy revolution must re-electrify the blacks whom vengeance and resentment have electrified for so long, and it is not with punishments that the effect of this upheaval will be repressed. From one insurrection badly pacified will twenty others be born, of which one alone can ruin the colonists forever.

It is worthy of the first free Assembly of France to consecrate the principle of philanthropy which makes of humankind only one single family, to declare that it is horrified by this annual carnage which takes place on the coasts of Africa, that it has the intention of abolishing it one day, of mitigating the slavery that is the result, of looking for and preparing, from this moment, the means.

STUDY QUESTIONS

1. How does the Society of the Friends of the Blacks foresee ending slavery? What methods do they suggest will allow the promise of equality to apply to humans from Africa in addition to those from France?
2. What does this speech reveal about the limits of revolutionary ideology? What barriers kept revolutionaries from making instant changes to their society?

5.5 MAXIMILIEN ROBESPIERRE, SPEECH TO THE NATIONAL CONVENTION, FEBRUARY 5, 1794

The French Revolution became increasingly radical in 1793 after having abolished the monarchy and executed the king and queen. The ruling Jacobins ejected their opponents from the Convention, the revolutionary legislature, and conferred vast political power on the twelve-member Committee of Public Safety, which worked to identify "enemies of the Republic" and send them to the guillotine. Historians place the committee's work under the rubric of "the Terror," as did its leader, Maximilien Robespierre, a small-town lawyer nicknamed "the Incorruptible." In this speech, Robespierre outlines his inflexible approach to keeping the Revolution on track. He compares revolutionary values with those of the Old Regime (epitomized by Louis XIV, but embodied by Louis XVI) and advocates violence ("terror") to implement his political ideas ("virtue").

It is time to mark clearly the aim of the Revolution and the end toward which we wish to move; it is time to take stock of ourselves, of the obstacles which we still face, and of the means which we ought to adopt to attain our objectives. . . .

What is the goal for which we strive? A peaceful enjoyment of liberty and equality, the rule of that eternal justice whose laws are engraved, not upon marble or stone, but in the hearts of all men.

We wish an order of things where all low and cruel passions are enchained by the laws, all beneficent and generous feelings aroused; where ambition is the desire to merit glory and to serve one's fatherland; where distinctions are born only of equality itself; where the citizen is subject to the magistrate, the magistrate to the people, the people to justice; where the nation safe guards the welfare of each individual, and each individual proudly enjoys the prosperity and glory of his fatherland; where all spirits are enlarged by the constant exchange of republican sentiments and by the need of earning the respect of a great people; where the arts are the adornment of liberty, which ennobles them; and where commerce is the source of public wealth, not simply of monstrous opulence for a few families.

In our country we wish to substitute morality for egotism, probity for honor, principles for conventions, duties for etiquette, the empire of reason for the tyranny of customs, contempt for vice for contempt for misfortune, pride for insolence, the love of honor for the love of money . . . that is to say, all the virtues and miracles of the Republic for all the vices and snobbishness of the monarchy.

We wish in a word to fulfill the requirements of nature, to accomplish the destiny of mankind, to make good the promises of philosophy . . . that France, hitherto illustrious among slave states, may eclipse the glory of all free peoples that have existed, become the model of all nations. . . . That is our ambition; that is our aim.

What kind of government can realize these marvels? Only a democratic government. . . . But to found and to consolidate among us this democracy, to realize the peaceable rule of constitutional laws, it is necessary to conclude the war of liberty against tyranny and to pass successfully through the storms of revolution. Such is the aim of the revolutionary system which you have set up. . . .

Now what is the fundamental principle of democratic, or popular government—that is to say, the

From Raymond P. Stearns, *Pageant of Europe* (New York: Harcourt Brace Jovanovich, 1947), pp. 404–405.

essential mainspring upon which it depends and which makes it function? It is virtue: I mean public virtue . . . that virtue which is nothing else but love of fatherland and its laws. . . .

The splendor of the goal of the French Revolution is simultaneously the source of our strength and of our weakness: our strength, because it gives us an ascendancy of truth over falsehood, and of public rights over private interests; our weakness, because it rallies against us all vicious men, all those who in their hearts seek to despoil the people. . . . It is necessary to stifle the domestic and foreign enemies of the Republic or perish with them. Now in these circumstances, the first maxim of our politics ought to be to lead the people by means of reason and the enemies of the people by terror.

If the basis of popular government in time of peace is virtue, the basis of popular government in time of revolution is both virtue and terror: virtue without which terror is murderous, terror without which virtue is powerless. Terror is nothing else than swift, severe, indomitable justice; it flows, then, from virtue.

STUDY QUESTIONS

1. What problems does Robespierre identify in Old Regime (pre-Revolutionary) France? According to Robespierre, how has the Revolution solved these problems?
2. How did the revolutionaries use Enlightenment ideas to justify killing and terror?

5.6 NAPOLEON BONAPARTE, *PROCLAMATION TO THE PEOPLE OF EGYPT* WITH A RESPONSE FROM ABD AL-RAHMAN AL-JABARTI, JULY 2, 1798

By the mid-1790s, Great Britain had subdued its Jacobin sympathizers and joined the war against Revolutionary France. This move coincided with the rise to power of a brilliant military leader from Corsica called Napoleon Bonaparte (1769–1821). Aware of Britain's formidable navy, and reluctant to confront British warships in their home waters, Napoleon led his army across the Mediterranean to Egypt, where he hoped to disrupt Britain's lucrative trade with India, which it dominated militarily. But once the French fleet had deposited Napoleon and his troops on Egyptian soil in July 1798, the British navy stranded them there by destroying the French vessels anchored in Aboukir Bay.

Napoleon expected the Egyptians, whom he saw as being oppressed by cruel Ottoman overlords, to greet him as a liberator. Instead, they strenuously resisted him. But even as the French invasion went from bad to worse, Napoleon proved himself to be a master of propaganda, sending home to France images of military triumph and cultural discovery, and boasting of his successful effort to "civilize" the Egyptian people. To preserve his reputation in the face of an imminent military disaster, Napoleon slipped out of Egypt and returned to France before the collapse of the

From http://www.laits.utexas.edu/cairo/teachers/napoleon.pdf.

French forces, which could now be blamed on someone else. The Egyptian scholar and jurist Abd al-Rahman al-Jabarti responded with a lengthy letter to the Egyptian people, which explained Napoleon's letter according to his own interpretation.

NAPOLEON BONAPARTE, PROCLAMATION TO THE PEOPLE OF EGYPT

To the People of Egypt, H.Q. Alexandria, 2 July 1798.

In the name of God, the Merciful, the Compassionate. There is no god but God. He has no son, nor has He an associate in His domain. On behalf of the French Republic which is based upon the foundation of liberty and equality, General Bonaparte makes it known that the beys who govern Egypt have for long insulted the French nation and injured its merchants: the hour of their punishment has arrived. For too long this rabble of slaves bought in Georgia and Caucasia have tyrannized over the most beautiful part of the world; but God, from whom all depends, has ordered that their empire shall cease. Peoples of Egypt, you will be told that I have come to destroy your religion; do not believe it! Answer that I have come to restore your rights and punish the usurpers, and that, more than the Mamluks, I respect God, his prophet and the Koran. Say that all men are equal before God; wisdom, talent and virtue alone differentiate between them. But what wisdoms, what talents, what virtue have the Mamluks, that they exclusively have all that makes life desirable and sweet? Is there a fine estate? It belongs to the Mamluks. Is there a beautiful slave, a good horse, a pleasant house? They belong to the Mamluks. If Egypt is their farm, let them show the lease that God has given them. But God is just and merciful to the people. The Egyptians will be called upon to hold all offices; the wisest and most learned and most virtuous will govern, and the people will be happy. Once there were among you great cities, great canals, a great commerce. What has destroyed all this if not greed, the injustice and the tyranny of the Mamluks? Qadis, sheiks, imams, [In the French version] tell the people that we are friends of the true Muslims. [In the Arabic version] tell the people that the French are also faithful Muslims, and in confirmation of this, we have destroyed the Pope, who called for war against the Muslims. We have destroyed the knights of Malta because those madmen believed God wished them to fight the Muslims. We have been through the centuries the friends of the French in Egypt.

When the French forces commanded by Napoleon Bonaparte landed at Alexandria in June 1798, they found themselves in the position of needing to justify their presence in Egypt. There were only a few thousand Frenchmen, uninvited guests in a country where no one knew who they were or why they were there. Ever the diplomat, Napoleon wrote out a message to the Egyptian people, reproduced here: "Sultan (may God grant his desires) and the enemies of his enemies. But, as for the Mamluks, have they ever not been in revolt against the Sultan's authority, which even now they disown? Thrice happy those who shall be for us! They will prosper both in fortune and in rank. Happy those who shall be neutral! They will have time to learn to know us, and they will range themselves beside us. But woe, threefold woe to those who take up arms for the Mamluks and fight against us! For them there will be no hope: they will perish."

RESPONSE FROM ABD AL-RAHMAN AL-JABARTI

Here is an explanation of the incoherent words and vulgar constructions put into this miserable letter. His statement "In the name of God, the merciful, the Compassionate . . . etc." In mentioning these three phrases there is an indication that the French agree with the three religions, but at the same time they do not agree with them, nor with any religion. They are consistent with the Muslims in stating the formula "In the name of God," in denying that He has a son or an associate. They disagree with the Muslims in rejecting the mission of Muhammad. They agree with the Christians in most of their words and deeds but disagree with them by not mentioning the Trinity and furthermore by killing their priests and destroying their churches. . . . Their statement "On behalf of the French republic, etc." means that their proclamation is sent from their Republic, because they have no chief or sultan with whom they all agree, whose function is to speak on their behalf. For when they rebelled against their sultan six years ago and killed him, the people agreed unanimously that there was not to be a single ruler, but that their state, territories, laws and administrations of their affairs should be in the hands of the intelligent and wise among them. They made this the foundation and basis of their system. Their term "liberty" means that they are not slaves like the Mamluks. . . . They follow this rule: great and small, high and low, male and female are all equal. Sometimes they break this rule according to their whims and inclinations or reasoning. Their women do not veil themselves and have no modesty. Whenever a Frenchman has to perform an act of nature, he does so wherever he happens to be, even in full view of people. . . . As for his statement "destroyed the Pope," by this deed they have gone against the Christians as has already been pointed out. So those people are opposed to both Christians and Muslims, and do not hold to any religion."

STUDY QUESTIONS

1. How was Napoleon extending the principles of the Revolution in France to Egypt, and in a specifically Muslim context?
2. How was al-Jabarti extending the principle of "true religion" in a governmental context to Revolutionary France?

5.7 VISUAL SOURCE: SOUVENIR PLATE OF THE EXECUTION OF LOUIS XVI, C. 1793

The Convention put the king on trial for "conspiracy against national liberty and assault against national security" in late 1792. His family's flight to Varennes the previous year had angered many supporters of the revolution, and France's declaration of war against Austria, the home of Marie Antoinette, further endangered Louis XVI. The Jacobins blamed the king for the precarious military situation and the economic problems that continued to plague France. In September 1792 deputies voted to strip Louis of his titles, abolish the monarchy, and create a Republic; many believed they needed to eliminate the king himself. The legislature quickly found him guilty of treason but conducted a lengthy debate over how to punish him. Maximilien Robespierre gave a long speech in which he said, "I am no lover of long speeches on obvious matters; they augur ill for freedom. I vote for death." The artist Jacques-Louis David also voted for death. Thomas Paine, the Anglo-American author of *Common Sense* who had taken a seat in the French assembly, aimed for the middle ground, voting that Louis be imprisoned during the war and then sent into exile.

From "Commemorating the Revolution on Chinaware," *Liberty, Equality, Fraternity* http://chnm.gmu.edu/revolution/d/104

In the January 1793, the final votes were cast with a very narrow majority in favor of execution. The split in the Convention reflected a split across the nation. The Terror that followed the king's public execution might suggest that zealous revolutionaries had taken hold of France against the tide of public opinion. Yet this artifact reveals the deep well of public anger against the king.

Souvenir plates, made of porcelain to commemorate an important event, are still in production today. For example, Amazon.com sold plates to celebrate the 2018 marriage of Britain's Prince Harry to Meghan Markle. The dishes are usually put on display rather than used for food, but owners can, of course, do what they wish with them. This souvenir plate memorializing the execution of King Louis XVI graphically depicts his bloody death and implies a kind of symbolic feast of the enemy, hinting that the owner can (like a vampire) grow stronger from eating the blood of the sacrifice.

FIGURE 5.7 Souvenir Plate of the Execution of Louis XVI

STUDY QUESTIONS

1. What does the creation (and preservation) of this plate reveal about how contemporaries felt about the execution of King Louis XVI, called simply Louis Capet on the plate? What emotions are evoked here?

2. Look closely at what the artist chose to include. What aspect(s) of the execution seemed the most worthy of remembering? What details are left out of this image?

THE THESIS STATEMENT
AND ITS SUPPORTING IDEAS

In history papers, students' most common mistake is to write a simple narrative of events without a "controlling idea" or thesis. This mistake can be avoided using a method we call *X-1-2-3*.[1]

With X-1-2-3, you write a thesis statement (Sentence X) that can be parsed into at least three separate and distinct ideas. These ideas become your paper's main supporting points in a mini-outline.

A good thesis statement does not *require* a three-part structure. But if your thesis statement cannot easily be broken down into three supporting ideas, this may be a signal that it needs more thought. The X-1-2-3 method is both a diagnostic test and a preventive measure: it protects you from writing a purely narrative or descriptive paper.

EXAMPLE 1

Thesis (Sentence X)	The most important reason for the French monarchy's financial difficulties was its constant warfare, but the nobility's tax exemptions and venal office holding figured prominently as well. **(THESIS)**
Topic	The French monarchy's financial difficulties
1	The French monarchy's financial difficulties were caused primarily by its constant warfare. **(SUPPORTING IDEA)**
2	The French monarchy's financial difficulties were also caused by the nobility's tax exemptions. **(SUPPORTING IDEA)**
3	The French monarchy's financial difficulties were also caused by the nobility's venal office holding. **(SUPPORTING IDEA)**

Notice that the *topic* of this paper—the French monarchy's financial difficulties—is also the grammatical *subject* of sentences X, 1, 2, and 3. With the X-1-2-3 method, your thesis statement "controls" your supporting points via the structure of the sentence.

X-1-2-3 sentence sets work as simple outlines for papers of any length, and can easily be expanded into formal outlines, with smaller points and historical detail nested below sentences 1, 2, and 3. An X-1-2-3 sequence allows your argument to unfold gracefully over the pages of your paper, with historical narrative and description woven in.

---

[1] Adaptation of a method created by William J. Kerrigan (William J. Kerrigan and Allan A. Metcalf, *Writing to the Point*, 4th ed. (New York: Harcourt Brace Jovanovich, 1987), p. 19.

EXAMPLE 2

A comparative thesis statement and its supporting sentences:

X   French intellectuals were more likely to become radicalized politically than their British counterparts because the former were largely excluded from government and the latter often played a major role in it. **(THESIS)**

1   French intellectuals were more likely to become radicalized politically than their British counterparts. **(SUPPORTING IDEA)**

2   French intellectuals were largely excluded from government. **(SUPPORTING IDEA)**

3   British intellectuals often played a major role in government. **(SUPPORTING IDEA)**

EXAMPLE 3

X   Because the Terror continued after France had defeated its enemies and resolved its most pressing economic problems, the Terror did not result from the circumstances of war and economic crisis but rather from the ideology and paranoia of the Jacobins. **(THESIS)**

1   The Terror continued after France had defeated its enemies and resolved its most pressing economic problems. **(SUPPORTING IDEA)**

2   The Terror did not result from the circumstances of war and economic crisis. **(SUPPORTING IDEA)**

3   The Terror resulted from the ideology and paranoia of the Jacobins. **(SUPPORTING IDEA)**

EXERCISE: WRITE A SET OF SUPPORTING-IDEA SENTENCES FOR EACH THESIS STATEMENT

Instructions

For each thesis statement, write a set of supporting-idea sentences using words, phrases, and/or clauses contained in the thesis. Use the thesis statement's topic as the grammatical subject of sentences 1, 2, and 3.

1. X The French Revolution resulted from four profound crises that the government was unable to resolve—a financial crisis, political crisis, legitimacy crisis, and an economic crisis.
   1 The French Revolution resulted from a financial crisis the government was unable to resolve.
   2 The French Revolution resulted from a political crisis the government was unable to resolve.

   3 _____

   _____

   4 _____

   _____

2. Together, the bankruptcy of the treasury and the organized expression of public opinion precipitated the fall of the monarchy, and neither would have done so alone.

1 _____

_____

2 _____

_____

3 _____

_____

3. Both slaves and free people of color in Haiti came to believe that Haiti's social and economic system was incompatible with the ideals of the French Revolution, although each group had reasons of its own for understanding the Revolution in this way.

1 _____

_____

2 _____

_____

3 _____

_____

You will find suggested answers to the exercises in the back of this book. For more Writing History exercises, as well as study resources for this chapter, visit oup.com/us/berenson.

CHAPTER 6

THE INDUSTRIAL REVOLUTION, 1750–1850

6.1 SAMUEL SMILES ON RICHARD ARKWRIGHT, *SELF-HELP*, 1859

In *Self-Help*, an immensely popular book published in 1859, author Samuel Smiles lauded Richard Arkwright (1732–1792), the creator of England's first steam-powered textile factories, as a paragon of self-help. Although Arkwright's real life was much less self-actualized and self-driven than the book portrays, Smiles' famous account nonetheless consecrated Arkwright as one of the iconic figures of the Industrial Revolution.

To the nineteenth century's avid readers of biographies of great men, Arkwright's life story seemed a rare rags-to-riches tale. He opened his first mill (or factory) near a stream of falling water in 1772. This venture proved to be a four-year experiment that ultimately resulted in a smoothly working enterprise, after which he built a second factory incorporating everything he had learned from the first. The second mill, established in 1776 in the town of Cromford, became the proto-type for all of the cotton mills subsequently erected throughout Britain—and, eventually, the rest of the world—during the eighteenth and nineteenth centuries.

Arkwright was famous for figuring out how to mechanize the spinning of raw cotton into thread, vastly reducing the cost of cotton thread and thus of finished cloth, even though weaving thread into fabric was still done by hand. When he died at age 60 in 1792, he was one of the wealthiest men in Britain, with a fortune estimated at £500,000, the equivalent of a multibillion-aire today. In the process of amassing this great fortune, however, Arkwright cost a great many hand spinners their jobs.

Richard Arkwright, like most of our great mechani-cians, sprang from the ranks. He was born in Preston in 1732. His parents were very poor, and he was the youngest of thirteen children. He was never at school: the only education he received he gave to himself; and to the last he was only able to write with

From Samuel Smiles, *Self-Help with Illustrations of Conduct and Perseverance* (London: John Murray, 1876), pp.33-37.

difficulty. When a boy, he was apprenticed to a barber, and after learning the business, he set up for himself in Bolton, where he occupied an underground cellar, over which he put up the sign, "Come to the subterraneous barber—he shaves for a penny." The other barbers found their customers leaving them, and reduced their prices to his standard, when Arkwright, determined to push his trade, announced his determination to give "A clean shave for a halfpenny." After a few years he quitted his cellar, and became an itinerant dealer in hair. At that time wigs were worn, and wig-making formed an important branch of the barbering business. Arkwright went about buying hair for the wigs. He was accustomed to attend the hiring fairs throughout Lancashire resorted to by young women, for the purpose of securing their long tresses; and it is said that in negotiations of this sort he was very successful. He also dealt in a chemical hair dye, which he used adroitly, and thereby secured a considerable trade. But he does not seem, notwithstanding his pushing character, to have done more than earn a bare living.

The fashion of wig-wearing having undergone a change, distress fell upon the wig-makers, and Arkwright, being of a mechanical turn, was consequently induced to turn machine inventor or "conjurer," as the pursuit was then popularly termed. Many attempts were made about that time to invent a spinning-machine, and our barber determined to launch his little bark on the sea of invention with the rest. Like other self-taught men of the same bias, he had already been devoting his spare time to the invention of a perpetual-motion machine, and from that the transition to a spinning-machine was easy. He followed his experiments so assiduously that he neglected his business, lost the little money he had saved, and was reduced to great poverty. His wife—for he had by this time married—was impatient at what she conceived to be a wanton waste of time and money, and in a moment of sudden wrath she seized upon and destroyed his models, hoping thus to remove the cause of the family privations. Arkwright was a stubborn and enthusiastic man, and he was provoked beyond measure by this conduct of his wife, from whom he immediately separated.

In travelling about the country, Arkwright had become acquainted with a person named Kay, a clockmaker at Warrington, who assisted him in constructing some of the parts of his perpetual-motion machinery. It is supposed that he was informed by Kay of the principle of spinning by rollers; but it is also said that the idea was first suggested to him by accidentally observing a red-hot piece of iron become elongated by passing between iron rollers. However this may be, the idea at once took firm possession of his mind, and he proceeded to devise the process by which it was to be accomplished, Kay being able to tell him nothing on this point. Arkwright now abandoned his business of hair collecting, and devoted himself to the perfecting of his machine, a model of which, constructed by Kay under his directions, he set up in the parlour of the Free Grammar School at Preston. Being a burgess of the town, he voted at the contested election at which General Burgoyne was returned; but such was his poverty, and such the tattered state of his dress, that a number of persons subscribed a sum sufficient to have him put in a state fit to appear in the poll-room. The exhibition of his machine in a town where so many workpeople lived by the exercise of manual labour proved a dangerous experiment; ominous growlings were heard outside the school-room from time to time, and Arkwright,—remembering the fate of Kay, who was mobbed and compelled to fly from Lancashire because of his invention of the fly-shuttle, and of poor Hargreaves, whose spinning-jenny had been pulled to pieces only a short time before by a Blackburn mob,—wisely determined on packing up his model and removing to a less dangerous locality. He went accordingly to Nottingham, where he applied to some of the local bankers for pecuniary assistance; and the Messrs. Wright consented to advance him a sum of money on condition of sharing in the profits of the invention. The machine, however, not being perfected so soon as they had anticipated, the bankers recommended Arkwright to apply to Messrs. Strutt and Need, the former of whom was the ingenious inventor and patentee of the stocking-frame. Mr. Strutt at once appreciated the merits of the invention, and a partnership was entered into with Arkwright, whose road to fortune was now clear. The patent was secured in the name of "Richard Arkwright, of Nottingham, clockmaker," and it is a circumstance worthy of note, that it was taken out in 1769, the same year in which Watt secured the patent for his steam-engine. A cotton-mill was first erected at Nottingham, driven by horses; and another was shortly after built, on a much larger scale, at Cromford, in Derbyshire, turned by a water-wheel, from which circumstance the spinning-machine came to be called the water-frame.

Arkwright's labours, however, were, comparatively speaking, only begun. He had still to perfect all the working details of his machine. It was in his hands the subject of constant modification and improvement, until eventually it was rendered practicable and profitable in an eminent degree. But success was only secured by long and patient labour: for some years, indeed, the speculation was disheartening and unprofitable, swallowing up a very large amount of capital without any result. When success began to appear more certain, then the Lancashire manufacturers fell upon Arkwright's patent to pull it in pieces, as the Cornish miners fell upon Boulton and Watt to rob them of the profits of their steam-engine. Arkwright was even denounced as the enemy of the working people; and a mill which he built near Chorley was destroyed by a mob in the presence of a strong force of police and military. The Lancashire men refused to buy his materials, though they were confessedly the best in the market. Then they refused to pay patent-right for the use of his machines, and combined to crush him in the courts of law. To the disgust of right-minded people, Arkwright's patent was upset. After the trial, when passing the hotel at which his opponents were staying, one of them said, loud enough to be heard by him, "Well, we've done the old shaver at last;" to which he coolly replied, "Never mind, I've a razor left that will shave you all." He established new mills in Lancashire, Derbyshire, and at New Lanark, in Scotland. The mills at Cromford also came into his hands at the expiry of his partnership with Strutt, and the amount and the excellence of his products were such, that in a short time he obtained so complete a control of the trade, that the prices were fixed by him, and he governed the main operations of the other cotton-spinners.

Arkwright was a man of great force of character, indomitable courage, much worldly shrewdness, with a business faculty almost amounting to genius. At one period his time was engrossed by severe and continuous labour, occasioned by the organising and conducting of his numerous manufactories, sometimes from four in the morning till nine at night. At fifty years of age he set to work to learn English grammar, and improve himself in writing and orthography. After overcoming every obstacle, he had the satisfaction of reaping the reward of his enterprise. Eighteen years after he had constructed his first machine, he rose to such estimation in Derbyshire that he was appointed High Sheriff of the county, and shortly after George III. conferred upon him the honour of knighthood. He died in 1792. Be it for good or for evil, Arkwright was the founder in England of the modern factory system, a branch of industry which has unquestionably proved a source of immense wealth to individuals and to the nation.

STUDY QUESTIONS

1. Was Arkwright's success due more to his ability to capitalize on an opportunity or to his native ingenuity?
2. Is it accurate to call Arkwright the founder of England's modern factory system?

6.2 THOMAS HOOD,
"THE SONG OF THE SHIRT," 1843

Industrialization in England brought special challenges, as well as some rewards, to the country's women. In the past, it had not been uncommon for whole families to work together as a domestic unit, enabling wives and children to contribute to the family income without leaving their homes. Perhaps the most important changes in family life stemmed from the new possibilities for women to work outside the home. As technological transformation moved cotton spinning from home to factory, women followed.

Partly because women had traditionally done the textile spinning and partly because entrepreneurs found it possible to pay women and children less than men, large numbers of urban women were recruited for the low-skilled, repetitive tasks of the textile mills. For the most part, these women "operatives" were young and single; if married, they tended to be childless. In taking wives and daughters out of their homes, industrial labor did much to disrupt traditional family life, especially when wives worked and their husbands were unemployed.

By the mid-nineteenth century, the presence of women in these new industrial fields was noticeable enough for male writers to speculate about the long-term effects of employing women in this kind of work—both on the women themselves and on their families. This poem was published in *Punch* on December 16, 1843 shortly before Christmas, attempting to rouse sympathy for these workers, some of whom were probably sewing the shirts that would appear under Victorian Christmas trees in the coming weeks.

With fingers weary and worn,
With eyelids heavy and red,
A woman sat in unwomanly rags,
Plying her needle and thread—
Stitch! stitch! stitch!
In poverty, hunger, and dirt,
And still with a voice of dolorous pitch
She sang the "Song of the Shirt." . . .

Work—work—work,
Till the brain begins to swim;
Work—work—work,
Till the eyes are heavy and dim!
Seam, and gusset, and band,
Band, and gusset, and seam,
Till over the buttons I fall asleep,
And sew them on in a dream!

O, men, with sisters dear!
O, men, with mothers and wives!
It is not linen you're wearing out,
But human creatures' lives!
Stitch—stitch—stitch,
In poverty, hunger and dirt,
Sewing at once, with a double thread,
A Shroud as well as a Shirt. . . .

Work—work—work!
From weary chime to chime,
Work—work—work,
As prisoners work for crime!
Band, and gusset, and seam,
Seam, and gusset, and band,
Till the heart is sick, and the brain benumbed,
As well as the weary hand.

From Rewey Belle Inglis, Donald A. Stauffer, and Cecil Evva Larsen, *Adventures in English Literature* (Toronto: W. J. Gage, 1952), pp. 436-437; originally published in *Punch, or the London Charivari*, reprinted http://www.victorianweb.org/authors/hood/shirt.html.

Work—work—work,
In the dull December light,
And work—work—work,
When the weather is warm and bright—
While underneath the eaves
The brooding swallows cling
As if to show me their sunny backs
And twit me with the spring. . . .

With fingers weary and worn,

With eyelids heavy and red,
A woman sat in unwomanly rags,
Plying her needle and thread—

Stitch! stitch! stitch!
In poverty, hunger, and dirt,
And still with a voice of dolorous pitch,—
Would that its tone could reach the Rich!—
She sang this "Song of the Shirt!"

STUDY QUESTIONS

1. How does this poem replicate the rhythms of industrial sewing in the mid-nineteenth century?
2. Was a male poet able fully to appreciate the gender issues related to industrialization?

6.3 YOUNG MINERS TESTIFY TO THE ASHLEY COMMISSION, 1842

In the mid-nineteenth century, the British Parliament launched a series of initiatives to investigate the lives of women and children working in factories and mines. Individuals testified directly—in this case, before Lord Ashley's Mines Commission of 1842. The resulting testimonies, presented by women and children to the various parliamentary commissions, make for fascinating—and uniquely visceral—reading because they starkly reveal the harsh working conditions. The lives of working children are rarely detailed in historical sources from any era; in this instance, their statements had a direct impact on the lives of British laborers. These shocking testimonies, and others like them, resulted in the Mines Act of 1842, prohibiting the employment in the mines of all women and of boys under 13 years of age.

NO. 116.—SARAH GOODER, AGED 8 YEARS

I'm a trapper in the Gawber pit. It does not tire me, but I have to trap without a light and I'm scared. I go at four and sometimes half past three in the morning, and come out at five and half past. I never go to sleep. Sometimes I sing when I've light, but not in the dark; I dare not sing then. I don't like being in the pit. I am very sleepy when I go sometimes in the morning. I go

From *Readings in European History Since 1814*, edited by Jonathan F. Scott and Alexander Baltzly (New York: Appleton-Century-Crofts, Inc., 1930), drawing on Parliamentary Papers, 1842, vols. XV–XVII, Appendix I, pp. 252, 258, 439, 461; Appendix II, pp. 107, 122, 205, reprinted http://www.victorianweb.org/history/ashley.html.

to Sunday-schools and read Reading made Easy. She knows her letters, and can read little words. They teach me to pray. She repeated the Lord's Prayer, not very perfectly, and ran on with the following addition:—"God bless my father and mother, and sister and brother, uncles and aunts and cousins, and everybody else, and God bless me and make me a good servant. Amen." I have heard tell of Jesus many a time. I don't know why he came on earth, I'm sure, and I don't know why he died, but he had stones for his head to rest on. I would like to be at school far better than in the pit.

NO. 14.—ISABELLA READ, 12 YEARS OLD, COAL-BEARER

Works on mother's account, as father has been dead two years. Mother bides at home, she is troubled with bad breath, and is sair weak in her body from early labour. I am wrought with sister and brother, it is very sore work; cannot say how many rakes or journeys I make from pit's bottom to wall face and back, thinks about 30 or 25 on the average; the distance varies from 100 to 250 fathom.

I carry about 1 cwt. and a quarter on my back; have to stoop much and creep through water, which is frequently up to the calves of my legs. When first down fell frequently asleep while waiting for coal from heat and fatigue.

I do not like the work, nor do the lassies, but they are made to like it. When the weather is warm there is difficulty in breathing, and frequently the lights go out.

NO. 26.—PATIENCE KERSHAW, AGED 17, MAY 15

My father has been dead about a year; my mother is living and has ten children, five lads and five lasses; the oldest is about thirty, the youngest is four; three lasses go to mill; all the lads are colliers, two getters and three hurriers; one lives at home and does nothing; mother does nought but look after home.

All my sisters have been hurriers, but three went to the mill. Alice went because her legs swelled from hurrying in cold water when she was hot. I never went to day-school; I go to Sunday-school, but I cannot read or write; I go to pit at five o'clock in the morning and come out at five in the evening; I get my breakfast of porridge and milk first; I take my dinner with me, a cake, and eat it as I go; I do not stop or rest any time for the purpose; I get nothing else until I get home, and then have potatoes and meat, not every day meat. I hurry in the clothes I have now got on, trousers and ragged jacket; the bald place upon my head is made by thrusting the corves; my legs have never swelled, but sisters' did when they went to mill; I hurry the corves a mile and more under ground and back; they weigh 300 cwt.; I hurry 11 a-day; I wear a belt and chain at the workings, to get the corves out; the getters that I work for are naked except their caps; they pull off all their clothes; I see them at work when I go up; sometimes they beat me, if I am not quick enough, with their hands; they strike me upon my back; the boys take liberties with me sometimes they pull me about; I am the only girl in the pit; there are about 20 boys and 15 men; all the men are naked; I would rather work in mill than in coal-pit.

This girl is an ignorant, filthy, ragged, and deplorable-looking object, and such a one as the uncivilized natives of the prairies would be shocked to look upon.

NO. 72.—MARY BARRETT, AGED 14, JUNE 15

I have worked down in pit five years; father is working in next pit; I have 12 brothers and sisters—all of them but one live at home; they weave, and wind, and hurry, and one is a counter, one of them can read, none of the rest can, or write; they never went to day-school, but three of them go to Sunday-school; I hurry for my brother John, and come down at seven o'clock about; I go up at six, sometimes seven; I do not like working in pit, but I am obliged to get a living; I work always without stockings, or shoes, or trousers; I wear nothing but my chemise; I have to go up to the headings with the men; they are all naked there; I am got well used to that, and don't care now much about it; I was afraid at first, and did not like it; they never behave rudely to me; I cannot read or write.

STUDY QUESTIONS

1. Do the employers of these workers seem to have taken into account the unique conditions of their age and gender?
2. How does the recorder of these interviews interject his own reactions to these narratives, and why does he do this?

6.4 FRIEDRICH ENGELS ON WOMEN'S WORK IN *THE CONDITION OF THE WORKING CLASS IN ENGLAND*, 1845

Friedrich Engels (1820–1895) came from a German family that invested in British textile mills. As a young man, Engels ran in German intellectual circles while studying factory management. He moved to Manchester in 1842 to oversee his father's mill, a position that led him to develop a strong interest in the fate of laborers working in the factory system. In 1845 he published *The Condition of the Working Class in England*, which described the effects of industry on individuals and society and became a highly influential work. Engels would subsequently begin a long intellectual and political collaboration with Karl Marx. In this excerpt, Engels discusses the effects of women's factory work on society, calling attention to the ways in which the capitalist economy dissolved traditional relationships.

Working Men!

To you I dedicate a work, in which I have tried to lay before my German Countrymen a faithful picture of your condition, of your sufferings and struggles, of your hopes and prospects. I have lived long enough amidst you to know something about your circumstances; I have devoted to their knowledge my most serious attention, I have studied the various official and non-official documents as far as I was able to get hold of them—I have not been satisfied with this, I wanted more than a mere abstract knowledge of my subject, I wanted to see you in your own homes, to observe you in your everyday life, to chat with you on your condition and grievances, to witness your struggles against the social and political power of your oppressors. I have done so: I forsook the company and the dinner-parties, the port-wine and champagne of the middle-classes, and devoted my leisure-hours almost exclusively to the intercourse with plain Working-Men; I am both glad and proud of having done so. Glad, because thus I was induced to spend many a happy hour in obtaining a knowledge of the realities of life—many an hour, which else would have been wasted in fashionable talk and tiresome etiquette; proud, because thus I got an opportunity of doing justice to an oppressed and calumniated class of men who with all their faults and under all the disadvantages of their situation, yet

From Frederick Engels, *The Condition of the Working Class in England in 1844*, with a Preface written in 1892, translated by Florence Kelley Wischnewetzky (London: Allen and Unwin LTD, 1952), xx–xxi, 141–148.

command the respect of every one but an English money-monger; proud, too, because thus I was placed in a position to save the English people from the growing contempt which on the Continent has been the necessary consequence of the brutally selfish policy and general behaviour of your ruling middle-class.

. . .

Let us examine somewhat more closely the fact that machinery more and more supersedes the work of men. The human labour, involved in both spinning and weaving, consists chiefly in piecing broken threads, as the machine does all the rest. This work requires no muscular strength, but only flexibility of finger. Men are, therefore, not only not needed for it, but actually, by reason of the greater muscular development of the hand, less fit for it than women and children, and are, therefore, naturally almost superseded by them. Hence, the more the use of the arms, the expenditure of strength, can be transferred to steam or waterpower, the fewer men need be employed; and as women and children work more cheaply, and in these branches better than men, they take their places. . . . At the power-looms women, from fifteen to twenty years, are chiefly employed, and a few men; these, however, rarely remain at this trade after their twenty-first year. Among the preparatory machinery, too, women alone are to be found, with here and there a man to clean and sharpen the carding-frames. Besides all these, the factories employ numbers of children—doffers—for mounting and taking down bobbins, and a few men as overlookers, a mechanic and an engineer for the steam- engines, carpenters, porters, etc.; but the actual work of the mills is done by women and children. This the manufacturers deny.

They published last year elaborate tables to prove that machinery does not supersede adult male operatives. According to these tables, rather more than half of all the factory-workers employed, viz., 52 per cent, were females and 48 per cent males, and of these operatives more than half were over eighteen years old. So far, so good. But the manufacturers are very careful not to tell us, how many of the adults were men and how many women. And this is just the point. Besides this, they have evidently counted the

mechanics, engineers, carpenters, all the men employed in any way in the factories, perhaps even the clerks, and still they have not the courage to tell the whole truth. . . . Let us take some of the statements of a speech with which Lord Ashley introduced the Ten Hours' Bill, March 15th, 1844, into the House of Commons. Here he gives some data as to the relations of sex and age of the operatives, not yet refuted by the manufacturers, whose statements, as quoted above, cover moreover only a part of the manufacturing industry of England. Of 419,590 factory operatives of the British Empire in 1839, 192,887, or nearly half, were under eighteen years of age, and 242,296 of the female sex, of whom 112,192 were less than eighteen years old. There remain, therefore, 80,695 male operatives under eighteen years, and 96,599 adult male operatives, *or not one full quarter of the whole number.* In the cotton factories, 56¼ per cent; in the woolen mills, 69½ per cent; in the silk mills, 70½ per cent; in the flax-spinning mills, 70½ per cent of all operatives are of the female sex. These numbers suffice to prove the crowding out of adult males. But you have only to go into the nearest mill to see the fact confirmed. Hence follows of necessity that inversion of the existing social order which, being forced upon them, has the most ruinous consequences for the workers. The employment of women at once breaks up the family; for when the wife spends twelve or thirteen hours every day in the mill, and the husband works the same length of time there or elsewhere, what becomes of the children? They grow up like wild weeds; they are put out to nurse for a shilling or eighteenpence a week, and how they are treated may be imagined. Hence the accidents to which little children fall victims multiply in the factory districts to a terrible extent. . . . That the general mortality among young children must be increased by the employment of the mothers is self-evident, and is placed beyond all doubt by notorious facts. Women often return to the mill three or four days after confinement, leaving the baby, of course; in the dinner-hour they must hurry home to feed the child and eat something, and what sort of suckling that can be is also evident. . . . The use of narcotics to keep the children still is fostered by this infamous system, and has reached a great extent in the factory districts.

Dr. Johns, Registrar in Chief for Manchester, is of opinion that this custom is the chief source of the many deaths from convulsions. The employment of the wife dissolves the family utterly and of necessity, and this dissolution, in our present society, which is based upon the family, brings the most demoralising consequences for parents as well as children. A mother who has no time to trouble herself about her child, to perform the most ordinary loving services for it during its first year, who scarcely indeed sees it, can be no real mother to the child, must inevitably grow indifferent to it, treat it unlovingly like a stranger. The children who grow up under such conditions are utterly ruined for later family life, can never feel at home in the family which they themselves found, because they have always been accustomed to isolation, and they contribute therefore to the already general undermining of the family in the working-class. A similar dissolution of the family is brought about by the employment of the children. When they get on far enough to earn more than they cost their parents from week to week, they begin to pay the parents a fixed sum for board and lodging, and keep the rest for themselves. This often happens from the fourteenth or fifteenth year. . . .

In many cases the family is not wholly dissolved by the employment of the wife, but turned upside down. The wife supports the family, the husband sits at home, tends the children, sweeps the room and cooks. This case happens very frequently; in Manchester alone, many hundred such men could be cited, condemned to domestic occupations. It is easy to imagine the wrath aroused among the workingmen by this reversal of all relations within the family, while the other social conditions remain unchanged. . . .

. . . And yet this condition, which unsexes the man and takes from the woman all womanliness without being able to bestow upon the man true womanliness, or the woman true manliness—this condition which degrades, in the most shameful way, both sexes, and, through them, Humanity, is the last result of our much-praised civilisation, the final achievement of all the efforts and struggles of hundreds of generations to improve their own situation and that of their posterity. We must either despair of

mankind, and its aims and efforts, when we see all our labour and toil result in such a mockery, or we must admit that human society has hitherto sought salvation in a false direction; we must admit that so total a reversal of the position of the sexes can have come to pass only because the sexes have been placed in a false position from the beginning. If the reign of the wife over the husband, as inevitably brought about by the factory system, is inhuman, the pristine rule of the husband over the wife must have been inhuman too. If the wife can now base her supremacy upon the fact that she supplies the greater part, nay, the whole of the common possession, the necessary inference is that this community of possession is no true and rational one, since one member of the family boasts offensively of contributing the greater share. If the family of our present society is being thus dissolved, this dissolution merely shows that, at bottom, the binding tie of this family was not family affection, but private interest lurking under the cloak of a pretended community of possessions. . . .

The unmarried women, who have grown up in mills, are no better off than the married ones. It is self-evident that a girl who has worked in a mill from her ninth year is in no position to understand domestic work, whence it follows that female operatives prove wholly inexperienced and unfit as housekeepers. They cannot knit or sew, cook or wash, are unacquainted with the most ordinary duties of a housekeeper, and when they have young children to take care of, have not the vaguest idea how to set about it. The Factories' Inquiry Commission's Report gives dozens of examples of this. . . .

But that is the least of the evil. The moral consequences of the employment of women in factories are even worse. The collecting of persons of both sexes and all ages in a single work-room, the inevitable contact, the crowding into a small space of people, to whom neither mental nor moral education has been given, is not calculated for the favourable development of the female character. The manufacturer, if he pays any attention to the matter, can interfere only when something scandalous actually happens; the permanent, less conspicuous influence of persons of dissolute character upon the more moral, and especially upon the younger ones, he cannot ascertain, and consequently cannot prevent. But precisely this influence is the injurious. The language used in the mills is characterised by many witnesses in the report of 1833, as "indecent," "bad," "filthy," etc. It is the same process upon a small scale which we have already witnessed upon a large one in the great cities. The centralisation of population has the same influence upon the same persons, whether it affects them in a great city or a small factory. The smaller the mill the closer the packing, and the more unavoidable the contact; and the consequences are not wanting. A witness in Leicester said that he would rather let his daughter beg than go into a factory; that they are perfect gates of hell; that most of the prostitutes of the town had their employment in the mills to thank for their present situation.

STUDY QUESTIONS

1. What does Engels reveal about how widespread industrialization is in England? Which abuses of factory labor most outrage him?
2. According to Engels, what are the effects of so many women working in the factory system? Who suffered from their employment?

6.5 CHARLOTTE BRONTË, *SHIRLEY*, 1849

When her novel *Jane Eyre* appeared in 1847 to great critical acclaim, Charlotte Brontë (1816–1855) began to consider the theme of her next project. She was living through a period of profound social unrest and would work on the new novel, *Shirley*, during the revolutionary year of 1848. For this reason, perhaps, Brontë set the book an earlier period of social upheaval and took an actual incident as its starting point. Having been born in Yorkshire (northern England), Brontë decided to spin her tale around several bouts of "Luddite" (machine-breaking) violence that had occurred there in 1811 and 1812, during the Napoleonic Wars.

After diligent study of detailed eyewitness reports of the uprising, recorded in back issues of the *Leeds Mercury* newspaper, Brontë focused *Shirley's* plot on two female characters, Caroline Helstone and Shirley Keeldar, and the men in their lives. Caroline's beau, Robert Moore, was an innovator who built a small enterprise on the strength of industrial machines. Mr. Moore "loved his machinery"—but in the Yorkshire dialect Brontë captured in the novel, he was a "Divil" whose "hellish machinery" had thrown the men of the region out of work and made them extremely hostile to him.

At the time this history commences, Robert Moore had lived but two years in the district; during which period he had at least proved himself possessed of the quality of activity. The dingy cottage was converted into a neat, tasteful residence. Of part of the rough land he had made garden-ground, which

From Charlotte Brontë, *Shirley*, edited by Herbert Rosengarten and Margaret Smith (Oxford: Oxford University Press, 1979), pp. 29–33.

he cultivated with singular, even with Flemish, exactness and care. As to the mill, which was an old structure, and fitted up with old machinery, now become inefficient and out of date, he had from the first evinced the strongest contempt for all its arrangements and appointments: his aim had been to effect a radical reform, which he had executed as fast as his very limited capital would allow; and the narrowness of that capital, and consequent check on his progress, was a restraint which galled his spirit sorely. Moore ever wanted to push on: "Forward" was the device stamped upon his soul; but poverty curbed him; sometimes (figuratively) he foamed at the mouth when the reins were drawn very tight.

In this state of feeling, it is not to be expected that he would deliberate much as to whether his advance was or was not prejudicial to others. Not being a native, nor for any length of time a resident of the neighbourhood, he did not sufficiently care when the new inventions threw the old work-people out of employ: he never asked himself where those to whom he no longer paid weekly wages found daily bread; and in this negligence he only resembled thousands besides, on whom the starving poor of Yorkshire seemed to have a closer claim.

The period of which I write was an overshadowed one in British history, and especially in the history of the northern provinces. War was then at its height. Europe was all involved therein. England, if not weary, was worn with long resistance; yes, and half her people were weary too, and cried out for peace on any terms. National honour was become a mere empty name of no value in the eyes of many, because their sight was dim with famine, and for a morsel of meat they would have sold their birthright. . . .

Misery generates hate: these sufferers hated the machines which they believed took their bread from them; they hated the buildings which contained those machines; they hated the manufacturers who owned those buildings. In the parish of Briarfield, with which we have at present to do, Hollow's-mill was the place held most abominable; Gérard Moore, in his double character of semi-foreigner and thoroughgoing progressist, the man most abominated. And it perhaps rather agreed with Moore's temperament than otherwise to be generally hated, especially

when he believed the thing for which he was hated a right and an expedient thing. . . .

He returned to the counting-house and lit a lantern, with which he walked down the mill-yard, and proceeded to open the gates. The big waggons were coming on; the dray-horses' huge hoofs were heard splashing in the mud and water. Moore hailed them.

"Hey, Joe Scott! Is all right?"

Probably Joe Scott was yet at too great a distance to hear the inquiry; he did not answer it.

"Is all right, I say?" again asked Moore, when the elephant-like leader's nose almost touched his.

Some one jumped out from the foremost waggon into the road; a voice cried aloud, "Ay, ay, divil, all's raight! We've smashed 'em."

And there was a run. The waggons stood still; they were now deserted.

"Joe Scott!" No Joe Scott answered. "Murgatroyd! Pighills! Sykes!" No reply. Mr. Moore lifted his lantern, and looked into the vehicles; there was neither man nor machinery; they were empty and abandoned.

Now Mr. Moore loved his machinery. He had risked the last of his capital on the purchase of these frames and shears which to-night had been expected; speculations most important to his interests depended on the results to be wrought by them: where were they? . . .

An impatient trampling of one of the horses made him presently look up; his eye, in the movement, caught the gleam of something white attached to a part of the harness. Examined by the light of the lantern, this proved to be a folded paper—a billet. It bore no address without; within was the superscription:—

"To the Divil of Hollow's-miln."

We will not copy the rest of the orthography, which was very peculiar, but translate it into legible English. It ran thus:—

"Your hellish machinery is shivered to smash on Stilbro' Moor, and your men are lying bound hand and foot in a ditch by the roadside. Take this as a warning from men that are starving, and have starving wives and children to go home to when they have done this deed. If you get new machines, or if you otherwise go on as you have done, you shall hear from us again. Beware!"

1. How does Brontë characterize Moore and the connection to his machinery? Why?
2. How does Brontë create sympathy for both the industrialist entrepreneur and those whose jobs were destroyed by his innovations?

6.6 VISUAL SOURCE: ENGLISH WOMEN'S DAY DRESSES, C. 1850

Textile mills drove the early process of industrialization in England and later across Europe, making clothing much more affordable to many more people. Studying the material objects, especially clothing, made during this revolution can give scholars new insights into the history of women and gender. The historian Leonore Auslander has explored the intimate relation of clothing to the body, noting that it plays not only a physical but also a psychological role in daily life. Women's fashion conveyed status, and more ornate decorations and layers of fabric signified wealth and respectability.

The two dresses shown here, held in the Metropolitan Museum of Art's Costume Institute, were made around 1850 of silk, linen, and wool. They were typical of daytime wear for affluent women, who had enough money to afford an excess of fabric and enough time to spend getting dressed in multiple layers. Such women put together an outfit from separate, detachable pieces, including the skirt, bodice, collar, and cuff, allowing them to change their look by changing one of its elements. Undergarments included a tight corset on top and layers of petticoats or a crinoline cage below, creating a voluminous figure with an hourglass shape. Outdoors, women wore bonnets with their hair swept off their necks in a bun, with or without ringlets. Eveningwear was less cumbersome, featuring an open neckline and allowing more freedom of movement.

From https://www.metmuseum.org/art/collection/search/108416.

FIGURE 6.6 English Women's Day Dresses, c. 1850

STUDY QUESTIONS

1. What do these dresses signify about the women who wore them and how they spent their time?
2. What do these outfits say about the role of English women as both producers of fabric and consumers of fashion?

COHESION ACROSS SENTENCES

Cohesion ("sticking tightly together") is the property that makes a text a *text*, not a list of sentences.

Old-to-new principle: In cohesive writing, each sentence typically begins with content that has appeared in the preceding sentence (or sentences) and ends with content that is new.

There are three principal ways of writing sentences that move from old to new.

1. The subject of each sentence is the same.

From his home base in the town of Bolton, **Arkwright** traveled the region offering to buy women's hair. **He** [OLD] cut it for them first and then used the human hair to make wigs, which were highly fashionable at the time. **He** [OLD] experimented with different dyes and soon invented a chemical process that could create the hair colors his customers wanted.

2. In each two-sentence pair, information included in the *predicate* of Sentence 1 becomes the *subject* of Sentence 2. In other words, content toward the end of Sentence 1 appears in the beginning of Sentence 2.

The Glorious Revolution of 1688 produced **a government dedicated to the protection of private property**. **The new political system** [OLD] fostered *confidence* [NEW] that owners could improve their land without interference from the state. *This confidence* [OLD] gave them the sense that such investments would remain secure. [NEW]

3. In paragraphs, a list of details follows a topic sentence.

Accompanying these cultural developments were profoundly important changes in the nature of society. [TOPIC SENTENCE] In 1750, most people still lived in the country and worked in agriculture and cottage industries; [DETAIL] a century later the majority congregated in urban centers, having left farming to just 20% of the population. [DETAIL] In 1750, family members tended to work together in household units; [DETAIL] in 1850, they were employed separately, with most working members laboring in a different shop, firm, factory, or residence. [DETAIL] In 1750, women and children seldom worked outside the home, except in the case of domestic servants or apprentices who worked in someone else's home. [DETAIL] One hundred years later, women and children were routinely employed in mills, mines, and the mansions of the rich. [DETAIL]

SPECIAL CASE: USING PASSIVE VOICE TO CREATE COHESION

Textbooks often recommend avoiding the passive voice because, taken out of context, the active voice usually sounds better to our ears.

The Combination Acts outlawed trade unions [ACTIVE]

Trade unions were outlawed by the Combination Acts. [PASSIVE]

Taken *in* context, however, active-voice sentences may sound worse, depending upon the sentences that immediately precede and follow them. In particular, active-voice sentences tend to sound worse when they begin with new information and end with old, violating the old-to-new principle. When that happens, the passive voice allows writers to create cohesion by swapping the content between subject and predicate.

Cotton was most efficiently grown on large plantations in the Deep South. Africans forced into bondage [NEW] staffed these plantations. [OLD]

[ACTIVE] Cotton was most efficiently grown on large plantations in the Deep South. These plantations [OLD] were staffed [PASSIVE VOICE] by Africans forced into bondage. [NEW]

[PASSIVE] The rule for choosing between active and passive voice:

When use of the active voice requires placing new information before old, consider using the passive voice instead.

EXERCISE: CHOOSE THE VERSION OF SENTENCE 2 THAT BEST FOLLOWS SENTENCE 1

Use the old-to-new principle to make your choice.

Worked example

Sentence 1 Farmers also grew turnips and potatoes on fallow lands.
Sentence 2
A. **This process** [OLD] resulted in better soil and livestock. [NEW]
B. Better soil and livestock resulted from [NEW] **this process.** [OLD]

Combined: Farmers also grew turnips and potatoes on formerly fallow lands. This process resulted in better soil and livestock.

---

1. Sentence 1 As the British economy grew, increasing numbers of people could afford to have their children educated.
Sentence 2
A. Opportunities were opened by education.
B. Education opened opportunities.

---

2. Sentence 1 The English woolen industry produced better-quality fabrics than either the Belgians or Italians could make.
Sentence 2
A. Sheep had far more land to graze on in England, which produced the English advantage.
B. The English advantage came from their sheep, which had far more land to graze on.

---

3. Sentence 1 British manufacturers needed vastly increased quantities of raw cotton.
Sentence 2
A. The manufacturers' insatiable demand transformed the economy of the American South.
B. The economy of the American South was transformed by the manufacturer's insatiable demand.

EXERCISE: CHOOSE THE VERSION OF SENTENCE 2 THAT FITS BEST BETWEEN SENTENCES 1 AND 3

4. Sentence 1 During London's great home-construction boom of the seventeenth century, builders equipped the new dwellings with coal-burning stoves.
Sentence 2 (Choose A or B)
A. The stoves resulted in a skyrocketing demand for coal.
B. A skyrocketing demand for coal resulted from the stoves.
Sentence 3 In 1800, British coal production was 60 times what it had been two centuries earlier.

EXERCISE: REWRITE SENTENCES TO PRODUCE COHESION

Rewrite Sentence 2A, reversing the sequence of information. Then choose the version—2A or 2B—that follows best from Sentence 1.

Worked example

Sentence 1 In the early and mid-eighteenth century, Britain manufactured a number of goods useful to consumers at home and abroad.
Sentence 2
A. Cotton textiles were by far the most successful product.

Your revision of Sentence A, with subject and predicate reversed:
B. By far the most successful product was cotton textiles.
Sentence 3 Cotton cloth was ideal for both home and overseas markets, because it could be worn comfortably in cool as well as warm climates.

Combined: In the early and mid-eighteenth century, Britain manufactured a number of goods useful to consumers at home and abroad. *By far the most successful product was cotton textiles.* Cotton cloth was ideal for both home and overseas markets, because it could be worn comfortably in cool as well as warm climates.

5. Sentence 1 It became increasingly rare for a tailor to work alone making whole articles of clothing from start to finish.
Sentence 2
A. By the mid-nineteenth century, sizable workshops employed most tailors.
Your revision of Sentence A, with subject and predicate reversed:
B. By the mid-nineteenth century,

6. Sentence 1 Trade unions were outlawed by the Combination Acts of 1799.
   Sentence 2
   A. Banding together for the purpose of striking for higher wages or better working conditions was forbidden by the Acts.
   B. The Acts

You will find suggested answers to the exercises in the back of this book. For more Writing History exercises, as well as study resources for this chapter, visit oup.com/us/berenson.

CHAPTER 7

CONSERVATISM, REFORM, AND REVOLUTION, 1815–1852

7.1 GEORGE SAND, LETTER TO GIUSEPPE MAZZINI, JUNE 15, 1848

Aurore Dupin (1804–1876), commonly known by her pseudonym George Sand, was France's most famous and prolific woman writer of the nineteenth century. While establishing herself as a major literary figure, Sand pursued political interests, friendships, and romantic attachments with equal élan. Introduced to France's leading republican and socialist activists by the militant republican lawyer Michel de Bourges, Sand became a committed socialist by the early 1840s, although hers was a temperate Christian socialism that did not espouse violent revolution. She also developed a deep friendship with the Italian revolutionary Giuseppe Mazzini. Although they fell out later, they were close at the time of this letter.

Sand advocated a "moral revolution" grounded in "the religious and philosophical conviction of equality," rather than class warfare and rebellion in the streets. These views shaped her writing and activism during the Revolution of 1848, which began with an uprising in Paris and resulted four months later in the slaughter of many thousands of workingmen. Sand launched herself into the revolutionary vortex, writing everything from circulars for the new provisional government to newspaper articles and philosophical tracts. Although she refused to stand for a seat in the new legislature and disavowed the women who proposed her candidacy, she was actively involved in promoting the revolution, albeit a relatively moderate version of it. In this letter, she confronts the promises and pitfalls of the revolution and explains her vision for the future of France and of socialist democracy.

To Giuseppe [Joseph] Mazzini, Milan
15th June 1848

What can those do who have devoted their lives to the idea of paternal equality, who have ardently loved mankind, and who worship in Christ the symbol of the people redeemed and saved? In short, what can Socialists do when ideal deserts the bosoms of men, when humanity despairs of itself, when the people

From George Sand, *Letters of George Sand*, trans. and ed. by Raphael Ledos de Beaufort, volume II (London: Ward and Downey, 1886), 49–58.

disown their own cause? Is not that what threatens to happen to-day, perchance to-morrow?

You are full of courage, friend; that is to say, you preserve your hopes. As for me, I shall keep my creed; the pure and bright idea, eternal truth, will always shine in the sky, unless I should grow blind. But hope is the belief in the near triumph of creed, and I should lack sincerity were I to say that that disposition of my soul has undergone no modification within the last two months.

I see civilised Europe rushing, through the impulse of Providence, along the road to great struggles. I see the idea of the future grappling with the past. That vast movement of ideas is an immense progress, after the long years of stupor which marked period of stagnation in the formation of oppressed societies. . . .

As for France, the question has reached its last stage, and stares us in the face unmistakably, without complication, as being one between wealth and poverty. It might still be resolved peaceably; the *pretenders* are not serious obstacles, they will vanish like bubbles in the air. The *bourgeoisie* wants to reign. For the last sixty years it has been striving to realise its motto: *"What is the tiers état [third estate, the common people]? Nothing. What should it be? Everything."* Yes, the *tiers état* wants to be everything in the State, and the 24th of February freed it from the obstacle of royalty. It is thus indubitable that France must henceforth be a Republic, since on the one hand the poorest and most numerous class prefers that form of government which throws open to it the gates of the future; and, on the other hand, the wealthiest, most influential, politically the most powerful class, finds its interest in an oligarchy.

Some day, universal suffrage will do justice to that pretension of the *tiers état*. The former is an invincible weapon which the people did not know how to handle, and which at the first trial was turned against them. The political education of the masses will be achieved quicker than is supposed, and an equality, progressive but uninterrupted in its onward course, can and must proceed from the principle of the sovereign rights of the people. That is the logical fact it presents itself. But are logical deductions always the normal law of man's history? No! in most cases there is another logic than that of the general

fact: it is that of the particular fact, which confuses the whole, and with us the particular fact is, that the majority of the *tiers état* fails to understand the situation.

That want of intelligence may cause our next revolution to be violent and terrible, and, through attempts at domination (*liberticide*), it may exasperate the sufferings of the masses. Then the solemn progress of time will be interrupted. Excessive poverty will not call its sufferings virtue, but abjection. It will have recourse to its own strength; it will violently dispossess the rich, and wage a fearful contest in which the importance of the aim in view will seem to justify any means. Fatal epochs in the lives of nations are those when the victors, for having committed excesses in the exercise of their power, become vanquished in their turn!

The Socialists of the times we live in do not wish for the solutions of despair. Profiting by the lessons of the past, enlightened by a loftier comprehension of Christian civilization, all those who deserve that appellation, whatever the social doctrine they may belong to, repudiate for the future the tragic part played by the old Jacobins, and beseech, with folded hands, the conscience of man to get enlightened and to decide in favour of God's law.

But the idea of despotism is in its essence so identical with that of fear, that the bourgeoisie trembles and threatens as the same time. It is so afraid of Socialism that it wants to annihilate it through calumny and persecution; and whenever some far-seeing one's voice is raised in order to point out the danger, a thousand others are at once raised to bring anathema upon the obnoxious prophet.

"You are provoking hatred," they will say; "you are calling down vengeance upon us. You *make* the people *believe* that they are miserable; you point us out as objects for their fury. You only pity them in order to excite them. You remind them of their poverty only because we are rich." In short, charity, brotherly love, all that which Christ used to preach to men of His time, has become a fiery predication, and, were Jesus to appear among us, He would be attacked by the National Guards as an anarchist and a factious citizen.

That is what I fear for France, the Christ of nations, as she has been lately very rightly termed. I fear the want of intelligence of the rich and the despair of the poor. I fear the state of struggle which is not yet in men's minds, but which may become acts, if the ruling class does not enter upon a frankly democratic and sincerely fraternal path. Then, I declare, there will be great confusion and sore misfortune, for the people are not ripe for self-government. They possess powerful individualities, intellects able to cope with any situation. But such are not known. They do not exercise over the people the prestige which the masses require in order to love and believe. The masses have no faith in their own element, they have just proved it at the last general elections; they seek for guides above them, they love great names and celebrities, whoever they may be.

The people will therefore again look for among bourgeois, self-styled democrats, Socialists, or others, and they will once more be deceived in their expectations, for, but with a few exceptions, perhaps, there does not exist in France a democratic party sufficiently enlightened to undertake a dictatorship of public safety. Will they rely upon the wisdom or the inspiration of a single individual? That would be a retrograde step, reversing all the progress of mankind during the last twenty years.

No man will ever be superior to a principle, and the principle which must impart life to new societies is universal suffrage, the sovereignty of all. . . .

Proper names are the enemies of principles, and yet they alone stir the people. The latter seek who shall represent them, they, the eternally represented, and look, among extreme individualities, some for M. Thiers, others for M. Cabet, others for Louis Bonaparte, others again for Victor Hugo, a strange and monstrous product of the poll, and which proves how little the people know of where they go and what they want.

It is, however, easy to throw sufficient light on the question for the people, "To be or not to be?" but the people are not aware of the means. In order to dazzle and bewilder them, the great phantom of political falsehood has been invented, and, when I say falsehood, I am doing too much honour to the odd and ridiculous element which, just now, is guiding public opinion in France. We possess a trivial expression which you will translate by some equivalent in your language. It is the political *canard* (hoax). Every morning, some wonderful, in most cases absurd, ignoble story, starts from I know not what cesspools in Paris, and goes the round of France, exciting the population on its passage, proclaiming to them the advent of a fresh saviour, or of an ogre ready to devour them, thus rousing foolish hopes or stupid fears in their bosoms, and, through a mysterious community of feeling, impersonating itself in the individuals who are liked or disliked in each locality. Thus they endeavour to brutify that intelligent but credulous and impressible people; but, as that is not an easy task, they only succeed in exciting and maddening it. The masses are nowhere quiet, nowhere do they understand. Here, they shout, "Down with the Republic!" and "Equality for ever!" Elsewhere, "Down with Equality!" and "The Republic for ever!"

Whence can light proceed amidst such a conflict of false ideas and deceiving formulæ? Grand and noble laws can alone explain to the masses that the Republic is not the property of each and such a class, of such and such a person, but the doctrine of the safety of all.

Who will make those laws? A truly National Assembly. The present one is unfortunately subjected to every sort of prejudice, and gives way to all the influences which bring about the downfall of monarchies.

You see, my friend, how difficult it is for a society to transform itself without struggle and violence. And yet our very ideal was to bring about that transformation without internecine discord, without an impious struggle between citizens of the same nation. . . .

Let us still hope that our nation will be stronger and grander than the baneful passions which they seek to arouse in it. Let us hope that it will turn a deaf ear to the provoking agents who try to excite it to their advantage, and who fancy that after they have let it loose upon us, it will not rush the next day against them. It rests with the reactionary *bourgeoisie* whether the people of France will imitate the lazzaroni of Naples. . . .

. . . Ah! how little they know us, those who believe us to be their enemies and inexorable judges! Are they not aware that it is impossible to love the people without detesting the evil which the people might commit! Do they not perceive that the work they pursue, in trying to foster brutal and sanguinary ideas in the people, grieves us far more than all the evil which they might do us! We love the people one loves a child; we love them as one loves that which is miserable, feeble, deceived, and sacrificed; as one loves what is young, ignorant, pure, and bearing within itself the germ of an ideal future. We love it as one loves the innocent victim snatched from the altar, as one loves Christ on the cross, hope, the idea of justice, in short, as one loves God in the person of mankind! Can we love thus and desire the object of our love to debase itself in misery or tarnish itself with pillage?

You might well ask a mother whether she wishes the offspring of her bosom to become a bandit and a murderer!

And yet such are the accusations brought against us. People say that our ideas of fraternal equality are the signal bell for murder and arson, and, in so saying, they ring in the ears of the masses the maddening tocsin, pointing out to them invisible enemies whom they incite them to murder. They mark the doors of our houses. They would wish for a St. Bartholomew of new heretics, and they shout to the masses: "Kill! so that there may be no one left between you, the people, and us, the *bourgeoisie*, and then we shall reckon together."

But the people will not kill. Yet, what would I care if they killed me, provided my blood could the wrath of heaven or even that of the *bourgeoisie*? But blood intoxicates and fills the atmosphere with a contagious influence. Murder maddens; insults, harsh words, threatening utterances kill morally those who give expression to them. The education of hatred is a school of brutality and impiety which ends in slavery. *Bourgeois, bourgeois!* be yourselves. Speak about charity and fraternity; for when you have morally killed the people, you will find yourselves confronted by Cossacks, Neapolitan lazzaroni, and Gallician peasants.

STUDY QUESTIONS

1. According to Sand, what contributed to the failure of the Revolution of 1848 in Paris?
2. Her discussion of "political falsehood" sounds very similar to present day conversations about "fake news." What kind of damage does she warn that such falsehoods can do in a democratic society?

7.2 PERCY BYSSHE SHELLEY ON THE PETERLOO MASSACRE OF 1819 IN *THE MASQUE OF ANARCHY*, 1832

The rules for electing representatives to the British House of Commons had remained essentially unchanged since the Middle Ages, in spite of the profound demographic transformation taking place. As a result, by the early 1800s—after two centuries of urbanization—the largest British

From Percy Bysshe Shelley, *The Mask of Anarchy, A Poem*, edited by Thomas J. Wise (London: Reeves and Turner, 1892), https://archive.org/details/ofanarchypmasque00shelrich.

cities were vastly underrepresented in Parliament while the countryside was almost absurdly overrepresented.

The Tory party, however, had no intention of changing a political system that kept it in power. Seeing even peaceful protest as a prelude to revolution, the government banned public demonstrations and subjected protesters to arbitrary arrest. When some 50,000 protesters gathered at St. Peter's Field in Manchester in 1819 to advocate for reform, heavily armed soldiers fired on the crowd, killing eleven and wounding hundreds more. The massacre came to be known as "Peterloo," a label that combined Peter's Field with Waterloo, the famous battle in which the British army had helped defeat Napoleon. At Peterloo, the British army was accused of attacking its own people, rather than the French enemy. But the Tories were unrepentant. In the wake of the massacre, they tightened the screws of repression, passing the Six Acts, a series of laws intended to suppress all efforts to reform the British system.

Incensed by the government's violent suppression of protest, the Romantic poet Percy Bysshe Shelley (1792–1822) wrote a lengthy work entitled *The Masque of Anarchy*, which harshly criticized the Tory government. The work remained unpublished until ten years after Shelley's death, when Leigh Hunt, a leading radical reformer, believed the country was finally ready to hear to Shelley's critique.

[From Leigh Hunt's Preface:]

This Poem was written by Mr. Shelley on occasion of the bloodshed at Manchester, in the year 1819. I was editor of the Examiner at that time, and it was sent to me to be inserted or not in that journal, as I thought fit. I did not insert it, because I thought that the public at large had not become sufficiently discerning to do justice to the sincerity and kindheartedness of the spirit that walked in this flaming robe of verse. His charity was avowedly more than proportionate to his indignation; yet I thought that even the suffering part of the people, judging, not unnaturally, from their own feelings, and from the exasperation which suffering produces before it produces knowledge, would believe a hundred-fold in his anger, to what they would in his good intention; and this made me fear that the common enemy would take advantage of the mistake to do them both a disservice. Mr. Shelley's writings have since aided the general progress of knowledge in bringing about a wiser period; and an effusion, which would have got him cruelly misrepresented a few years back, will now do unequivocal honour to his memory, and shew everybody what a most considerate and kind, as well as fervent heart, the cause of the world has lost.

I.

As I lay asleep in Italy,
There came a voice from over the sea
And with great power it forth led me
To walk in the visions of Poesy.

II.

I met Murder on the way—
He had a mask like Castlereagh—
Very smooth he look'd, yet grim;
Seven bloodhounds followed him:

III.

All were fat; and well they might
Be in admirable plight,
For one by one, and two by two,
He tossed them human hearts to chew,
Which from his wide cloak he drew.

IV.

Next came Fraud, and he had on,
Like Lord E, an ermined gown;
His big tears, for he wept well,
Turned to mill-stones as they fell;

V.

And the little children, who
Round his feet played to and fro.
Thinking every tear a gem.

Had their brains knocked out by them.

. . .

VIII.

Last came Anarchy; he rode
On a white horse, splashed with blood;
He was pale even to the lips,
Like Death in the Apocalypse.

IX.

And he wore a kingly crown;
And in his grasp a sceptre shone;
And on his brow this mark I saw:
"I am God, and King, and Law!"

X.

With a pace stately and fast,
Over English land he past.
Trampling to a mire of blood
The adoring multitude.

XI.

And a mighty troop around,
With their trampling shook the ground,
Waving each a bloody sword,
For the service of their Lord.

. . .

XXXV.

(As if their own indignant earth,
Which gave the sons of England birth,
Had felt their blood upon her brow,
And shuddering with a mother's throe,

XXXVI.

Had turned every drop of blood,
By which her face had been bedewed,
To an accent unwithstood,
As if her heart had cried aloud:)

. . .

LXXVI.

"Let the charged artillery drive,
Till the dead air seems alive
With the clash of clanging wheels,
And the tramp of horses' heels.

LXXVII.

"Let the fixed bayonet
Gleam with sharp desire to wet
Its bright point in English blood,
Looking keen as one for food.

LXXVIII.

"Let the horsemen's scimitars
Wheel and flash, like sphereless stars,
Thirsting to eclipse their burning
In a sea of death and mourning.

LXXIX.

"Stand ye calm and resolute,
Like a forest close and mute,
With folded arms, and looks which are
Weapons of an unvanquished war.

. . .

LXXXIV.

"And if then the tyrants dare.
Let them ride among you there;
Slash, and stab, and maim, and hew;
What they like, that let them do.

LXXXV.

"With folded arms and steady eyes,
And little fear and less surprise,
Look upon them as they stay
Till their rage has died away:

LXXXVI.

"Then they will return with shame,
To the place from which they came,
And the blood thus shed will speak
In hot blushes on their cheek:

. . .

LXXXIX.

"And that slaughter to the nation
Shall steam up like inspiration,
Eloquent, oracular,
A volcano heard afar:

XC.

And these words shall then become
Like Oppression's thundered doom,
Ringing through each heart and brain,
Heard again—again—again.

XCI.

Rise like lions after slumber
In unvanquishable number!
Shake your chains to earth, like dew
Which in sleep had fall'n on you:
Ye are many—they are few.

STUDY QUESTIONS

1. How does Shelley describe physical violence, in both concrete and allegorical terms?
2. Why do the forces of "order" welcome and contribute to the advance of "Anarchy"?

7.3 *THE PEOPLE'S CHARTER*, 1839

The Chartist movement took its name from the *People's Charter*, created by William Lovett (1800–1877) and Francis Place (1771–1854). Chartists demanded political reforms that would allow working-class men to participate directly in politics. The Reform Act of 1832 had expanded the number of adults eligible to vote, but that figure stood at only 7 percent of Britain's population. The Charter called for reforms that would have ushered in an era of mass (male) democracy. Although hundreds of thousands of supporters signed petitions that were presented to Parliament in 1839 (the version reprinted here), and again in 1842 and 1848, the Chartist demands were rebuffed. Mass suffrage for male citizens would be granted only later in the century.

Being an Outline of an Act to provide for the just Representation of the People of Great Britain and Ireland in the Commons' House of Parliament: **embracing the Principles of Universal Suffrage, no Property Qualification, Annual Parliaments, Equal Representation, Payment of Members, and Vote by Ballot.**

Prepared by a Committee of twelve persons, six members of Parliament and six members of the London Working Men's Association, and addressed to the People of the United Kingdom.

An Act to provide for the just Representation of the People of Great Britain and Ireland, in the Commons' House of Parliament.

Whereas to insure, in as far as it is best possible by human forethought and wisdom, the just government of the people, it is necessary to subject those who have the power of making the laws, to a wholesome and strict responsibility to those whose duty it is to obey them when made:

And, whereas, this responsibility is best enforced through the instrumentality of a body which emanates directly from, and is itself immediately subject to, the whole people, and which completely represents their feelings and their interests:

And, whereas, as the Common's House of Parliament now exercises in the name and on the supposed behalf of the people, the power of making the laws, it ought, in order to fulfil with wisdom and with honesty the great duties imposed in it, to be made the faithful and accurate representation of the people's wishes, feelings and interests.

Be it therefore Enacted,

1. That from and after the passing of this Act, every male inhabitant of these realms be entitled to vote for the election of a Member of Parliament, subject however to the following conditions.
2. That he be a native of these realms, or a foreigner who has lived in this country upwards of two years, and been naturalised.
3. That he be twenty-one years of age.
4. That he be not proved insane when the list of voters are revised.
5. That he be not convicted of felony within six months from and after the passing of this Act.

From https://www.marxists.org/history/england/chartists/peoples-charter.htm.

6. That his electoral rights be not suspended for bribery at elections, or for personation, or for forgery of election certificates, according to the penalties of this Act . . .

Electoral Districts

1. Be it enacted, that for the purpose of obtaining an equal representation of the people in the Commons' House of Parliament, the United Kingdom be divided into 300 electoral districts.
2. That each such district contain, as nearly as may be, an equal number of inhabitants.
3. That the number of inhabitants be taken from the last census, and as soon as possible after the next ensuing decennial census shall have been taken, the electoral districts be made to conform thereto.
4. That each electoral district be named after the principal city or borough within its limits.
5. That each electoral district return one representative to sit in the Commons' House of Parliament, and no more. . . .

Returning Officer and his Duties

I–III [Returning officers to be elected for each electoral district every three years.]

Arrangement for Nominations

1. Be it enacted, that for the purpose of guarding against too great a number of candidates, who might otherwise be heedlessly proposed, as well as for giving time for the electors to enquire into the merits of the persons who may be nominated for Members of Parliament, as well as for returning officers, that all nominations be taken as hereinafter directed.
2. That for all general elections of Members of Parliament, a requisition of the following form,

signed by at least one hundred qualified electors of the district, be delivered to the returning officer of the district between the 1st and 10th day of May in each year; and that such requisition constitute the nomination of such person as a candidate for the district. . . .

11. that no other qualification shall be required for members to serve in the Commons' House of Parliament, than the choice of the electors. . . .

Arrangement of Elections

I–VI [Election of Members of Parliament to take place annually in June; electors to vote only in the district in which they are registered; voting to be by secret ballot.]

Duration of Parliament

1. Be it enacted, that Members of the House of Commons chosen as aforesaid, shall meet on the first Monday in June in each year, and continue their sittings from time to time as they may deem it convenient, till the first Monday in June the following, when the next new Parliament is to be chosen: they shall be eligible to be re-elected.
2. That during an adjournment, they be liable to be called together by the executive, in cases of emergency.
3. That a register be kept of the daily attendance of each member, which at the close of the session shall be printed as a sessional paper, showing how the members have attended. . . .

Payment of Members

1. Be it enacted, that every Member of the House of Commons by entitles, at the close of the session, to a writ of expenses on the Treasury, for his legislative duties in the public service, and shall be paid £500 per annum.

STUDY QUESTIONS

1. What do the Chartist demands reveal about working-class frustrations with the British political system?
2. Why would working-class men choose this set of reforms to fight for? What changes would they want enacted once they gained suffrage?

7.4 FLORA TRISTAN, *L'UNION OUVRIÈRE* (THE WORKERS' UNION), 1843

Flora Tristan (1803–1844) was one of the most important woman activists of the early nineteenth century. Inspired by her own financial difficulties and the ideas of "Utopian" socialists such as Henri de Saint Simon and Charles Fourier, Tristan called for improvements for women and for all working people. At a time when respectable middle-class women seldom went out in public unaccompanied, Tristan traveled France alone, giving powerful speeches advocating for equal pay for men and women, a radical reform that, she maintained, would eliminate economic competition between the sexes and unite all workers as a class. In *L'Union Ouvrière* (The Workers' Union) she argued for the creation of a universal workers' union that would recognize both men and women as essential contributors to society.

What happened for the proletarians is surely a good omen for the future of women when their '89 will have rung. By a very simple calculation it is obvious that wealth will increase indefinitely when women (half of the human race) are summoned to bring into social service their intelligence, strength, and ability. This is as easy to understand as that two is double one. But alas! We are not there yet and while waiting for that happy '89 let us note what is happening in 1843. . . .

I know of nothing so powerful as the forced, inevitable logic that issues from a principle laid down or from the hypothesis that represents it. Once woman's inferiority is proclaimed and posed as a principle, see what disastrous consequences result for the universal well-being of all men and all women.

Believing that woman, because of her structure, lacked strength, intelligence, and ability and was unsuited for serious and useful work, it has been concluded very logically that it would be a waste of time to give her a rational, solid, strict education capable of making her a useful member of society. Therefore she has been raised to be an amiable doll and a slave destined to entertain her master and serve him. To be sure, from time to time a few intelligent and compassionate men, suffering for their mothers, wives, and daughters, have cried out against such barbarousness and absurdity and have protested energetically against so unjust a condemnation. . . . Occasionally society has been momentarily sympathetic; but, under the pressure of logic it has responded: Well! Granted that women are not what the sages thought, suppose even that they have a great deal of moral force and much intelligence; well, in that case what purpose would it serve to develop their faculties, since they would have no opportunity to employ them usefully in this society that rejects them? What more frightful punishment than to feel in oneself the strength and ability to act and to see oneself condemned to inactivity! . . .

Notice that in all the trades engaged in by men and women, the woman worker gets only half what a man does for a day's work, or, if she does piecework, her rate is less than half. Not being able to imagine such a flagrant injustice, the first thought to strike us is this: because of his muscular strength, man doubtless does double the work of woman. Well, readers, just the contrary happens. In all the trades where skill and finger dexterity are necessary, women do almost twice as much work as men. For example, in printing, in setting type (to tell the truth they make many errors, but that is from their lack of education); in

Translated by Doris and Paul Beik

cotton or silk spinning mills, to fasten the threads; in a word, in all the trades where a certain lightness of touch is needed, women excel. A printer said to me one day with a naiveté completely characteristic: "Oh, they are paid a half less, it is true, since they work more quickly than men; they would earn too much if they were paid the same." Yes, they are paid, not according to the work they do, but because of their low cost, a result of the privations they impose on themselves. Workers, you have not foreseen the disastrous consequences that would result for you from a similar injustice done to the detriment of your mothers, sisters, wives, and daughters. What is happening? The manufacturers, seeing the women laborers work more quickly and at half price, day by day dismiss men from their workshops and replace them with women. Consequently the man crosses his arms and dies of hunger on the pavement! That is what the heads of factories in England have done. Once started in this direction, women will be dismissed in order to replace them with twelve-year-old children. A saving of half the wages! Finally one gets to the point of using only seven- and eight-year-old children. Overlook one injustice and you are sure to get thousands more. . . .

I demand rights for women because I am convinced that all the ills of the world come from this forgetfulness and scorn that until now have been inflicted on the natural and imprescriptible rights of the female. I demand rights for women because that is the only way that their education will be attended to and because on the education of women depends that of men in general, and particularly of the men of the people. I demand rights for women because it is the only means of obtaining their rehabilitation in the eyes of the church, the law, and society, and because that preliminary rehabilitation is necessary if the workers themselves are to be rehabilitated. All the ills of the working class are summed up by these two words: poverty and ignorance, ignorance and poverty. But to get out of this labyrinth, I see only one way: to start by educating women, because women are entrusted with raising the children, male and female. . . .

Workers, you who have good common sense, and with whom one can reason, because as Fourier says, your minds are not stuffed with a lot of theories, will you assume for a moment that woman is legally the equal of man? Well, what would be the result?

1. That from the moment one would no longer have to fear the dangerous consequences that, in the present state of their legal servitude, necessarily result from the moral and physical development of women's faculties, one would instruct them with great care in order to draw from their intelligence and work the best possible advantages;
2. That you, men of the people, would have for mothers skilled workers earning good wages, educated, well brought up, and very capable of instructing you, of raising you well, you, the workers, as is proper for free men;
3. That you would have for sisters, for lovers, for wives, for friends, educated women well brought up and whose everyday dealings could not be more agreeable for you; for nothing is sweeter, pleasanter for man than the conversation of women when they are educated, good, and converse with reason and good-will.

STUDY QUESTIONS

1. Did Tristan acknowledge any rationale for women being paid a lower wage than men?
2. Why does Tristan refuse to generate mere "sympathy" for the plight of women? How did she believe women should be educated for a modern society?

7.5 "LORD BYRON IN GREECE," *THE WESTMINSTER REVIEW,* JULY 1824

George Gordon, Lord Byron (1788–1824) was an English poet and a leading figure of the Romantic movement. Like other Romantics, Byron hoped to apply his aesthetic and moral convictions to real-world conflicts and issues—in Byron's case, to resurrecting "the glory that was Greece" (as Edgar Allan Poe put it). In August 1823, Byron enthusiastically joined the Greek war of independence against the Ottoman Empire in spite of his lack of military experience. He laid plans to lead the rebels in a raid on an Ottoman fort, but he fell ill with a fever before he could launch the attack. Tragically, he died at Messolonghi in April of the following year. He was immediately acclaimed a hero by the Greeks—and remained a hero of the revolution after Greek independence was finally declared in 1831. This review of Byron's final published work reflects the effect of his death on the larger British public of the time.

ART. XII.—*The Deformed Transformed; a drama.* By the Right Hon. Lord Byron. 2nd Ed. London J. and H. L. Hunt, 1824. 8vo.

This then is the last work we are to expect from the pen of this great poet. He closed the notice prefixed to it by saying that "the rest *may* hereafter appear"—that doubt is settled for ever. We had proposed some observations on this eccentric drama, and upon his writings in general, when the news of the noble author's decease reached us. We turn from the cold analysis we had made of his poetic powers with a changed heart, and view the work, which we had meditated with complacency, now with feelings little short of disgust. . . .

The motives which induced Lord Byron to leave Italy and join the Greeks struggling for emancipation from the yoke of their ignorant and cruel oppressors, are of so obvious a nature, that it is scarcely worthwhile to allude to them. It was in Greece that his high poetical faculties had been first most powerfully developed; and they who know the delight attendant, even in a very inferior degree, upon this intellectual process, will know how to appreciate the tender associations which, "soft as the memory of buried love," cling to the scenes and the persons that have first stimulated the dormant genius. Greece, a land of the most venerable and illustrious history, of a peculiarly grand and beautiful scenery, inhabited by various races of the most wild and picturesque manners, was to him the land of excitement,—never-cloying, never-wearying, ever-changing excitement:—such must necessarily have been the chosen and favourite spot of a man of powerful and original intellect, of quick and sensible feelings, of a restless and untameable spirit, of warm affections, of various information,—and, above all, of one satiated and disgusted with the formality, hypocrisy, and sameness of daily life. Dwelling upon that country, as it is clear from all Lord Byron's writings he did, with the fondest solicitude, and being, as he was well known to be, an ardent though perhaps not a very systematic lover of freedom, we may be certain that he was no unconcerned spectator of its recent revolution: and as soon as it appeared to him that his presence might be useful, he prepared to visit once more the shores of Greece. The imagination of Lord Byron, however, was the subject and servant of his reason—in this instance he did not act, and perhaps never did, under the influence of the

From John Bowring, Edward Blaquiere, William Fletcher, "Lord Byron in Greece," *Westminster Review* 2 (July 1824): pp. 225-227, 260, 262, http://www.lordbyron.org/doc.php?choose=WestminsterRev.1824.Byron.xml.

delusions of a wild enthusiasm, by which poets, very erroneously as regards great poets, are supposed to be generally led. It was not until after very serious deliberation of the advantages to be derived from this step, and after acquiring all possible information on the subject, that he determined on it; and in this as in every other act regarding this expedition, as we shall find, proved himself a wise and practical philanthropist. Like all men educated as he had been, Lord Byron too often probably obeyed the dictates of impulse, and threw up the reins to passions which he had never been taught the necessity of governing; but the world are under a grievous mistake if they fancy that Lord Byron embarked for Greece with the ignorant ardour of a schoolboy, or the flighty fanaticism of a crusader. It appeared to him that there was a good chance of his being useful in a country which he loved—a field of honourable distinction was open to him, and doubtless he expected to derive no mean gratification from witnessing so singular and instructive a spectacle as the emancipation of Greece.—A glorious career apparently presented itself, and he determined to try the event. When he had made up his mind to leave Italy for Greece, he wrote from Genoa to one of his most intimate friends, and constant companions, then at Rome, saying, "T——, you must have heard I am going to Greece; why do you not come to me? I am at last determined—Greece is the only place I ever was contented in—I am serious—and did not write before, as I might have given you a journey for nothing:—they all say I can be of great use in Greece. I do not know how, nor do they, but at all events let us try!" He had, says this friend, who knew him well, become ambitious of a name as distinguished for deeds, as it was already by his writings. It was but a short time before his decease, that he composed one of the most beautiful and touching of his songs on his 36th birthday, which remarkably proves the birth of this new passion. One stanza runs as follows:

If thou regret thy youth, why live?
The land of honourable death
Is here—Up to the field, and give
Away thy breath—

Awake not Greece—*She* is awake,
Awake *my* spirit! —

. . .

Lord Byron's death was a severe blow to the people of Messolonghi, and they testified their sincere and deep sorrow by paying his remains all the honours their state could by any possibility invent and carry into execution. But a people, when really animated by the passion of grief, requires no teaching or marshalling into the expression of its feelings. The rude and military mode in which the inhabitants and soldiers of Messolonghi, and of other places, vented their lamentations over the body of their deceased patron and benefactor, touches the heart more deeply than the vain and empty pageantry of much more civilized states. . . .

. . .By these and a multitude of other causes which might be enumerated, the fate of Greece is certain. We repeat with the most earnest assurance to those who still doubt, and with the most intimate knowledge of all the facts which have taken place, that the ultimate *independence* of Greece is secure. The only question at stake is the rapidity of the events which may lead to so desirable a consummation—so desirable to those who delight in the happiness and improvement of mankind—so delightful to those who have the increased prosperity of England at heart. It is here that Lord Byron might have been useful; by healing divisions, by exciting dormant energies, by ennobling and celebrating the cause, he might perhaps have accelerated the progress of Greece towards the wished-for goal. But even here, though his life was not to be spared, his death may be useful—the death-place of such a man must be in itself illustrious. The Greeks will not despair when they think how great a sacrifice has been made for them: the eyes of all Europe are turned to the spot in which he breathed his last. No man who knows that Lord Byron's name and fame were more universal than those of any other then or now existing, can be indifferent to the cause for which he spent his last energies—on which he bent his last thoughts—the cause for which he DIED.

STUDY QUESTIONS

1. To what factors do the reviewers attribute Byron's *personal* concern for the freedom of the Greeks?
2. What elements of cultural condescension for the Greeks remain in this review?

7.6 GIUSEPPE MAZZINI, *INSTRUCTIONS FOR THE MEMBERS OF YOUNG ITALY*, 1831

The Genoese writer and political activist Giuseppe Mazzini (1805–1872) became known as the "soul of Italian unification." He is best remembered today as the founder of Young Italy (*Giovine Italia*, in the Genoese dialect of the era), a secret organization devoted to the achievement of a united Italy. He formed a vast network of intellectuals and activists determined to undermine the political status quo. By 1833, Young Italy claimed 60,000 members, and Mazzini had begun to instruct them in what he saw as the proper structure of a unified nation. Conservative leaders feared his influence; Klemens von Metternich came to consider him the most dangerous man in Europe. Mazzini was particularly opposed to aristocratic and religious power, as well as to the Italian practice of *campanilismo*, the privileging of one's local or regional identity (in the form of a "bell tower") over that of Italy as a whole. Mazzini was briefly able to implement some of his ideas in 1849, when he became head of a "Republic" in Rome. Although he lived most of his life in exile in London, he witnessed the unification of Italy in 1861, a project completed two years before his death with the incorporation of Rome in 1870.

Young Italy is a brotherhood of Italians who believe in a law of Progress and Duty, and are convinced that Italy is destined to become a nation—convinced also that she possesses sufficient strength within herself to become one, and that the ill success of her former tentative efforts is to be attributed not to the weakness, but to the misdirection of the revolutionary elements within her—that the secret of force lies in constancy and unity of effort. Joined in association, they are consecrating both thought and action to the great aim of re-constituting Italy as one independent sovereign nation of free men and equals. . . .

Young Italy is Republican and Unitarian.

Republican—because theoretically all the men of a nation are called by the law of God and humanity, to form a free and equal community of brothers; and the republican is the only form of government that insures this future. Because all sovereignty resides essentially in the nation, the sole progressive and continuous interpreter of the supreme moral law.

Because, whatever be the form of privilege that constitutes the apex of the social edifice, its tendency is to spread among the other classes, and by undermining the equality of the citizens, to endanger the

Adapted from Giuseppe Mazzini, "General Instructions for the Members of Young Italy" (1831), in *Selected Writings*, edited by N. Gangulee (London, 1945), pp. 129–131 and http://users.dickinson.edu/~rhyne/232/Four/Mazzini_instructions.html.

liberty of the country. Because, when the sovereignty is recognized as existing not in the whole body, but in several distinct powers, the path to usurpation is laid open, and the struggle for supremacy between these powers is inevitable; distrust and organized hostility take the place of harmony, which is the law of life for society.

Because the monarchical element being incapable of sustaining itself alone by the side of the popular element, it necessarily involves the existence of the intermediate element of an aristocracy—the source of inequality and corruption to the whole nation. Because both history and the nature of things teach us that elective monarchy tends to generate anarchy; and hereditary monarchy tends generate despotism. Because, when monarchy is not—as in the Middle Ages—based upon the belief now rejected in divine right, it becomes too weak to be a bond of unity and authority in the state.

Because the Italian tradition is completely republican; our great memories are republican; the whole history of our national progress is republican; whereas the introduction of monarchy amongst us was coëval with our decay, and consummated our ruin by its constant servility to the foreigner, and the antagonism to the people, as well as to the unity of the nation.

Young Italy is Unitarian—Because, without unity, there is no true nation. Because, without unity, there is no real strength; and Italy, surrounded as she is by powerful, united and jealous nations, has need of strength before all things. Because federalism, by reducing her to the political impotence of Switzerland, would necessarily place her under the influence of one of the neighbouring nations.

Because federalism, by reviving the local rivalries now extinct, would throw Italy back upon the Middle Ages. Because federalism would divide the great national sphere into a number of smaller spheres; and, by thus leaving the field to paltry ambitions, become a source of aristocracy. Because federalism, by

destroying the unity of the great Italian family, would strike at the roots of the great mission Italy is destined to accomplish towards humanity.

Because Europe is undergoing a progressive series of transformations, which are gradually and irresistibly guiding European society to form itself into vast and united masses. Because the entire work of international civilization in Italy will be seen, if rightly studied, as to have been tending for ages to the formation of unity. Because all objections raised against the Unitarian system do but apply, in fact, to a system of administrative centralization and despotism, which has really nothing in common with unity.

National unity, as understood by Young Italy, does not imply the despotism of any, but the association and concord of all. The life inherent in each locality is sacred. Young Italy would have the administrative organization designed upon a broad basis of religious respect for the liberty of each commune, but the political organization, destined to represent the nation in Europe, should be one and central. Without unity of religious belief, and unity of social pact; without unity of civil, political, and penal legislation, there is no true nation.

Both initiators and initiated must never forget that the moral application of every principle is the first and most essential; that without morality there is no true citizen; that the first step towards the achievement of a holy enterprise is the purification of the soul by virtue; that, where the daily life of the individual is not in harmony with the principles he preaches, the inculcation of those principles is an infamous profanation and hypocrisy; that it is only by virtue that the members of Young Italy can win over the others to their belief; that if we do not show ourselves far superior to those who deny our principles, we are but miserable sectarians; and that Young Italy must be neither a sect nor a party, but a faith and an apostolate.

As the precursors of Italian regeneration, it is our duty to lay the first stone of its religion.

STUDY QUESTIONS

1. Was the ultimate establishment of a unified Italy as a monarchy contrary to Mazzini's goals? Why?
2. Why did Mazzini believe that a national Italy could only come into existence by rejecting local and regional allegiances?

7.7 VISUAL SOURCE: JANOS HORVAY, *LAJOS KOSSUTH MEMORIAL*, BUDAPEST, INAUGURATED 1927, REDEDICATED 2015

During the revolutions of 1848, the most important challenge to the integrity of the Austrian Empire came from the Hungarians, or Magyars, under the able leadership of the nobleman and lawyer Lajos (Louis) Kossuth (1802–1894). The Hungarians quickly took advantage of the March 1848 revolution in Vienna by declaring their region independent of the empire in all fundamental respects. In April 1849, Kossuth became president of a new Magyar republic, but Hungarian independence was short-lived. Tsar Nicolas I of Russia, horrified by the idea of a neighboring republic, joined forces with the Austrians, and the combined armies soon overwhelmed the Magyar troops. Kossuth, forced to live in exile, traveled around Europe and the United States on the lecture circuit, attempting to rouse international sympathy for the Hungarians' cause.

Despite his failure, Kossuth is recognized as the father of modern Hungary. This monument, sculpted in the 1920s by Janos Horvay, was designed to face the parliament building in Budapest's Kossuth Square. The monument celebrates Kossuth and eight members of the first Hungarian government (in this image, two figures at each end are cut off). In the 1950s, Hungary's new communist rulers moved the monument out of the capital to a less prominent location and then reimagined Kossuth surrounded by peasants and workers rather than parliamentarians. More than a half-century later, Hungarians returned to the original image of Kossuth as leader of a great Hungarian nation. In 2015, the government recast Horvay's statue and restored it to the newly renovated Kossuth Square.

Monuments show historians which people and events their society deems worthy of remembrance and how influential contemporaries wanted them to be remembered. As the history of this sculpture shows, these memories and their depiction can change over time. Someone who seemed to represent the community's ideals may later fall out of favor, a process playing out in numerous American neighborhoods today with memorials of the Civil War. Kossuth has never fallen completely out of favor, but the way successive governments portrayed him has changed over time.

FIGURE 7.7   Janos Horvay, Lajos Kossuth Memorial

STUDY QUESTIONS

1. What does this monument reveal about Kossuth's place in Hungarian memory?
2. How does the history of Horvay's sculpture reflect Hungarian national history?

PARAGRAPH FLOW

There are three principal ways to make writing flow within paragraphs.

BEGINNING-TO-BEGINNING:

Content that appears in the beginning of a sentence reappears in the beginning of the next sentence. Usually this means that the subject of most sentences in a paragraph is the same or closely related. *(Nationalism emerged from . . . Nationalists believe that . . .)*

END-TO-BEGINNING:

Content toward the end of one sentence becomes the beginning of the next sentence. **(Another reaction was the development of *liberalism*. *Liberalism* focused on . . .)**

LIST OF DETAILS:

A list of details follows a topic sentence (for example: Two groups opposed the tsar. The first group was . . . The second group was . . .)

The following paragraph uses both the beginning-to-beginning and the end-to-beginning principles:

₁Russia reached its zenith of autocracy in 1825, when Alexander was succeeded by his son, **Nicholas**. ₂**Nicholas's** conservatism stemmed, in part, from a serious rebellion on the eve of his ascension to the throne by two distinct groups: **liberal noblemen and intellectuals, and impoverished army officers**. ₃**Members of these two groups** emerged from their clandestine existence to challenge the new tsar via two secret societies. ₄ **Some 3,000 soldiers** marched to St. Petersburg's Senate Square, where they demanded a constitution and the abdication of Nicholas. ₅Poorly organized and unsure of what to do next, **the rebels** were dispersed by troops loyal to the new tsar.

Sentence pair	Cohesion method	Words from sentences
Sentence 1 to Sentence 2	End-to-beginning	Nicholas → Nicholas's [conservatism]
Sentence 2 to Sentence 3	End-to-beginning	liberal noblemen and intellectuals, and impoverished officers → members of these two groups
Sentence 3 to Sentence 4	Beginning-to-beginning	members of these two groups → some 3,000 soldiers
Sentence 4 to Sentence 5	Beginning to beginning	Some 3,000 soldiers → the rebels

EXERCISE: IDENTIFY THE COHESION PRINCIPLE

Instructions

Underline or highlight the words that tie each two-sentence pair together, and name the principle used.

EXAMPLE

The tsar exercised direct control over his ministries, which were staffed by **autocratic and often-corrupt bureaucrats**. Even the highest <u>Russian civil servants</u> possessed little independent authority.

Words connected: *Principle used:*

autocratic and often-corrupt bureaucrats → Russian civil servants   End-to-beginning

---

1. Metternich had hoped to end the age of revolution once and for all. But the revolution and its Napoleonic aftermath remained very much alive in the minds of kings and statesmen, poets and painters, and ordinary members of the increasingly active middle and working classes.

---

2. Louis XVIII adopted a series of repressive measures, which became even more severe when his brother, Charles X, assumed the throne. Charles tightened censorship and infuriated the middle classes by paying former émigrés some 26 million francs in compensation for their confiscated lands.

---

3. For Metternich any constitution, no matter how weak, opened the door to revolution. He quickly moved to undermine Bavaria's new system.

WHOLE-PARAGRAPH COHESION *VERSUS* SENTENCE-TO-SENTENCE COHESION

As a general rule:

- **End-to-beginning** ties make *neighboring sentences* cohesive.
- **Beginning-to-beginning** ties make *whole paragraphs* cohesive[1]

In practice, this means that although end-to-beginning ties always make neighboring sentences flow, a paragraph with *only* end-to-beginning ties quickly becomes hard to follow (grammatical subjects in boldface):

> **Hostility to the regime** was further inflamed by The Congress of Vienna. **The Congress** imposed significant reparations on France. **These payments** required the government to raise taxes. **Higher taxes** created severe economic hardship. **This hardship** led to attacks by hungry people on markets, bakeries, and rural administrative centers. **The unrest** persisted, leading to the assassination of the Duc de Berry, Louis XVIII's nephew and

---

[1] Joseph Williams, *Style: Lessons in Clarity and Grace*, 11th edition (New York: Longman, 2013).

potential heir to the throne, by a worker. **Berry's murder** struck conservatives as part of a Europe-wide conspiracy to once again engulf the continent in revolution. **This worry** led some more extreme conservatives to convince Louis XVIII to adopt a series of repressive measures. . . .

This paragraph is difficult to read because its sentences have seven distinct grammatical subjects:

1. hostility to the regime
2. the Congress
3. these payments
4. higher taxes
5. this hardship
6. the unrest
7. Berry's murder
8. this worry

Rewritten with beginning-to-beginning ties (subjects in boldface):

French citizens grew more hostile to the regime in the wake of reparation payments imposed by The Congress of Vienna. **They** suffered severe economic hardship when the government raised taxes to meet the payments, and violence ensued. **Crowds of hungry people** attacked markets, looted bakeries, besieged rural administrative centers, and rioted in rage and desperation. Finally, in 1820, **a worker** assassinated the Duc de Berry, Louis XVIII's nephew and potential heir to the throne. Although **the assassin** had acted alone, **the citizenry** was now subjected to a series of repressive measures adopted by the King at the behest of conservatives who perceived a Europe-wide conspiracy to once again engulf the continent in revolution.

The revision is much easier to read because it has just two distinct subjects:

Four variants of "the people":
French citizens
they
crowds of hungry people
the citizeny

Two variants of "the assassin":
a worker
the assassin [grammatical subject of a dependent clause]

In nonfiction writing, it is rarely possible to use the same subject in every sentence of a paragraph (and it may not be desirable, either). A reasonable rule of thumb is to use the same (or closely related) grammatical subject in roughly three-quarters of each paragraph's sentences.

EXERCISE: REVISE FOR FLOW

Instructions

Rewrite the passage below making *liberalism* the subject of Sentence 2.

---

4. ₁In Western Europe, liberalism emerged in the wake of Britain and France's revolutions of the seventeenth and eighteenth centuries. ₂The perceived dangers of absolutism, revolutionary dictatorship and popular democracy were things that **liberalism**

responded to. ₃Liberals thus wanted not only to guarantee individual rights—speech, assembly, and religious worship, among others—but to protect private property from potential encroachment by the state.

WORDS THAT REFER TO OTHER WORDS

In cohesive writing, most sentences explicitly refer to the preceding sentence, often through the use of pronouns (e.g., *he, she, it, they*):

> <u>Metternich</u> wanted a balance of power. To guard against future revolutions, **he** sought to create an alliance of all the great powers.

The word "he," a pronoun, refers to Metternich. Synonyms and other expressions (e.g., *the latter, the former*) are used as well:

> <u>Metternich</u> wanted a balance of power. To guard against future revolutions, **the Austrian prince** sought to create an alliance of all the great powers.

"The Austrian prince" refers to Metternich.

> The "naked" *this*
> For most Russians **this period** was not a happy time.
> Naked "this": For most Russians **this** was not a happy time.

As a general rule, novice writers should avoid using the naked *this* (as well as the naked *that, these,* and *those*) because these terms can be confusing:

> The result was a harsh economic recession that caused widespread unemployment, misery, and hunger. Rather than alleviate **this**, the government made things worse.

What did the government fail to alleviate? The recession? The suffering caused by the recession? Both? Revision:

> The result was a harsh economic recession that caused widespread unemployment, misery, and hunger. Rather than alleviate **this suffering**, the government made things worse.

The revision makes it clear that the writer is referring to "widespread unemployment, misery, and hunger."

EXERCISE: IDENTIFY WHAT THE BOLDFACED WORDS REFER TO

Instructions

Tell what the two boldfaced words in this paragraph refer to.

---

5. In 1815, the Napoleonic legal code remained in force, as did the deposed Emperor's Concordat with the pope making the French clergy servants of the state. The new regime retained Napoleon's highly centralized administrative structure and educational system, and **it** confirmed the ownership titles of those who had purchased land confiscated during the Revolution. The Charter called for an independent judiciary with trial by jury, and **it** guaranteed freedom of the press, although not without leaving open a major loophole: the government could impose restraints on journalists if it became necessary to "curb their abuses." Finally, Louis XVIII accepted the idea that government officials should be chosen on the basis of talent and skills not aristocratic birth.

Refers to:

it

it

EXERCISE: USE PRONOUNS AND SYNONYMS TO CONNECT SENTENCES AND THOUGHTS

Instructions

Replace the boldfaced words with pronouns, synonyms, or other expressions. Numerous possibilities exist for each item.
Example:

> The army's unwillingness to fight left the government defenseless and in disarray. **The army's unwillingness to fight** enabled insurgents to take control of the city in what came to be known as the Revolution of 1830.

Revision:

> The army's unwillingness to fight left the government defenseless and in disarray. **Its collapse** enabled insurgents to take control of the city in what came to be known as the Revolution of 1830.

In number 6, replace "the" with a pronoun, and cut "of France's leading republican and socialist activists."

6. One of George Sand's greatest loves was for the militant republican lawyer Michel de Bourges, who introduced her to France's leading republican and socialist activists. Under **the influence of France's leading republican and socialist activists**, she wrote the novel **Spiridion**.

In number 7, keep "protests" and replace the words "that were like the weavers' rebellion" with another expression.

7. In 1844, the weavers rebelled, threatening the region's wealthiest merchants and demanding higher pay. When the protests turned violent, the government called in military force. **Protests that were like the weavers' rebellion** erupted regularly throughout continental Europe as severe economic difficulties created what contemporaries called the "hungry forties."

You will find suggested answers to the exercises in the back of this book. For more Writing History exercises, as well as study resources for this chapter, visit oup.com/us/berenson.

CHAPTER 8

FROM NATIONAL UNIFICATION TO RELIGIOUS REVIVAL, 1850–1880

8.1 OTTO VON BISMARCK, "IRON AND BLOOD" SPEECH, SEPTEMBER 30, 1862

Otto von Bismarck (1815–1898), the prime minister of Prussia, was the architect of a new German Reich. During the 1860s, Bismarck achieved what had so conspicuously eluded the revolutionaries of 1848: the unification of the various German states into a single and coherent national whole. His ruthless approach made him the master of *Realpolitik*, the pure pursuit of power unleavened by considerations of ethics or morality.

When he became prime minister in 1862, Bismarck's charge was to resolve a tense standoff between the king and a newly elected parliament dominated by liberals, who refused to approve the king's military budget unless he agreed to limit his powers and increase their own. Bismarck responded by collecting taxes illegally and allocating funds without parliament's consent. He dared the liberals to block him, and they backed down.

Having asserted his dominance over parliament, Bismarck proceeded to unify Germany under Prussian leadership through a series of ruthless and often brilliant moves. The three wars he fought (against Denmark, Austria, and France) for German unity created a new and distinctive German state, whose progressive economy and conservative politics combined the two poles of his being—a daring personality and aristocratic political inclinations. In his famous "Iron and Blood" speech, Bismarck signals both aspects of his plans for Prussia—and Germany.

From Germany History in Documents and Images/Jeremiah Riemer

Bismarck responds to [Max von] Forckenbeck's lengthy arguments about appropriation rights and Art. 99 of the constitution and the people's wish for a shortened military service:

He would like to go into the budget for 1862, though without making a prejudicial statement. An abuse of constitutional rights could be undertaken by any side; this would then lead to a reaction from the other side. The Crown, e.g., could dissolve [Parliament] twelve times in a row—that would certainly be permitted according to the letter of the constitution—but it would be an abuse. It could just as easily reject cuts in the budget, immoderately; it would be hard to tell where to draw the line there; would it be at 6 million? At 16? Or at 60?—There are members of the National Association [*Nationalverein*]—of this association that has achieved a reputation owing to the justness of its demands—highly esteemed members who have stated that all standing armies are superfluous. Well, what if a public assembly had this view! Would not a government have to reject this?!—There was talk about the "sobriety" of the Prussian people. Yes, the great independence of the individual makes it difficult in Prussia to govern with the constitution (or to consolidate the constitution?); in France things are different, there this individual independence is lacking. A constitutional crisis would not be disgraceful, but honorable instead.—Furthermore, we are perhaps too "well-educated" to support a constitution; we are too critical; the ability to assess government measures and records of the public assembly is too common; in the country there are a lot of Catiline [a ruthless politician who had—at least according to Cicero—failed to launch a revolt against the ancient Roman Republic in 63 BCE] characters who have a great interest in upheavals. This may sound paradoxical, but everything proves how hard constitutional life is in Prussia.—Furthermore, one is too sensitive about the government's mistakes; as if it were enough to say "this and that [cabinet] minister made mistakes," as if one wasn't adversely affected oneself. Public opinion changes, the press is not [the same as] public opinion; one knows how the press is written; members of parliament have a higher duty, to lead opinion, to stand above it. We are too hot-blooded, we have a preference for putting on armor that is too big for our small body; and now we're actually supposed to utilize it. Germany is not looking to Prussia's liberalism, but to its power; Bavaria, Württemberg, Baden may indulge liberalism, and yet no one will assign them Prussia's role; Prussia has to coalesce and concentrate its power for the opportune moment, which has already been missed several times; Prussia's borders according to the Vienna Treaties [of 1814–1815] are not favorable for a healthy, vital state; it is not by speeches and majority resolutions that the great questions of the time are decided—that was the big mistake of 1848 and 1849—but by iron and blood. Last year's appropriation has been carried out; for whatever reasons, it is a matter of indifference; he [i.e., Bismarck himself] is sincerely seeking the path of agreement: whether he finds it does not depend on him alone. It would have been better if one had not made a fait accompli on the part of the Chamber of Deputies.—If no budget comes about, then there is a tabula rasa; the constitution offers no way out, for then it is one interpretation against another interpretation; *summum ius, summa iniuria* [the highest law, the highest injury]; the letter killeth. He is pleased that the speaker's remark about the possibility of another resolution of the House on account of a possible bill allows for the prospect of agreement; he, too, is looking for this bridge; when it might be found is uncertain.—Bringing about a budget this year is hardly possible given the time; we are in exceptional circumstances; the principle of promptly presenting the budget is also recognized by the government; but it is said that this was already promised and not kept; [and] now [it's] "You can certainly trust us as honest people." He does not agree with the interpellation that it is unconstitutional to make expenditures [whose authorization had been] refused; for every interpretation, it is necessary to agree on the three factors.

STUDY QUESTIONS

1. Why does Bismarck mention France and other German states in this context?
2. How were Prussia's domestic politics and foreign policy connected in his mind?

8.2 FLORENCE NIGHTINGALE, *NOTES ON NURSING*, 1860

At the beginning of the Crimean War (1853–1856), citizens cheered their soldiers with patriotic zeal, but as the conflict reached a stalemate and reports of hideous suffering appeared on the front pages of newspapers, public opinion soured. When it became clear that far more soldiers were dying from inadequate food, shelter, and medical supplies than from the fighting itself, influential people in Britain and France began to complain, but few openly opposed the war or tried to alleviate the suffering it had caused.

One notable exception was Florence Nightingale (1820–1910), a well-to-do and well-educated English woman who embraced nursing both to address the humanitarian crisis and to escape the constraints of British society, which saw a woman's place as being in the home. Nightingale could not solve the problems created by her country's military malfeasance, but as a nurse, she helped to save so many lives that she quickly became a national hero. Her work in the Crimean War as well as her bestselling book, *Notes on Nursing*, did much to raise the status of her profession and improve care for the sick. In the process, she also became a model for women throughout Europe who wanted to take the caring, nurturing role that society had thrust upon them and apply it outside the confines of their own families.

And remember every nurse should be one who is to be depended upon, in other words, capable of being a "confidential" nurse. She does not know how soon she may find herself placed in such a situation; she must be no gossip, no vain talker; she should never answer questions about her sick [patient] except to those who have a right to ask them; she must, I need not say, be strictly sober and honest; but more than this, she must be a religious and devoted woman; she must have a respect for her own calling, because God's precious gift of life is often literally placed in her hands; she must be a sound, and close, and quick observer; and she must be a woman of delicate and decent feeling.

To return to the question of what observation is for:—It would really seem as if some had considered it as its own end, as if detection, not cure, was their business; nay more, in a recent celebrated trial, three medical men, according to their own account, suspected poison, prescribed for dysentery, and left the patient to the poisoner. This is an extreme case. But in a small way, the same manner of acting falls under the cognizance of us all. How often the attendants of a case have stated that they knew perfectly well that the patient could not get well in such an air, in such a room, or under such circumstances, yet they have gone on dosing him with medicine, and making no effort to remove the poison from him, or him from the poison which they knew was killing him; nay, more, have sometimes not so much as mentioned their conviction in the right quarter—that is, to the only person who could act in the matter.

. . .

It may again be added, that, with very weak adult patients, these causes [of "sudden death"] are also (not often "suddenly fatal," it is true, but) very much oftener than is at all generally known, irreparable in their consequences.

Both for children and for adults, both for sick and for well (although more certainly in the case of sick

From Florence Nightingale, *Notes on Nursing* (reprint, London: Brandon/Systems Press, 1970), pp. 70–74.

children than in any others), I would here again repeat, the most frequent and most fatal cause of all is sleeping, for even a few hours, much more for weeks and months, in foul air, a condition which, more than any other condition, disturbs the respiratory process, and tends to produce "accidental" death in disease.

I need hardly here repeat the warning against any confusion of ideas between cold and fresh air. You may chill a patient fatally without giving him fresh air at all. And you can quite well, nay, much better, give him fresh air without chilling him. This is the test of a good nurse.

In cases of long recurring faintnesses from disease, for instance, especially disease which affects the organs of breathing, fresh air to the lungs, warmth to the surface, and often (as soon as the patient can swallow) hot drink, these are the right remedies and the only ones. Yet, oftener than not, you see the nurse or mother just reversing this; shutting up every cranny through which fresh air can enter, and leaving the body cold, or perhaps throwing a greater weight of clothes upon it, when already it is generating too little heat.

. . .

To sum up:—the answer to two of the commonest objections urged, one by women themselves, the other by men, against the desirableness of sanitary knowledge for women, *plus* a caution, comprises the whole argument for the art of nursing.

1. It is often said by men, that it is unwise to teach women anything about these laws of health, because they will take to physicking,—that there is a great deal too much of amateur physicking as it is, which is indeed true. One eminent physician told me that he had known more calomel [the common name for mercury chloride, a powder that was given to patients as a purgative—and inadvertently poisoned them in the process] given, both at a pinch and for a continuance, by mothers, governesses, and nurses, to children than he had ever heard of a physician prescribing in all his experience. Another says, that women's only idea in medicine is calomel and aperients [laxatives]. This is undeniably too often the case. There is nothing ever seen in any professional practice like the reckless physicking by amateur females. But this is just what the really experienced and observing nurse does *not* do; she neither physics herself nor others. And to cultivate in things pertaining to health observation and experience in women who are mothers, governesses or nurses, is just the way to do away with amateur physicking, and if the doctors did but know it, to make the nurses obedient to them,—helps to them instead of hindrances. Such education in women would indeed diminish the doctor's work—but no one really believes that doctors wish that there should be more illness, in order to have more work.

STUDY QUESTIONS

1. In what specific ways does Nightingale argue that nurses are actually medical *professionals*? Why does she insist on the point?
2. Does the prejudice of some male doctors against nurses result from the latter being women? Does Nightingale think female nurses could actually be superior to male doctors in certain respects?

8.3 KARL MARX AND FRIEDRICH ENGELS, *THE COMMUNIST MANIFESTO*, 1848

The Communist Manifesto was the brainchild of two prominent German intellectuals, Karl Marx (1818–1883) and Friedrich Engels (1820–1895). Although Marx and Engels first met in Cologne, Germany in 1842, they began their collaboration two years later in Paris, after Marx's incendiary journalism forced him to leave Germany. They continued to work together, living in exile in Brussels and then England. Their mutual concern for the working class formed the basis of their life-long partnership.

When they were commissioned to spell out the beliefs of the fledgling Communist Party, Marx and Engels offered more than just a list of goals. In *The Communist Manifesto* they called attention to the problems created by industrialization, notably the oppression of workers (proletariat) by factory owners (bourgeoisie). Looking back at history they found recurring tensions between the oppressed and the oppressor, a class struggle that, they predicted, would end only with the victory of the proletariat and the creation of a communist society. Their pamphlet did not make much of an impression in 1848, despite the numerous revolutions that broke out that year, but it attracted a great deal of attention later in the century and took on global importance after 1917 with the rise of the Bolsheviks in Russia and the Communist Party in China.

The history of all hitherto existing society is the history of class struggles.

Freeman and slave, patrician and plebeian, lord and serf, guild-master and journeyman, in a word, oppressor and oppressed, stood in constant opposition to one another, carried on an uninterrupted, now hidden, now open fight, a fight that each time ended, either in a revolutionary reconstitution of society at large, or in the common ruin of the contending classes.

In the earlier epochs of history, we find almost everywhere a complicated arrangement of society into various orders, a manifold gradation of social rank. In ancient Rome we have patricians, knights, plebeians, slaves; in the Middle Ages, feudal lords, vassals, guild-masters, journeymen, apprentices, serfs; in almost all of these classes, again, subordinate gradations.

The modern bourgeois society that has sprouted from the ruins of feudal society has not done away with class antagonisms. It has but established new classes, new conditions of oppression, new forms of struggle in place of the old ones.

Our epoch, the epoch of the bourgeoisie, possesses, however, this distinct feature: it has simplified class antagonisms. Society as a whole is more and more splitting up into two great hostile camps, into two great classes directly facing each other—Bourgeoisie and Proletariat. . . .

Modern industry has established the world market, for which the discovery of America paved the way. This market has given an immense development to commerce, to navigation, to communication by land. This development has, in its turn, reacted on the extension of industry; and in proportion as industry, commerce, navigation, railways extended, in

Excerpted from https://www.marxists.org/archive/marx/works/1848/communist-manifesto/. Source: Karl Marx and Friedrich Engels, "The Communist Manifesto" in Marx/Engels Selected Works, Vol. One, trans. by Samuel Moore in cooperation with Friedrich Engels (Moscow: Progress Publishers, 1969), 98-137.

the same proportion the bourgeoisie developed, increased its capital, and pushed into the background every class handed down from the Middle Ages. We see, therefore, how the modern bourgeoisie is itself the product of a long course of development, of a series of revolutions in the modes of production and of exchange. . . .

The bourgeoisie, wherever it has got the upper hand, has put an end to all feudal, patriarchal, idyllic relations. It has pitilessly torn asunder the motley feudal ties that bound man to his "natural superiors," and has left remaining no other nexus between man and man than naked self-interest, than callous "cash payment." It has drowned the most heavenly ecstasies of religious fervour, of chivalrous enthusiasm, of philistine sentimentalism, in the icy water of egotistical calculation. It has resolved personal worth into exchange value, and in place of the numberless indefeasible chartered freedoms, has set up that single, unconscionable freedom—Free Trade. In one word, for exploitation, veiled by religious and political illusions, it has substituted naked, shameless, direct, brutal exploitation.

The bourgeoisie has stripped of its halo every occupation hitherto honoured and looked up to with reverent awe. It has converted the physician, the lawyer, the priest, the poet, the man of science, into its paid wage labourers.

The bourgeoisie has torn away from the family its sentimental veil, and has reduced the family relation to a mere money relation. . . .

The bourgeoisie has subjected the country to the rule of the towns. It has created enormous cities, has greatly increased the urban population as compared with the rural, and has thus rescued a considerable part of the population from the idiocy of rural life. Just as it has made the country dependent on the towns, so it has made barbarian and semi-barbarian countries dependent on the civilised ones, nations of peasants on nations of bourgeois, the East on the West. . . .

The bourgeoisie, during its rule of scarce one hundred years, has created more massive and more colossal productive forces than have all preceding generations together. Subjection of Nature's forces to man, machinery, application of chemistry to industry and agriculture, steam-navigation, railways,

electric telegraphs, clearing of whole continents for cultivation, canalisation or rivers, whole populations conjured out of the ground—what earlier century had even a presentiment that such productive forces slumbered in the lap of social labour? . . .

But not only has the bourgeoisie forged the weapons that bring death to itself; it has also called into existence the men who are to wield those weapons—the modern working class—the proletarians. . . .

In what relation do the Communists stand to the proletarians as a whole? The Communists do not form a separate party opposed to the other working-class parties. They have no interests separate and apart from those of the proletariat as a whole. They do not set up any sectarian principles of their own, by which to shape and mould the proletarian movement. . . .

The immediate aim of the Communists is the same as that of all other proletarian parties: formation of the proletariat into a class, overthrow of the bourgeois supremacy, conquest of political power by the proletariat. . . .

In this sense, the theory of the Communists may be summed up in the single sentence: Abolition of private property. . . .

You are horrified at our intending to do away with private property. But in your existing society, private property is already done away with for nine-tenths of the population; its existence for the few is solely due to its non-existence in the hands of those nine-tenths. You reproach us, therefore, with intending to do away with a form of property, the necessary condition for whose existence is the non-existence of any property for the immense majority of society. In one word, you reproach us with intending to do away with your property. Precisely so; that is just what we intend. . . .

Communism deprives no man of the power to appropriate the products of society; all that it does is to deprive him of the power to subjugate the labour of others by means of such appropriations.

It has been objected that upon the abolition of private property, all work will cease, and universal laziness will overtake us.

According to this, bourgeois society ought long ago to have gone to the dogs through sheer idleness; for those of its members who work, acquire nothing, and those who acquire anything do not work. The whole of this objection is but another expression of the tautology: that there can no longer be any wage-labour when there is no longer any capital. . . .

The Communists are reproached with desiring to abolish countries and nationality. The working men have no country. We cannot take from them what they have not got. Since the proletariat must first of all acquire political supremacy, must rise to be the leading class of the nation, must constitute itself the nation, it is so far, itself national, though not in the bourgeois sense of the word. . . .

The proletariat will use its political supremacy to wrest, by degree, all capital from the bourgeoisie, to centralise all instruments of production in the hands of the State, i.e., of the proletariat organised as the ruling class; and to increase the total productive forces as rapidly as possible.

Of course, in the beginning, this cannot be effected except by means of despotic inroads on the rights of property, and on the conditions of bourgeois production; by means of measures, therefore, which appear economically insufficient and untenable, but which, in the course of the movement, outstrip themselves, necessitate further inroads upon the old social order, and are unavoidable as a means of entirely revolutionising the mode of production.

These measures will, of course, be different in different countries.

Nevertheless, in most advanced countries, the following will be pretty generally applicable:

1. Abolition of property in land and application of all rents of land to public purposes.
2. A heavy progressive or graduated income tax.
3. Abolition of all rights of inheritance.
4. Confiscation of the property of all emigrants and rebels.
5. Centralisation of credit in the banks of the state, by means of a national bank with State capital and an exclusive monopoly.
6. Centralisation of the means of communication and transport in the hands of the State.
7. Extension of factories and instruments of production owned by the State; the bringing into cultivation of waste-lands, and the improvement of the soil generally in accordance with a common plan.
8. Equal liability of all to work. Establishment of industrial armies, especially for agriculture.
9. Combination of agriculture with manufacturing industries; gradual abolition of all the distinction between town and country by a more equable distribution of the populace over the country.
10. Free education for all children in public schools. Abolition of children's factory labour in its present form. Combination of education with industrial production, etc, etc.

In short, the Communists everywhere support every revolutionary movement against the existing social and political order of things.

In all these movements, they bring to the front, as the leading question in each, the property question, no matter what its degree of development at the time.

Finally, they labour everywhere for the union and agreement of the democratic parties of all countries.

The Communists disdain to conceal their views and aims. They openly declare that their ends can be attained only by the forcible overthrow of all existing social conditions. Let the ruling classes tremble at a Communistic revolution. The proletarians have nothing to lose but their chains. They have a world to win. Workingmen of all countries, unite!

STUDY QUESTIONS

1. According to *The Communist Manifesto,* what have the bourgeoisie accomplished in the last one hundred years?
2. What problems did Marx and Engels identify in 1840s Europe? How would Communism solve these problems in society?

8.4 CHARLES DARWIN,
ON THE ORIGIN OF SPECIES, 1859

The name of Charles Darwin (1809–1882) is inextricably linked to the earth-shattering and—even today—controversial theory of evolution he proposed in 1859. The controversy surrounding him stemmed in part from his exceptional skill as a writer, even though many of his observations and conclusions were difficult for nonspecialists to appreciate. The 200th anniversary of his birth—and the 150th anniversary of the appearance of *On The Origin of Species*—in 2009 resulted in a series of commemorative events around the world, a brief sample of which can be viewed at http://darwin-online.org.uk/2009.html. Among the most famous elements of the book are the tangled riverbank image introduced in the long book's final paragraph and Darwin's stimulating view of the "grandeur in this view of life."

As this whole volume is one long argument, it may be convenient to the reader to have the leading facts and inferences briefly recapitulated.

That many and serious objections may be advanced against the theory of descent with modification through variation and natural selection, I do not deny. I have endeavoured to give to them their full force. Nothing at first can appear more difficult to believe than that the more complex organs and instincts have been perfected, not by means superior to, though analogous with, human reason, but by the accumulation of innumerable slight variations, each good for the individual possessor. Nevertheless, this difficulty, though appearing to our imagination insuperably great, cannot be considered real if we admit the following propositions, namely, that all parts of the organisation and instincts offer, at least individual differences—that there is a struggle for existence leading to the preservation of profitable deviations of structure or instinct—and, lastly, that gradations in the state of perfection of each organ may have existed, each good of its kind. The truth of these propositions cannot, I think, be disputed.

It is, no doubt, extremely difficult even to conjecture by what gradations many structures have been perfected, more especially among broken and failing groups of organic beings, which have suffered much extinction; but we see so many strange gradations in nature, that we ought to be extremely cautious in saying that any organ or instinct, or any whole structure, could not have arrived at its present state by many graduated steps. There are, it must be admitted, cases of special difficulty opposed to the theory of natural selection; and one of the most curious of these is the existence in the same community of two or three defined castes of workers or sterile female ants; but I have attempted to show how these difficulties can be mastered.

. . .

A grand and almost untrodden field of inquiry will be opened, on the causes and laws of variation, on correlation, on the effects of use and disuse, on the direct action of external conditions, and so forth. The study of domestic productions will rise immensely in value. A new variety raised by man will be a far more important and interesting subject for study

From Charles Darwin, *On the Origin of Species by Means of Natural Selection, or the Preservation of Favored Races in the Struggle for Life and The Descent of Man, and Selection in Relation to Sex* (New York: Modern Library, 1936), pp. 353, 372, and 373–374.

than one more species added to the infinitude of already recorded species. Our classifications will come to be, as far as they can be so made, genealogies; and will then truly give what may be called the plan of creation. The rules for classifying will no doubt become simpler when we have a definite object in view. We possess no pedigrees or armorial bearings; and we have to discover and trace the many diverging lines of descent in our natural genealogies, by characters of any kind which have long been inherited. Rudimentary organs will speak infallibly with respect to the nature of long-lost structures. Species and groups of species which are called aberrant, and which may fancifully be called living fossils, will aid us in forming a picture of the ancient forms of life. Embryology will often reveal to us the structure, in some degree obscured, of the prototypes of each great class.

When we can feel assured that all the individuals of the same species, and all the closely allied species of most genera, have, within a not very remote period descended from one parent, and have migrated from some one birth-place; and when we better know the many means of migration, then, by the light which geology now throws, and will continue to throw, on former changes of climate and of the level of the land, we shall surely be enabled to trace in an admirable manner the former migrations of the inhabitants of the whole world. Even at present, by comparing the differences between the inhabitants of the sea on the opposite sides of a continent, and the nature of the various inhabitants of that continent in relation to their apparent means of immigration, some light can be thrown on ancient geography.

. . .

It is interesting to contemplate a tangled bank, clothed with many plants of many kinds, with birds singing on the bushes, with various insects flitting about, and with worms crawling through the damp earth, and to reflect that these elaborately constructed forms, so different from each other, and dependent upon each other in so complex a manner, have all been produced by laws acting around us. These laws, taken in the largest sense, being Growth with Reproduction; Inheritance which is almost implied by reproduction; Variability from the indirect and direct action of the conditions of life, and from use and disuse; a Ratio of Increase so high as to lead to a Struggle for Life, and as a consequence to Natural Selection, entailing Divergence of Character and the Extinction of less-improved forms. Thus, from the war of nature, from famine and death, the most exalted object which we are capable of conceiving, namely, the production of the higher animals, directly follows. There is grandeur in this view of life, with its several powers, having been originally breathed by the Creator into a few forms or into one; and that, whilst this planet has gone cycling on according to the fixed law of gravity, from so simple a beginning endless forms most beautiful and most wonderful have been, and are being evolved.

STUDY QUESTIONS

1. How does Darwin convey the excitement that he feels for this new scientific field and the possibilities for applying his theory to other disciplines?
2. How does his quest for common ancestors underscore the interconnected nature of all species on our planet?

8.5 POPE PIUS IX,
THE SYLLABUS OF ERRORS, 1864

In 1864, Pope Pius IX (Giovanni Maria Mastai-Ferretti, 1792–1878; papacy 1846–1878) sought to counter what he considered a dangerous secularizing trend by releasing a document entitled *The Syllabus of Errors*. This document denounced "rationalism," "indifferentism," and "secularism," the three "isms" said to separate people from God, and declared it heretical to claim that "the Roman Pontiff can and ought to reconcile himself to, and agree with, progress, liberalism, and modern civilization." The *Syllabus* horrified the Catholics who sought to reconcile religion, science, and liberalism. Even so, the pope went one step further in 1870 by promulgating the doctrine of papal infallibility, the notion that any official pronouncement by the pope *ex cathedra* ("from his chair of office") was necessarily true.

In the following excerpts, each of the numbers identifies an "error" that Catholics are instructed not to believe. Another way to read this list of errors is to imagine that each of them begins with the statement, "It is not true that . . ." Thus, the fifth error should read, "It is not true that divine revelation is imperfect, and therefore subject to a continual and indefinite progress, corresponding with the advancement of human reason." The dates that follow each error refer to the moment when Pius IX or his predecessors declared the particular belief to be false. Thus, Pius IX announced on June 9, 1862 that it is an error to believe that "human reason, without any reference whatsoever to God, is the sole arbiter of truth."

THE SYLLABUS OF ERRORS CONDEMNED BY PIUS IX

I. Pantheism, Naturalism and Absolute Rationalism

1. There exists no Supreme, all-wise, all-provident Divine Being, distinct from the universe, and God is identical with the nature of things, and is, therefore, subject to changes. In effect, God is produced in man and in the world, and all things are God and have the very substance of God, and God is one and the same thing with the world, and, therefore, spirit with matter, necessity with liberty, good with evil, justice with injustice.—Allocution "Maxima quidem," June 9, 1862.

2. All action of God upon man and the world is to be denied.—Ibid.

3. Human reason, without any reference whatsoever to God, is the sole arbiter of truth and falsehood, and of good and evil; it is law to itself, and suffices, by its natural force, to secure the welfare of men and of nations.—Ibid.

4. All the truths of religion proceed from the innate strength of human reason; hence reason is the ultimate standard by which man can and ought to arrive at the knowledge of all truths of every kind.—Ibid. and Encyclical "Qui pluribus," Nov. 9, 1846, etc.

5. Divine revelation is imperfect, and therefore subject to a continual and indefinite progress, corresponding with the advancement of human reason.—Ibid.

6. The faith of Christ is in opposition to human reason and divine revelation not only is not useful, but is even hurtful to the perfection of man.—Ibid.

From Pope Bl. Pius IX, "The Syllabus of Errors," https://www.papalencyclicals.net/pius09/p9syll.htm.

7. The prophecies and miracles set forth and recorded in the Sacred Scriptures are the fiction of poets, and the mysteries of the Christian faith the result of philosophical investigations. In the books of the Old and the New Testament there are contained mythical inventions, and Jesus Christ is Himself a myth.

VI. Errors About Civil Society, Considered Both in Itself and in its Relation to the Church

39. The State, as being the origin and source of all rights, is endowed with a certain right not circumscribed by any limits.—Allocution "Maxima quidem," June 9, 1862.

40. The teaching of the Catholic Church is hostile to the well-being and interests of society.—Encyclical "Qui pluribus," Nov. 9, 1846; Allocution "Quibus quantisque," April 20, 1849.

41. The civil government, even when in the hands of an infidel sovereign, has a right to an indirect negative power over religious affairs. It therefore possesses not only the right called that of "exsequatur," but also that of appeal, called "appellatio ab abusu."—Apostolic Letter "Ad Apostolicae," Aug. 22, 1851.

42. In the case of conflicting laws enacted by the two powers, the civil law prevails.—Ibid.

43. The secular power has authority to rescind, declare and render null, solemn conventions, commonly called concordats, entered into with the Apostolic See, regarding the use of rights appertaining to ecclesiastical immunity, without the consent of the Apostolic See, and even in spite of its protest.—Allocution "Multis gravibusque," Dec. 17, 1860; Allocution "In consistoriali," Nov. 1, 1850.

44. The civil authority may interfere in matters relating to religion, morality and spiritual government: hence, it can pass judgment on the instructions issued for the guidance of consciences, conformably with their mission, by the pastors of the Church. Further, it has the right to make enactments regarding the administration of the divine sacraments, and the dispositions necessary for receiving them.—Allocutions "In consistoriali," Nov. 1, 1850, and "Maxima quidem," June 9, 1862.

45. The entire government of public schools in which the youth of a Christian state is educated, except (to a certain extent) in the case of episcopal seminaries, may and ought to appertain to the civil power, and belong to it so far that no other authority whatsoever shall be recognized as having any right to interfere in the discipline of the schools, the arrangement of the studies, the conferring of degrees, in the choice or approval of the teachers.—Allocutions "Quibus luctuosissimis," Sept. 5, 1851, and "In consistoriali," Nov. 1, 1850.

46. Moreover, even in ecclesiastical seminaries, the method of studies to be adopted is subject to the civil authority.—Allocution "Nunquam fore," Dec. 15, 1856.

47. The best theory of civil society requires that popular schools open to children of every class of the people, and, generally, all public institutes intended for instruction in letters and philosophical sciences and for carrying on the education of youth, should be freed from all ecclesiastical authority, control and interference, and should be fully subjected to the civil and political power at the pleasure of the rulers, and according to the standard of the prevalent opinions of the age.—Epistle to the Archbishop of Freiburg, "Cum non sine," July 14, 1864.

48. Catholics may approve of the system of educating youth unconnected with Catholic faith and the power of the Church, and which regards the knowledge of merely natural things, and only, or at least primarily, the ends of earthly social life.—Ibid.

49. The civil power may prevent the prelates of the Church and the faithful from communicating freely and mutually with the Roman pontiff.—Allocution "Maxima quidem," June 9, 1862.

54. Kings and princes are not only exempt from the jurisdiction of the Church, but are superior to the Church in deciding questions of jurisdiction.—Damnatio "Multiplices inter," June 10, 1851.

55. The Church ought to be separated from the State, and the State from the Church.—Allocution "Acerbissimum," Sept. 27, 1852.

X. Errors Having Reference to Modern Liberalism

77. In the present day it is no longer expedient that the Catholic religion should be held as the only religion of the State, to the exclusion of all other forms of

worship.—Allocution "Nemo vestrum," July 26, 1855.

78. Hence it has been wisely decided by law, in some Catholic countries, that persons coming to reside therein shall enjoy the public exercise of their own peculiar worship.—Allocution "Acerbissimum," Sept. 27, 1852.

79. Moreover, it is false that the civil liberty of every form of worship, and the full power, given to

all, of overtly and publicly manifesting any opinions whatsoever and thoughts, conduce more easily to corrupt the morals and minds of the people, and to propagate the pest of indifferentism.—Allocution "Nunquam fore," Dec. 15, 1856.

80. The Roman Pontiff can, and ought to, reconcile himself, and come to terms with progress, liberalism and modern civilization.—Allocution "Jamdudum cernimus," March 18, 1861.

STUDY QUESTIONS

1. Why did the Church see State authority as a particular challenge to its sovereignty? Was it correct to evaluate secular authorities in that light?
2. Which seems to be the most significant and potentially devastating to the Church's authority of the "errors" listed here? Why?

8.6 VISUAL SOURCE: ADVERTISMENT FOR WOMBWELL'S ROYAL NATIONAL ZOOLOGICAL COLLECTION, 1853

Cheaper printing methods and increased literacy in the nineteenth century resulted in a flood of new publications in Europe, from self-help books to science fiction novels. Newspapers especially flourished in this era, offering daily news, society gossip, and installments of fiction. Around 1830, there were seven morning papers and six evening papers printed in London and about 150 more in the provinces.

Paperboys in London began their day three hours before dawn and finished at the stroke of six p.m. They delivered newspapers to the homes of the wealthy, where they were ironed by servants before being laid out at breakfast, and to local inns, chop houses, and taverns for sharing. Because it was possible to rent a paper for an hour each day—or even to rent the previous day's paper—paperboys spent much of their day shuffling rented papers back and forth to different clients, calling out headlines in the streets as they went.

Newspapers, of course, printed the events of the day, but to earn revenue, they also published large numbers of advertisements. The one shown here, published in Colchester, England in 1853, promotes George Wombwell's collection of exotic animals. He dubbed it the Royal National Zoological Collection, but in truth it was a private business that had nothing to do with the monarchy

From British Library, *Wombwell's Royal National Zoological Collection*, https://www.bl.uk/collection-items/poster-wombwells-royal-national-zoological-collection-which-contains-his-unequalled-group-of-lions.

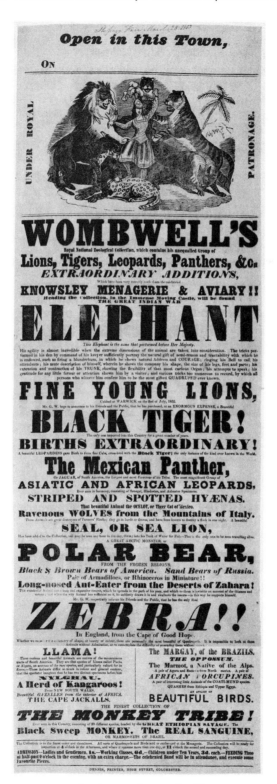

FIGURE 8.6   Advertisement for Wombwell's

or the state. In fact Wombwell himself had died three years earlier, but his successors kept the popular attraction going. Wombwell's traveling menagerie toured the country, appealing to people whose earnings enabled them to afford paid entertainment. The fine print at the bottom lists the admissions prices—1 shilling for ladies and gentlemen, 6 pence for working classes, and 3 pence for children. Note that the advertisement sensationalizes the most sought-after animals using large letters and bold print instead of pictures because illustrations were more expensive to print than text.

STUDY QUESTIONS

1. What aspects of this advertisement would get a reader's attention? What does the success of such a traveling menagerie reveal about social life in this era?
2. What does the variety of exotic animals advertised by Wombwell reveal about Britain's relationship with other nations and British people's interest in foreign lands?

TEXT RECONSTRUCTION

Text reconstruction is the latter-day term for the method Ben Franklin invented to teach himself to write. In a modern text-reconstruction exercise, the sentences in a paragraph are listed out of order, and you rearrange them to form a coherent paragraph. When you organize sentences someone else has written, your mind is freed to focus exclusively on structure and the connecting devices writers use to create flow.

Ben Franklin teaches himself to write:

About this time I met with an odd volume of the *Spectator*—I thought the writing excellent, and wished, if possible, to imitate it. With this view I took some of the papers, and, making short hints of the sentiment in each sentence laid them by a few days, and then, without looking at the book, try'd to compleat the papers again, by expressing each hinted sentiment at length, and as fully as it had been expressed before, in any suitable words that should come to hand. . . . I also sometimes jumbled my collections of hints into confusion, and after some weeks endeavored to reduce them into the best order, before I began to form the full sentences and compleat the paper. This was to teach me method in the arrangement of thoughts. By comparing my work afterwards with the original, I discovered many faults and amended them; but I sometimes had the pleasure of fancying that, in certain particulars of small import, I had been lucky enough to improve the method or the language.

EXERCISE: RECONSTRUCT PARAGRAPHS

Instructions

Number the sentences in the order you think they appear in the original paragraphs. Some of the numbering has been provided.

1.

    Later on, this paradox would help account for many of his political and diplomatic achievements.

  3 His radicalism allowed him to see new possibilities and to take the gamble they often required, while his conservatism enabled him to maintain the confidence and preserve the interests of his fellow aristocrats and the king.

    By temperament he was a radical, by background and upbringing a conservative through and through.

  1 Here, then, was the paradox that would characterize Bismarck's life.

2.

  2 For example, small, specialized workshops were best for the building of locomotives, which required detailed engineering skills..

    Even though industrialization forced significant numbers of small textile and metallurgical firms out of business, it called a great many other small firms into being.

4 In construction, which expanded rapidly during the Industrial Revolution, small crews of builders working by hand did most of the work.

In addition, members of the Industrial Revolution's growing middle class could now afford luxury products that had to be carefully crafted by hand, usually in workshops of modest size.

3.

Each serf drafted into the army was condemned to serve for 25 years, and although promised emancipation at the end, draftees found this dim prospect unmotivating at best.

5 To make matters worse, the low productivity of Russia's system of unfree labor limited the number of serfs who could be spared from the land and conscripted into the army, thus restricting its size and strength.

A cadre of Russian officials examined their army and economy to pinpoint the needed reforms.

2 Beyond its outmoded transport system, the military's essential problem was low morale, which resulted from a conscription process that relied almost exclusively on Russia's serfs.

How many would survive the decades of harsh barracks conditions and dangerous battles to take advantage of freedom at the end?

EXERCISE: COPY PARAGRAPHS WORD FOR WORD

Once you have reordered the sentences in a paragraph, the next step is direct transcription: copying the text verbatim, holding five to ten words in memory at a time. Direct transcription is useful because our brains read for content, not form. Reading for meaning is natural and normal, but in learning to write we must read for style and technique too. "Copywork" helps.

Instructions

On a separate sheet of paper, copy by hand each of the original paragraphs verbatim, holding five to ten words in memory at a time.

You will find suggested answers to the exercises in the back of this book. For more Writing History exercises, as well as study resources for this chapter, visit oup.com/us/berenson.

CHAPTER 9

EUROPEAN SOCIETY AND THE ROAD TO WAR, 1880–1914

9.1 MARIA MONTESSORI, *DR. MONTESSORI'S OWN HANDBOOK*, 1914

No one exemplified the New (emancipated) Woman of the late nineteenth century more than Italy's Maria Montessori (1870–1952), who is best known in the United States for her pioneering efforts to reform early childhood education. In January 1907, Montessori established a school for young children in one of Rome's low-income housing projects. Known as the Children's House, this tenement school became the laboratory for an experiment in early childhood education that would ultimately become an international movement, with Montessori schools located throughout the world.

In the United States, where Montessori was invited to lecture in 1913, her ideas became central to the kindergarten curriculum, and in the 1960s, her teaching methods helped inspire Head Start, the government-funded early education program. After World War I, Montessori developed into something of a cult figure, the increasingly authoritarian leader of what was becoming a quasi-religious sect. She had disciples but never collaborators, and she isolated herself and her movement from other educational reforms. Nevertheless, she broke through the barriers of sex discrimination in her time and set an example of what women could do.

As the child's body must draw nourishment and oxygen from its external environment, in order to accomplish a great physiological work, the *work of growth*, so also the spirit must take from its environment the nourishment which it needs to develop according to its own "laws of growth." It cannot be denied that the phenomena of development are a great work in themselves. The consolidation of the bones, the growth of the whole body, the completion of the minute construction of the brain, the formation of the teeth, all these are very real labors of the physiological organism, as is also the transformation

From Maria Montessori, *Dr. Montessori's Own Handbook* (New York: Frederick A. Stokes Company, 1914), pp. 4–10.

which the organism undergoes during the period of puberty.

These exertions are very different from those put forth by mankind in so-called *external work*, that is to say, in "social production," whether in the schools where man is taught, or in the world where, by the activity of his intelligence, he produces wealth and transforms his environment.

It is none the less true, however, that they are both "work." In fact, the organism during these periods of greatest physiological work is least capable of performing external tasks, and sometimes the work of growth is of such extent and difficulty that the individual is overburdened, as with an excessive strain, and for this reason alone becomes exhausted or even dies.

Man will always be able to avoid "external work" by making use of the labor of others, but there is no possibility of shirking that inner work. Together with birth and death it has been imposed by nature itself, and each man must accomplish it for himself. This difficult, inevitable labor, this is the "work of the child."

When we say then that little children should *rest*, we are referring to one side only of the question of work. We mean that they should rest from that *external* visible work to which the little child through his weakness and incapacity cannot make any contribution useful either to himself or to others.

Our assertion, therefore, is not absolute; the child in reality is not resting, he is performing the mysterious inner work of his autoformation. He is working to make a man, and to accomplish this it is not enough that the child's body should grow in actual size; the most intimate functions of the motor and nervous systems must also be established and the intelligence developed.

. . .

A "CHILDREN'S HOUSE"

The "Children's House" is the *environment* which is offered to the child that he may be given the opportunity of developing his activities. This kind of school is not of a fixed type, but may vary according to the financial resources at disposal and to the opportunities afforded by the environment. It ought to be a real house; that is to say, a set of rooms with a garden of which the children are the masters. A garden which contains shelters is ideal, because the children can play or sleep under them, and can also bring their tables out to work or dine. In this way they may live almost entirely in the open air, and are protected at the same time from rain and sun.

The central and principal room of the building, often also the only room at the disposal of the children, is the room for "intellectual work." To this central room can be added other smaller rooms according to the means and opportunities of the place: for example, a bathroom, a dining-room, a little parlor or common-room, a room for manual work, a gymnasium and rest-room.

The special characteristic of the equipment of these houses is that it is adapted for children and not adults. They contain not only didactic material specially fitted for the intellectual development of the child, but also a complete equipment for the management of the miniature family. The furniture is light so that the children can move it about, and it is painted in some light color so that the children can wash it with soap and water. There are low tables of various sizes and shapes— square, rectangular and round, large and small. The rectangular shape is the most common as two or more children can work at it together. The seats are small wooden chairs, but there are also small wicker armchairs and sofas.

STUDY QUESTIONS

1. Why did Dr. Montessori see "work" as a fundamental concept in a child's development? Which form of "work" was especially significant?
2. How can Montessori's method be connected to the daily rhythms of industrialization?

9.2 JULES FERRY, SPEECH ON IMPERIALISM, JULY 28, 1883

How exactly to explain the Europeans' late-nineteenth-century race for colonies has long been the subject of heated debate. Some historians have attributed it mostly to economic motives, others to chiefly political and cultural ones. In reality imperialism, like most other complex historical phenomena, grew from a combination of economic, political, and cultural roots: all countries had political motives, and most had economic and cultural motives as well.

In the case of France, colonies in Asia and Africa brought prestige to the mother country and confirmed its status as a great power. Such confirmation was especially valuable because Prussia had dealt France a humiliating military defeat in 1870, followed by a humbling relative decline of the French economy from second place in 1850 to fourth in the 1880s. To compensate for these losses, French leaders turned to imperialism with a vengeance. They brought Algeria (first invaded in 1830) into their trading zone, then expanded eastward into Tunisia in 1881, into the Congo the following year, and into West Africa over the next two decades. In Southeast Asia, they turned what had been little more than trading posts into actual colonies.

Jules Ferry (1832–1893) served twice as prime minister and was in power during many of these imperialist ventures. Here, he responds to his critics in a particularly frank discussion of his government's plans for these far-flung corners of the world. Notice how the legacy of the French Revolution continued to be up for debate.

M. JULES FERRY

Gentlemen, it embarrasses me to make such a prolonged demand upon the gracious attention of the Chamber, but I believe that the duty I am fulfilling upon this platform is not a useless one: It is as strenuous for me as for you, but I believe that there is some benefit in summarizing and condensing, in the form of arguments, the principles, the motives, and the various interests by which a policy of colonial expansion may be justified; it goes without saying that I will try to remain reasonable, moderate, and never lose sight of the major continental interests which are the primary concern of this country. What I wish to say, to support this proposition, is that in fact, just as in word, the policy of colonial expansion is a political and economic system; I wish to say that one can relate this system to three orders of ideas: economic ideas, ideas of civilization in its highest sense, and ideas of politics and patriotism.

In the area of economics, I allow myself to place before you, with the support of some figures, the considerations which justify a policy of colonial expansion from the point of view of that need, felt more and more strongly by the industrial populations of Europe and particularly those of our own rich and hard-working Country: the need for export markets. Is this some kind of chimera? Is this a view of the future or is it not rather a pressing need, and, we could say, the cry of our industrial population? I will formulate only in a general way what each of you, in the different parts of France, is in a position to confirm. Yes, what is lacking for our great industry, drawn irrevocably on to the path of exportation by the (free trade) treaties of 1860, what it lacks more and more is export markets. Why? Because next door to us Germany is surrounded by barriers, because beyond the ocean, the United States of America has become protectionist, protectionist in the most extreme sense, because not only have these great markets, I will not say closed but shrunk, and thus become more difficult of access for our industrial products, but also these great scares are beginning to pour products not seen heretofore into our own markets . . . It is not necessary to pursue this demonstration any further. . . .

. . . Gentlemen, there is a second point, a second order of ideas to which I have to give equal attention, but as quickly as possible, believe me; it is the humanitarian and civilizing side of the question. On this point the honorable M. Camille Pelletan has jeered in his own refined and clever manner; he jeers, he condemns, and he says "What is this civilization which you impose with cannon-balls? What is it but another form of barbarism? Don't these populations, these inferior races, have the same rights as you? Aren't they masters of their own houses? Have they called upon you? You come to them against their will, you offer them violence, but not civilization." There, gentlemen, is the thesis I do not hesitate to say that this is not politics, nor is it history: it is political metaphysics. (*"Ah, Ah" on far left.*)

. . . Gentlemen, I must speak from a higher and more truthful plane. It must be stated openly that, in effect, Superior races have rights over inferior races. (*Movement on many benches on the far left.*)

M. JULES MAIGNE: Oh! You dare to say this in the country which has proclaimed the rights of man!

M. DE GUILLOUTET: This is a justification of slavery and the slave trade!

M. JULES FERRY: If M. Maigne is right, if the declaration of the rights of man was written for the blacks of equatorial Africa, then by what right do you impose regular commerce upon them? They have not called upon you.

M. RAOUL DUVAL: We do not want to impose anything upon them. It is you who wish to do so!

M. JULES MAIGNE: To propose and to impose are two different things!

M. GEORGES PERIN: In any case, you cannot bring about commerce by force.

M. JULES FERRY: I repeat that superior races have a right, because they have a duty. They have the duty to civilize inferior races. . . . (*Approbation from the left. New interruptions on the extreme left and from the right.*) . . .

That is what I have to answer M. Pelletan in regard to the second point upon which he touched.

He then touched upon a third, more delicate, more serious point, and upon which I ask your permission to express myself quite frankly. It is the political side of the question. The honorable M. Pelletan, who is a distinguished writer, always comes up with remarkably precise formulations. I will borrow from him the one which he applied the other day to this aspect of colonial policy.

". . . It is a system," he says, "which consists of seeking out compensations in the Orient with a circumspect and peaceful seclusion which is actually imposed upon us in Europe."

I would like to explain myself in regard to this. I do not like this word "compensation," and, in effect, not here but elsewhere it has often been used in a treacherous way. If what is being said or insinuated is that a republican minister could possibly believe that there are in any part of the world compensations for the disasters which we have experienced, an injury is being inflicted . . . and an injury undeserved by that government. (*Applause at the center and left.*) I will ward off this injury with all the force of my patriotism! (*New applause and bravos from the same benches.*)

Gentlemen, there are certain considerations which merit the attention of all patriots. The conditions of naval warfare have been profoundly altered. ("Very true, Very true.")

At this time, as you know, a warship cannot carry more than fourteen days' worth of coal, no matter how perfectly it is organized, and a ship which is out of coal is a derelict on the surface of the sea, abandoned to the first person who comes along. Thence the necessity of having on the oceans provision stations, shelters, ports for defense arid revictualling. (*Applause at the center and left. Various interruptions.*) And it is for this that we needed Tunisia, for this that we needed Saigon and the Mekong Delta, for this that we need Madagascar, that we are at Diego-Suarez and Vohemar and will never leave them! (*Applause from a great number of benches.*) Gentlemen, in

Europe as it is today, in this competition of so many rivals which we see growing around us some by perfecting their military or maritime forces, others by the prodigious development of an ever growing population; in a Europe, or rather in a universe of this sort, a policy of peaceful seclusion or abstention is simply the highway to decadence! Nations are great in our times only by means of the activities which they develop; it is not simply by the peaceful shining forth of "institutions" (*Interruptions and laughter on the left and right*) that they are great at this hour. . . .

As for me, I am astounded to find the monarchist parties becoming indignant over the fact that the Republic of France is following a policy which does not confine itself to that ideal of modesty, of reserve, and, if you will allow me the expression, of bread and butter (*Interruptions and laughter on the left*) which the representatives of fallen monarchies wish to impose upon France. (*Applause at the center.*) . . .

(The Republican Party) has shown that it is quite aware that one cannot impose upon France a political ideal conforming to that of nations like independent Belgium and the Swiss Republic; that something else is needed for France: that she cannot be merely a free country, that she must also be a great country, exercising all of her rightful influence over the destiny of Europe, that she ought to propagate this influence throughout the world and carry everywhere that she can her language, her customs, her flag, her arms, and her genius. (*Applause at center and left.*)

STUDY QUESTIONS

1. Are economic and commercial interests the main supports for Ferry's position?
2. Was Ferry winning over his audience throughout the oration? What arguments seem to have been the most persuasive?

9.3 RUDYARD KIPLING, *THE WHITE MAN'S BURDEN*, 1899

Rudyard Kipling (1865–1936) came from a prominent family with strong connections to the British Empire. His father was an artist and teacher who spent much of his career in India and designed Queen Victoria's Durbar Room, which she used to showcase her Indian artifacts. Kipling was born in Mumbai, went to England for schooling, and returned to Lahore, India, as a young man to work as a journalist. A prolific poet and short story writer, he eventually made his way back to Britain and then to the United States, where he wrote *The Jungle Book*. He set many of his tales, such as *Kim* and the *Just So Stories*, in lands that were exotic to his British and American readers. He won the Nobel Prize for literature in 1907.

The White Man's Burden celebrated the American acquisition of the Philippines and remains one of the most quoted defenses of imperialism. Note his devotion to the concept of empire and his glorification of conquest as noble and heroic. Although Kipling admitted that such commitments abroad encouraged parents to "bind your sons to exile/To serve your captives' needs," his own son did not choose exile for himself. He remained in Europe and was killed in the First World War.

From https://rpo.library.utoronto.ca/poems/white-mans-burden.

Take up the White Man's burden—
Send forth the best ye breed—
Go bind your sons to exile
To serve your captives' need;
To wait in heavy harness,
On fluttered folk and wild—
Your new-caught, sullen peoples,
Half-devil and half-child.

Take up the White Man's burden—
In patience to abide,
To veil the threat of terror
And check the show of pride;
By open speech and simple,
An hundred times made plain
To seek another's profit,
And work another's gain.

Take up the White Man's burden—
The savage wars of peace—
Fill full the mouth of Famine
And bid the sickness cease;
And when your goal is nearest
The end for others sought,
Watch sloth and heathen Folly
Bring all your hopes to nought.

Take up the White Man's burden—
No tawdry rule of kings,
But toil of serf and sweeper—
The tale of common things.

The ports ye shall not enter,
The roads ye shall not tread,
Go mark them with your living,
And mark them with your dead.

Take up the White Man's burden—
And reap his old reward:
The blame of those ye better,
The hate of those ye guard—
The cry of hosts ye humour
(Ah, slowly!) toward the light:—
"Why brought he us from bondage,
Our loved Egyptian night?"

Take up the White Man's burden—
Ye dare not stoop to less—
Nor call too loud on Freedom
To cloke your weariness;
By all ye cry or whisper,
By all ye leave or do,
The silent, sullen peoples
Shall weigh your gods and you.

Take up the White Man's burden—
Have done with childish days—
The lightly proferred laurel,
The easy, ungrudged praise.
Comes now, to search your manhood
Through all the thankless years
Cold, edged with dear-bought wisdom,
The judgment of your peers!

STUDY QUESTIONS

1. For Kipling, what benefits did locals get from the imperialist project and what did it cost Americans and Europeans?
2. How does Kipling characterize the relationship between the locals and the colonizers; how accepting were locals of the "benefits" brought by the "white man"?

9.4 MARK TWAIN, "TO THE PERSON SITTING IN DARKNESS," 1901

Not everyone agreed that the project of imperialism was worthwhile. Mark Twain (Samuel Clemens, 1835–1910), the eminent American man of letters, was incensed by the blatant racism of Kipling's exhortation and lashed out at Kipling in this satirical essay, written in Twain's later years when he became increasingly embittered about the chances of "civilization" overcoming barbarism. In this essay he assumes the voice of a preacher addressing an American audience. The huckster-preacher conveys what, to him, seems the perfect synergy of moral and financial considerations. In his mind, obtaining the willing incorporation of the Filipinos into the "Blessings-of-Civilization Trust" is just a matter of public relations, of persuading the "Brother who Sits in Darkness" that he would be better off under an imperialist regime.

Extending the Blessings of Civilization to our Brother who Sits in Darkness has been a good trade and has paid well, on the whole; and there is money in it yet, if carefully worked—but not enough, in my judgment, to make any considerable risk advisable. The People that Sit in Darkness are getting to be too scarce—too scarce and too shy. And such darkness as is now left is really of but an indifferent quality, and not dark enough for the game. The most of those People that Sit in Darkness have been furnished with more light than was good for them or profitable for us. We have been injudicious.

The Blessings-of-Civilization Trust, wisely and cautiously administered, is a Daisy. There is more money in it, more territory, more sovereignty, and other kinds of emolument, than there is in any other game that is played. But Christendom has been playing it badly of late years, and must certainly suffer by it, in my opinion. She has been so eager to get every stake that appeared on the green cloth, that the People who Sit in Darkness have noticed it—they have noticed it, and have begun to show alarm. They have become suspicious of the Blessings of Civilization. More—they have begun to examine them. This is not well. The Blessings of Civilization are all right, and a good commercial property; there could not be a better, in a dim light. In the right kind of a light, and at a proper distance, with the goods a little out of focus, they furnish this desirable exhibit to the Gentlemen who Sit in Darkness:

Love,	Law and Order,
Justice,	Liberty,
Gentleness,	Equality,
Christianity,	Honorable Dealing,
Protection to the Weak,	Mercy,
Temperance,	Education,
—and so on.	

There. Is it good? Sir, it is pie. It will bring into camp any idiot that sits in darkness anywhere. But not if we adulterate it. It is proper to be emphatic upon that point. This brand is strictly for Export—apparently. *Apparently.* Privately and confidentially, it is nothing of the kind. Privately and confidentially, it is merely an outside cover, gay and pretty and attractive, displaying the special patterns of our Civilization which we reserve for Home Consumption, while

From Mark Twain, *The Family Mark Twain* (New York: Harper & Brothers, 1935), pp. 1390–1391, 1394–1395, 1397, and 1398.

inside the bale is the Actual Thing that the Customer Sitting in Darkness buys with his blood and tears and land and liberty. That Actual Thing is, indeed, Civilization, but it is only for Export. Is there a difference between the two brands? In some of the details, yes.

. . .

The more we examine the mistake, the more clearly we perceive that it is going to be bad for the Business. The Person Sitting in Darkness is almost sure to say: "There is something curious about this—curious and unaccountable. There must be two Americas: one that sets the captive free, and one that takes a once-captive's new freedom away from him, and picks a quarrel with him with nothing to found it on; then kills him to get his land."

The truth is, the Person Sitting in Darkness *is* saying things like that; and for the sake of the Business we must persuade him to look at the Philippine matter in another and healthier way. We must arrange his opinions for him. I believe it can be done; for Mr. Chamberlain has arranged England's opinion of the South African matter, and done it most cleverly and successfully. He presented the facts—some of the facts—and showed those confiding people what the facts meant. He did it statistically, which is a good way. He used the formula: "Twice 2 are 14, and 2 from 9 leaves 35." Figures are effective; figures will convince the elect.

. . .

We must bring him to, and coax him and coddle him, and assure him that the ways of Providence are best, and that it would not become us to find fault with them; and then, to show him that we are only imitators, not originators, we must read the following passage from the letter of an American soldier-lad in the Philippines to his mother, published in *Public Opinion*, of Decorah, Iowa, describing the finish of a victorious battle:

"WE NEVER LEFT ONE ALIVE. IF ONE WAS WOUNDED, WE WOULD RUN OUR BAYONETS THROUGH HIM."

. . .

Now then, that will convince the Person. You will see. It will restore the Business. Also, it will elect the Master of the Game to the vacant place in the Trinity of our national gods; and there on their high thrones the Three will sit, age after age, in the people's sight, each bearing the Emblem of his service: Washington, the Sword of the Liberator; Lincoln, the Slave's Broken Chains; the Master, the Chains Repaired.

. . .

[And as for a flag for the Philippine Province], it is easily managed. We can have a special one—our states do it: we can have just our usual flag, with the white stripes painted black and the stars replaced by the skull and crossbones.

STUDY QUESTIONS

1. How does Twain incorporate the language of the marketplace into this oration, and why?
2. Is Twain justified in seeing the conquest of the Philippines as a betrayal of American values and historical development?

9.5 KARL LUEGER, FIRST ANTI-SEMITIC SPEECH, OCTOBER 2, 1887

Karl Lueger (1844–1910), a lawyer and self-made man, made his reputation as a politician in Vienna, the capital of Austria-Hungary, by exploiting the deep anti-Jewish hostility of the late nineteenth century. Lueger assiduously courted the landed aristocracy as well as certain radical elements within the Catholic Church, but his primary constituency was the newly enfranchised lower middle class of skilled craftsmen and small shopkeepers. These groups were angry over their inability to compete with large factories and with the era's newest commercial institution, the department store. Lueger wooed these disaffected citizens by blaming the Jews, who were falsely believed to dominate the economy. His popularity earned him several terms as mayor of Vienna, an office he held until 1910, shortly after a young Austrian man named Adolf Hitler had come to live there.

For my part, I like to ignore the small differences which might exist between one or other of the parties about the method of the struggle; I have very little regard for words and names, and much more for the cause. Whether Democrat or anti-Semite, the matter really comes to one and the same thing. The Democrats in their struggle against corruption come up against the Jews at every step, and the anti-Semites, if they want to carry out their economic programme, have to overcome not only the bad Jews but the bad Christians also.

All my party comrades share my opinion that it is the first duty of a Democrat to take the side of the poor oppressed people and to take up the fight with all determination against the unjustified and even harmful domination of a small fraction of the population. To be sure, the Manchester-Liberal papers have the habit of describing a Democrat in somewhat different terms. They aim, for instance, that it would be the duty of such a Democrat to come forward as an enemy of the Christian religion, to mock and ridicule its believers and priests. But we know that the motive of such a manoeuvre is solely to mislead the people, which we may deduce from the remarkable fact that were anybody to come forward against the Jewish religion and ridicule its doctrines and believers he would be branded by the same organs as a reactionary obscurantist. However, this strange conception can be seen even more clearly in an economic question. Quite shamelessly the Liberal organs threaten the confiscation of the property of the Church and claim that the goods of the "dead hand" are harmful. By this means an attempt is made to divert the attention of the people from the property of the "living hand" which, in my view, harms the people in a most grievous way. But what a yell of rage would go up from the Liberal press if one were to substitute the slogan "confiscation of Church property" with the slogan "confiscation of the goods of the conscious, living hand!" He who would dare this would risk at once being portrayed as injuring the sacred rights of property, as an anarchist, a columnist who wanted to subvert the social order and destroy all existing things. And now I ask: is the title of property of the conscious, living hand stronger or more sacred than the title to the property of the Church? Surely not. And so it is more than extraordinary if one were to confiscate the property of the comparatively poor priests and through this help the rich of another denomination to increase their wealth!

STUDY QUESTIONS

1. How does Lueger conflate economic grievances with anti-Semitic charges? Why?
2. Why does Lueger bring up the concept of confiscating Church-owned lands? What does this reference suggest about his audience in late-nineteenth-century Vienna?

From Peter Pulzer, *The Rise of Political Anti-Semitism in Germany and Austria* (Cambridge, MA: Harvard University Press, 1964).

9.6 EMMELINE PANKHURST, *WHY WE ARE MILITANT*, OCTOBER 21, 1913

In 1903 Emmeline Pankhurst (1858–1928) re-animated the fight for women's suffrage in Britain by founding the Women's Social and Political Union (WSPU). She and her daughters, Christabel (1880–1958) and Sylvia (1882–1928), turned to militancy to win support for their campaign, calling for "Deeds, Not Words," and appropriating the techniques used by the Irish independence movement. WSPU supporters held giant marches and demonstrations, chained themselves to railings, rushed Parliament, damaged mailboxes, boycotted the census, and smashed windows. In 1913 they began a bombing campaign that targeted small businesses and private homes. When arrested, they went on hunger strikes; the government responded by force-feeding the women inmates with thick rubber tubes shoved down their throats. Force-feeding amounted to torture and called further attention to the government's heavy-handed response to the issue of women's suffrage.

In this speech, Pankhurst explains to an American audience why she feels violent protest is the best way for women to achieve political equality. Note the manner in which she addresses the men in her audience and how she links her struggle to those of other revolutions in the past, notably the American and French Revolutions.

know that in your minds there are questions like these; you are saying, "Woman Suffrage is sure to come; the emancipation of humanity is an evolutionary process, and how is it that some women, instead of trusting to that evolution, instead of educating the masses of people of their country, instead of educating their own sex to prepare them for citizenship, how is it that these militant women are using violence and upsetting the business arrangements of the country in their undue impatience to attain their end?"

Let me try to explain to you the situation.

Although we have a so-called democracy, and so-called representative government there, England is the most conservative country on earth. Why, your forefathers found that out a great many years ago! If you had passed your life in England as I have, you would know that there are certain words which certainly, during the last two generations, certainly till about ten years ago, arouse a feeling of horror and fear in the minds of the mass of the people. The word revolution, for instance, was identified in England with all kind of horrible ideas. The idea of change, the idea of unsettling the established order of things was repugnant.

. . . All my life I have people talking in advocacy of reforms which it was self-evident would be for the good of the people, and yet it has all ended in talk; they are still talking about these reforms, and unless something happens of a volcanic nature they will go on talking about it until the end of time. Nothing has ever been got out of the British Parliament without something very nearly approaching a revolution. You need something dynamic in order to force legislation through the House of Commons; in fact the whole machinery of government in England may almost be said to be an elaborate arrangement for not doing anything.

The extensions of the franchise to the men of my country have been preceded by very great violence, by something like a revolution, by something like civil war. . . .

Meanwhile, during the '80's, women, like men, were asking for the franchise. Appeals, larger and more numerous than for any other reform, were presented in support of Woman's Suffrage. . . . More

From Jane Marcus, *Suffrage and the Pankhursts* (London: Routledge & Keegan Paul, 1987), 153–162.

meetings were held, and larger, for Woman Suffrage than were held for votes for men, and yet the women did not get it. Men got the vote because they were and would be violent. The women did not get it because they were constitutional and law-abiding. . . .

Well, we in Great Britain, on the eve of the General Election of 1905, a mere handful of us—why, you could almost count us on the fingers of both hands—set out on the wonderful adventure of forcing the strongest Government of modern times to give the women the vote. . . .

The Suffrage movement was almost dead. The women had lost heart. You could not get a Suffrage meeting that was attended by members of the general public. . . .

Two women changed that in a twinkling of an eye at a great Liberal demonstration in Manchester, where a Liberal leader, Sir Edward Grey, was explaining the programme to be carried out during the Liberals' next turn of office. The two women put the fateful question, "When are you going to give votes to women?" and refused to sit down until they had been answered. These two women were sent to gaol, and from that day to this the women's movement, both militant and constitutional, has never looked back. We had little more than one moribund society for Woman Suffrage in those days. Now we have nearly 50 societies for Woman Suffrage, and they are large in membership, they are rich in money, and their ranks are swelling every day that passes . . .

I want to say here and now that the only justification for violence, the only justification for damage to property, the only justification for risk to the comfort of other human beings is the fact that you have tried all other available means and have failed to secure justice, and as a law-abiding person—and I am by nature a law-abiding person, as one hating violence, hating disorder—I want to say that from the moment we began our militant agitation to this day I have felt absolutely guiltless in this matter.

I tell you that in Great Britain there is no other way. . . .

We are fighting to get the power to alter bad laws; but some people say to us, "Go to the representatives in the House of Commons, point out to them that these laws are bad, and you will find them quite ready to alter them."

Ladies and gentlemen, there are women in my country who have spent long and useful lives trying to get reforms, and because of their vote-less condition, they are unable even to get the ear of Members of Parliament, much less are they able to secure those reforms.

Our marriage and divorce laws are a disgrace to civilisation. I sometimes wonder, looking back from the serenity of past middle age, at the courage of women. I wonder that women have the courage to take upon themselves the responsibilities of marriage and motherhood when I see how little protection the law of my country affords them. I wonder that a woman will face the ordeal of childbirth with the knowledge that after she has risked her life to bring a child into the world she has absolutely no parental rights over the future of that child. Think what trust women have in men when a woman will marry a man, knowing, if she has knowledge of the law, that if that man is not all she in her love for him thinks him, he may even bring a strange woman into the house, bring his mistress into the house to live with her, and she cannot get legal relief from such a marriage as that. . . .

. . . Yet women have done it, and as we get to know more of life we militant Suffragists have nerved ourselves and forced ourselves to learn how other people live. As we get that knowledge we realise how political power, how political influence, which would enable us to get better laws, would make it possible for thousands upon thousands of unhappy women to live happier lives. . . .

I want to ask you whether, in all the revolutions of the past, in your own revolt against British rule, you had deeper or greater reasons for revolt than women here to-day?

Take the industrial side of the question: have men's wages for a hard day's work ever been so low and inadequate as are women's wages today? Have men ever had to suffer from the laws, more injustice than women suffer? Is there a single reason which men have had for demanding liberty that does not also apply to women?

Why, if you were talking to the *men* of any other nation you would not hesitate to reply in the affirmative. There is not a man in this meeting who has not felt sympathy with the uprising of the men of other lands when suffering from intolerable tyranny, when deprived of all representative rights. . . .

All my life I have tried to understand why it is that men who value their citizenship as their dearest possession seem to think citizenship ridiculous when it is to be applied to the women of their race. And I find an explanation, and it is the only one I can think of. It came to me when I was in a prison cell, remembering how I had seen men laugh at the idea of women going to prison. Why they would confess they could not bear a cell door to be shut upon themselves for a single hour without asking to be let out. A thought came to me in my prison cell, and it was this: that to men women are not human beings like themselves. Some men think we are superhuman; they put us on pedestals; they revere us; they think we are too fine and too delicate to come down into the hurly-burly of life. Other men think us sub-human; they think we are a strange species unfortunately having to exist for the perpetuation of the race. They think that we are fit for drudgery, but that in some strange way our minds are not like theirs, our love for great things is not like theirs, and so we are a sort of subhuman species.

We are neither superhuman nor are we subhuman. We are just human beings like yourselves.

Our hearts burn within us when we read the great mottoes which celebrate the liberty of your country; when we go to France and we read the words, liberty, fraternity and equality, don't you think that we appreciate the meaning of those words? And then when we wake to the knowledge that these things are not for us, they are only for our brothers, then there comes a sense of bitterness into the hearts of some women, and they say to themselves, "Will men never understand?" But so far as we in England are concerned, we have come to the conclusion that we are not going to leave men any illusions upon the question. . . .

. . .You know perfectly well that if the situation were reversed, if you had no constitutional rights and we had all of them, if you had the duty of paying and obeying and trying to look as pleasant, and we were the proud citizens who could decide our fate and yours, because we knew what was good for you better than you knew yourselves, you know perfectly well that you wouldn't stand it for a single day, and you would be perfectly justified in rebelling against such intolerable conditions.

Well, in Great Britain, we have tried persuasion, we have tried the plan of showing (by going upon public bodies, where they allowed us to do work they hadn't much time to do themselves) that we are capable people. We did it in the hope that we should convince them and persuade them to do the right and proper thing. But we had all our labour for our pains, and now we are fighting for our rights, and we are growing stronger and better women in the process. We are getting more fit to use our rights because we have such difficulty in getting them. . . .

We know the joy of battle. When we have come out of the gates of Holloway at the point of death, battered, starved, forcibly fed as some of our women have been—their mouths forced open by iron gags—their bodies bruised, they have felt when the prison bars were broken and the doors have opened, even at the point of death, they have felt the joy of battle and the exultation of victory.

People have said that women could never vote, never share in the government, because government rests upon force. We have that this is not true. Government rests not upon force; government rests upon the consent of the governed; and the weakest woman, the very poorest woman, if she withholds her consent cannot be governed. . . .

And so we are glad we have had the fighting experience, and we are glad to do all the fighting for all the women all over the world. All that we ask of you is to back us up. We ask you to show that although, perhaps, you may not mean to fight as we do, yet you understand the meaning of our fight; that you realise we are women fighting for a great idea; that we wish the betterment of the human race, and that we believe this betterment is coming through the emancipation and uplifting of women.

STUDY QUESTIONS

1. According to Pankhurst, what caused a revival of the movement for women's suffrage in Britain, dormant since the failed struggle of the 1880s?
2. What did Pankhurst think women would gain by having a vote in Parliament? What kinds of rights and privileges did British women lack in 1913?

9.7 VISUAL SOURCE: IMPERIALISM BOARD GAME, SPAIN, C. NINETEENTH CENTURY

Historians of material culture draw meaning from a variety of objects. This *Game of Assault*, published in nineteenth-century Barcelona, is a strategy game played with dice, the goal being to conquer a country by advancing troops across the squares. The game highlight Spanish efforts against the Moors, probably from the war against Morocco; similar boards exist for French, Italian, and British conquests. The illustrations in the game's corners capture an attitude shared by many westerners: that invading other lands was a game. Quite apart from the profit and prestige to be gained from overseas expansion, the exploits of soldiers and adventurers in foreign lands fascinated people back home. Notice the representation of the Spanish soldiers–how they are dressed and the weapons they use compared with those of their enemy.

FIGURE 9.7 Imperialism Board Game

From http://www.giochidelloca.it/images/a/asalto1121a.jpg.

STUDY QUESTIONS

1. What do the images on the game show about the advantages held by Europeans in their encounters with locals in faraway places?
2. What kinds of values are conveyed to players of this game about Europeans' place in the world in this era?

TEXT RECONSTRUCTION AND COMPOSITION

In this set of exercises, you continue to follow in the footsteps of Benjamin Franklin, first arranging sentences into a coherent paragraph and then, a day later, writing the paragraph in your own words, using the notes provided and without looking back at the original.

EXERCISE: TEXT RECONSTRUCTION AND COMPOSITION

Instructions

Number the sentences below in the order in which you believe they appeared in the original. (Some of the numbering has been provided.) Then copy the paragraph verbatim on another sheet of paper. Please do not copy word by word. Instead, try to remember and transcribe five to ten words at a time.

1.

the old empires of Spain and Portugal had declined almost to nothing.

1 Before 1880, only Britain and France possessed colonies of any significance;

As for France, it controlled some dots of territory in West Africa, Southeast Asia, and the Caribbean but encouraged settlement only in Algeria, whose European population came mostly from Spain, Italy, Greece, and Malta rather than France.

True, Britain possessed a large "informal" empire of countries it dominated economically, but it did not seek to govern them.

And although Canada, Australia, and New Zealand still belonged to Britain's "formal" empire, these countries had become largely independent by the late nineteenth century.

3 And even Britain and France did not devote much attention to empire, with the great exceptions of India, crucial for British trade and political prestige, and Algeria, which France claimed in 1830 and struggled for 50 years to subdue.

At least two effective arrangements are possible for #2.

2.

In Great Britain, just 2,184 landowners, with an average of 5,000 acres each, possessed fully half of the country's property.

The rest belonged to smallholding peasants, who remained France's largest social group, despite substantial migration to cities and towns.

1 France's cacophony of political voices revealed considerably more social equality than existed in many of its European neighbors.

In France, 50,000 owners, averaging 250 acres each, together held only one-quarter of their country's land.

3.

To supply themselves with this material, the French, Germans, and Belgians looked longingly at the Congo, since the British and Americans already controlled the rubber trade in Brazil.

Bicycles and cars, for example, ran on tires made of rubber, a resource found mainly in the Congo and Amazon basins.

One of the key economic reasons for imperialism was the growing competition among the industrialized countries for the raw materials and natural resources crucial to their new technology and inventions but largely unavailable in Europe.

EXERCISE: TEXT (RE)COMPOSITION

Instructions

Once you have ordered the sentences in exercises 1–3, wait a day and then write your own versions of paragraphs 1 and 2, in your own words. Use the notes provided in 4 and 5 to remember the points that you need to cover, and do not look back at the originals until you are finished. Then compare your version to the original. Remember the principles of paragraph cohesion you practiced in Chapters 5 and 6:

1. **Beginning-to-beginning:** Content appearing in the beginning of a sentence reappears in the beginning of the next sentence.
2. **End-to-beginning:** Content toward the end of one sentence appears in the beginning of the next sentence.
3. **List of details:** A list of details follows a topic sentence.

And be sure to use pronouns (*this, those, another, his, their*) and synonyms to refer back to earlier content.

4.

PARAGRAPH TOPIC	Before 1880 only Britain and France had important colonies, but even Britain and France didn't care strongly about building empires
SUPPORTING IDEAS	• Before 1880 Spain and Portugal's empires declined to almost nothing
	• Before 1880 Britain and France cared only about India and Algeria
	England:
	• By 1880 Canada, Australia, and New Zealand were mostly independent
	• India was important for British trade and political prestige
	• Britain had a big "informal" empire of countries it didn't try to run
	• Britain dominated its informal empire economically
	France:
	• Settlers in Algeria mostly came from Spain, Italy, Malta, and Greece
	• Most settlers in Algeria did not come from France
	• France tried to subdue Algeria for 50 years, starting in 1830
	• In 1880, France encouraged Europeans to move to Algeria
	• By 1880, France had some tiny territories in Africa and the Caribbean

5.

PARAGRAPH TOPIC	France had more equality than other countries

SUPPORTING
IDEAS

England:
- 2,184 landowners owned half of all land; average of 5,000 acres per landowner

France:
- 50,000 landowners owned one quarter of all land; average of 250 acres per landowner
- Peasants owned three quarters of the land
- Peasants were the largest group even though many peasants had moved to the city.

You will find suggested answers to the exercises in the back of this book. For more Writing History exercises, as well as study resources for this chapter, visit oup.com/us/berenson.

CHAPTER 10

THE FIRST WORLD WAR, 1914–1919

10.1 SIEGFRIED SASSOON, "DOES IT MATTER?" AND "SUICIDE IN THE TRENCHES," 1918

The First World War drew an entire generation of young men into its vortex of death and destruction, transforming the lives of those who survived. No one reveals this process better than the British poet Siegfried Sassoon (1886–1967), whose autobiographical writings convey a powerful sense of the disillusionment war could produce and what it meant and felt like to be a soldier at the front.

The 28-year-old Sassoon rushed to enlist in his country's cause in 1914, but he soon lost many relatives and friends—and was himself wounded twice, once by a German sniper and once by friendly fire. By 1917, he was firmly a pacifist, writing a series of poems that chronicled both the horrors of the Western Front and the cynical ineptitude of his military superiors. Published as *Counter-Attack and Other Poems* (1918), these works made him one of the best known of Britain's "war poets."

Having survived the war, Sassoon's best poetry was behind him, but he wrote obsessively, publishing five volumes of poems in the 1920s before turning to prose. His three-part fictionalized memoir, based on real-time diary entries, not only provided a gripping account of the war but also helped shape the way future generations would perceive it. Sassoon found the entire Great War a futile, meaningless, and tragic waste, as these famous poems underscore.

Does It Matter?
DOES it matter?—losing your legs? . . .
For people will always be kind,
And you need not show that you mind
When the others come in after hunting
To gobble their muffins and eggs.
Does it matter?—losing your sight? . . .
There's such splendid work for the blind;

And people will always be kind,
As you sit on the terrace remembering
And turning your face to the light.
Do they matter?—those dreams from the pit? . . .
You can drink and forget and be glad,
And people won't say that you're mad;
For they'll know you've fought for your country
And no one will worry a bit.

Suicide in the Trenches
I knew a simple soldier boy
Who grinned at life in empty joy,
Slept soundly through the lonesome dark,
And whistled early with the lark.
In winter trenches, cowed and glum,
With crumps and lice and lack of rum,

He put a bullet through his brain.
No one spoke of him again.
You smug-faced crowds with kindling eye
Who cheer when soldier lads march by,
Sneak home and pray you'll never know
The hell where youth and laughter go.

STUDY QUESTIONS

1. Does Sassoon accurately predict the effects of the war, even after it reached its conclusion?
2. How does he contrast average civilian life with that of a soldier at the front? What are the consequences of this gap in knowledge?

10.2 ERNST JÜNGER, *BATTLE AS AN INNER EXPERIENCE*, 1929

German soldiers also produced beautifully worded—and equally frustrated—accounts of their time as soldiers in the "War That Will End War," as H. G. Wells termed it in 1914. Ernst Jünger (1895–1998) was wounded seven times in battle and received the highest military decoration of the German government for his exceptional bravery under fire. After the war he published his memoir, a graphic account of trench warfare based on his diaries and entitled *Storm of Steel* (*In Stahlgewittern*, 1920). By the late 1920s, he, like many young German combat veterans, was still trying to come to terms with what he had experienced in the trenches.

There are moments when from above the horizon of the mind a new constellation dazzles the eyes of all those who cannot find inner peace, an annunciation and storm-siren betokening a turning-point in world history, just as it once did for the kings from the East. From this point on the surrounding stars are engulfed in a fiery blaze, idols shatter into shards of clay, and everything that has taken shape hitherto is melted down in a thousand furnaces to be cast into new values.

The waves of such an age are surging around us from all sides. Brain, society, state, god, art, eros, morality: decay, ferment—resurrection? Still the images flit restlessly past our eyes, still the atoms seethe in the cauldrons of the city. And yet this tempest too will ebb, and even this lava stream will freeze into order. Every madness has always disintegrated against a grey wall, unless someone is found who harnesses it to his wagon with a fist of steel.

From Ernst Jünger, *Der Kampf als inneres Erlebnis* (Berlin: E. G. Mittler & Son, 1929), pp. xi–xv, 1–5, as quoted in Roger Griffin, *Fascism* (New York: Oxford University Press, 1995), pp. 108–109.

Why is it that our age in particular is so overflowing with destructive and productive energies? Why is this age in particular so pregnant with such enormous promise? For while much may perish in the feverish heat, the same flame is simultaneously brewing future wonders in a thousand retorts. A walk in the street, a glance in the newspaper is enough to confirm this, confounding all the prophets.

It is War which has made human beings and their age what they are. Never before has a race of men like ours stridden into the arena of the earth to decide who is to wield power over the epoch. For never before has a generation entered the daylight of life from a gateway so dark and awesome as when they emerged from this War. And this we cannot deny, no matter how much some would like to: War, father of all things, is also ours; he has hammered us, chiselled and tempered us into what we are. . . .

As sons of an age intoxicated by matter, progress seemed to us perfection, the machine the key to godliness, telescopes and microscopes organs of enlightenment. Yet underneath the ever more polished exterior, beneath all the clothes in which we bedecked ourselves, we remained naked and raw like men of the forest and the steppes.

That showed itself when the War ripped asunder the community of Europe, when we confronted each other in a primordial contest behind flags and symbols which many sceptics had long mocked. Then it was that, in an orgy of frenzy, the true human being made up for everything he had missed. At this point his drives, too long pent up by society and its laws, became once more the ultimate form of reality, holiness, and reason. . . .

What actually went on? The carriers of War and its creatures, human beings, whose lives had to lead towards War and through Him, were flung into new paths, new goals. This is what we were to Him, but what was He to us? That is a question which many now seek to ask. This is what these pages are concerned with.

STUDY QUESTIONS

1. Why could the First World War not have happened at it did earlier in history?
2. How was war, in Jünger's opinion, comparable to a communicable disease that is endemic to the human species? Is he correct?

10.3 C. E. W. BEAN, *THE OFFICIAL HISTORY OF AUSTRALIA IN THE WAR OF 1914–1918*, 1941

After the First World War ended in November 1918, all of the Allied nations undertook official or authorized histories of the conflict. Perhaps unintentionally, some of these projects revealed serious errors of judgment on the part of military commanders and the terrible loss of life that resulted from their decisions. One of the costliest and most futile campaigns of the war occurred on the Gallipoli Peninsula, the narrow finger of land separating the European and Asian parts of

From C.E.W. Bean, The Story of ANZAC from 4 May, 1915, to the evacuation of the Gallipoli Peninsula, *The Official History of Australia in the War of 1914–1918*, Volume 2 (Sydney: Angus and Robertson, 1941)

Turkey. In this excerpt from his multivolume history of Australian war efforts, C. E. W. Bean describes the attempt by Allied forces to land in Gallipoli on their way to capture the Ottoman capital Constantinople (Istanbul).

The campaign proved a disastrous failure. The Allies underestimated the Ottoman Turks' strength and coordinated their own efforts poorly. The Australian and New Zealand Army Corps (ANZAC) suffered particularly heavy losses, and leaders of these two countries later blamed the British for using their men as cannon fodder in an ill-conceived military campaign. The screenplay for the award-winning film *Gallipoli* (1981) was adapted from an incident described in Bean's work. The excerpt below recounts another segment of the battle and highlights the incompetence of the war effort and the toll it took on the ANZAC soldiers.

Perceiving the difficulty of advancing under such an enfilade, Major Powles directed the next platoons to swing to the left and advance northwards or north-eastwards in order to subdue the fire from that direction. This attempt was quickly shattered. A part of the third company, under Major Lane, advancing towards Goodsell's left, succeeded in reaching the same trench and pushed along it towards the east. These later lines, however, only reached the trench in fragments, and the situation of the left flank was desperate. From a point of vantage in a cross-trench the Turks were flinging bombs with impunity among the Australians. An unauthorised order to retire had been given to some of Lane's men, and in withdrawing over the open they had lost heavily. At 7 o'clock the battalion was urged by a message from Russell to push on and seize the summit, but such an attempt would have been hopeless. Goodsell's left gradually withdrew southward along the trench. With such parts of the later lines as reached him he had extended farther to his right along the same sap and, finding there some of the Hampshire, discovered that he was actually in the trench which had been captured by the New Zealanders, and which encircled the lower slope of the hill. By 10 o'clock the remnant of Goodsell's men had retired along it until they reached the flank of the New Zealanders, where they remained, stubbornly holding fifty yards of the trench.

The attempt to round off the capture of Hill 60 by setting a raw battalion, without reconnaissance, to rush the main part of a position on which the experienced troops of Anzac had only succeeded in obtaining a slight foothold, ended in failure. Its initiation was due to the fact that Russell and his brigade-major, Powles, both careful and capable officers, lacked the realisation—which came to many commanders only after sharp experience—that the attack upon such a position required minute preparation, and that the unskillfulness of raw troops, however brave, was likely to involve them in heavy losses for the sake of results too small to justify the expense. Within a few hours the 18th Battalion, which appears to have marched out 750 strong, had lost 11 officers and 372 men, of whom half had been killed. The action had been a severe one for all the troops engaged, the losses of the comparatively small force which attacked from Anzac amounting to over 1,300. The flank had been brought up to Susak Kuyu, and a lodgment had been obtained in the enemy's strongly entrenched position at Hill 60. Slight though it was, this gain was the only one achieved on the whole battle-front. In the Suvla area the position at first secured by the 29th Division on the crest of Scimitar Hill was untenable, a brave advance by the reserve—the 2nd Mounted Division—availing nothing. On the plain the 11th Division was unable to maintain its unconnected line in the first Turkish trench. A barricade built across the Asmak creek-bed was blown down by the enemy, and the British flank was forced back to Kazlar Chair, from which it had started, 1,000 yards in rear of the Gurkha post at Susak Kuyu, the Turks still intervening near the "poplars." To fill this dangerous space, the 19th Battalion of the new Australian brigade was marched to the left and stationed near the gap. Cox reported that he believed the new line could be held, although the position on Hill 60 "cannot be considered satisfactory."

If the Battle of Sari Bair was the climax of the Gallipoli campaign, that of Scimitar Hill was its anticlimax. With it the great offensive ended. In the words of Kitchener's message received by Hamilton on July 11th: ". . . When the surprise ceases to be operative, in so far that the advance is checked and the enemy begin to collect from all sides to oppose the attackers, then perseverance becomes merely a useless waste of life." The attempt to prolong the offensive by driving through the flank of the enemy's now established trench-line had utterly failed; and Hamilton had not the troops, nor had all the troops the morale, necessary for a fresh attack. Birdwood, however, in agreement with his subordinate commanders, desired to strengthen his flank by capturing the summit of Hill 60, and he obtained leave to renew this effort on August 27th.

The two regiments of the mounted rifles, Otago and Canterbury, which had won the footing on the hill—together with a number of Maoris who had reinforced them, and the fragments of the 18th Battalion-were relieved on the night of August 23rd by the two remaining regiments of the Mounted Rifles Brigade, which had been brought into General Cox's area for the purpose. The 4th Australian Brigade, which was equally weary, was strengthened by the addition of the 17th Battalion from the new Australian brigade. Except for a dangerous enfilade by a Turkish battery near Hill 971 on the main range, the New Zealanders at the foot of Hill 60 were not seriously disturbed. The Turks were, however, at work nightly upon the upper part of the hill, and the New Zealand Howitzer Battery, which shot exceedingly well, was directed to hinder them by firing during the dark. It was decided that the attack should be made by the same units which had undertaken the previous assault. Repeated demands had, however, already been made on these troops. Moreover, the number of men who were being sent away through sickness was so great that general orders appear to have been issued to the medical service to exercise greater strictness. Accordingly the chief medical officer of the N.Z. & A. Division urged upon his subordinates that no man should be sent away who was fit, not to fight, but

to stand in a trench and hold a rifle. A consequence of the sickness and previous losses was that the assaulting force-on this occasion 1000 strong-was necessarily composed of numerous small detachments, each consisting of comparatively fit men from a number of regiments. . . .

As the attempt was certain to be met by heavy fire of all arms, General Russell, Colonel Monash, and all their officers, relying on the ability of colonial troops to find their way in the dark, favoured a night attack without bombardment. General Cox, however, decided to attack by daylight, having first crushed the opposition by an hour's heavy shelling. The available land artillery consisted of forty-five guns and howitzers, most of which were to bombard Hill 60 and the spur leading to it, while the cruisers *Talbot* and *Grafton* and two destroyers, together with some of the land guns, covered the approaches and silenced the enemy's batteries on the main range. The bombardment was to commence at 4, the troops at 5 o'clock assaulting Hill 60 on three sides.

The course of the fight which followed—one of the most difficult in which Australian troops were ever engaged—was conditioned by the inaccuracy of the knowledge which the staff had so far succeeded in obtaining of the complicated defences of the hill. The simple method which was applied a few years later—that of sending an aeroplane to photograph the region from above—does not seem to have suggested itself, and the local staff based its maps upon what it could see from the front line on Damakjelik and from the Suvla area. But the hill was clothed with scrub four feet high, through which the trenches were difficult to trace. . . .

. . . The bombardment upon Hill 60 was heavy. But for some reason, although General Russell had urged that special attention should be given to the trenches facing the Australian detachment, these were not bombarded. Only two shells of small calibre are said to have fallen upon them; so far, indeed, as this sector was concerned, the bombardment merely served to announce to the enemy that he was about to be attacked. While the men in the advanced trench awaited the order to charge, hostile rifle and machine-gun fire was tearing the parapet above their heads. When the whistle blew, and Captain Connelly of the 14th led out the first line on to the wheatfield, it was at once swept away. Connelly, who had just returned from sick leave, was hit in three places and killed, and Captain Graham wounded. Captain Cooper with eight men got as far as a smaller oaktree, growing near the larger one, and lay there in the shelter of a low hedge. eventually crawling back with a few survivors.

The line which attempted to charge up the little re-entrant was annihilated, except on the extreme left near the New Zealanders; there a few men, swerving somewhat to their left, succeeded in reaching the point "B1" on the extreme flank of their objective, and joined the New Zealanders. Meanwhile the Turks, standing breast-high along their trench to shoot at the attacking party, had been observed by Captain Black of the 16th, who swept their parapet with his machine-gun, and one of Fergusson's mountain-guns burst shell after shell on the edge of the trench. But the assault by the Australian detachment had already completely failed, and, two-thirds of his men and all his officers, except Captain Cooper, being killed or wounded, Colonel Adams did not call upon his reserves. The fighting on the right flank therefore quickly ended.

. . .

Thus ended the action at Hill 60. Birdwood believed that the actual knoll had been captured, and so reported to Hamilton, who wrote: "Knoll 60, now ours throughout, commands the Biyuk Anafarta valley with view and fire—a big tactical scoop." As a matter of fact half the summit—or possibly rather more—was still in possession of the Turks. The fighting of August 27th, 28th, and 29th had, however, given the troops on the left of Anzac a position astride the spur from which a fairly satisfactory view could be had over the plain to the "W" Hills. The cost was over 1,100 casualties. The burden of the work had been sustained by war-worn troops. The magnificent brigade of New Zealand Mounted Rifles, which was responsible for the main advances, had been worked until it was almost entirely consumed, its four regiments at the end numbering only 365 all told. The 4th Australian Infantry Brigade which, through defective co-ordination with the artillery, had been twice thrown against a difficult objective without a chance of success, was reduced to 968. General Russell and his brigade-major, Powles, had worked untiringly, the latter personally guiding almost every attacking party to its starting point in the dangerous maze of trenches. It was not their fault that at this stage of the war both staff and commanders were only learning the science of trench-warfare. Had the experience and the instruments of later years been available, the action at Hill 60 would doubtless have been fought differently.

STUDY QUESTIONS

1. What factors, in Bean's estimation, led to the very high casualty figures among the Allied troops in this campaign?
2. Did Bean consider the loss of these troops a "useless waste of life"? Were the leaders of the effort incompetent?

10.4 ARNO DOSCH-FLEUROT, INTERVIEW WITH MARY GOTOUBYOVA, JULY 31, 1917

Arno Dosch-Fleurot (1879–1951), was an American journalist stationed in Europe during the First World War. The son of a German immigrant, he gained fame as a war correspondent, covering the Russian Revolution and conflicts in Eastern Europe and Ireland.

In this column, published in the *Chicago Daily Tribune*, he describes meeting Mary Gotoubyova (1899–?), an 18-year-old soldier fighting on the Eastern Front. Nothing else is known about Gotoubyova, except that she was one of the small number of Russian women allowed to serve openly as soldiers at the front in the First Russian Women's Battalion of Death. This all-female fighting unit had been formed by Maria Bochkareva both to promote women's equality and to shame recalcitrant men into fighting. The idea of women in combat was very new, and only Russia committed to accepting women *en masse* into the military; some individual women served in other nations, mostly in secret as cross-dressers or in individual cases of a nurse separated from her base. Most countries were grappling with the novelty of seeing women in public roles, such as working in factories or conducting buses and trams. Many felt threatened by the appearance of independent women working outside the home with their own incomes, not to mention women involved in the business of killing. Note how Dosch-Fleurot frames Gotoubyova's testimony about being a patriotic soldier with descriptions of her physical beauty and charm, trying to make her story more palatable to his American readers.

RUSSIAN GIRL, FIRST TO SLAY FOE, IS WOUNDED: MODEST HEROINE TELLS OF BATTLE IN WHICH WOMEN FOUGHT.

PETROGRAD, July 30—The story of the first girl in the woman's battalion who killed a German has just been given me by the heroine herself as she lay in the hospital, wounded.

She is Mary Gotoubyova, an 18 year old high school student. Mary is tall and graceful, with pretty blue eyes, her blonder hair, now short, giving her the appearance of a handsome boy. Laughing at the wounds which caused her to be sent to the hospital, she showed her brilliant white teeth. Even the rough hospital nightgown could not conceal her well developed, beautiful figure.

Dictating to me her tale, she constantly made girlish gestures. She hid her face in her pillow and blushed when I asked her if admirers had objected to her going to the front. She trifled with a locket and a little bag at her neck. On asking, I learned the bag contained cyanide of potassium in case she was captured. In the battalion all carried the same.

HEROINE TELLS HER STORY.

"I am wounded they say. I call it mere scratches," she said, "but it may keep me from the front several weeks after only two days' fighting. At any rate, I was in the front trenches and I got my German. I am feeling better already, and hope I go right back. I must go; my country needs me. That is why I enlisted.

"I saw soldiers in Petrograd demanding not to be sent to the front, and I realized that the country needed every man and woman who was not a coward. Then the woman's battalion was formed and I joined

From *Chicago Daily Tribune*, July 31, 1917, available at www.newspapers.com.

immediately. I have never regretted it. I was never afraid, and I ask only the privilege to bear a gun against the enemy again. I must fill the place of men who will not fight.

FORGOT SHE WAS A WOMAN.

"Going to war is not too much for a woman. I was always strong. Still, being a woman, I wondered if it would be too fatiguing. Once at the front, I forgot whether I was a man or a woman. I was just a soldier. The only preparation I made against contact with the enemy was to wrap the upper portion of my body firmly. In the burning battle I was never hampered for an instant on account of my sex. The soldiers, the real brave soldiers, treated me like a comrade. Only the cowards jeered.

"We went into action a fortnight after our arrival at the front, under heavy German fire. Given the order to advance, we rushed out of our trenches.

KILLED A GERMAN.

"After the first attack I was attached to a machine gun, carrying ammunition to advanced position under the fire of hidden German machine guns. We were advancing and constantly in danger of capture by the Germans. On one trip over newly captured ground I saw what I considered a wounded German officer lying on the ground. I went to help him with my gun in my right hand and the machine gun ammunition in my left.

"Seeing me he jumped to his knees and pulled out his revolver, but before could shoot I dropped the ammunition and killed him.

READY TO DIE FOR RUSSIA.

"How did I feel on taking a human life? I had no sensation, except to rid my country of an enemy. There was no sentimentality. We were trying to kill them and they were trying to kill us—that is all. Any Russian girl or any American girl in the same position would have the same feeling.

"No, I do not feel that I did anything exceptional. Any well girl can do the same.

"I never knew when I was hit. Shells were breaking everywhere. One got me. The next time one may really get me."

As she finished dictating, the girl took her cap from a table beside the bed, put it on at a fetching angle, and gave a comic salute. Then suddenly overcome with blushes, she hid her face in the pillow.

STUDY QUESTIONS

1. How did Gotoubyova understand her life as a soldier? How did she account for her status as a woman doing what had always been thought of as a man's job?
2. How did Dosch-Fleurot describe Gotoubyova to his American audience? Was he impressed or dismissive of her accomplishments on the battlefield? Would a reader be more likely to support expanding women's roles after reading this account?

10.5 WOODROW WILSON, *THE FOURTEEN POINTS*, JANUARY 8, 1918

Even before the First World War ended, President Woodrow Wilson (1856–1924) articulated his vision for the postwar order in his famous Fourteen Points speech presented on January 8, 1918, to the United States Congress. The Fourteen Points framed much of the discussion at the Paris Peace Conference in 1919, which Wilson attended in person—the first sitting American president to travel abroad. Wilson enjoyed great esteem among European populations, if not among their leaders, and he used his prestige and popularity to exhort his counterparts to enact his idealistic Fourteen Points. His call for national self-determination held widespread appeal, but in practice, not every aspirant nation was allowed to determine its own fate, leaving a huge gap between Wilsonian ideals and the realities of geopolitics. Millions of people remained unsatisfied after the war's end, including those in the Middle East who were now subjected to a new form of colonial rule.

Gentlemen of the Congress . . .

It will be our wish and purpose that the processes of peace, when they are begun, shall be absolutely open and that they shall involve and permit henceforth no secret understandings of any kind. The day of conquest and aggrandizement is gone by; so is also the day of secret covenants entered into in the interest of particular governments and likely at some unlooked-for moment to upset the peace of the world. It is this happy fact, now clear to the view of every public man whose thoughts do not still linger in an age that is dead and gone, which makes it possible for every nation whose purposes are consistent with justice and the peace of the world to avow nor or at any other time the objects it has in view.

We entered this war because violations of right had occurred which touched us to the quick and made the life of our own people impossible unless they were corrected and the world secure once for all against their recurrence. What we demand in this war, therefore, is nothing peculiar to ourselves. It is that the world be made fit and safe to live in; and particularly that it be made safe for every peace-loving nation which, like our own, wishes to live its own life, determine its own institutions, be assured of justice and fair dealing by the other peoples of the world as against force and selfish aggression. All the peoples of the world are in effect partners in this interest, and for our own part we see very clearly that unless justice be done to others it will not be done to us. The program of the world's peace, therefore, is our program; and that program, the only possible program, as we see it, is this:

I.   Open covenants of peace, openly arrived at, after which there shall be no private international understandings of any kind but diplomacy shall proceed always frankly and in the public view.

II. Absolute freedom of navigation upon the seas, outside territorial waters, alike in peace and in war, except as the seas may be closed in whole or in part by international action for the enforcement of international covenants.

III. The removal, so far as possible, of all economic barriers and the establishment of an equality of

From https://kr.usembassy.gov/education-culture/infopedia-usa/living-documents-american-history-democracy/woodrow-wilson-fourteen-points-speech-1918/.

trade conditions among all the nations consenting to the peace and associating themselves for its maintenance.

IV. Adequate guarantees given and taken that national armaments will be reduced to the lowest point consistent with domestic safety.

V. A free, open-minded, and absolutely impartial adjustment of all colonial claims, based upon a strict observance of the principle that in determining all such questions of sovereignty the interests of the populations concerned must have equal weight with the equitable claims of the government whose title is to be determined.

VI. The evacuation of all Russian territory and such a settlement of all questions affecting Russia as will secure the best and freest cooperation of the other nations of the world in obtaining for her an unhampered and unembarrassed opportunity for the independent determination of her own political development and national policy and assure her of a sincere welcome into the society of free nations under institutions of her own choosing; and, more than a welcome, assistance also of every kind that she may need and may herself desire. The treatment accorded Russia by her sister nations in the months to come will be the acid test of their good will, of their comprehension of her needs as distinguished from their own interests, and of their intelligent and unselfish sympathy.

VII. Belgium, the whole world will agree, must be evacuated and restored, without any attempt to limit the sovereignty which she enjoys in common with all other free nations. No other single act will serve as this will serve to restore confidence among the nations in the laws which they have themselves set and determined for the government of their relations with one another. Without this healing act the whole structure and validity of international law is forever impaired.

VIII. All French territory should be freed and the invaded portions restored, and the wrong done to France by Prussia in 1871 in the matter of Alsace-Lorraine, which has unsettled the peace of the world for nearly fifty years, should be righted, in order that peace may once more be made secure in the interest of all.

IX. A readjustment of the frontiers of Italy should be effected along clearly recognizable lines of nationality.

X. The peoples of Austria-Hungary, whose place among the nations we wish to see safeguarded and assured, should be accorded the freest opportunity to autonomous development.

XI. Rumania, Serbia, and Montenegro should be evacuated; occupied territories restored; Serbia accorded free and secure access to the sea; and the relations of the several Balkan states to one another determined by friendly counsel along historically established lines of allegiance and nationality; and international guarantees of the political and economic independence and territorial integrity of the several Balkan states should be entered into.

XII. The Turkish portion of the present Ottoman Empire should be assured a secure sovereignty, but the other nationalities which are now under Turkish rule should be assured an undoubted security of life and an absolutely unmolested opportunity of autonomous development, and the Dardanelles should be permanently opened as a free passage to the ships and commerce of all nations under international guarantees.

XIII. An independent Polish state should be erected which should include the territories inhabited by indisputably Polish populations, which should be assured a free and secure access to the sea, and whose political and economic independence and territorial integrity should be guaranteed by international covenant.

XIV. A general association of nations must be formed under specific covenants for the purpose of affording mutual guarantees of political independence and territorial integrity to great and small states alike.

In regard to these essential rectifications of wrong and assertions of right we feel ourselves to be intimate partners of all the governments and peoples associated together against the Imperialists. We cannot be separated in interest or divided in purpose. We stand together until the end.

For such arrangements and covenants we are willing to fight and to continue to fight until they are achieved; but only because we wish the right to prevail and desire a just and stable peace such as can be secured only by removing the chief provocations to war, which this program does remove. We have no jealousy of German greatness, and there is nothing in this program that impairs it. We grudge her no achievement or distinction of learning or of pacific enterprise such as have made her record very bright and very enviable. We do not wish to injure her or to block in any way her legitimate influence or power. We do not wish to fight her either with arms or with hostile arrangements of trade if she is willing to associate herself with us and the other peace-loving nations of the world in covenants of justice and law and fair dealing. We wish her only to accept a place of equality among the peoples of the world,—the new world in which we now live,—instead of a place of mastery.

Neither do we presume to suggest to her any alteration or modification of her institutions. But it is necessary, we must frankly say, and necessary as a preliminary to any intelligent dealings with her on our part, that we should know whom her spokesmen speak for when they speak to us, whether for the Reichstag majority or for the military party and the men whose creed is imperial domination.

We have spoken now, surely, in terms too concrete to admit of any further doubt or question. An evident principle runs through the whole program I have outlined. It is the principle of justice to all peoples and nationalities, and their right to live on equal terms of liberty and safety with one another, whether they be strong or weak. Unless this principle be made its foundation no part of the structure of international justice can stand. The people of the United States could act upon no other principle; and to the vindication of this principle they are ready to devote their lives, their honor, and everything they possess. The moral climax of this the culminating and final war for human liberty has come, and they are ready to put their own strength, their own highest purpose, their own integrity and devotion to the test.

STUDY QUESTIONS

1. What main principles underlie Wilson's idealistic vision?
2. What measures did Wilson assume would preserve peace in the postwar world?

10.6 JOHN MAYNARD KEYNES, *THE ECONOMIC CONSEQUENCES OF THE PEACE*, 1920

Germany's representatives at the Versailles Peace Conference in 1919 bitterly opposed most provisions of the treaty that had been drafted. They argued that the punitive measures it contained would frustrate efforts to rebuild their damaged economy and to re-create imperial Germany as a stable democratic state. The economic weakness the treaty imposed on their country, they maintained, would also shackle the rest of the European economy, which depended on trade with an economically viable Germany. These points were echoed and endorsed by the economist John Maynard Keynes (1883–1946), who participated in the British delegation at Versailles, in an extraordinarily influential book entitled *The Economic Consequences of the Peace*.

From J. M. Keynes, *The Economic Consequences of the Peace* (New York: Harcourt, 1920; Penguin edition, 1988), pp. 216–225.

In fact, the treaty did not hamstring the German economy or turn it into a second-rate power, although the onerous reparations payments imposed on Germany at Versailles would play a major role in the German hyperinflation of 1923. Keynes had argued against reparations, and on this point, he proved to be right. Because the inflation proved so devastating, the British and American governments ultimately agreed with Keynes on reparations; after 1923, they only lightly enforced them while offering Germany lenient terms for repaying wartime debts.

The comments on this of the German Financial Commission at Versailles were hardly an exaggeration:—"German democracy is thus annihilated at the very moment when the German people was about to build it up after a severe struggle—annihilated by the very persons who throughout the war never tired of maintaining that they sought to bring democracy to us. . . . Germany is no longer a people and a State, but becomes a mere trade concern placed by its creditors in the hands of a receiver, without its being granted so much as the opportunity to prove its willingness to meet its obligations of its own accord. The Commission, which is to have its permanent headquarters outside Germany, will possess in Germany incomparably greater rights than the German Emperor ever possessed; the German people under its régime would remain for decades to come shorn of all rights, and deprived, to a far greater extent than any people in the days of absolutism, of any independence of action, of any individual aspiration in its economic or even in its ethical progress."

In their reply to these observations the Allies refused to admit that there was any substance, ground, or force in them. "The observations of the German Delegation," they pronounced, "present a view of this Commission so distorted and so inexact that it is difficult to believe that the clauses of the Treaty have been calmly or carefully examined. It is not an engine of oppression or a device for interfering with German sovereignty. It has no forces at its command; it has no executive powers within the territory of Germany; it cannot, as is suggested, direct or control the educational or other systems of the country. Its business is to ask what is to be paid; to satisfy itself that Germany can pay; and to report to the Powers, whose delegation it is, in case Germany makes default. If Germany raises the money required in her own way, the Commission cannot order that it shall be raised in some other way; if Germany offers payment in kind, the Commission may accept such payment, but, except as specified in the Treaty itself, the Commission cannot require such a payment."

This is not a candid statement of the scope and authority of the Reparation Committee, as will be seen by a comparison of its terms with the summary given above or with the Treaty itself. . . .

I cannot leave this subject as though its just treatment wholly depended either on our own pledges or on economic facts. The policy of reducing Germany to servitude for a generation, of degrading the lives of millions of human beings, and of depriving a whole nation of happiness should be abhorrent and detestable,—abhorrent and detestable, even if it were possible, even if it enriched ourselves, even if it did not sow the decay of the whole civilized life of Europe. Some preach it in the name of Justice. In the great events of man's history, in the unwinding of the complex fates of nations Justice is not so simple. And if it were, nations are not authorized, by religion or by natural morals, to visit on the children of their enemies the misdoings of parents or of rulers.

STUDY QUESTIONS

1. Could one justify the stance of the Allies, in spite of Keynes' criticism?
2. Was Keynes making a reasonable case for the consequences of this peace, especially for German democracy?

10.7 VISUAL SOURCE: KÄTHE KOLLWITZ, *THE GRIEVING PARENTS*, 1932

In 1914, Peter Kollwitz (1895–1914), the 18-year-old only child of Käthe and Karl Kollwitz, signed up to fight in the first wave of German volunteers and was killed only 10 days after departing for the front. Consumed with grief, his parents left his childhood bedroom intact for years, creating a household shrine that they graced with flowers each year on his birthday. They lit eighteen candles on their Christmas tree in the first year of the war, then added one candle in each subsequent year as a reminder of the adult he would have become had he survived.

Käthe Kollwitz (1867–1945) was an artist well versed in multiple types of media whose work focused on women and the working class. In her grief, she created the pair of granite sculptures pictured here as a memorial to her son and his friends who died in the war. We see a mother and father lost in sorrow, separated not only from their child but also from each other. Both are on their knees as if in prayer, the mother doubled over, seemingly in pain, the father staring grimly ahead at his son's grave with his arms wrapped tightly around himself, as if to contain his grief. *The Grieving Parents* took Kollwitz years to design, but the figures were sculpted by other artists. Kollwitz exhibited the completed pair in Berlin's National Gallery before it was installed in the Roggeveld military cemetery in Belgium overlooking the graves of German dead. When the Nazis came to power, they classified Kollwitz's work as "degenerate" and removed it from art galleries nationwide. In 1956 the *Grieving Parents* memorial moved three miles, along with Peter's grave and those of 25,000 other Germans, to their current site at Vladslo German Military cemetery.

FIGURE 10.7   Käthe Kollwitz

STUDY QUESTIONS

1. What does Kollwitz's memorial reveal to later generations about the First World War?
2. What role does gender identity play both in the creation of this memorial and in its depiction of a man and a woman? What does the memorial say about how contemporaries thought about masculinity and femininity in this era?

PAPER RECONSTRUCTION

In this exercise, you will reconstruct the order of paragraphs in a student paper written for a survey course in modern European history.

The prompt: In his essay, "Thoughts for the Times on War and Death," Sigmund Freud wrote: "Our mortification and painful disillusionment on account of the uncivilized behavior of our fellow-citizens of the world during this war were unjustified. They were based on an illusion to which we had given way. In reality our fellow-citizens have not sunk so low as we feared, because they had never risen so high as we believed."

Please write an essay that analyses Freud's view of human nature and human behavior and compares his view with those represented in at least THREE of the following sources: Ernest Renan, Joseph Conrad, Erich Maria Remarque, Wilfred Owen, and Alexandra Kollontai.

"THE REFLECTIONS OF SIGMUND FREUD AND HIS CONTEMPORARIES ON WORLD WAR I"

Instructions

Number the paragraphs in the order in which you believe they appeared in the original. Some of the numbering has been provided.

---

1 In "Thoughts for the Times on War and Death" (1915), Freud maintains that the common attitude of shock and disillusionment over the brutality and bloodshed of World War I reveals the public's ignorance about human nature. Freud argues that "civilized" Europeans have always been capable of terrible violence, since violence is inherent to human beings. Joseph Conrad largely shares Freud's view, while Ernest Renan and Erich Maria Remarque differ from both of them in maintaining that it is the state or other forces external to individuals that move them to act violently.

Even before 1914, Conrad anticipated Freud's beliefs about the violence inherent to human beings. In *Heart of Darkness* (1899), Conrad portrays the unspeakable acts of brutality that "civilized" European imperialists committed against the native peoples of Africa's Congo region. Colonialism, declares Marlow, the book's protagonist, is "just robbery with violence, aggravated murder on a great scale, and men going at it blind" (Conrad, 7). Throughout his novel, Conrad suggests that individuals who behaved peacefully in Europe readily turned to violence in Africa, where there was no civilization to suppress their instincts.

2 Addressing the public shock over the brutality of World War I, Freud writes, "our mortification and our painful disillusionment over the uncivilized behavior of our fellow-citizens of the world during this war were unjustified," based as they were on "an illusion to which we had given way" (Freud, 5–6). This "illusion" is the idea that the advanced state of civilization in Europe cured people of their natural capacity for violence. In fact, Freud says, society has merely "forced its members into . . . an unceasing suppression of instinct." During wartime, those instincts are no longer suppressed, resulting in the extreme violence of the war (Freud, 5).

Had he lived long enough to witness the First World War, Renan would have recognized, as Freud and Conrad did, that the violence of World War I was not unprecedented. Where Renan differs from Freud and Conrad is in his beliefs about the origins of this violence. Renan thinks it comes from sources external to individuals, especially religion and the state, and not from their own inherent inclinations, as Freud and Conrad believe.

4 Like Conrad, Ernest Renan anticipated Freud with regard to the European capacity for violence. In "What Is a Nation" (1882), Renan maintains that even within Europe itself, nations and peoples have throughout history been extraordinarily violent and bloodthirsty. The St. Bartholomew's Day massacre (1572), for example, left some five thousand French Protestants dead. Events such as this are so terrible, Renan writes, that people must forget them in order to coexist as members of the same nation (Renan, 145). It is no surprise, then, that by the time World War I erupted, the European populace had forgotten the atrocious violence of the past.

Although World War I turned the world upside down and horrified those who lived through it, there were thinkers and writers who saw the Great War as just another expression of the brutality that had long been a part of "civilized" European culture. These writers differed, however, in their views of the sources of this violence—whether it came from within the individual or without. Less than 25 years after the end of the war, another bloody conflict would take the lives of an estimated 60 million people and revive this debate. Was violence innate to human beings or the result of living under governments that regularly called for violence to achieve their ends?

At certain times, the state, in particular, encourages people to be merciless and violent, as the novelist Erich Maria Remarque underscores. In Remarque's *All Quiet on the Western Front* (1929), a young German soldier named Paul declares that the state has made him into a killing machine. Speaking of the enemy, Paul remarks, "a word of command has made these silent figures our enemies" (Remarque, 193–194). Here, the motivation to kill comes not from the individual himself, but from a command given by an authority figure representing the state. Unlike Freud, Remarque suggests that the individual has no inherent desire to kill.

EXERCISE: TEXT (RE)COMPOSITION

Instructions

Once you have ordered the paragraphs, wait a day before writing your own version of the paper. Reconstruct **PARAGRAPH 1**—the introduction—via the following steps:

Introduce the subject matter of the paper by summarizing the main idea of Freud's essay, "Thoughts for the Times on War and Death."

Construct a THESIS STATEMENT that includes the following elements:

- Conrad shares Freud's views about the sources of violence.
- Renan and Remarque differ from Freud and Conrad.
- Renan and Remarque think violence comes from forces outside the individual.

Reconstruct **PARAGRAPHS 2–6** by opening each paragraph with the main idea or TOPIC. Then, elaborate on the topic by including three SUPPORTING IDEAS. For each paragraph, the topic and supporting ideas are given below; your task is to shape them into an essay using the principles of effective writing we have studied so far.

Paragraph 2

TOPIC:
- According to Freud, our disillusionment over the uncivilized behavior of the war is unjustified.

SUPPORTING IDEAS:
- People are disillusioned because they are suffering from an illusion.
- The illusion is that civilization has cured people of their violent tendencies.
- Instead, civilization has merely suppressed their violent instincts.

Paragraph 3

TOPIC:
- Conrad's *Heart of Darkness* shows that Europeans were capable of extreme violence.

SUPPORTING IDEAS:
- European imperialists committed terrible atrocities against the people of the Congo region.
- Colonialism, according to Conrad, is "just robbery and violence."
- According to Conrad, people who behave peacefully at home in Europe become violent in Africa because there is no civilization there to suppress instincts.

Paragraph 4

TOPIC:

- Renan anticipated Freud's ideas about people's capacity for violence.

SUPPORTING IDEAS:

- Throughout history, Europeans have been violent and bloodthirsty.
- The St. Bartholomew's Day massacre is an example of extreme violence.
- Because events like this massacre are so terrible, people must forget them in order to co-exist as members of the same nation.

Paragraph 5

TOPIC:

- Renan's views about the sources of violence differ from those of Freud and Conrad.

SUPPORTING IDEAS:

- Renan thinks violence comes from sources external to the individual.
- Those sources are religion and the state.
- Freud thinks violence is part of human nature.

Paragraph 6

TOPIC:

- Remarque thinks the state encourages people to be brutal and merciless.

SUPPORTING IDEAS:

- Remarque quote: "A word of command has made [enemy soldiers] our enemies."
- The motivation to kill comes from authority figures representing the state.
- Remarque thinks individuals have no inherent desire to kill.

Paragraph 7 (conclusion)

Please construct a CONCLUSION using the following elements:

- Many people were horrified and disillusioned by the violence of World War I, but certain intellectuals were not surprised by it.
- These intellectuals expected that human beings would readily commit acts of extreme violence.
- The four writers examined in this essay can be divided into two opposing views of the sources of this violence.
- Intellectuals still debate whether violence comes from within the individual or from without.

You will find suggested answers to the exercises in the back of this book. For more Writing History exercises, as well as study resources for this chapter, visit oup.com/us/berenson.

CHAPTER 11

THE RUSSIAN REVOLUTION AND THE RISE OF THE SOVIET UNION, 1905–1940

11.1 ALEKSANDRA KOLLONTAI, *THE AUTOBIOGRAPHY OF A SEXUALLY EMANCIPATED COMMUNIST WOMAN*, 1926

Aleksandra Kollontai (1872–1952) turned out to be one of the rare "Old Bolsheviks" (original revolutionaries) who did not fall under the "wheel of history" that Josef Stalin had set in motion. Before 1917, Kollontai was a single mother and a fiercely emancipated woman. A tireless speaker and organizer, Kollontai traveled to a dozen European countries, often leaving her son behind. In her romantic relationships with men, mostly fellow revolutionaries, she expected to be treated as an intellectual and political equal, not merely as an object of desire.

After the Bolsheviks' October Revolution, she became the People's Commissar of Social Welfare, making her the lone woman in the new Soviet government. At first exhilarated and optimistic, she was quickly overwhelmed by the tasks of providing social welfare to an immense population shattered by revolution and war. She did not retain her government position for long. Irritated by her support of the "workers' opposition," an effort to create an independent trade union movement, officials sent her to Norway, where she lived in de facto exile as a diplomat.

Three years later, Kollontai returned home and rejoined the debate over the future of women under the new communist system. Just as communists foresaw the "withering away of the state" in a harmonious socialist utopia, Kollontai looked forward to the "withering away of the family." Such views—as expressed in this book from 1926—attracted interest in the 1920s, when younger Russians began to think about new socialist ways to live. The words printed in italics signify what she deleted from her original manuscript before publishing her book so as not to irritate Stalin as he consolidated his power.

From The Autobiography of a Sexually Emancipated Communist Woman (New York: Herder and Herder, 1971), translated by Salvator Attansio. Marxist Internet Archive, https://www.marxists.org/archive/kollonta/1926/autobiography.htm.

Now began a dark time of my life which I cannot treat of here since the events are still too fresh in my mind. *But the day will also come when I will give an account of them.*

There were differences of opinion in the Party. I resigned from my post as People's Commissar *on the ground of total disagreement with the current policy. Little by little I was also relieved of all my other tasks. I again gave lectures and espoused my ideas on "the new woman" and "the new morality."* The Revolution was in full swing. The struggle was becoming increasingly irreconcilable and bloodier, *much of what was happening did not fit in with my outlook.* But after all there was still the unfinished task, women's liberation. Women, of course, had received all rights but in practice, of course, they still lived under the old yoke: without authority in family life, enslaved by a thousand menial household chores, bearing the whole burden of maternity, even the material cares, because many women now found life alone as a result of the war and other circumstances.

In the autumn of 1916 when I devoted all my energies to drawing up systematic guidelines for the liberation of working women in all areas, I found a valuable support in the first President of the Soviets, Sverdlov, now dead. Thus the first Congress of Women Workers and Women Peasants could be called as early as November of 1918; some 1147 delegates were present. Thus the foundation was laid for methodical work in the whole country for the liberation of the women of the working and the peasant classes. A flood of new work was waiting for me. The question now was one of drawing women into the people's kitchens and of educating them to devote their energies to children's homes and day-care centers, the school system, household reforms, and still many other pressing matters. The main thrust of all this activity was to implement, in fact, equal rights for women as a labor unit in the national economy and as a citizen in the political sphere and, of course, with the special proviso: maternity was to be appraised as a social function and therefore protected and provided for by the State.

Under the guidance of Dr. Lebedevo, the State institutes for pre-natal care also flourished then. At the same time, central officers were established in the whole country to deal with issues and tasks connected with women's liberation and to draw women into Soviet work.

. . .

At the eighth Soviet Congress, as a member of the Soviet executive *(now there were already several women on this body)*, I proposed a motion that the Soviets in all areas contribute to the creation of a consciousness of the struggle for equal rights for women and, accordingly, to involve them in State and communal work. I managed to push the motion through and to get it accepted but not without resistance. It was a great, an enduring victory.

A heated debate flared up when I published my thesis on the new morality. *For our Soviet marriage law, separated from the Church to be sure, is not essentially more progressive than the same laws that after all exist in other progressive democratic countries. Marriage, civil marriage and although the illegitimate child was in Soviet Russia* placed on a legal par with the legitimate child, in practice a great deal of hypocrisy and injustice still exists in this area. When one speaks of the "immorality" which the Bolsheviks purportedly propagated, it suffices to submit our marriage laws to a close scrutiny to note that in the divorce question we are on a par with North America whereas in the question of the illegitimate child we have *not yet even* progressed as far as the Norwegians.

The most radical wing of the Party was formed around this question. My theses, my *sexual and moral* views, were bitterly fought *by many Party comrades of both sexes: as were still other differences of opinion in the Party regarding political guiding principles.* Personal and family cares were added thereto and thus months in 1922 went by without fruitful work. Then in the autumn of 1922 came my official appointment to the legation of the Russian Soviet representation in Norway. I really believed that this appointment would be purely formal and that therefore in Norway I would find time to devote to myself, to my literary activity. Things turned out quite differently. With the day of my entry into office in Norway I also entered upon a wholly new course of work in my life which drew upon all my energies to the highest degree. During my diplo-matic activity, therefore, *I wrote only one article, "The Winged Eros," which caused an extraordinarily great flutter. Added to this were three short novels, "Paths of Love," which have been published by* *Malik-Verlag in Berlin.* My book "The New Morality and the Working Class" and a socio-economic study, "The Condition of Women in the Evolution of Political Economy," were written when I was still in Russia.

STUDY QUESTIONS

1. What were the sources of and justifications for resistance to women's liberation in the new Soviet Union?
2. How did Kollontai use comparative evidence from other countries to shame her own into progress?

11.2 TSAR NICHOLAS II, *MANIFESTO*, OCTOBER 17, 1905

In the summer of 1905, peasants throughout Russia rebelled against the nobility in what was to be the most extensive rural uprising since the Pugachev revolt of the late eighteenth century. Peasants sacked and burned nobles' residences and attacked landowners and government officials. By August, the rebellion had grown to the point that the tsar felt he had no alternative but to allow the creation of an elected Duma, or parliament, with the ability to advise him but no right to frame legislation or shape policy. By this point, however, the demands for change had become so widespread and impassioned that the tsar's opponents rejected a purely advisory Duma.

Agitation intensified, and at the end of October, the months-long crescendo of labor unrest coalesced into a massive general strike in St. Petersburg, which paralyzed the Russian capital for nearly two weeks. To direct the strike, workers formed a leadership council—a "*soviet*" in Russian—whose members made the work stoppage one of the most successful in history. On October 30, the tsar gave in and issued the October Manifesto, which granted Russians civil liberties and established a Duma with real legislative powers. Nevertheless, many Russians thought it did not go far enough.

We, Nicholas II, By the Grace of God Emperor and Autocrat of all Russia, King of Poland, Grand Duke of Finland, etc., proclaim to all Our loyal subjects: Rioting and disturbances in the capitals [St. Petersburg and the old capital, Moscow] and in many localities of Our Empire fill Our heart with great and

Translated by Daniel Field

From http://academic.shu.edu/russianhistory/index.php/Manifesto_of_October_17th,_1905

heavy grief. The well-being of the Russian Sovereign is inseparable from the well-being of the nation, and the nation's sorrow is his sorrow. The disturbances that have taken place may cause grave tension in the nation and may threaten the integrity and unity of Our state.

By the great vow of service as tsar We are obliged to use every resource of wisdom and of Our authority to bring a speedy end to unrest that is dangerous to Our state. We have ordered the responsible authorities to take measures to terminate direct manifestations of disorder, lawlessness, and violence and to protect peaceful people who quietly seek to fulfill their duties. To carry out successfully the general measures that we have conceived to restore peace to the life of the state, We believe that it is essential to coordinate activities at the highest level of government.

We require the government dutifully to execute our unshakeable will:

1. To grant to the population the essential foundations of civil freedom, based on the principles of genuine inviolability of the person, freedom of conscience, speech, assembly and association.

2. Without postponing the scheduled elections to the State Duma, to admit to participation in the Duma (insofar as possible in the short time that remains before it is scheduled to convene) of all those classes of the population that now are completely deprived of voting rights; and to leave the further development of a general statute on elections to the future legislative order.

3. To establish as an unbreakable rule that no law shall take effect without confirmation by the State Duma and that the elected representatives of the people shall be guaranteed the opportunity to participate in the supervision of the legality of the actions of Our appointed officials.

We summon all loyal sons of Russia to remember their duties toward their country, to assist in terminating the unprecedented unrest now prevailing, and together with Us to make every effort to restore peace and tranquility to Our native land.

Given at Peterhof the 17th of October in the 1905th year of Our Lord and of Our reign the eleventh.

STUDY QUESTIONS

1. Was this document misleading in certain key respects? What does it say about the right of "assembly"?
2. Was the offer of voting rights in the Duma a reasonable solution to the problem?

11.3 N. N. SUKHANOV, *THE RUSSIAN REVOLUTION, 1917: EYEWITNESS ACCOUNT*, 1922

N.N. Sukhanov (1882–1940), a leader of the Mensheviks (the moderate wing of the Social Democrats), published in 1922 his account of the events that unfolded in 1917, providing historians with an insider view of the Russian Revolution. In this excerpt, Sukhanov describes the impressive oratorical skill of the Bolshevik leader Leon Trotsky (1879–1940), whose speech on November 4 (marked as October 22 on the old calendar still in effect in Russia) announced the beginning of a Bolshevik revolution. Just three days later, Bolsheviks stormed the tsar's feebly defended Winter

The Russian Revolution. By Sheila Fitzpatrick. Oxford and New York: Oxford University Press, 1982

Palace in Petrograd. With little bloodshed and minimal effort, they took the building and deposed the Provisional Government. On November 9, the Bolsheviks created a new revolutionary government directed by a Council of People's Commissars. Vladimir Lenin (1870–1924) served as chairman, Trotsky as commissar for foreign affairs, and Josef Stalin (1878–1953) as commissar for national minorities. Stalin and Trotsky became fierce rivals, and Stalin, who took control of the party bureaucracy, ultimately had Trotsky removed from power, exiled, and killed.

CHAPTER 28: THE FINAL REVIEW

I should like to mention just this about the front [in the First World War]. Once more strings of delegations from the front were not only filing into Smolny appearing at big Soviet meetings with their messages and speeches: besides this they were stubbornly seeking *intimate conversations* and authoritative direct explanations from the old Soviet leaders. But there was no time for them. They were almost never received. When they did succeed in getting hold of a leader they could get no satisfaction from him. . . . Disappointed and angry, [they] immediately turned to the Bolsheviks. They poured out their hearts to them at Smolny, and at the front became conductors of their influence. Our editorial office (and others too no doubt) was literally swamped at this time with letters from the trenches. These were remarkable human documents. Pouring their souls out to the dregs, the soldiers showed what the unbearable suffering of wartime had turned them into. If only it would end: nothing else mattered—parties, politics, or revolution. Anyone would be supported who produced even a ghost of peace. . . .

Besides the Soviet organizations there were also some municipalities in the hands of the Bolsheviks. One way or another in such conditions the overturn definitely did not recall either a military conspiracy or a Blanquist experiment.

But the active and deciding role belonged to Petersburg, and partly to its suburbs. Forces were mobilized here most of all, in the main arena of the drama.

Trotsky, tearing himself away from work on the revolutionary staff, personally rushed . . . [all around]; he seemed to be speaking at all points simultaneously. His influence, both among the masses and on the staff, was overwhelming. He was the central figure of those days and the principal hero of this remarkable page of history.

* * *

On October 21st the Petersburg garrison *conclusively acknowledged the Soviet as sole power, and the Military Revolutionary Committee as the immediate organ of authority.*

Two days earlier the District Commander had again reported to the Premier: "There is no reason to think the garrison will refuse to obey the orders of the military authorities."

One could remain calm. The Winter Palace was calm. "Steps had been taken."

* * *

I spent that night in the Karpovka because I had to speak the next day at noon at a mass-meeting in the People's House.

The decisive day came. The Cyclopean building of the People's House was packed to the doors with a countless throng. They filled the enormous theatres to overflowing in the expectation of mass-meetings. The foyer, buffet, and corridors were also full. Behind the scenes people kept asking me: Just what did I intend to talk about? I replied—about the "current moment," of course. Did that mean—*against the coup?* They began trying to persuade me to speak on foreign policy. After all, that was my specialty! The discussion with the organizers took on such a character I absolutely refused to speak at all. But that was no use either.

Irritated, I went out from backstage, to watch events from the hall. Trotsky was flying along the corridor towards me on to the stage. He glanced at me angrily and rushed by without any greeting. . . .

The mood of the people, more than 3,000, who filled the hall was definitely tense: they were all silently waiting for something. The audience was of course primarily workers and soldiers, but more than a few typically lower-middle-class men's and women's figures were visible.

Trotsky's ovation seemed to be cut short prematurely, out of curiosity and impatience: what was he going to say? Trotsky at once began to heat up the atmosphere, with his skill and brilliance. I remember that at length and with extraordinary power he drew a picture (difficult through its simplicity) of the suffering of the trenches. Thoughts flashed through my mind of the inevitable incongruity of the parts in this oratorical whole. But Trotsky knew what he was doing. The whole point lay in the mood. The political conclusions had long been familiar. They could be condensed, as long as there were enough highlights.

Trotsky did this—with enough highlights. The Soviet regime was not only called upon to put an end to the suffering of the trenches. It would give land and heal the internal disorder. Once again the recipes against hunger were repeated: a soldier, a sailor, and a working girl, who would requisition bread from those who had it and distribute it gratis to the cities and front. But Trotsky went even further on this decisive "Day of the Petersburg Soviet."

"The Soviet Government will give everything the country contains to the poor and the men in the trenches. You, bourgeois, have got two fur caps!—give one of them to the soldier, who's freezing in the trenches. Have you got warm boots? Stay at home. The worker needs your boots . . ."

These were very good and just ideas. They could not but excite the enthusiasm of a crowd who had been reared on the Tsarist whip. In any case, I certify as a direct witness that this was what was said on this last day.

All round me was a mood bordering on ecstasy. It seemed as though the crowd, spontaneously and of its own accord, would break into some religious hymn. Trotsky formulated a brief and general resolution, or pronounced some general formula like "we will defend the worker-peasant cause to the last drop of our blood."

Who was—for? The crowd of thousands, as one man, raised their hands. I saw the raised hands and burning eyes of men, women, youths, soldiers, peasants, and typically lower-middle-class faces. Were

they in spiritual transports? Did they see, through the raised curtain, a corner of the "righteous land" of their longing? Or were they penetrated by a consciousness of the *political occasion*, under the influence of the political agitation of a *Socialist*? Ask no questions! Accept it as it was. . . .

Trotsky went on speaking. The innumerable crowd went on holding their hands up. Trotsky rapped out the words: "Let this vote of yours be your vow with all your strength and at any sacrifice to support the Soviet that has taken on itself the glorious burden of bringing to a conclusion the victory of the revolution and of giving land, bread, and peace!"

The vast crowd was holding up its hands. It agreed. It vowed. Once again, accept this as it was. With an unusual feeling of oppression I looked on at this really magnificent scene.

Trotsky finished. Someone else went out on to the stage. But there was no point in waiting and looking any more.

Throughout Petersburg more or less the same thing was going on. Everywhere there were final reviews and final vows. Thousands, tens of thousands and hundreds of thousands of people. . . . This, actually, was already an insurrection. Things had started. . . .

* * *

At about 5 or 6 o'clock, I don't remember just why, a meeting of our Pre-Parliament fraction was scheduled in the Marian Palace. But almost no one was there. In the reading-room I came across two or three comrades, in deep arm-chairs, lazily exchanging remarks. I began to tell them what I had seen and heard that day. But I don't think it made much impression. Dr. Mandelberg, coming to the point, began talking about what was going to happen in the Pre-Parliament on Tuesday or Wednesday.

"What?" I stopped him. "D'you think there's still going to be a Pre-Parliament on Tuesday and Wednesday? Don't delude yourself! In two or three days the Pre-Parliament will no longer exist . . ."

But they ironically waved me aside. Two hours passed. The time assigned for our fraction meeting had already gone by. I didn't go away because at about 8 or 9 o'clock an *inter-fraction* meeting was scheduled on the question of a peace formula. While waiting I wandered about the empty half-dark rooms. All at once a group of people from other fractions appeared—Peshekhonov, Kuskov, Skobelev, and someone else. They were already looking for the other delegates in order to begin the conference. Well, what had they seen and heard today? What did they think? I went up to them and abruptly flung out: "So the insurrection's begun! What are your impressions?"

For a long moment the group looked at me in frowning silence, not knowing what to say. Insurrection? No, they didn't know a thing. Should they believe me? How should they reply? Whether you believed it or not you shouldn't get into this sort of conversation. After all, if the insurrection really had begun Sukhanov of course would be in it . . .

The inter-fraction meeting began, but we didn't have time to finish. We were interrupted by a group of people who had rushed over from Smolny with extraordinary news.

CHAPTER 29: OVERTURE

In actual fact the overturn was accomplished the moment the Petersburg garrison acknowledged the Soviet as its supreme authority and the Military Revolutionary Committee as its direct command. Such a decision, as we know, was made at the meeting of the garrison representatives on October 21st. But in the unprecedented setting this act may be said to have had an abstract character. No one took it for a coup d'etat.

And no wonder. The decision, after all, did not really change the situation: even earlier the Government had had no real power or authority. The real power in the capital had already been in the hands of the Bolsheviks of the Petersburg Soviet long before, and nevertheless the Winter Palace had remained the Government. . . .

Nevertheless the Government was already overthrown on October 21st, as Tsar Nicholas had been on February 28th What remained now was essentially to *complete* what had been done—first of all, to make the overturn official by proclaiming a new government, and secondly, to liquidate *de facto* the pretenders to power, thus achieving general acknowledgement of the accomplished fact.

The significance of what was accomplished on October 21st was obscure not only to the man-in-the-street and the spectator; it was not clear to the revolutionary leaders themselves.

STUDY QUESTIONS

1. What does Sukhanov reveal about the ways the Russian First World War experience contributed to the revolutions in 1917?
2. How does Sukhanov, a rival leader, describe Trotsky's skill and the Bolshevik path to power?

11.4 VLADIMIR LENIN, *THE NEW ECONOMIC POLICY AND THE TASKS OF THE POLITICAL EDUCATION DEPARTMENTS*, OCTOBER 17, 1921

The Bolsheviks' attempt to collectivize the economy quickly through a harsh policy of "War Communism" was a catastrophic failure. Surveying the damage, Lenin decided in 1921 to replace War Communism with a New Economic Policy (NEP) designed above all to encourage peasants to

Vladimir Lenin, *The New Economic Policy and the Tasks of the Political Education Departments* (October 17, 1921). Translated by: David Skvirsky and George Hanna. Marxist Internet Archive, https://www.marxists.org/archive/lenin/works/1921/oct/17.htm.

grow food for a starving country. In this excerpt, Lenin explains the reasons for the NEP: to re-build Russia's war-shattered economy, it was necessary to restore key features of capitalism, de-spite the danger that capitalists would take advantage of the Bolshevik's retreat from War Communism to overturn socialism itself.

As Lenin explains, the NEP featured the denationalization of the country's small-scale indus-try and trade, and—most importantly—the end of grain requisitions for Russia's 25 million peas-ant families. To finance government operations, the regime imposed a relatively modest tax in kind (paid in crops, not money) on the farmers' agricultural produce, rather than simply taking it from them. Once peasants had settled their tax obligations, the more crops they grew, the more they could either keep for themselves or (the government hoped) sell for a profit on a market now released from most political controls. Peasant profits would fuel the revival of Russia's moribund industrial economy, and this revival would re-create the proletariat, which, together with the peasantry, would lay the groundwork for the transition to communism.

OUR MISTAKE

At the beginning of 1918 we expected a period in which peaceful construction would be possible. When the Brest peace was signed it seemed that danger had subsided for a time and that it would be possible to start peaceful construction. But we were mistaken, because in 1918 a real military danger overtook us in the shape of the Czechoslovak mutiny and the outbreak of civil war, which dragged on until 1920. Partly owing to the war problems that overwhelmed us and partly owing to the desperate position in which the Republic found itself when the imperialist war ended—owing to these circum-stances, and a number of others, we made the mis-take of deciding to go over directly to communist production and distribution. We thought that under the surplus-food appropriation system the peasants would provide us with the required quantity of grain, which we could distribute among the facto-ries and thus achieve communist production and distribution.

I cannot say that we pictured this plan as defi-nitely and as clearly as that; but we acted approxi-mately on those lines. That, unfortunately, is a fact. I say unfortunately, because brief experience con-vinced us that that line was wrong, that it ran counter to what we had previously written about the transi-tion from capitalism to socialism, namely, that it would be impossible to bypass the period of socialist accounting and control in approaching even the lower stage of communism. Ever since 1917, when the problem of taking power arose and the Bolsheviks explained it to the whole people, our theoretical lit-erature has been definitely stressing the necessity for a prolonged, complex transition through socialist ac-counting and control from capitalist society (and the less developed it is the longer the transition will take) to even one of the approaches to communist society.

A STRATEGICAL RETREAT

At that time, when in the heat of the Civil War we had to take the necessary steps in economic organization, it seemed to have been forgotten. In substance, our New Economic Policy signifies that, having sustained severe defeat on this point, we have started a strategi-cal retreat. We said in effect: "Before we are completely routed, let us retreat and reorganize everything, but on a firmer basis." If Communists deliberately exam-ine the question of the New Economic Policy there cannot be the slightest doubt in their minds that we have sustained a very severe defeat on the economic front. In the circumstances it is inevitable, of course, for some people to become very despondent, almost panic-stricken, and because of the retreat, these people will begin to give way to panic. That is inevi-table. When the Red Army retreated, was its flight from the enemy not the prelude to its victory? Every retreat on every front, however, caused some people to give way to panic for a time. But on each occasion—on the Kolchak front, on the Denikin front, on the Yudenich front, on the Polish front and on the Wrangel front—once we had been badly battered (and sometimes more than once) we proved the truth of the proverb: "A man who has been beaten is worth two who haven't." After being beaten we began to advance slowly, systematically and cautiously.

Of course, tasks on the economic front are much more difficult than tasks on the war front, although there is a general similarity between the two elementary outlines of strategy. In attempting to go over straight to communism we, in the spring of 1921, sustained a more serious defeat on the economic front than any defeat inflicted upon us by Kolchak, Denikin or Pilsudski. This defeat was much more serious, significant and dangerous. It was expressed in the isolation of the higher administrators of our economic policy from the lower and their failure to produce that development of the productive forces which the Program of our Party regards as vital and urgent.

The surplus-food appropriation system in the rural districts—this direct communist approach to the problem of urban development—hindered the growth of the productive forces and proved to be the main cause of the profound economic and political crisis that we experienced in the spring of 1921. That was why we had to take a step which from the point of view of our line, of our policy, cannot be called anything else than a very severe defeat and retreat. Moreover, it cannot be said that this retreat is—like retreats of the Red Army—a completely orderly retreat to previously prepared positions. True, the positions for our present retreat were prepared beforehand. That can be proved by comparing the decisions adopted by our Party in the spring of 1921 with the one adopted in April 1918, which I have mentioned. The positions were prepared beforehand; but the retreat to these positions took place (and is still taking place in many parts of the country) in disorder, and even in extreme disorder.

PURPORT OF THE NEW ECONOMIC POLICY

It is here that the task of the Political Education Departments to combat this comes to the forefront. The

main problem in the light of the New Economic Policy is to take advantage of the situation that has arisen as speedily as possible.

The New Economic Policy means substituting a tax for the requisitioning of food; it means reverting to capitalism to a considerable extent—to what extent we do not know. Concessions to foreign capitalists (true, only very few have been accepted, especially when compared with the number we have offered) and leasing enterprises to private capitalists definitely mean restoring capitalism, and this is part and parcel of the New Economic Policy; for the abolition of the surplus-food appropriation system means allowing the peasants to trade freely in their surplus agricultural produce, in whatever is left over after the tax is collected—and the tax~ takes only a small share of that produce. The peasants constitute a huge section of our population and of our entire economy, and that is why capitalism must grow out of this soil of free trading.

That is the very ABC of economics as taught by the rudiments of that science, and in Russia taught, furthermore, by the profiteer, the creature who needs no economic or political science to teach us economics with. From the point of view of strategy the root question is: who will take advantage of the new situation first? The whole question is—whom will the peasantry follow? The proletariat, which wants to build socialist society? Or the capitalist, who says, "Let us turn back; it is safer that way; we don't know anything about this socialism they have invented"?

WHO WILL WIN, THE CAPITALIST OR SOVIET POWER?

The issue in the present war is—who will win, who will first take advantage of the situation: the capitalist, whom we are allowing to come in by the door, and even by several doors (and by many doors we are not aware of, and which open without us, and in spite of us), or proletarian state power? What has the latter to rely on economically? On the one hand, the improved position of the people. In this connection we must remember the peasants. It is absolutely incontrovertible and obvious to all that in spite of the awful disaster of the famine—and leaving that disaster out of the reckoning for the moment—the improvement that has taken place in the position of the people has been due to the change in our economic policy.

On the other hand, if capitalism gains by it, industrial production will grow, and the proletariat will grow too. The capitalists will gain from our policy and will create an industrial proletariat, which in our country, owing to the war and to the desperate poverty and ruin, has become declassed, i. e., dislodged from its class groove, and has ceased to exist as a proletariat. The proletariat is the class which is engaged in the production of material values in large-scale capitalist industry. Since large-scale capitalist industry has been destroyed, since the factories are at a standstill, the proletariat has disappeared. It has sometimes figured in statistics, but it has not been held together economically.

The restoration of capitalism would mean the restoration of a proletarian class engaged in the production of socially useful material values in big factories employing machinery, and not in profiteering, not in making cigarette-lighters for sale, and in other "work" which is not very useful, but which is inevitable when our industry is in a state of ruin.

The whole question is who will take the lead. We must face this issue squarely—who will come out on top? Either the capitalists succeed in organising first—in which case they will drive out the Communists and that will be the end of it. Or the proletarian state power, with the support of the peasantry, will prove capable of keeping a proper rein on those gentlemen, the capitalists, so as to direct capitalism along state channels and to create a capitalism that will be subordinate to the state and serve the state. . . .

We must say: either those who wanted to crush us—and who we think ought to be destroyed—must perish, in which case our Soviet Republic will live or the capitalists will live, and in that case the Republic will perish. In an impoverished country either those who cannot stand the pace will perish, or the workers' and peasants' republic will perish. There is not and cannot be any choice or any room for sentiment. Sentiment is no less a crime than cowardice in wartime. Whoever now departs from order and discipline is permitting the enemy to penetrate our midst. . . .

SHALL WE BE ABLE TO WORK FOR OUR OWN BENEFIT?

We had deserters from the army, and also from the labour front. We must say that in the past you worked for the benefit of the capitalists, of the exploiters, and of course you did not do your best. But now you are working for yourselves, for the workers' and peasants' state. Remember that the question at issue is whether we shall be able to work for ourselves, for if we cannot, I repeat, our Republic will perish. And we say, as we said in the army. that either those who want to cause our destruction must perish, or we must adopt the sternest disciplinary measures and thereby save our country—and our Republic will live.

That is what our line must be, that is why (among other things) we need the New Economic Policy.

Get down to business, all of you! You will have capitalists beside you, including foreign capitalists, concessionaires and leaseholders. They will squeeze profits out of you amounting to hundreds per cent; they will enrich themselves, operating alongside of you. Let them. Meanwhile you will learn from them the business of running the economy, and only when you do that will you be able to build up a communist republic. Since we must necessarily learn quickly, any slackness in this respect is a serious crime. And we must undergo this training, this severe, stern and sometimes even cruel training, because we have no other way out.

You must remember that our Soviet land is impoverished after many years of trial and suffering, and has no socialist France or socialist England as neighbors which could help us with their highly developed technology and their highly developed industry. Bear that in mind! We must remember that at present all their highly developed technology and their highly developed industry belong to the capitalists, who are fighting us.

We must remember that we must either strain every nerve in everyday effort, or we shall inevitably go under.

Owing to the present circumstances the whole world is developing faster than we are. While developing, the capitalist world is directing all its forces against us. That is how the matter stands! That is why we must devote special attention to this struggle.

Owing to our cultural backwardness we cannot crush capitalism by a frontal attack. Had we been on a different cultural level we could have approached the problem more directly; perhaps other countries will do it in this way when their turn comes to build their communist republics. But we cannot do it in the direct way.

The state must learn to trade in such a way that industry satisfies the needs of the peasantry, so that the peasantry may satisfy their needs by means of trade. We must see to it that everyone who works devotes himself to strengthening the workers' and peasants' state. Only then shall we be able to create large-scale industry.

STUDY QUESTIONS

1. Why did Lenin believe that a New Economic Policy was necessary?
2. What pitfalls does Lenin see in this new approach?

11.5 JOSEF STALIN, *THE RESULTS OF THE FIRST FIVE-YEAR PLAN*, JANUARY 7, 1933

Stalin's economic development plan focused on the construction of several gigantic factories modeled after the largest plants in the United States. His goal was to catch up with, and eventually overtake, the world's leading manufacturing power. Stalin considered this effort a matter of life or death for Soviet Russia, for, as he put it, "the pace of Soviet industrialization would determine whether the socialist fatherland survived or crumbled before its enemies." Stalin's version of socialism stood in contrast to classical Marxist theory, which understood industrial capitalism, achieved through large-scale, mechanized private enterprise, to precede socialism and lead to it. Capitalism, in the classical Marxist view, could not exist simultaneously with the socialist state. In essence, Stalin believed he could bypass capitalism to rapidly industrialize his country using the levers of an all-powerful state.

Stalin established goals for the development of his country in a series of Five-Year Plans that outlined what the economy was to look like a half-decade later. The first Five-Year Plan soon squeezed into four years (1928–1932), focused on iron and steel. It assigned each industry and industrial plant quotas specifying the quantities to be produced, creating what looked like an organized and rational set of goals. By 1933, although the goals had not been met, Stalin claimed that they had, and he immediately announced plans for a second Five-Year Plan.

What is the five-year plan?

What was the fundamental task of the five-year plan?

The fundamental task of the five-year plan was to transfer our country, with its backward, and in part medieval, technology, on to the lines of new, modern technology.

The fundamental task of the five-year plan was to convert the U.S.S.R. from an agrarian and weak country, dependent upon the caprices of the capitalist

Marxists Internet Archive
https://www.marxists.org/reference/archive/stalin/works/1933/01/07.htm.

countries, into an industrial and powerful country, fully self-reliant and independent of the caprices of world capitalism.

The fundamental task of the five-year plan was, in converting the U.S.S.R. into an industrial country, to completely oust the capitalist elements, to widen the front of socialist forms of economy, and to create the economic basis for the abolition of classes in the U.S.S.R., for the building of a socialist society.

The fundamental task of the five-year plan was to create in our country an industry that would be capable of re-equipping and re-organizing, not only industry as a whole, but also transport and agriculture—on the basis of socialism.

The fundamental task of the five-year plan was to transfer small and scattered agriculture on to the lines of large-scale collective farming, so as to ensure the economic basis of socialism in the countryside and thus to eliminate the possibility of the restoration of capitalism in the U.S.S.R.

Finally, the task of the five-year plan was to create all the necessary technical and economic prerequisites for increasing to the utmost the defence capacity of the country, enabling it to organize determined resistance to any attempt at military intervention from abroad, to any attempt at military attack from abroad . . .

These propositions formed the basis of those considerations of the Party that led to the drawing up of the five-year plan and to determining its fundamental task.

That is how matters stand with regard to the fundamental task of the five-year plan.

But the execution of such a gigantic plan cannot be started haphazardly, just anyhow.

In order to carry out such a plan it is necessary first of all to find its main link; for only after finding and grasping this main link could a pull be exerted on all the other links of the plan.

What was the main link in the five-year plan?

The main link in the five-year plan was heavy industry, with machine building as its core. For only heavy industry is capable of reconstructing both industry as a whole, transport and agriculture, and of putting them on their feet. It was necessary to begin the fulfilment of the five-year plan with heavy industry. Consequently, the restoration of heavy industry had to be made the basis of the fulfilment of the five-year plan. . . .

But the restoration and development of heavy industry, particularly in such a backward and poor country as ours was at the beginning of the five-year plan period, is an extremely difficult task; for, as is well known, heavy industry calls for enormous financial expenditure and the existence of a certain minimum of experienced technical forces, without which, generally speaking, the restoration of heavy industry is impossible. Did the Party know this, and did it take this into account? Yes, it did. Not only did the Party know this, but it announced it for all to hear. The Party knew how heavy industry had been built in Britain, Germany and America. It knew that in those countries heavy industry had been built either with the aid of big loans, or by plundering other countries, or by both methods simultaneously. The Party knew that those paths were closed to our country. What, then, did it count on? It counted on our country's own resources. It counted on the fact that, with a Soviet government at the helm, and the land, industry, transport, the banks and trade organizations, we could pursue a regime of the strictest economy in order to accumulate sufficient resources for the restoration and development of heavy industry. The Party declared frankly that this would call for serious sacrifices, and that it was our duty openly and consciously to make these sacrifices if we wanted to achieve our goal. The Party counted on carrying through this task with the aid of the internal resources of our country—without enslaving.

STUDY QUESTIONS

1. Is Stalin employing merely empty rhetoric in his explanation of the Five-Year Plan?
2. Was *actual* industrial development possible under the Soviet system? If so, how?

11.6 NIKOLAI BUKHARIN, *CULTURE IN TWO WORLDS*, 1934

During Lenin's era, Nikolai Bukharin (1888–1938), a key Bolshevik theoretician, led the more right-wing faction of the party. Bukahrin maintained that the Soviets should not waste their meager resources in futile attempts to foment revolution abroad but rather focus on their own country and allow it to evolve gently but steadily toward socialism by maintaining the New Economic Policy, or NEP. After Lenin's death, Bukharin may have been the Party's most prestigious policymaker and editor of its official newspaper, *Pravda* (*Truth*), but the real, everyday political muscle increasingly belonged to Stalin.

In this excerpt, Bukharin, a more subtle thinker than Stalin, nonetheless pays homage to the latter's analysis of fascism, which simplistically explained fascism as resulting from a "general crisis of capitalism." In the long run, Bukharin's show of obeisance did not matter: in 1938, Stalin staged an elaborate "show trial" for Bukharin and two others—all of them longstanding, prominent Bolshevik leaders—in which they were forced to confess to efforts to sabotage the regime. As "enemies of the people," they were summarily shot.

I: THE "PARADOX" OF FASCISM

It is now generally admitted that we are living in a period of very great historical cataclysms, of violent upheaval in all social life, of the most radical changes, and of the crash of old systems of material existence and the old outlook on life. Wars, revolutions, the crisis, the dictatorship of the proletariat, fascism, the threat of new wars, the heroic struggle of the Austrian workers—all these facts are extremely ominous for capitalism, which might say, with Horatio [a quote from Shakespeare's *Hamlet*, Act I, Scene I]:

> In what particular thought to work I know not; But, in the gross and scope of my opinion, This bodes some strange eruption to our state.

The strain of the contradictions which are under constant pressure in the unbearably stuffy atmosphere of the capitalist world may at any moment end in some new catastrophe quite unexpected in its form.

However, we can trace a basic historical "tendency of development" through the cinematographic swiftness and motley change of events. This tendency is expressed first and foremost in the unusually intensive process of the polarization of the classes—the great differentiation in all social forces and ideologies—the sharpening of the struggle between fascism and communism, as two class camps—two doctrines—two cultures. If we were to characterize the entire historical situation briefly from this point of view, we might say that great class forces are forming in military array for coming battles—for the battles which will be really final (in the world-historic sense) and really decisive.

For this reason, fascism must be subjected to thoughtful study in all its aspects, from its economics down to its philosophy. And all these already exist; for the bourgeois ranks are being reorganized with enormous swiftness, both in the form of so-called "national revolutions" and in the form of "plain

From Nikolai Bukharin, *Culture in Two Worlds: The Crisis of Capitalist Culture and the Problems of Culture in the U. S. S. R.*, International Pamphlets #42 (New York: privately published, 1934), pp. 2–4.

fascism." These forms vary greatly, but one cannot doubt their common historical tendency and the common root of their social and political class significance. . . .

Fascist "order" is the "order" of military, political and economic *barracks*; it is the military capitalist system of a state of "emergency." This expresses itself in a number of most important facts: in the tendency towards state capitalism; in the "common national," "corporate," etc., dictatorship, with the suppression of a number of internal contradictions; in the establishment of various "mono" systems—"mono-nation," "mono-party," "mono-state" ("totalitarian state"), etc.; in the organization of mass human reserves—petty-bourgeois and, in part, working class; in a whole "incorporated" ideology, attuned to the basic interests of finance capital; and, finally, in the creation of a material and ideological war base.

The so-called fascist "national revolutions," with their anti-capitalist slogans, are really in essence but a speedy reorganization of the bourgeois ranks, eliminating parliamentary changes and the system of competing parties, introducing uniform military discipline all along the line, and organizing mass reserves.

The petty-bourgeois Philistines of the "centre" will say: "But you Communists also do many of these things." Or, as the Social-Democratic petty-bourgeois phrase it: "There is dictatorship here and dictatorship there, both equally abominable." Or: "There is 'Left' Bolshevism and there is 'Right' Bolshevism; and there is no difference in principle between them."

These miserable people, who receive blows both from the left and from the right, do not understand that the *formal* side of the matter alone ("dictatorship" in general), which they understood incorrectly at that, does not decide anything: *the important thing is its class meaning; its content—material and ideological; the dynamics of its development*; its relationship with the general current of world historical development. Only imbeciles can fail to understand that the dictatorship of the *proletariat* and the dictatorship of the *capitalists* are polar opposites, and that their content and historical significance are entirely different. Those who cannot—or will not—understand this will inevitably be crushed and plunged into the inglorious refuse of history.

II: THE CRISIS AND FASCIST IDEOLOGY

Thus fascism, in its essence, is a product of the general crisis of capitalism—as Joseph Stalin has emphasized. But from this it follows that the coming of fascism, in creating something *new* (*reactionarily* new) in the capitalist ways of living and thinking that had been formed before its coming, could not but bring with it a profound crisis in certain important bourgeois orientations. It should be stated that not all aspects of this complex reorientation are of the same depth or of the same stability: doubtless, many aspects are changing and will change—depending to a great extent on the curve of the economic cycle. But many aspects, of course, will remain, until the development and conclusion of the class struggle puts forward problems of an entirely different nature.

STUDY QUESTIONS

1. Why did Bukharin consider fascism and communism as completely different ideologies despite their shared origins?
2. Did any of the *results* of fascism and communism appear similar?

11.7 VISUAL SOURCE: *WHAT THE OCTOBER REVOLUTION GAVE WORKER AND PEASANT WOMEN, 1920*

After the Bolsheviks successfully toppled the Provisional Government, they still faced resistance as civil war broke out across Russia. To shore up support and disseminate their socialist message, the new Bolshevik government produced huge numbers of vivid posters aimed at Russia's large semiliterate population. In 1920 alone, the government printed 3.2 million lithographic posters, which it plastered across towns and throughout the countryside. One goal of this propaganda campaign, as Aleksandra Kollontai (see document 11.1) declared in a speech in 1921, was to "win

FIGURE 11.7   What the October Revolution Gave

Nikolai Kupreyanov/Wikipedia
https://en.wikipedia.org/wiki/Women_in_the_Russian_Revolution#/media/File:SovietWoman1920.jpg.

over the women workers and turn them into defenders of Soviet power." Although men appeared more often, women were featured in Bolshevik posters as more than allegorical or symbolic figures. Posters showed proud women taking active roles in society—as factory workers, farmers, and protestors against capitalism who benefitted from new state institutions dedicated to relieving them of the burdens of household work.

The poster shown here, *What the October Revolution Gave Worker and Peasant Women*, portrays a female factory worker wearing a blacksmith's apron gesturing to the social services provided by the new Bolshevik state: a library, a maternity home, a cafeteria, a kindergarten, an adult school, a worker's club, a daycare center, and more. The sun shines brightly over her shoulders, charging her with its power, while the clouds dissipate on the left, blown away by the new opportunities now available to women. Notice the hammer and sickle, the symbols of communism, prominently displayed—the hammer in her hands, the sickle by her feet. The government printed twenty-five thousand copies of this poster, which became an iconic Soviet image, although the artist remains unknown.

STUDY QUESTIONS

1. What were the ideal qualities for women to have in postrevolutionary Russia? How did the state intend to foster women's participation in society?
2. What does the existence and popularity of this poster reveal about how willing women were to take on new roles in society?

ANALYZING AND SORTING MATERIAL INTO MAIN IDEAS

To create a thesis statement, writers and scholars often begin by listing everything relevant to the topic: facts, quotations, observations, and ideas. Then they analyze the list, looking to answer three questions.

1. What goes with what?
2. What contradicts what? (And what explains the contradiction?)
3. What three or four central categories can the items be sorted into?

The central categories become the paper's main ideas and the elements of the thesis statement.

EXERCISE: ANALYZE AND SORT MATERIAL INTO MAIN IDEAS

EXAMPLE

PROMPT: Write an essay arguing that, on the whole, Lenin's New Economic Policy (NEP) was a success.

Step 1: Draw up a list of facts about NEP's success.

- People had enough to eat (1921–1928)
- The majority of peasants became landowners (1921–1928)
- Women were encouraged to join the workforce (1921–1928)
- There was a precipitous drop in illiteracy because peasants could afford some schooling for their children (1921–1928)
- Divorce and family planning were accepted (1921–1928)
- There was a 30% drop in infant mortality due to better nutrition (1921–1928)
- Laborers were able to rise to managerial positions in industry (1921–1928)
- There was an 11% rise in real wages (1921–1928)
- The new state welfare system helped women care for their children (1921–1928)
- Laborers were able to rise to bureaucratic posts in the rapidly expanding Communist state (1921–1928)

Step 2: Organize the list into three or more central categories.

NEP IMPROVED EVERYDAY LIFE

- People had enough to eat (1921–1928)
- There was an 11% rise in real wages (1921–1928)
- There was a 30% drop in infant mortality due to better nutrition (1921–1928)

NEP FOSTERED SOCIAL MOBILITY

- There was a precipitous drop in illiteracy because peasants could afford some schooling for their children (1921–1928)
- Laborers were able to rise to managerial positions in industry (1921–1928)

- Laborers were able to rise to bureaucratic posts in the rapidly expanding Communist state (1921–1928)
- The majority of peasants became landowners (1921–1928)

NEP PRODUCED MORE OPPORTUNITIES FOR WOMEN

- Divorce and family planning were accepted (1921–1928)
- The new state welfare system helped women care for their children (1921–1928)
- Women were encouraged to join the workforce (1921–1928)

Step 3: Write a thesis statement and three or more supporting statements:

X. On the whole, the NEP was a success because it improved everyday life, fostered social mobility, and improved opportunities for women. (THESIS)

1. The NEP improved everyday life.
2. The NEP fostered social mobility.
3. The NEP improved opportunities for women.

INSTRUCTIONS

Use the following list of material to create a thesis statement and its supporting ideas. Sort the list into categories, and then turn the categories into an X-1-2-3 set. Please note that you will be able to use most or all of the items on the list below. Some of your categories may contain more items than others.

PROMPT: Write an essay arguing that, on the whole, the NEP was a failure.
List of facts to organize into categories:

- Stalin's first step once he gained full control was the collectivization of Russian peasantry (beginning in 1927)
- Stalin was disillusioned with NEP because it did not industrialize the country fast enough (1927)
- Russia needed high investment to build heavy industry like steel, automobiles, coal, electricity, and chemicals (beginning in 1928)
- Organized religion was abolished (by 1923)
- The more free and open the economic system became, the more Russia's leaders clamped down politically (1921–1928)
- Stalin was appointed General Secretary of the Communist Party (1922)
- All parties were banned, except for the Bolsheviks (by 1923)
- Bukharin, Trotsky, and Stalin fought for control of the Communist Party (1924–1929)
- Trotsky was expelled from the Party (1927) and banished from the country after Bukharin and Stalin joined forces against him. Assassinated in Mexico City in 1940.
- Mensheviks were purged after the suppression of the sailors' rebellion at Kronstadt (1921).
- Power struggle to succeed Lenin (1924–1929)
- Russia could not attract significant foreign investment (1921–1928)
- Democratic centralism (Bolshevik leaders agreed not to disagree in public) always presented a completely unified front to the Russian people (circa 1923)
- Bukharin was expelled from Politburo (1929) (sentenced to death in a "show trial" in 1938)
- According to Stalin, peasants were the problem because they were unwilling or unable to sell enough grain (1927)
- NEP's peasant-based market economy did not produce enough money to support industrialization (1921–1928):

   a. Mediocre consumer-goods sector did not produce enough consumer products to buy, so peasants hoarded grain or produced less grain and ate more of their yield (1921–1928)

   b. Breaking up large estates and canceling peasant debts created "millions of mostly tiny plots" so there were no economies of scale in agriculture—many peasants could not produce larger crops even if they wanted to (1921–1928)

- Stalin appointed General Secretary of the Communist Party (1922)
- As General Secretary, Stalin controlled bureaucratic appointments, so he appointed only those loyal to him (1922–1929)
- Communist officials probably agreed with Stalin more than Bukharin (1924–1929)
- "Terror famine" (1932–1933)
- Real wages for industrial workers dropped by 50% across Russia (1928–1933)
- Bukharin could not appeal to the Russian people for support because he believed in democratic centralism—he believed in a monolithic, authoritarian Communist Party
- One writer has called the Soviet period from 1928 to 1933 "the culmination of the most precipitous peace-time decline in living standards known in recorded history."
- Stalin: "liquidation of the kulaks as a class" (1929)
- Lenin expanded the secret police (1921–1928)
- Suppression of sailors' rebellion at Kronstadt naval base (March 1921)

You will find suggested answers to the exercises in the back of this book. For more Writing History exercises, as well as study resources for this chapter, visit oup.com/us/berenson.

CHAPTER 12

FASCISM AND NAZISM: MASS POLITICS AND MASS CULTURE, 1919–1939

12.1 LENI RIEFENSTAHL, *A MEMOIR*, 1987

A talented dancer, actor, and filmmaker, Leni Riefenstahl (1902–2003) is best known for her lyrical propaganda film *Triumph of the Will* (1934), which glorified Hitler and his Nazi movement. Although Riefenstahl also made excellent films that had nothing to do with Nazism, *Triumph of the Will* identified her for all time as a "Nazi filmmaker" and implicated Riefenstahl in Hitler's crimes against humanity. Her Nazi connections do not, however, negate the artistry of her work. The quality of her photography and editing made *Triumph of the Will* a masterpiece of visual propaganda, and she later claimed that she would have filmed fruits or vegetables with the same artistry as she did the speeches of Hitler and his henchmen.

Riefenstahl's next film, *Olympia: Festival of Nations and Festival of Beauty* (1938), was commissioned by the International Olympics Committee, not by the Nazi Party. *Olympia* depicted the 1936 Olympic Games held in Berlin. The games were extraordinarily controversial, for they seemed to lend international recognition to the Nazi regime. Hitler very much wanted the Olympics to take place in his country precisely to win a measure of legitimacy abroad and as a means of advertising the achievements of his regime. Thus, to the extent that the Olympics itself obscured the terror and racism that were central to Nazi policy, Riefenstahl's film did as well. Beyond this important effect, however, *Olympia* had little overt propaganda value. The film itself beautifully depicted the grace, strength, and elegance of the human form.

In this excerpt from her memoir, Riefenstahl recalls her conversation with Hitler about her decision to make a documentary of the 1936 Olympic Games.

HITLER IN PRIVATE

On Christmas Eve 1935 I went off to the mountains as I had done every year. Shortly before my departure I received a phone call from Schaub: could I visit Hitler in his Munich home the morning of the first day of the Christmas holiday? Schaub could not tell me the reason for this surprising invitation but, since I would be passing through Munich anyhow, there was no difficulty. . . .

Trying to change the subject, I asked Hitler, "How did you spend Christmas Eve?" There was sadness in his voice: "I had my chauffeur drive me around aimlessly, along highways and through villages, until I became tired." I looked at him, amazed. "I do that every Christmas Eve." After a pause: "I have no family and I am lonely."

"Why don't you get married?"

"Because it would be irresponsible of me to bind a woman in marriage. What would she get from me? She would have to be alone most of the time. My love belongs wholly and only to my nation—and if I had children, what would become of them if fate should turn against me? I would then not have a single friend left, and my children would be bound to suffer humiliation and perhaps even die of starvation." His words were bitter and he seemed agitated. Becoming calmer, he went on, "I have tried to express my gratitude wherever I can, for gratitude is a virtue insufficiently valued. I have people at my side who helped me in my bad years. I will remain true to them, even if they do not always have the abilities demanded by their positions." He then gave me a searching look and said quite abruptly, "And what about you, what are your plans?"

My heart leaped. "Hasn't Dr Goebbels told you?"

He shook his head. Relieved, I told him that after a long period of reluctance, I had decided to make a film about the Olympic Games in Berlin.

Hitler looked at me in surprise. "That's an interesting challenge for you. But I thought you didn't want to make any more documentaries, that you only wanted to work as an actress?"

"That's true," I said, "and this is definitely my last documentary. I thought it over for a long time. But I finally said yes because of the great opportunity that the IOC [International Olympic Committee] offered me, the wonderful contract with Tobis, and, last but not least, the realization that we won't be having another Olympics in Germany for a long time." Then I told Hitler about the difficulties of the project and the great responsibility, which made me uneasy about doing it.

"That's a mistake: you have to have a lot more self-confidence. What you do will be valuable, even if it remains incomplete in your eyes. Who else but you should make an Olympic film? And this time you won't have any problems with Dr Goebbels if the IOC organizes the games and we are merely hosts." To my surprise, he said, "I myself am not very interested in the games. I would rather stay away . . ."

"But why?" I asked.

Hitler hesitated. Then he said, "We have no chance of winning medals. The Americans will win most of the victories, and the Negroes will be their stars. I won't enjoy watching that. And then many foreigners will come who reject National Socialism. There could be trouble." He also mentioned that he didn't like the Olympic Stadium: the pillars were too slender, the overall construction not imposing enough.

"But don't be discouraged," he added. "You are sure to make a good film."

. . .

With four gold medals and two world records, Jesse Owens was the athletic phenomenon of the games. One of the legends is that Hitler refused to shake hands with the great champion for racist reasons. Karl von Halt, a member of the IOC and president of the German Olympic Committee, who was in charge of the light athletic contests, told me the true story. It is also recorded in the official American report on the Olympic Games. This, it appears, is what really happened: on the first day of the games, Hitler received the winners on the rostrum, but this was then prohibited by Count Baillet-Latour, the French president of the Olympic Committee, because it was against Olympic protocol. That was why Hitler did not shake hands with any more athletes.

STUDY QUESTIONS

1. Does Riefenstahl's narrative strike you as being a reliable one?
2. Were Hitler's general reactions to the Olympic Games plausible? Is Riefenstahl's version of the Jesse Owens story plausible?

12.2 JOSÉ ORTEGA Y GASSET, *THE REVOLT OF THE MASSES*, 1930

The Spanish philosopher and essayist José Ortega y Gasset (1883–1955) attempted to bring his countrymen into contact with Western—and specifically German—thought. His most famous work, published in 1930 and excerpted here, analyzes the role of "mass politics" in contemporary societies. Ortega y Gasset sought not just to engage philosophically with the dramatic changes of the early twentieth century, but also to participate directly in ongoing events. One year after the publication of *Masses*, he played a celebrated role in the overthrow of the Spanish king Alfonso XIII, but he quickly became disillusioned with politics and left the country after the outbreak of the Spanish Civil War in 1936. When he returned to Spain in 1945, several of his former republican comrades criticized him for appearing to accept Francisco Franco's authoritarian regime.

Whenever the mass acts on its own, it does so in only one manner, for it has no other: in effect it carries out a lynching. It is not entirely by chance that lynch law comes from America, for America is, in its own fashion, the paradise of the masses. It is even less surprising that now, when the masses are in the ascendant, violence is also in the ascendant and is made the ultimate *ratio*, the final reason, the only doctrine. For some time now, the process of violence has become the norm. Nowadays it has reached its height of development, and that can be a good symptom, for it means that its decline is at hand. Violence is now the rhetoric of the day: inane dogmatic rhetoricians have made it their own. When a human reality has run its course, completed its history, when it has been lost and cast away, the waves throw it up on the shore, on the rocks of rhetoric, and there, although already a corpse, it remains for some time. Rhetoric is the cemetery of realities. At best, it is a hospital. A dead reality is survived by its name, which though it is only a word, preserves some of a word's magic power.

Even though the prestige of violence as a cynically established norm may have begun to diminish, we shall continue to live under its rule, though it be under another form.

I refer to the gravest danger now threatening Western civilization. Like all the other dangers which menace it, this one is a creature of civilization itself, one of its glories, in fact: the modern state. We find here a replica of the situation confronting science: the fertility of its principles impels it toward fabulous progress, but this progress inexorably imposes upon it a specialization which threatens to strangle it.

The same process holds true for the state.

. . .

The contemporary state is the most visible and striking product of civilization. It is an interesting revelation to note the attitude adopted toward it by the mass-man. He can see it, admire it, know *it is there*, safeguarding his existence; but he has no notion that it is a creation of human beings, invented by certain men and maintained by certain virtues and presuppositions which were held by men in the past, but could disappear tomorrow. Moreover, the mass-man sees in the state an anonymous power, and since he feels himself to be anonymous too, he believes that the state is something of his own. When conflict or crisis occurs in public life, the mass-man will tend to look to the state to assume the burden, take on the

From José Ortega y Gasset, *The Revolt of the Masses*, translated by Anthony Kerrigan and edited by Kenneth Moore (Notre Dame, Indiana: University of Notre Dame Press, 1985), pp. 102–107.

problem, take charge directly of solving the matter with its unsurpassable means.

And this is the greatest danger threatening civilization today: the stratification of life, state intervention, the taking over by the state of all social spontaneity. And this amounts to the annulment of historical spontaneity, which is what sustains, nourishes, and impels all human destiny. Whenever the mass suspects some misfortune, or when it is moved by its prurient appetite, the temptation is there to look to the permanent and secure possibility of getting everything—without effort, argument, doubt, or risk—to call on this marvelous machinery which goes into action with the touch of a button. The mass tells itself: "The state is me," its own version of *L'État,*

c'est moi. And that is a complete mistake. The state is the mass only in the same sense that two men can say they are identical merely because neither of them is called John. The contemporary state and the mass are the same only in being anonymous. But the mass-man nevertheless believes that he is the state, and he will increasingly tend to want it to be set in motion on the least pretext, to crush any creative minority which disturbs it, disturbs it in any way whatsoever: in politics, ideas, industry.

The result of this tendency will prove fatal. Social spontaneity will be constantly violated by state intervention; no new seeds will bear fruit. Society will have to live *for* the state, man *for* the governmental machine.

STUDY QUESTIONS

1. Does Ortega y Gasset have the political systems of any countries other than the United States in mind as he writes?
2. Does he make a convincing case for the drive of the "mass-man" toward anonymity? Might the circumstances of average people in the 1930s be interpreted differently?

12.3 BENITO MUSSOLINI, "THE DOCTRINE OF FASCISM" FROM THE *ITALIAN ENCYCLOPEDIA*, 1932

A former socialist who broke with his party over his support for Italian participation in the First World War, Benito Mussolini (1883–1945) returned from war embittered that Italy had not gained more in the peace settlement. In 1919 he created the Fascist Party, named for the *fasces*, an ancient Roman symbol of power depicting a bundle of rods tied together. Appointed prime minister in 1922, he used every means available to him—legislation and exploitation of the media as well as political violence—to establish himself as ruler of an authoritarian state.

Fascism relied on emotional appeals that prioritized loyalty to the state over individual needs and desires. The excerpt below is drawn from the *Italian Encyclopedia* entry on Fascism, written by Mussolini and the philosopher Giovanni Gentile, Mussolini's first minister of education, and published ten years after Mussolini's rise to power. Scholars have noted the rambling nature of the article and its obvious inconsistencies. Nevertheless, it represents his thinking about the origins and meaning of fascist ideology.

From Charles Delzell, ed., *Mediterranean Fascism, 1919–1945* (New York: Harper and Row, 1971), pp. 91–93, 99–106.

Like all sound political conceptions, Fascism is action and it is thought; action in which doctrine is immanent, and doctrine arising from a given system of historical forces in which it is inserted, and working on them from within. . . .

Thus many of the practical expressions of Fascism—such as party organization, system of education, discipline—can only be understood when considered in relation to its general attitude toward life. A spiritual attitude. Fascism sees in the world not only those superficial, material aspects in which man appears as an individual, standing by himself, self-centered, subject to natural law which instinctively urges him toward a life of selfish momentary pleasure; it sees not only the individual but the nation and the country; individuals and generations bound together by a moral law, with common traditions and a mission which, suppressing the instinct for life closed in a brief circle of pleasure, builds up a higher life, founded on duty, a life free from the limitations of time and space, in which the individual, by self-sacrifice, the renunciation of self-interest, by death itself, can achieve that purely spiritual existence in which his value as a man exists. . . .

Fascism wants man to be active and to engage in action with all his energies; it wants him to be manfully aware of the difficulties besetting him and ready to face them. It conceives of life as a struggle in which it behooves a man to win for himself a really worthy place (physically, morally, intellectually) to become the implement required for winning it. As for the individual, so for the nation, and so for mankind. Hence the high value of culture in all its forms (artistic, religious, scientific), and the outstanding importance of education. Hence also the essential value of work, by which man subjugates nature and creates the human world (economic, political, ethical, intellectual).

. . . The Fascist disdains an "easy" life.

. . .

And above all, Fascism, the more it considers and observes the future and the development of humanity quite apart from political considerations of the moment, believes neither in the possibility nor the utility of perpetual peace. It thus repudiates the doctrine of Pacifism—born of a renunciation of the struggle and an act of cowardice in the face of sacrifice. War alone brings up to its highest tension all human energy and puts the stamp of nobility upon the peoples who have the courage to meet it. All other trials are substitutes. . . . Thus the Fascist accepts life and loves it, knowing nothing of and despising suicide: he rather conceives of life as a duty and a struggle and conquest, life which should be high and full, lived for oneself, but above all for others—those who are at hand and those who are far distant, contemporaries, and those who will come after.

Such a conception of life makes Fascism the complete opposite of that doctrine, the base of the so-called scientific and Marxian Socialism, the materialist conception of history; according to which the history of human civilization can be explained simply through the conflict of interests among the various social groups and by the change and development in the means and instruments of production. That the changes in the economic field . . . have their importance no one can deny; but that these factors are sufficient to explain the history of humanity excluding all others is an absurd delusion. Fascism now and always, believes in holiness and in heroism; that is to say, in actions influenced by no economic motive, direct or indirect . . . And above all Fascism denies that class war can be the preponderant force in the transformation of society. . . .

After Socialism, Fascism combats the whole complex system of democratic ideology; and repudiates it, whether in its theoretical premises or in its practical application. Fascism denies that the majority, by the simple fact that it is a majority, can direct human society; it denies that numbers alone can govern by means of a periodical consultation, and it affirms the immutable, beneficial, and fruitful inequality of mankind, which can never be permanently leveled through the mere operation of a mechanical process such as universal suffrage. The democratic regime may be defined as from time to time giving the people the illusion of sovereignty, while the real effective sovereignty lies in the hands of other concealed and irresponsible forces. Democracy is a regime nominally without a king, but it is ruled by many kings—more absolute, tyrannical, and ruinous than one sole king, even though a tyrant.

. . .

But the Fascist negation of Socialism, Democracy, and Liberalism must not be taken to mean that Fascism desires to lead the world back to the state of affairs before 1789, the date which seems to be indicated as the opening year of the succeeding semi-Liberal century; we do not desire to turn back. . . .

. . . Fascism uses in its construction whatever elements in the Liberal, Social, or Democratic doctrines still have a living value; it maintains what may be called the certainties which we owe to history, but it rejects all the rest—that is to say, the conception that there can be any doctrine of unquestioned efficiency for all times and all peoples. Given that the nineteenth century was the century of Socialism, Liberalism and Democracy, it does not necessarily follow that the twentieth century must also be a century of Socialism, Liberalism, and Democracy: political doctrines pass, but humanity remains; and it may rather be expected that this will be a century of authority, a century of the Right, a century of Fascism. For if the nineteenth century was a century of individualism (Liberalism always signifying individualism) it may be expected that this will be the century of collectivism, and hence the century of the State. It is a perfectly logical deduction that a new doctrine can utilize all the still vital elements of previous doctrines.

. . .

The Fascist State is not indifferent to the fact of religion in general, or to that particular and positive faith which is Italian Catholicism. The State professes no theology, but a morality, and in the Fascist State religion is considered as one of the deepest manifestations of the spirit of man; thus it is not only respected but defended and protected. The Fascist State has never tried to create its own God, as at one moment Robespierre and the wildest extremists of the Convention tried to do, nor does it vainly seek to obliterate religion from the hearts of men as does Bolshevism; Fascism respects the God of the ascetics, the saints and heroes, and, equally, God as He is perceived and worshipped by simple people.

The Fascist State is an embodied will to power and government; the Roman tradition is here an ideal of force in action. According to Facsism, government is not so much a thing to be expressed in territorial or military terms of morality and the spirit. It must be thought of as an empire—that is to say, a nation which directly or indirectly rules other nations, without the need for conquering a single square yard of territory. For Fascism, the growth of empire, that is to say the expansion of the nation, is an essential manifestation of vitality, and its opposite a sign of decadence. Peoples which are rising, or rising again after a period of decadence, are always imperialist: any renunciation is a sign of decay and death.

Fascism is the doctrine best adapted to represent the tendencies and the aspirations of a people, like the people of Italy, who are rising again after many centuries of abasement and foreign servitude. But empire demands discipline, the coordination of all forces and a deeply felt sense of duty and sacrifice: this fact explains many aspects of the practical working of the regime, the character of many forces in the State, and the necessarily severe measures which must be taken against those who would oppose this spontaneous and inevitable moment of Italy in the twentieth century, and would oppose it by recalling the outworn ideology of the nineteenth century—repudiated wheresoever there has been the courage to undertake great experiments of social and political transformation: for never before has the nation stood more in need of authority, of direction, and of order. If every age has its own characteristic doctrine, there are a thousand signs which point to Fascism as the characteristic doctrine of our time. For if a doctrine must be a living thing, this is proved by the fact that Fascism has created a living faith; and that this faith is very powerful in the minds of men, is demonstrated by those who have suffered and died for it.

STUDY QUESTIONS

1. What frustrated Mussolini about the political ideas and governments that emerged in the wake of the French Revolution in 1789, making the nineteenth century, as he called it, "the century of Socialism, Liberalism, and Democracy"?
2. How was Fascism imbued with both the language and the reality of violence?

12.4 ADOLF HITLER, *MEIN KAMPF*, 1925

In November 1923, after the failure of his "Beer Hall Putsch," Adolf Hitler (1889–1945) was sentenced to five years in a minimum-security prison, but thanks to judges sympathetic to him, he served less than nine months. He emerged from prison with the manuscript of a book, *Mein Kampf* (*My Struggle*), which outlined his political philosophy and plans to achieve radical change. He spoke as well of his early life and vented his extreme hatred of Jewish people. Recently discovered documents reveal that he hoped to parlay the proceeds from the sale of *Mein Kampf* into funding for his political organization, the National Socialist German Workers Party—and for the purchase of a new car with special features. This section of *Mein Kampf* reveals what he had already learned about rhetoric and political action in his nascent career.

I have already stated in the first volume that all great, world-shaking events have been brought about, not by written matter, but by the spoken word. This led to a lengthy discussion in a part of the press, where, of course, such an assertion was sharply attacked, particularly by our bourgeois wiseacres. But the very reason why this occurred confutes the doubters. For the bourgeois intelligentsia protest against such a view only because they themselves obviously lack the power and ability to influence the masses by the spoken word, since they have thrown themselves more and more into purely literary activity and renounced the real agitational activity of the spoken word. Such habits necessarily lead in time to what distinguishes our bourgeoisie today; that is, to the loss of the psychological instinct for *mass effect* and *mass influence*.

While the speaker gets a continuous correction of his speech from the crowd he is addressing, since he can always see in the faces of his listeners to what extent they can follow his arguments with understanding and whether the impression and the effect of his words lead to the desired goal—the writer does not know his readers at all. Therefore, to begin with, he will not aim at a definite mass before his eyes, but will keep his arguments entirely general. By this to a certain degree he loses psychological subtlety and in consequence suppleness. And so, by and large, a brilliant speaker will be able to write better than a brilliant writer can speak, unless he continuously practices this art. On top of this there is the fact that the mass of people as such is lazy; that they remain inertly in the spirit of their old habits and, left to themselves, will take up a piece of written matter only reluctantly if it is not in agreement with what they themselves believe and does not bring them what they had hoped for. Therefore, an article with a definite tendency is for the most part read only by people who can already be reckoned to this tendency. At most a leaflet or a poster can, by its brevity, count on getting a moment's attention from someone who thinks differently. The picture in all its forms up to the film has greater possibilities. Here a man needs to use his brains even less; it suffices to look, or at most to read extremely brief texts, and thus many will more readily accept a *pictorial presentation* than *read* an *article* of any *length*. The picture brings them in a much briefer time, I might almost say at one stroke, the enlightenment which they obtain from written matter only after arduous reading.

The essential point, however, is that a piece of literature never knows into what hands it will fall, and yet must retain its definite form. In general the effect will be the greater, the more this form corresponds to the intellectual level and nature of those very people who will be

Adolf Hitler, Mein Kampf, translated by Ralph Mannheim (Boston: Houghton Mifflin, 1998), pp. 469–471.

its readers. A book that is destined for the broad masses must, therefore, attempt from the very beginning to have an effect, both in style and elevation, different from a work intended for higher intellectual classes.

Only by this kind of adaptability does written matter approach the spoken word. To my mind, the speaker can treat the same theme as the book; he will, if he is a brilliant popular orator, not be likely to repeat the same reproach and the same substance twice in the same form. He will always let himself be borne by the great masses in such a way that instinctively the very words come to his lips that he needs to speak to the hearts of his audience. And if he errs, even in the slightest, he has the living correction before him. As I have said, he can read from the facial expression of his audience whether, firstly, they *understand* what he is saying, whether, secondly, they can *follow the speech as a whole*, and to what extent, thirdly, he has *convinced* them of the *soundness* of what he has said. If—firstly—he sees that they do not understand him, he will become so primitive and clear in his explanations that even the last member of his audience has to understand him; if he feels—secondly—that they cannot follow him, he will construct his ideas so cautiously and slowly that even the weakest member of the audience is not left behind, and he will—thirdly—if he suspects that they do not seem convinced of the soundness of his argument, repeat it over and over in constantly new examples. He himself will utter their objections, which he senses though unspoken, and go on confuting them and exploding them, until at length even the last group of an opposition, by its very bearing and facial expression, enables him to recognize its capitulation to his arguments.

Here again it is not seldom a question of overcoming prejudices which are not based on reason, but, for the most part unconsciously, are supported only by sentiment. To overcome this barrier of instinctive aversion, of emotional hatred, of prejudiced rejection, is a thousand times harder than to correct a faulty or erroneous scientific opinion. False concepts and poor knowledge can be eliminated by instruction, the resistance of the emotions never. Here only an appeal to these mysterious powers themselves can be effective; and the writer can hardly ever accomplish this, but almost exclusively the orator.

STUDY QUESTIONS

1. What advantages does the orator have over the writer, in Hitler's assessment? Is he convincing on this point?
2. How does a skillful speaker manipulate an audience? Does the substance of the speech matter at all, as Hitler describes the process of public speaking?

12.5 HANNA SCHMITT, *THE DISFRANCHISEMENT OF WOMEN*, 1937

In a speech to the National Socialist *Frauenschaft* (Womanhood) in September 1934, Adolf Hitler told his audience that "the slogan 'Emancipation of women' was invented by Jewish intellectuals and its content was formed by the same spirit." Hitler and the Nazis valorized "exemplary"

From Hanna Schmitt, "Die Entrechtung der Frauen," in *Deutsche Frauenschicksale*, ed. by Union für Recht und Freiheit (2nd edition; London, 1937), pp. 17–25, translated and reprinted in Eleanor S. Riemer and John C. Fout, eds., *European Women: A Documentary History 1789–1945* (New York: Schocken Books, 1980), pp. 111–113.

motherhood above all, but not all women wanted to be confined to their maternal roles or prized by the state for the number of children they bore. In the following excerpt, from 1937, Hanna Schmitt, a Swiss woman who had worked closely with German feminists in the days before Hitler took power, offers foreigners a countervailing view of events inside Germany. She published her article (written in German) in England, where it would reach an international audience.

In 1918 German women were given the active and passive franchise. From that time on, they were represented in the parliaments of the Reich, the states and the communities. The progressive and socialist parties in particular sent women representatives to these bodies. The only exception was the Nazi party and once the dictatorship was in power, it was this party that expelled women from parliaments and deprived them again of their public functions. Thousands of women who formerly had been active in state and communal positions experienced the hostile attitude of the new regime. In numerous cases they were turned out of hospitals and schools where they were employed as physicians, school principals and valuable teachers.

Mr. Goebbels tried to explain the measure in his own peculiar brand of dishonest pathos: "When we exclude women from public life, we give them back their honor." . . .

I have observed for years the activities of this organization [International Women's League for Peace and Freedom] and learned to appreciate the labor of those women who, after the dissolution of the League [by the Nazis] had to leave their homeland to escape suffering in German prisons and concentration camps. Frieda Perlen, the chairwoman of the Stuttgart chapter, a tireless worker especially for German-French rapprochement, did not escape her persecutors. Her detention in a concentration camp broke her health and after her discharge she succumbed to her suffering. Three other friends, genuine and upright personalities, became stateless refugees. Why? Only because they wanted the best for their country, because they stood up for peace and freedom. . . .

Women when they are admitted to the universities are subject to work service duty in the so-called *Frauendienst* or "women's service." They are trained in anti-aircraft defense, for the signal corps and ambulance service, and get practice in the use of gas masks; in short, the first stage of their studies is given over to one theme only: readiness for war.

Women have disappeared from editorial offices and are deprived of professorships. There is no room for them in laboratories. If they are suspect for racial and ideological reasons, the regime persecutes them even more ruthlessly than men. For they are out of favor not only because of their convictions but also because of their sex, which, according to National Socialism, places them on a lower level than the male.

This is particularly evident in the economic and social life of women. An official decree issued on April 27, 1933, shortly after Hitler's seizure of power, said: "Management is to see to it that all married women employees ask for their discharge. If they do not comply voluntarily, the employer is free to dismiss them upon ascertaining that they are economically protected some other way." Thousands of employees lost their positions by this decree, married as well as single women, who were simply told that parents or other members of their families could take care of them. It goes without saying that such a loss of income seriously threatens the existence of a family, considering the low wage level in Germany. Besides, the men who take the place of the women are not paid any better. Thus, poorly paid husbands are supposed to take care of their wives. If they cannot manage, the wives will look for work, but these days married women are treated worse than ever. Their wages are minimal for a maximum amount of work. Wage contracts are ignored. Only in munitions factories are they sought after as a reserve labor force in case of war. Due to the slavedriver system and the unsanitary conditions in the war industry, the health of the women is most seriously endangered.

And what about the private life of women? The Nazis claim to honor housewives and mothers above all. But this honor is denied to a great number of mothers. It does not cover, for example, the mothers of illegitimate children. They bear the burden of care but are morally disqualified and do not get the benefit of the necessary legal protection.

Marriage is subject to the severest restrictions. Women who have been in a concentration camp must provide proof before marriage that they are in perfect physical and mental health, racially pure and not dependent on public relief. The threat of sterilization hangs over many women like the sword of Damocles. Every woman with a physical defect, be it ever so slight, must make it known to the authorities. The doors are wide open for denunciations and vindictive vengeance.

According to official German statistics, more than 500,000 people were sterilized in the last few years; of these, 30,000 cases resulted in death. While in the U.S.A., which has sterilization laws also, 19,000 people were sterilized in 28 years, 55,000 people were subjected to this dangerous operation in a single year in Germany. With such massive surgical intervention, the necessary precautionary measures are naturally not observed. The magazine *German Justice* [*Die deutsche Justiz*] reports that by the end of 1934, 27,958 women were sterilized, with five percent of the cases resulting in death.

The most tender and intimate relationship held sacred by all civilized peoples is that between mother and child. But with what brutality does National Socialism often tear asunder these bonds. If, for example, a mother is Jewish and the father Aryan, the child is taken away from the mother in case of divorce to avoid exposure to "Jewish influences." The fate of Jewish mothers is especially tragic in small towns. They must look on as their children grow up in isolation which has a devastating effect on the young minds. How heart-rending is the authentic report of a Jewish mother forced to live with husband and child in such a town. When she asked her little daughter what she wanted for Christmas, she tearfully replied, "Only a little playmate, mommy!" It is not surprising that Jewish families of means send their children abroad to be educated. There is a tragic saying among them, "Our children become letters." . . .

Women who are silent, women who serve, are not free women. For only free women can develop their characters to the fullest, be it in pursuit of studies or at work, as housewives and mothers. A nation that honors its women honors itself. However much it may ask of national virtues, a regime that oppresses the women shows contempt for the people and at the same time for those who are responsible for the future, the mothers of its children.

STUDY QUESTIONS

1. In what specific ways did the Nazi government limit the opportunities of its women citizens?
2. What falsehoods did Schmitt expose regarding the Nazi conception of gender roles? What outrageous acts did Schmitt want the world to know about in 1937?

12.6 THE NUREMBERG RACE LAWS, SEPTEMBER 15, 1935

Immediately after Hitler became Chancellor in January 1933, members of the Sturmabteilung and other Nazi supporters celebrated by assaulting Jews and vandalizing and looting Jewish-owned businesses. Hitler then made the persecution systematic by ordering the dismissal of Jewish civil

Adapted from http://archive.is/ess.uwe.ac.uk.

servants, teachers, and professors. A "Law against the Overcrowding of German Schools" denied young Jewish adults the right to enroll in universities, while a further decree excluded Jews from the world of arts and letters. In 1935, all German Jews lost their citizenship, and a Law for the Protection of German Blood and German Honor outlawed marriages between Jews and other Germans and made sexual relations between them a criminal offense. After less than two years in office, the Nazis had reduced Jews to political and social outcasts within their own society.

But these steps marked only the first stages of their persecution. In 1938, the regime launched a nationwide pogrom against Germany's Jewish communities, directly ordering brutal attacks against individuals, homes, businesses, and houses of worship. The pogrom of November 8, 1938, known as *Kristallnacht* (the Night of Broken Glass), took a particularly devastating toll: 100 dead, scores of synagogues burned to the ground, thousands of Jewish homes and businesses pillaged, 30,000 Jewish people condemned to concentration camps.

Although the Nazis' prewar violence against Jews did not reach its peak until *Kristallnacht* in 1938, the legal framework that prefigured this violence was fully in place by 1935. The two laws excerpted below give a clear indication of what the Nazi government intended for Germany's Jewish population.

REICH CITIZENSHIP LAW, SEPTEMBER 15, 1935

The Reichstag has unanimously enacted the following law, which is promulgated herewith:

§ 1

1. A subject of the State is a person who enjoys the protection of the German Reich and who in consequence has specific obligations towards it.
2. The status of subject of the State is acquired in accordance with the provisions of the Reich and State Citizenship Law.

§ 2

1. A Reich citizen is a subject of the State who is of German or related blood, who proves by his conduct that he is willing and fit faithfully to serve the German people and Reich.

Reich citizenship is acquired through the granting of a Reich Citizenship Certificate.
The Reich citizen is the sole bearer of full political rights in accordance with the Law.

§ 3

The Reich Minister of the Interior, in coordination with the Deputy of the Führer will issue the Legal and Administrative orders required to implement and complete this Law.

Nuremberg, September 15, 1935, at the Reich Party Congress of Freedom
The Führer and Reich Chancellor Adolf Hitler
The Reich Minister of the Interior Frick

NUREMBERG LAW FOR THE PROTECTION OF GERMAN BLOOD AND GERMAN HONOR, SEPTEMBER 15, 1935

Moved by the understanding that the purity of German Blood is the essential condition for the continued existence of the German people, and inspired by the inflexible determination to ensure the existence of the German Nation for all time, the Reichstag has unanimously adopted the following law, which is promulgated herewith:

Article 1.

1. Marriages between Jews and subjects of the state of German or related blood are forbidden. Marriages nevertheless concluded are invalid, even if concluded abroad to circumvent this law.
2. Annulment proceedings can be initiated only by the State Prosecutor.

Article 2.

Extramarital intercourse [the German word *Verkehr* could also be translated, crudely, as "traffic"] between Jews and subjects of the state of German or related blood is forbidden.

Article 3.

Jews may not employ in their households female subjects of the state of German or related blood who are under 45 years old.

Article 4.

(1) Jews are forbidden to fly the Reich or National flag or to display the Reich colors.

(2) They are, on the other hand, permitted to display the Jewish colors. The exercise of this right is protected by the State.

Article 5.

(1) Any person who violates the prohibition under §1 will be punished by a prison sentence with hard labor.

(2) A male who violates the prohibition under §2 will be punished with a prison sentence with or without hard labor.

(3) Any person violating the provisions under §3 or §4 will be punished with a prison sentence of up to one year and a fine, or with one or the other of these penalties.

Article 6.

The Reich Minister of the Interior, in coordination with the Deputy of the Führer and the Reich Minister of Justice, will issue the legal and administrative regulations required to implement and complete this law.

Article 7.

The law takes effect on the day following promulgations except for §3, which goes into force on January 1, 1936.

Nuremberg, September 15, 1935, at the Reich Party Congress of Freedom
The Führer and Reich Chancellor Adolf Hitler
The Reich Minister of the Interior Frick
The Reich Minister of Justice Dr. Gürtner
The Deputy of the Führer R. Hess

STUDY QUESTIONS

1. What are the connections between these two laws?
2. Why was the law applied differently to men and women?

12.7 VISUAL SOURCE: PALAZZO DELLA CIVILTÀ ITALIANA, EUR, ROME, 1938–1942

For many Italians, part of Fascism's appeal was Mussolini's claim that he would return Italy to its former glory, specifically harkening back to ancient Rome. Unlike Hitler, whose artistic taste was conservative, Mussolini supported both modern and classical styles. In the 1930s he began planning for a new site on the outskirts of Rome to host a 1942 world's fair. This event would celebrate the twentieth anniversary of Fascist rule, and its site would be called the Esposizione Universale Roma, or EUR.

OperaJoeGreen at English Wikipedia

EUR's most distinctive building is the Palazzo della Civiltà Italiana, built to house an Exhibition of Italian Civilization. Representing different schools of design, three architects collaborated on the project. With its rows of repeating arches, the building echoes the Colosseum—so much so that it is better known today as the "Square Colosseum." The Palazzo is constructed of reinforced concrete covered with travertine marble; its eight stories sit high on a podium, making the Square Colosseum visible across the city of Rome. Four statues from Greek mythology occupy the four corners of the podium; another twenty-eight statues fill the arches along the first floor of the building. At the top of the building, an inscription praises Italian genius: "A nation of poets, of artists, of heroes, of saints, of thinkers, of scientists, of navigators, of migrants."

The celebratory world's fair was not to be. In 1943, when the Germans invaded Italy, the first floor of the Palazzo became a repair shop for German vehicles, and the building suffered damage from the impact of grenades. The wider EUR project was finally completed in 1960 when Rome hosted the Olympics. Since 2015, the Palazzo has served as the headquarters for the fashion giant Fendi.

FIGURE 12.7 Palazzo Della Civilta Italiana

STUDY QUESTIONS

1. What does this building reveal about Fascist ideology and Mussolini's attempt to appeal to Italians?
2. Considering its different functions during the last nine decades, what endures about the style of the Palazzo della Civiltà Italiana?

CREATING THE COMPLEX NOUN PHRASES OF ACADEMIC WRITING

Over the past two centuries, noun phrases in academic writing have grown steadily more common and more complex. Composition handbooks often warn against heavy reliance on noun phrases, but when used well, noun phrases allow writers to communicate more content in fewer words.

A "noun phrase" is a phrase whose main word is a noun:

Conditions[1]
The *conditions*
The chaotic *conditions*
The chaotic *conditions* that prevailed in Italy
The chaotic *conditions* that prevailed in Italy after the war

Noun phrases are used the same way a single noun is used:

Conditions were difficult.
The conditions were difficult.
The chaotic conditions were difficult.
The chaotic conditions that prevailed in Italy were difficult.
The chaotic conditions that prevailed in Italy after the war were difficult.

COMBINING SENTENCES USING NOUN PHRASES

Rye bread was a staple of the German diet.
A kilo of rye bread weighed 2.2 lbs.
A kilo of rye bread cost 163 marks on January 3, 1923.
(3 sentences / 3 verbs / 29 words)

COMBINED by turning two of the sentences into noun phrases (underlined):

A kilo (2.2 lbs.) of rye bread, a staple of the German diet, cost 163 marks on January 3, 1923.

(1 sentence / 1 verb / 20 words)

PUNCTUATION: The underlined noun phrases in this example are set off from the rest of the sentence by commas and parentheses because they are "supplemental," meaning that you don't need them to understand the sentence. Supplemental noun phrases can also be set off by dashes or brackets.

---

[1] Inside a clause or sentence, a noun phrase can consist of just one word.

EXERCISE: USE NOUN PHRASES TO COMBINE SENTENCES

Instructions

Use one or more noun phrases to combine the sentences below, adding punctuation as needed.

EXAMPLE:

Gabriele D'Annunzio was a nationalist writer.
> He sought to improve his country's share of postwar spoils.

Combined:

Gabriele D'Annunzio, *a nationalist writer*, sought to improve his country's share of postwar spoils.
> *Or:*
> A nationalist writer, *Gabriele D'Annunzio*, sought to improve his country's share of postwar spoils.

---

1. By 1924, the German National People's Party had garnered 20 percent of the vote and stood as the country's second largest party after the SPD. The People's Party was known as the DNVP.
   COMBINED: By 1924, the German National People's Party _____ had garnered 20 percent of the vote and stood as the country's second largest party after the SPD.

---

2. Members of traditionally monarchist social groups did little to instill respect for democracy. These groups included teachers, professors, and administrators.
   COMBINED: Members of traditionally monarchist social groups— _____ —did little to instill respect for democracy.

---

3. Nationalism lay at the core of fascist belief. Nationalism was the ideology that glorified the nation.
   COMBINED:

---

4. Leni Riefenstahl was a talented dancer, actress, and filmmaker. She is best known for her lyrical propaganda film, *Triumph of the Will* (1934).
   COMBINED:

---

5. In Hitler's mind, the Final Solution was already taking shape. The Final Solution was the genocide of the Jews.
COMBINED:

EXERCISE: USE NOUN PHRASES TO SHORTEN SENTENCES

Academic writers often shorten sentences by using noun phrases in place of subordinate clauses (see Chapter 2 Writing History). Keep in mind, though, that sentence length is less important than rhythm and style. The goal is not to write shorter sentences per se, but sentences that flow.

Instructions

Shorten—or "reduce"—the underlined clauses to phrases.

EXAMPLE:

Hitler created a national highway system, called the *Autobahnen*, that was more advanced than any in the world.

Noun phrase in place of subordinate clause:

Hitler created a national highway system, the Autobahnen, that was more advanced than any in the world.

6. By the mid-1920s, *Il Duce (which means "leader")* had created an absolutist dictatorship built on political terror and mass propaganda.
SHORTENED:

7. In 1932, Riefenstahl read Hitler's book, which he titled *Mein Kampf*.
SHORTENED:

8. *Kristallnacht*, which means Night of the Broken Glass, took a devastating toll.
SHORTENED:

Turning verbs, adjectives, and clauses into nouns and noun phrases.

CLAUSE	NOUN PHRASE
The army was unwilling to defend the republic.	The army's unwillingness to defend the republic
Postwar parliamentary regimes were fragile.	The fragility of postwar parliamentary regimes
Thomas Mann, who was a great German writer	Thomas Mann, the great German writer

EXERCISE: COMBINE SENTENCES USING NOUN PHRASES (ADVANCED)

Instructions

Combine each set of sentences by replacing the italicized words with a noun phrase.

EXAMPLES:

The number of people who did not have jobs was already high in 1928.
By the beginning of 1930, *the number of people who did not have jobs* had risen to three million. (2 sentences, 33 words)

Combination:

By the beginning of 1930, *joblessness*, already high in 1928, had risen to three million. (1 sentence, 15 words)
   Or:
Already high in 1928, *joblessness* had risen to three million by the beginning of 1930. (1 sentence, 15 words)

The army was unwilling to defend the regime when attacked by nationalist opponents.
The fact that *the army was unwilling* to defend the regime did not bode well for the future. (2 sentences, 31 words)

Combination:

The army's unwillingness to defend the regime when attacked by nationalist opponents did not bode well for the future. (1 sentence, 19 words)

---

9. In Hungary, a fascist-style movement surfaced immediately after the war.
   But *the country lacked democratic institutions*, so the fascists were prevented from taking control.
   HINT: Try beginning your sentence with "In Hungary, where a fascist-style movement surfaced immediately after the war, . . ."
   SECOND HINT: Use the noun form of "lacked" (*lack*, usually expressed as *"the lack of"*).
   COMBINED:

---

10. The Nazi regime was the most extreme to emerge in Europe (outside of the Soviet Union).
    The Nazi regime was far from alone *in rejecting liberalism and democracy*.
    HINT: Use the noun form of the verb "reject" (*rejection*).
    COMBINED:

You will find suggested answers to the exercises in the back of this book. For more Writing History exercises, as well as study resources for this chapter, visit oup.com/us/berenson.

CHAPTER 13

THE SECOND WORLD WAR, 1939–1945

13.1 PRIMO LEVI, *SURVIVAL IN AUSCHWITZ*, 1947

Primo Levi (1919–1987) was one of about 6,400 Italian Jews (of a total Italian Jewish population of roughly 44,000) deported by his country's German occupiers to the Nazi death camp at Auschwitz, in Poland. Italian Jews were relatively fortunate because the Nazis did not begin sending them away until late in the war. In contrast, Jews from Poland, Russia, and elsewhere in Eastern Europe found themselves the objects of Hitler's "final solution" beginning in 1941. In camps specifically designed as murder facilities, the Nazis killed nearly three million Jews—about half the number they slaughtered altogether. The rare survivors stayed alive, in Levi's words, by sheer "luck."

Levi's *Survival in Auschwitz* (1947) is one of the most harrowing and lyrical accounts of the Holocaust. Although he never overcame his guilt for having survived when so many others did not, he wanted "to tell the story, to bear witness" to the incomprehensible horrors the Nazis had devised. Hoping that in the future others might be spared his fate, Levi used his gift of prose "not to live *and* to tell, but to live *in order* to tell."

Already for some months now the distant booming of the Russian guns had been heard at intervals when, on 11 January 1945, I fell ill of scarlet fever and was once more sent into Ka-Be. "*Infektionsabteilung*": it meant a small room, really quite clean, with ten bunks on two levels, a wardrobe, three stools and a closet seat with the pail for corporal needs. All in a space of three yards by five.

It was difficult to climb to the upper bunks as there was no ladder; so, when a patient got worse he was transferred to the lower bunks.

When I was admitted I was the thirteenth in the room. Four of the others—two French political prisoners and two young Hungarian Jews—had scarlet fever; there were three with diphtheria, two with typhus, while one suffered from a repellent facial erysipelas. The other two had more than one illness and were incredibly wasted away.

I had a high fever. I was lucky enough to have a bunk entirely to myself: I lay down with relief knowing that I had the right to forty days' isolation and therefore of rest, while I felt myself still sufficiently strong to fear neither the consequences of scarlet fever nor the selections.

Thanks to my by-now-long experience of camp life I managed to bring with me all my personal belongings: a belt of interlaced electric wire, the knife-spoon, a needle with three needlefuls, five buttons and last of all eighteen flints which I had stolen from the Laboratory. From each of these, shaping them patiently with a knife, it was possible to make three smaller flints, just the right gauge for a normal cigarette lighter. They were valued at six or seven rations of bread.

I enjoyed four peaceful days. Outside it was snowing and very cold, but the room was heated. I was given strong doses of sulpha drugs, I suffered from an intense feeling of sickness and was hardly able to eat; I did not want to talk.

The two Frenchmen with scarlet fever were quite pleasant. They were provincials from the Vosges who had entered the camp only a few days before with a large convoy of civilians swept up by the Germans in their retreat from Lorraine. The elder one was named Arthur, a peasant, small and thin. The other, his bed-companion, was Charles, a school teacher, thirty-two years old; instead of a shirt he had been given a summer vest, ridiculously short.

On the fifth day the barber came. He was a Greek from Salonica: he spoke only the beautiful Spanish of his people, but understood some words of all the languages spoken in the camp. He was called Askenazi and had been in the camp for almost three years. I do not know how he managed to get the post of *Frisör* [German for barber] of Ka-Be: he spoke neither German nor Polish, nor was he in fact excessively brutal. Before he entered, I heard him speaking excitedly for a long time in the corridor with one of the doctors, a compatriot of his. He seemed to have an unusual look on his face, but as the expressions of the Levantines are different from ours, I could not tell whether he was afraid or happy or merely upset. He knew me, or at least knew that I was Italian.

When it was my turn I climbed down laboriously from the bunk. I asked him in Italian if there was anything new: he stopped shaving me, winked in a serious and allusive manner, pointed to the window with his chin, and then made a sweeping gesture with his hand towards the west.

"Morgen, alle Kamarad weg." [German for "Tomorrow, all the soldiers are going."]

He looked at me for a moment with his eyes wide-open, as if waiting for a reaction, and then he added: *"todos, todos"* ["all, all" in Spanish] and returned to his work. He knew about my flints and shaved me with a certain gentleness.

The news excited no direct emotion in me. Already for many months I had no longer felt any pain, joy or fear, except in that detached and distant manner characteristic of the Lager, which might be described as conditional: if I still had my former sensitivity, I thought, this would be an extremely moving moment.

. . .

18 January. During the night of the evacuation the camp-kitchens continued to function, and on the following morning the last distribution of soup took place in the hospital. The central-heating plant had been abandoned; in the huts a little heat still lingered on, but hour by hour the temperature dropped and it was evident that we would soon suffer from the cold. Outside it must have been at least 5°F. below zero; most of the patients had only a shirt and some of them not even that.

Nobody knew what our fate would be. Some SS men had remained, some of the guard towers were still occupied.

About midday an SS officer made a tour of the huts. He appointed a chief in each of them, selecting from among the remaining non-Jews, and ordered a list of the patients to be made at once, divided into Jews and non-Jews. The matter seemed clear. No one was surprised that the Germans preserved their national love of classification until the very end, nor did any Jew seriously expect to live until the following day.

. . .

[Later that evening.] The Germans were no longer there. The towers were empty.

Today I think that if for no other reason than that an Auschwitz existed, no one in our age should speak of Providence. But without doubt in that hour the memory of biblical salvations in times of extreme adversity passed like a wind through all our minds.

STUDY QUESTIONS

STUDY QUESTIONS

1. What does Levi's account reveal about the international aspects of life among Auschwitz prisoners?
2. How was information gathered and disseminated in the camps?

13.2 MARC BLOCH, *STRANGE DEFEAT*, 1940

Professor Marc Bloch (1886–1944) was one of the most influential historians of the twentieth century. He was born into an assimilated Jewish family of Alsatian descent and had his childhood shadowed by the Dreyfus Affair and the vicious anti-Semitism that it revealed. After his service in the First World War, Bloch became a professor at the University of Strasbourg, where he would become internationally famous for the journal he founded in 1929 with his colleague Lucien Febvre: *Annales* (*Yearly [Papers]*). Today the historiographical method Bloch and Lebvre pioneered is called the "Annales" school of historical research. Bloch's most influential historical study, *Feudal Society*, appearing in two volumes in 1939 and 1940, was written against the backdrop of pervasive anti-Semitism in France.

In 1939, when he was fifty-three, Bloch joined the French army again. Sadly, he witnessed the "Strange Defeat" of France a year later, described in the following excerpt. Finding himself returned to civilian status and living in unoccupied Vichy France, Bloch joined the resistance and was captured and jailed for his activities. While in prison, he continued work on his final book, *The Historian's Craft*, a manual for an "apprentice historian" that was published after the war—and after he had been shot by the Gestapo in the summer of 1944.

Naturally, much inquiry is necessary into, and a great deal can be said about, the underlying causes of these weaknesses. Our middle class, which, in spite of everything, remains the brain of the nation, was a great deal more addicted to serious studies when most of its members had independent means than it is to-day. The business man, the doctor, the lawyer, has to put in a hard day's work at his office. When he leaves it he is in no fit state, it would seem, for anything but amusement. Perhaps a better organization of the working day might, without diminishing the intensity of his labours, assure him a rather greater degree of leisure. But how about these amusements of his? Do they take an intellectual form? One thing is certain: they rarely have any connexion, even indirect, with his active life. For it is an ancient tradition among us, that intelligence should be enjoyed, like art, for its own sake, and should be kept carefully shut away from all possibility of practical application. We are a nation of great scientists, yet no technicians are less scientific than ours. We read, when we do read, with the object of acquiring culture. I have nothing against that. But it never seems to occur to us that culture can, and should, be a great help to us in our daily lives.

But what the French people really need is to be pupils once again in the school of true intellectual freedom.

. . .

A university professor will be forgiven if he lays a great part of the responsibility for all this on education, and, himself an educator, does his best to expose, without undue beating about the bush, the defects of our teaching methods.

Our system of secondary education has been continuously oscillating, for a long time past, between an old-fashioned humanism which, aesthetically at least, has strong claims on its loyalty, and a taste—often excessive—for the new. But it is neither capable of preserving the aesthetic and moral standards of classical culture, nor of creating fresh ones to take their place. Consequently it has done little to develop the intellectual vitality of the nation. It lays upon its pupils the dead weight of examinations, and in this respect the universities are no better. It makes little room in its curriculum for those sciences which depend upon observation and might play so large a part in the training of visual concentration and the use of the grey matter of the brain. It pays a great deal of attention to the physiology of plants—and quite rightly, but it almost entirely neglects field botany, and, in so doing, commits a grievous fault. In English schools the authorities make a great point of encouraging "hobbies" (natural history, fossil-collecting, photography, and all sorts of odd pastimes). Our own pastors and masters, on the contrary, modestly avert their eyes from every kind of "queer taste" or else leave such matters to the tender mercy of the Boy Scouts. Indeed, the success of the Scout movement probably shows more clearly than does anything else where the most yawning gaps are to be found in our national system of education. I know more than one boy who was an excellent performer in the classroom but never once so much as opened a serious book after he had left his secondary school. On the other hand, it is no rare thing to find that those who had the reputation with their masters of being dunces or near-dunces have since developed a real taste for the things of the mind. If such occurrences were occasional only, they would not be particularly significant. It is when they become multiplied that one begins uncomfortably to feel that "something is wrong."

Am I moved to say all this by the same sort of perversity that urges a lover to hurt the beloved? As an historian I am naturally inclined to be especially hard on the teaching of history. It is not only the Staff College that equips its pupils inadequately to face the test of action. I do not mean that the secondary schools can be accused with justice of neglecting the contemporary scene. On the contrary, they tend to give it an increasingly dominant place in the curriculum. But just because our teachers of history are inclined to focus their attention *only* on the present, or at most on the very recent past, they find the present more and more difficult to explain. They are like oceanographers who refuse to look up at the stars because they are too remote from the sea, and consequently are unable to discover the causes of the tides. I do not say that the past entirely governs the present, but I do maintain that we shall never satisfactorily understand the present unless we take the past into account. But there is still worse to come. Because our system of historical teaching deliberately cuts itself off from a wide field of vision and comparison, it can no longer impart to those whose minds it claims to form anything like a true sense of difference and change. . . .

STUDY QUESTIONS

1. What did Bloch see as the consequences of French habits of mind in the prewar period?
2. Did the teaching of History in particular contribute to the fall of France in 1940?

13.3 VIDKUN QUISLING, "THE NORDIC REVIVAL" AND "A GREATER NORWAY," 1931 AND 1942

In 1933, shortly after Hitler took power in Germany, the Norwegian anti-Communist Vidkun Quisling (1887–1945) founded a party he named the Nasjonal Samling, or "Rallying of the Nation." Quisling and his followers quickly combined anti-Bolshevism with anti-Semitism, creating a toxic brew Quisling called "the Nordic Principle." Quisling welcomed the Nazis when Germany invaded Norway in April 1940 and was appointed head of the occupied state in 1942. Later that year he was granted an audience with Hitler himself.

When the war ended, Quisling was tried as a traitor and executed by firing squad. Today his name is a synonym for "traitor." Nevertheless, Quisling's name was invoked at trial by Anders Behring Breivik, a young Norwegian man who killed 77 people in coordinated terrorist attacks in July 2011. These excerpts come from two of Quisling's publications, *Russia and Ourselves* (1931) and *Quisling Calls Norway!* (1942).

RUSSIA AND OURSELVES

We have seen how the Bolshevists are working against the world. How is the world to defend itself against Bolshevism, and Bolshevist-ridden Russia, which, with her resources, her means, and her aims, is not only a danger, but the greatest of all dangers to the civilization of the world, and the welfare of mankind? . . .

The Nordic nations must strive towards a fuller knowledge of themselves, their own character, and their place and task in the world. We must realize that we do not stand alone, but that we are members of a common Northern stock, which represents the most valuable contribution to the human race, and has always been the chief exponent of world- civilization. Not only Greece and Rome, but Europe and America owe their greatness to the Nordic element, and the fate of the modern world is bound up with its preservation or decay, as was the case with the ancient civilizations. Efforts towards the national revival of our countries are futile unless the Nordic spirit is reanimated. The progress of our nations is inextricably bound up with the preservation of their Nordic blood; and in order to ensure this survival of our typical stock we must observe a set of rather primitive laws, already discovered by science. Unless we guard our Nordic character, it will be lost to us. . . .

QUISLING CALLS NORWAY!

The national decay and collapse of Norway are the result of a set of debilitating and corrosive forces which over generations have been able to gather momentum.

These currents of corruption are all closely linked with each other and finally merge in the mighty stream which we call Anglo-Jewish world capitalism. That is the Midgard snake which wraps itself round the world and gnaws at the roots of the Nordic tree of life [*Yggdrasil* in Norse mythology]. To remove Anglo-Jewish, capitalist influence from every area, dynastic, political, social, economic, and cultural, is the premise for the resurrection of Norway, and hence the principal goal of our movement for national unification [*Sammlung*]. . . . And England will go under with

From Roger Griffin, *Fascism* (New York: Oxford University Press, 1995), pp. 208–211.

the death of the doomed capitalist system, whose creators and leaders are the members of international Jewry resident there, and on whom English world dominion depends. It is now obvious that the English policy of "divide and rule" ["*divide et impera*" in Latin, which first appeared in political handbooks in the seventeenth century] in continental Europe is played out. It is precisely in the Balkans that the English attempt to balkanize Europe is rapidly approaching its moment of truth, in which the whole of Europe with a population of over 300 million people economically and militarily unified confront the English island, while its dominion in the East is being simultaneously threatened by Japan. . . .

The war has shocked the Norwegian people out of its deep slumber and the thought of national reconciliation is born once more. . . . With the foundation of the Nasjonal Samling we have safeguarded the new national autonomy of the Norwegian people and created the basis of a national rebirth in the spirit of the historical tradition of our people. And as good Norwegians we are now building the new Norway on this basis without regard to personal sacrifice. . . .

I am no prophet. But what I said in the past has come to pass. And today I tell you that what Norway was it will be again, despite the difficulties that lie in its path.

Norway will grow into a great political alliance and thus contribute to laying the spiritual and economic foundation of a new civilization.

Norway shall not only be free. Norway shall be great.

STUDY QUESTIONS

1. What evidence suggests that Quisling's philosophy was more anti-Semitic than anti-Communist?
2. What might Quisling have meant about "the Nordic element" in Western civilization? What evidence might he have offered to substantiate this claim?

13.4 ALBERT CAMUS, *THE MYTH OF SISYPHUS*, 1942

Albert Camus (1913–1960) was born in Algeria to European parents from the working class. His mother raised her two sons after their father was killed at the Battle of the Marne. Camus put himself through college at the University of Algiers and later worked as a journalist and directed a theater company. In the summer of 1942, he moved to France's unoccupied zone (Vichy) to recuperate from tuberculosis and began working with the famous resistance network Combat. When the Nazis crossed into Vichy, Camus moved to Paris and continued his involvement with intellectual resistance alongside Jean-Paul Sartre, Simone de Beauvoir, and others. After the war he enjoyed international fame for his writings, including the bestselling novels *The Stranger and The Plague*.

In the postwar era some people questioned Camus about his position on the Algerian struggle for independence. He remained neutral, refusing to choose between the Algerian Arabs and the European *pieds noirs*, the group to which his family belonged. Confronted by a young Algerian, Camus explained, "People are now planting bombs in the tramways of Algiers. My mother might be on one of those tramways. If that is justice, then I prefer my mother." This refusal to defend political violence was typical of the high value Camus routinely put on human life.

Among Camus's important ideas is the observation that life is "absurd" because there is no prescribed meaning that exists outside of our own actions. Although he is frequently classified as an Existentialist or an absurdist, he rejected the labels. He believed that humans must face irrationality and injustice yet still find joy in living, fully accepting that we will one day die. Camus received the Nobel Prize in Literature in 1957 and died three years later in a car accident.

In this essay from 1942, Camus re-examines the ancient Greek myth of Sisyphus, a man forced to spend eternity pushing a boulder uphill every day as punishment for defying the gods. He calls Sisyphus "the absurd hero." Camus was writing in the middle of war, at a time when his way of life and his values, like Sisyphus's daily labors, would have seemed doomed.

The gods had condemned Sisyphus to ceaselessly rolling a rock to the top of a mountain, whence the stone would fall back of its own weight. They had thought with some reason that there is no more dreadful punishment than futile and hopeless labor.

If one believes Homer, Sisyphus was the wisest and most prudent of mortals. According to another tradition, however, he was disposed to practice the profession of highwayman. I see no contradiction in this. Opinions differ as to the reasons why he became the futile laborer of the underworld. To begin with, he is accused of a certain levity in regard to the gods. He stole their secrets. Ægina, the daughter of Æsopus, was carried off by Jupiter. The father was shocked by that disappearance and complained to Sisyphus. He, who knew of the abduction, offered to tell about it on condition that Æsopus would give water to the citadel of Corinth. To the celestial thunderbolts he preferred the benediction of water. He was punished for this in the underworld. Homer tells us also that Sisyphus had put Death in chains. Pluto could not endure the sight of his deserted, silent empire. He dispatched the god of war, who liberated Death from the hands of her conqueror.

It is said that Sisyphus, being near to death, rashly wanted to test his wife's love. He ordered her to cast his unburied body into the middle of the public square. Sisyphus woke up in the underworld. And there, annoyed by an obedience so contrary to human love, he obtained from Pluto permission to return to earth in order to chastise his wife. But when he had seen again the face of this world, enjoyed water and sun, warm stones and the sea, he no longer wanted to go back to the infernal darkness. Recalls, signs of anger, warnings were of no avail. Many years more he lived facing the curve of the gulf, the sparkling sea, and the smiles of earth. A decree of the gods was necessary. Mercury came and seized the impudent man by the collar and, snatching him from his joys, lead him forcibly back to the underworld, where his rock was ready for him.

You have already grasped that Sisyphus is the absurd hero. He is, as much through his passions as through his torture. His scorn of the gods, his hatred of death, and his passion for life won him that unspeakable penalty in which the whole being is exerted toward accomplishing nothing. This is the price that must be paid for the passions of this earth. Nothing is told to us about Sisyphus in the underworld. Myths are made for the imagination to breathe life into them. As for this myth, one sees merely the whole effort of a body straining to raise the huge stone, to roll it, and push it up a slope a hundred times over; one sees the face screwed up, the cheek tight against the stone, the shoulder bracing the clay-covered mass, the foot wedging it, the fresh start with arms outstretched, the wholly human security of two earth-clotted hands. At the very end of his long effort measured by skyless space and time without depth, the purpose is achieved. Then Sisyphus watches the stone rush down in a few moments toward that lower world whence he will have to push it up again toward the summit. He goes back down to the plain.

It is during that return, that pause, that Sisyphus interests me. A face that toils so close to stones is already stone itself! I see that man going back down with a heavy yet measured step toward the torment of which he will never know the end. That hour like a breathing-space which returns as surely as his suffering, that is the hour of consciousness. At each of those moments when he leaves the heights and gradually sinks toward the lairs of the gods, he is superior to his fate. He is stronger than his rock.

If this myth is tragic, that is because its hero is conscious. Where would his torture be, indeed, if at every step the hope of succeeding upheld him? The workman of today works every day in his life at the same tasks, and his fate is no less absurd. But it is tragic only at the rare moments when it becomes conscious. Sisyphus, proletarian of the gods, powerless and rebellious, knows the whole extent of his wretched condition: it is what he thinks of during his descent. The lucidity that was to constitute his torture at the same time crowns his victory. There is no fate that cannot be surmounted by scorn.

* * *

If the descent is thus sometimes performed in sorrow, it can also take place in joy. This word is not too much. Again I fancy Sisyphus returning toward his rock, and the sorrow was in the beginning. When the images of earth cling too tightly to memory, when the call of happiness becomes too insistent, it happens that melancholy arises in man's heart: this is the rock's victory, this is the rock itself. The boundless grief is too heavy to bear. These are our nights of Gethsemane. But crushing truths perish from being acknowledged. Thus, Œdipus at the outset obeys fate without knowing it. But from the moment he knows,

his tragedy begins. Yet at the same moment, blind and desperate, he realizes that the only bond linking him to the world is the cool hand of a girl. Then a tremendous remark rings out: "Despite so many ordeals, my advanced age and the nobility of my soul make me conclude that all is well." Sophocles' Œdipus, like Dostoevsky's Kirilov, thus gives the recipe for the absurd victory. Ancient wisdom confirms modern heroism.

One does not discover the absurd without being tempted to write a manual of happiness. "What! by such narrow ways—?" There is but one world, however. Happiness and the absurd are two sons of the same earth. They are inseparable. It would be a mistake to say that happiness necessarily springs from the absurd discovery. It happens as well that the felling of the absurd springs from happiness. "I conclude that all is well," says Œdipus, and that remark is sacred. It echoes in the wild and limited universe of man. It teaches that all is not, has not been, exhausted. It drives out of this world a god who had come into it with dissatisfaction and a preference for futile suffering. It makes of fate a human matter, which must be settled among men.

All Sisyphus' silent joy is contained therein. His fate belongs to him. His rock is his thing. Likewise, the absurd man, when he contemplates his torment, silences all the idols. In the universe suddenly restored to its silence, the myriad wondering little voices of the earth rise up. Unconscious, secret calls, invitations from all the faces, they are the necessary reverse and price of victory. There is no sun without shadow, and it is essential to know the night. The absurd man says yes and his efforts will henceforth be unceasing. If there is a personal fate, there is no higher destiny, or at least there is, but one which he concludes is inevitable and despicable. For the rest, he knows himself to be the master of his days. At that subtle moment when man glances backward over his life, Sisyphus returning toward his rock, in that slight pivoting he contemplates that series of unrelated actions which become his fate, created by him, combined under his memory's eye and soon sealed by his death. Thus, convinced of the wholly human origin of all that is human, a blind man eager to see who knows that the night has no end, he is still on the go. The rock is still rolling.

I leave Sisyphus at the foot of the mountain! One always finds one's burden again. But Sisyphus teaches the higher fidelity that negates the gods and raises rocks. He too concludes that all is well. This universe henceforth without a master seems to him neither sterile nor futile. Each atom of that stone, each mineral flake of that night filled mountain, in itself forms a world. The struggle itself toward the heights is enough to fill a man's heart. One must imagine Sisyphus happy.

STUDY QUESTIONS

1. Most people have thought of Sisyphus as a symbol of failure. According to Camus, what is heroic about Sisyphus?
2. What does Camus's philosophy reveal about how it felt for millions of civilians to live under military occupation during the Second World War? What might this story mean to someone working in the resistance?

13.5 THE WANNSEE PROTOCOL, JANUARY 20, 1942

To kill large numbers of people at once, the Nazis built special concentration camps equipped with enormous gas chambers that could asphyxiate as many as 2,000 people at a time. Conceived in the fall of 1941, the camps would be the staging ground for the "final solution to the Jewish question."

The plan to murder Europe's 10 million Jews was communicated on January 20, 1942, to top civil servants, SS leaders, and Nazi Party officials at a meeting in Wannsee, Germany. One death camp, Chelmno in Poland, was already in operation, gassing a thousand people to death per day, and after the Wannsee Conference Nazi officials expanded their genocidal operation to four other Polish locations: Auschwitz-Birkenau, destined to be the largest factory of death, Treblinka, Sobibor, and Belsec.

To contend with the vast number of corpses, German bureaucrats designed special crematoria capable of incinerating dozens of bodies at once. The skill and efficiency with which German businesses manufactured goods now found a grotesque application in the murder factories designed to turn living human beings into dust.

* * * * * *Stamp: Top Secret 30 copies 16th copy, Minutes of discussion.

. . .

I.

The following persons took part in the discussion about the final solution of the Jewish question which took place in Berlin, am Grossen Wannsee [a suburb of Berlin] No. 56/58 on 20 January 1942.

. . .

II.

At the beginning of the discussion Chief of the Security Police and of the SD, SS-Obergruppenführer Heydrich, reported that the Reich Marshal had appointed him delegate for the preparations for the final solution of the Jewish question in Europe and pointed out that this discussion had been called for the purpose of clarifying fundamental questions. The wish of the Reich Marshal to have a draft sent to him concerning organizational, factual and material interests in relation to the final solution of the Jewish question in Europe makes necessary an initial common action of all central offices immediately concerned with these questions in order to bring their general activities into line. The Reichsführer-SS and the Chief of the German Police (Chief of the Security Police and the SD) was entrusted with the official central handling of the final solution of the Jewish question without regard to geographic borders. The Chief of the Security Police and the SD then gave a short report of the struggle which has been carried on thus far against this enemy, the essential points being the following:

   a) the expulsion of the Jews from every sphere of life of the German people,

   b) the expulsion of the Jews from the living space of the German people.

In carrying out these efforts, an increased and planned acceleration of the emigration of the Jews from Reich territory was started, as the only possible present solution.

By order of the Reich Marshal, a Reich Central Office for Jewish Emigration was set up in January 1939 and the Chief of the Security Police and SD was entrusted with the management. Its most important tasks were

   a) to make all necessary arrangements for the preparation for an increased emigration of the Jews,

   b) to direct the flow of emigration,

   c) to speed the procedure of emigration in each individual case.

The aim of all this was to cleanse German living space of Jews in a legal manner.

. . .

Under proper guidance, in the course of the final solution the Jews are to be allocated for appropriate labor in the East. Able-bodied Jews, separated according to sex, will be taken in large work columns to these areas for work on roads, in the course of which action doubtless a large portion will be eliminated by natural causes.

The possible final remnant will, since it will undoubtedly consist of the most resistant portion, have to be treated accordingly, because it is the product of natural selection and would, if released, act as the seed of a new Jewish revival (see the experience of history).

In the course of the practical execution of the final solution, Europe will be combed through from west to east. Germany proper, including the Protectorate of Bohemia and Moravia, will have to be handled first due to the housing problem and additional social and political necessities.

The evacuated Jews will first be sent, group by group, to so-called transit ghettos, from which they will be transported to the East.

SS-Obergruppenführer Heydrich went on to say that an important prerequisite for the evacuation as such is the exact definition of the persons involved.

. . .

IV.

In the course of the final solution plans, the Nuremberg Laws should provide a certain foundation, in which a prerequisite for the absolute solution of the problem is also the solution to the problem of mixed marriages and persons of mixed blood.

The Chief of the Security Police and the SD discusses the following points, at first theoretically, in regard to a letter from the chief of the Reich chancellery:

   1. Treatment of Persons of Mixed Blood of the First Degree

Persons of mixed blood of the first degree will, as regards the final solution of the Jewish question, be treated as Jews.

From this treatment the following exceptions will be made:

a) Persons of mixed blood of the first degree married to persons of German blood if their marriage has resulted in children (persons of mixed blood of the second degree). These persons of mixed blood of the second degree are to be treated essentially as Germans.

b) Persons of mixed blood of the first degree, for whom the highest offices of the Party and State have already issued exemption permits in any sphere of life. Each individual case must be examined, and it is not ruled out that the decision may be made to the detriment of the person of mixed blood.

The prerequisite for any exemption must always be the personal merit of the person of mixed blood. (Not the merit of the parent or spouse of German blood.)

Persons of mixed blood of the first degree who are exempted from evacuation will be sterilized in order to prevent any offspring and to eliminate the problem of persons of mixed blood once and for all. Such sterilization will be voluntary. But it is required to remain in the Reich. The sterilized "person of mixed blood" is thereafter free of all restrictions to which he was previously subjected.

2. Treatment of Persons of Mixed Blood of the Second Degree

Persons of mixed blood of the second degree will be treated fundamentally as persons of German blood, with the exception of the following cases, in which the persons of mixed blood of the second degree will be considered as Jews:

a) The person of mixed blood of the second degree was born of a marriage in which both parents are persons of mixed blood.

b) The person of mixed blood of the second degree has a racially especially undesirable appearance that marks him outwardly as a Jew.

c) The person of mixed blood of the second degree has a particularly bad police and political record that shows that he feels and behaves like a Jew.

Also in these cases exemptions should not be made if the person of mixed blood of the second degree has married a person of German blood.

3. Marriages between Full Jews and Persons of German Blood.

Here it must be decided from case to case whether the Jewish partner will be evacuated or whether, with regard to the effects of such a step on the German relatives, [this mixed marriage] should be sent to an old-age ghetto.

4. Marriages between Persons of Mixed Blood of the First Degree and Persons of German Blood.
a) Without Children.

If no children have resulted from the marriage, the person of mixed blood of the first degree will be evacuated or sent to an old-age ghetto (same treatment as in the case of marriages between full Jews and persons of German blood, point 3).

b) With Children.

If children have resulted from the marriage (persons of mixed blood of the second degree), they will, if they are to be treated as Jews, be evacuated or sent to a ghetto along with the parent of mixed blood of the first degree. If these children are to be treated as Germans (regular cases), they are exempted from evacuation as is therefore the parent of mixed blood of the first degree.

5. Marriages between Persons of Mixed Blood of the First Degree and Persons of Mixed Blood of the First Degree or Jews.

In these marriages (including the children) all members of the family will be treated as Jews and therefore be evacuated or sent to an old-age ghetto.

6. Marriages between Persons of Mixed Blood of the First Degree and Persons of Mixed Blood of the Second Degree.

In these marriages both partners will be evacuated or sent to an old-age ghetto without consideration of whether the marriage has produced children, since possible children will as a rule have stronger Jewish blood than the Jewish person of mixed blood of the second degree.

SS-Gruppenführer Hofmann advocates the opinion that sterilization will have to be widely used, since the person of mixed blood who is given the choice whether he will be evacuated or sterilized would rather undergo sterilization.

State Secretary Dr. Stuckart maintains that carrying out in practice of the just mentioned possibilities for solving the problem of mixed marriages and persons of mixed blood will create endless administrative work. In the second place, as the biological facts cannot be disregarded in any case, State Secretary Dr. Stuckart proposed proceeding to forced sterilization.

Furthermore, to simplify the problem of mixed marriages possibilities must be considered with the goal of the legislator saying something like: "These marriages have been dissolved."

With regard to the issue of the effect of the evacuation of Jews on the economy, State Secretary Neumann stated that Jews who are working in industries vital to the war effort, provided that no replacements are available, cannot be evacuated.

SS-Obergruppenführer Heydrich indicated that these Jews would not be evacuated according to the rules he had approved for carrying out the evacuations then underway.

State Secretary Dr. Bühler stated that the General Government would welcome it if the final solution of this problem could be begun in the General Government, since on the one hand transportation does not play such a large role here nor would problems of labor supply hamper this action. Jews must be removed from the territory of the General Government as quickly as possible, since it is especially here that the Jew as an epidemic carrier represents an extreme danger and on the other hand he is causing permanent chaos in the economic structure of the country through continued black market dealings. Moreover, of the approximately 2½ million Jews concerned, the majority is unfit for work.

State Secretary Dr. Bühler stated further that the solution to the Jewish question in the General Government is the responsibility of the Chief of the Security Police and the SD and that his efforts would be supported by the officials of the General Government. He had only one request, to solve the Jewish question in this area as quickly as possible.

In conclusion the different types of possible solutions were discussed, during which discussion both Gauleiter Dr. Meyer and State Secretary Dr. Bühler took the position that certain preparatory activities for the final solution should be carried out immediately in the territories in question, in which process alarming the populace must be avoided.

The meeting was closed with the request of the Chief of the Security Police and the SD to the participants that they afford him appropriate support during the carrying out of the tasks involved in the solution.

STUDY QUESTIONS

1. What specific points seem to have drawn the most discussion at this meeting? Why?
2. What considerations do *not* seem to have been brought up? Why?

13.6 IRIS ORIGO, *WAR IN VAL D'ORCIA,*
MAY 1944

Iris Cutting Origo (1902–1988) was a writer fascinated with the history of her adopted country, Italy. Born to aristocratic British and American parents, she married an Italian, Antonio Origo, with whom she owned La Foce, a large estate in Tuscany. The couple hoped to modernize agricultural practices and improve life for the fifty peasant families living on their land, each of whom farmed about a hundred acres.

Busy with local concerns, Origo did not pay much attention to Mussolini's rise until the Second World War broke out. In 1943 the war came to her doorstep. She took in two dozen refugee children and set up a network to help escaped Allied prisoners of war, Jewish and political refugees, and resistance fighters (called partisans)—all of this, as Allied planes dropped bombs and Nazi troops shored up control of the area. Throughout the war she managed to provide for her immediate family, including her two young daughters, both born during the war, while also looking after her tenants and strangers in need.

Origo recorded these events in a diary she kept hidden because it was illegal to take and preserve notes about the war. After the war's end, she published her account as *War in Val d'Orcia: An Italian War Diary* (1947). In it she describes her actions as "singularly undramatic and unheroic," but in fact she saved countless lives. Explaining the choices she made, she writes that the challenges she faced during the war "arose from a continual necessity to weigh, not between courage and cowardice or between right and wrong, but between conflicting duties and responsibilities, equally urgent."

May 19th

Cassino has fallen.

May 20th

The Gustav line has broken, and the Allies are advancing towards the Adolf Hitler line—which is said, however, to be very strong.

The local situation is becoming more stormy again. Partisans have broken into the barracks of San Casciano, disarming the Carabinieri; they have also taken prisoner one of the monks (an ardent Fascist) in the Montefollonico Monastery. He was subsequently sent back to his monastery, completely naked. Other partisans have disarmed two German soldiers at Contignano; with the consequence that this morning two lorries of German soldiers went to

the village and took nine men away with them as hostages. On their way back, at seven a.m., they stopped here, and sent up a message to Antonio to come down immediately.

Thinking it was some routine matter, Antonio dressed and shaved in a leisurely manner, until the officer, a captain, sent up an irate message to say that, if he didn't at once appear, he would come up himself and fetch him. When at last Antonio came downstairs the captain abused him for keeping him waiting, and then stated that he had come to search the house for rebels. His soldiers had already searched the surrounding houses and farms, but here they only entered the kitchen and servants' rooms, abstracting such small objects as caught their

From Iris Origo, *War in Val d'Orcia: An Italian War Diary, 1943–1944* (Boston: David R. Godine, 1984), pp. 185–188.

fancy. In the farm every room was examined, and everyone had to show their papers, and the captain then told Antonio to translate a little speech, in which he warned us all that any further help to the rebels would be given at the risk of our skins. He also asked Antonio to give him exact information as to the partisans' whereabouts, to which Antonio replied that they are to be found everywhere on the chain of hills running from Cetona to Montichiello—about fifty miles—and are seldom more than twenty four hours in any one place! The Germans then went off again.

May 21st

Leaflets have been dropped this morning by German planes in the Val d'Orcia, saying: "Whoever knows the place where a band of rebels is in hiding, and does not immediately inform the German Army, will be shot. Whoever gives food or shelter to a band or to individual rebels, will be shot. Every house in which rebels are found, or in which a rebel has stayed, will be blown up. So will every house from which anyone has fired on the German forces. In all such cases, all stores of food, wheat, and straw will be burned, the cattle will be taken away, and the inhabitants will be shot." The leaflet finishes with the reminder that "the German Army will proceed with justice, but with inflexible hardness."

Other leaflets scattered by Allied planes give precisely opposite instructions: "At all costs refrain from reporting yourselves to the Army. Commit acts of sabotage on the communication lines. Enter into contact with the foreigners in the German Army. Go on organizing groups. The moment for decisive action is near at hand."

The peasants read these leaflets with bewildered anxiety as to their own fate, and complete indifference (in most cases) to the main issue. *Che sarà di noi?* (What will become of us?) All that they want is peace—to get back to their land—and to save their sons.

All day a succession of young men come up, asking for advice, including the Sicilian and Calabrian soldiers who are working on the place. In the evening, too, we have a visit from some of the women from Contignano, whose husbands and brothers have been taken as hostages by the Germans. They have been to take food to them at Chianciano, where they are at present shut up. Antonio promises to try to help, but we believe that probably these men are merely being detained as a warning.

May 22nd

We were mistaken. This afternoon, the Bishop of Pienza arrived, and informed us that seven out of the hostages from Contignano are to be shot. He has succeeded in obtaining forty-eight hours' reprieve, but if, within that period, the arms which the rebels took away from the Germans are not returned, the execution will take place,

The Allied troops are advancing on Terracina.

Every day now, whenever I go out of the house, I find a little group of famished people sitting in the farm courtyard; haggard women, with babies in their arms and other children waiting for them at home; thin, ragged schoolboys or old men, carrying sacks or suitcases—all begging for food to take back to Rome. We give them all that we can, but Antonio begs me to remember that we must also go on providing food—for our own population and for the two hundred partisans in the woods.

None of our young men are going to report for military service. They will all leave home and hide in the woods—and they are trusting to luck, and to the Allied advance, to save their families from reprisals. But Antonio has already, this evening, received a note from the Fascio of Pienza, warning him that in a few days German troops will arrive there, to remain "until the mopping-up is finished." Our personal crisis is just beginning.

May 25th

Visit from the Maresciallo of Pienza. This is the last day of the amnesty, but it has been prolonged for a week, for this district at least, before the mopping-up is to begin. The little village of Castiglioncello, at the top of the hill, was surrounded this morning by German troops, who have found there the man responsible for disarming the Germans at Contignano. The seven hostages from Contignano have consequently been released, but two men from Castiglioncello have been shot.

The only recruit to join the Fascist Army is a boy with pleurisy who consequently believes that he will be sent home at once.

The Fifth Army, after occupying Terracina, joins up with the Eighth on the Anzio beach-head.

May 26th

Anti-aircraft guns, stationed at Spedaletto, bring down five Allied planes out of an unusually large bomber formation, which is attacking German columns on the road. Some of the airmen save themselves by parachute. From our terrace we can hear the firing, and see the little silver balloons opening and drifting down from the sky. One plane, laden with bombs, explodes as it hits the ground. We see the great column of black smoke soaring up, and long to hurry to the scene to bring first aid; but the Germans will be there before us.

The Allied Armies, still advancing, have broken through the Hitler line.

STUDY QUESTIONS

1. How were the Nazis and the Allies each trying to get the support of locals living in a war zone? According to Origo, how successful were their efforts?
2. How did the Origos get along with the Nazi military occupiers? What did they do to undermine Nazi control of the area?

13.7 VISUAL SOURCE: RONALD SEARLE, SKETCH FROM *TO THE KWAI—AND BACK*, 1939–1945

Ronald Searle (1920–2011), born in Cambridge, England, studied architecture as student. When the Second World War began, he joined the British army as an architectural draftsman and was sent to the Pacific Theater where he became, along with thousands of Allied troops, a prisoner of war in the wake of Singapore's fall in 1942. He was imprisoned in Changi and worked on the Thai Burma railway for the Japanese military, which notoriously did not respect international guidelines for the treatment of soldiers who had surrendered. Throughout his captivity, Searle managed to barter for art supplies and make drawings he preserved by burying them to avoid confiscation. His illustrations show his captors, his companions, and the landscape where he worked fifteen-hour days.

After the war Searle worked as an illustrator and cartoonist, publishing over fifty books. And his drawings of the girls at the imaginary school St. Trinian's were turned into popular movies and books.

From Ronald Searle, *To the Kwai—and Back: War Drawings, 1939–1945* (Boston: Atlantic Monthly Press, 1986), p.112.

Ronald Searle made this drawing under the eyes of the Japanese guards, and buried it, with others, to escape confiscation.

FIGURE 13.7 Ronald Searle, Sketch

STUDY QUESTIONS

1. What does this image tell us about life as a POW in the Pacific Theater during the Second World War? What can a drawing reveal than words cannot?
2. How does Searle depict his captors and his fellow prisoners?

USING PASSIVE VOICE, *IT*-SHIFTS, AND *WHAT*-SHIFTS TO TELL YOUR READER WHAT MATTERS MOST

Good writing is not just a matter of choosing the right words, important as that is. Good writing means choosing the right *order* for your words.

Writing is 15 percent word choice and 85 percent structure.

—George Gopen, Professor Emeritus of the Practice of Rhetoric, Duke University

---

Writers often use word order to place extra emphasis on the most important content in a sentence. In Chapters 1 and 2, we discussed *end focus*, the placement of the information or ideas we want to stress at the end of a sentence. By changing what comes at the end, we can alter emphasis—and in some cases even the meaning of a sentence.

Consider the difference between the following sentences:

1. Churchill, who was a conservative, opposed appeasement.
2. Churchill, who opposed appeasement, was a conservative.

In the first sentence, Churchill's opposition to appeasement receives the emphasis; in the second, his conservatism is underlined.

In the next sentence pair, changing the word order not only alters the emphasis, it modifies the meaning.

1. The French army, although well-prepared for war, allowed Germany to strike first.
2. The French army, although it allowed Germany to strike first, was well-prepared for war.

The first sentence suggests that the French squandered the great advantage of their strong preparation by allowing Germany to strike first. The second sentence suggests that Germany's first strike was insignificant because the French army was so well-prepared.

Beyond changing the placement of words in a sentence, there are three other sentence constructions especially useful for adding emphasis to particular information or ideas: the **passive voice**, the *it*-shift, and the ***what*-shift**. Although *it*- and *what*-shifts are usually called *it*- and *what*-clefts, we have followed Joseph Williams *Style: Lessons in Clarity and Grace* in using "*it*-shift" and "*what*-shift" because in both sentence types the original subject has been shifted to the right.

All three can be used to place extra emphasis on the most important content in a sentence.

Standard form: They turned the electricity off.

Passive voice: The electricity was turned off.

Standard form: We heard the neighbor's dog barking.

It-shift: It was the neighbor's dog we heard barking.

Standard form: I want ice cream.

What-shift: What I want is ice cream.

USING PASSIVE VOICE FOR EMPHASIS

Consider the following sentence, written in active voice, which places Germany in the stress position at the end of the sentence:

The British, French, Americans, and Russians occupied [ACTIVE VOICE] *Germany.*

If you want to stress the sheer number of occupying countries—four all told—the passive is a good choice:

Germany was occupied [PASSIVE VOICE] by the British, French, Americans, and Russians.

USING THE "*IT*-SHIFT" FOR EMPHASIS

The "*it*-shift" gives you another means of stressing the fact that Germany was occupied by no less than four countries:

It was the British, French, Americans, and Russians who occupied Germany.

Sentences of the form "it was X that did Y" place the emphasis on X, moving the stress position to the middle of the sentence.

We heard the neighbor's dog barking.
It was the neighbor's dog we heard barking. (Extra stress on "the neighbor's dog")

USING THE *WHAT*-SHIFT FOR EMPHASIS

A third option is the what-shift.
The Russians engineered a remarkable expansion of their military forces.
Versus:
What the Russians engineered was a remarkable expansion of their military forces.
Both sentences place "a remarkable expansion of their military forces" in the stress position at the end of the sentence, but the "*what*-shift" adds extra emphasis.

EXERCISE: USE PASSIVE VOICE, *IT*-SHIFTS, AND *WHAT*-SHIFTS TO ADD EMPHASIS

Instructions

Use passive voice, *it*-shifts, and *what*-shifts to add emphasis as indicated.

---

1. Use an *it*-shift to place emphasis on the words "only after Mussolini's alliance with Nazi Germany":
Italian officials began to enact anti-Semitic laws only after Mussolini's alliance with Nazi Germany in the late 1930s.
It was

---

2. Use a *what*-shift to place emphasis on the fact that the Germans decided to destroy or displace entire populations:
The fact that the Germans decided to destroy or displace entire populations made this war especially dangerous for European civilians.
What made

---

3. Use passive voice to emphasize "the settlement by the Nazis":
Despite these harsh conditions, the settlement with the Nazis relieved most French men and women.
Despite these harsh conditions, most

---

4. Use *it*-shifting, *what*-shifting, or passive voice to place emphasis on "Stalin's secret police":
Stalin's secret police systematically murdered the surviving officers.

---

5. Use *it*-shifting, *what*-shifting, or passive voice to place emphasis on the Allied bombing of German cities.
The Allied bombing of German cities really brought the war effort home to the Reich's population.

You will find suggested answers to the exercises in the back of this book. For more Writing History exercises, as well as study resources for this chapter, visit oup.com/us/berenson.

CHAPTER 14

THE POSTWAR, 1945–1970

14.1 HO CHI MINH, "THE PATH WHICH LED ME TO LENINISM," APRIL 1960

On September 2, 1945, the day of Japan's surrender to the United States, Ho Chi Minh (1890–1969), the leader of the communist resistance in Indochina, read a Vietnamese declaration of independence to half a million people in Hanoi. Ho addressed the declaration to France, which had ruled Vietnam since the late nineteenth century, and now—after France's liberation from Nazi Germany—wanted to reassert its primacy in Indochina. After French leaders persuaded the United States that this colonial conflict was an outgrowth of the larger Cold War between the West and the Soviet Union, the American administrations of Presidents Truman and Eisenhower provided financial and political support to France as it battled Vietnamese insurgents. But the French were unsuccessful, and they surrendered to Ho's victorious forces in 1954, leaving the northern half of the country in communist hands and the southern portion under conservative control.

A peace agreement promised the reunification of North and South, but Vietnam remained divided. North Vietnam and South Vietnam developed into separate states. South Vietnam was backed by the United States, which supplied military advisors and other personnel, while North Vietnam received support from the Soviet Union and Communist China, which saw US involvement as imperialist and their own involvement as liberationist. Ho endorsed the communist position, and in April 1960 published the statement excerpted here in the Soviet journal, *Problems of the East*. The statement outlines Ho's thinking about Lenin's struggle against Western imperialism.

After World War I, I made my living in Paris, now as a retoucher at a photographer's, now as painter of "Chinese antiquities" (made in France!). I would distribute leaflets denouncing the crimes committed by the French colonialists in Viet Nam.

At that time, I supported the October Revolution only instinctively, not yet grasping all its historic importance. I loved and admired Lenin because he was a great patriot who liberated his compatriots; until then, I had read none of his books.

From *Selected Works of Ho Chi Minh*, Vol. 4 (Foreign Languages Publishing House), transcription/markup: Roland Ferguson and Christian Liebl; online version: Ho Chi Minh Internet Archive (2003), http://www.marxists.org/reference/archive/ho-chi-minh/works/1960/04/x01.htm.

The reason for my joining the French Socialist Party was that these "ladies and gentlemen"—as I called my comrades at that moment—had shown their sympathy towards me, towards the struggle of the oppressed peoples. But I understood neither what was a party, a trade-union, nor what was socialism nor communism.

Heated discussions were then taking place in the branches of the Socialist Party, about the question whether the Socialist Party should remain in the Second International, should a Second and a half International be founded or should the Socialist Party join Lenin's Third International? I attended the meetings regularly, twice or thrice a week and attentively listened to the discussion. First, I could not understand thoroughly. Why were the discussions so heated? Either with the Second, Second and a half or Third International, the revolution could be waged. What was the use of arguing then? As for the First International, what had become of it?

What I wanted most to know—and this precisely was not debated in the meetings—was: which International sides with the peoples of colonial countries?

I raised this question—the most important in my opinion—in a meeting. Some comrades answered: It is the Third, not the Second International. And a comrade gave me Lenin's "Thesis on the national and colonial questions" published by *l'Humanité* to read.

There were political terms difficult to understand in this thesis. But by dint of reading it again and again, finally I could grasp the main part of it. What emotion, enthusiasm, clear-sightedness and confidence it instilled into me! I was overjoyed to tears. Though sitting alone in my room, I shouted out aloud as if addressing large crowds: "Dear martyr compatriots! This is what we need, this is the path to our liberation!"

After then, I had entire confidence in Lenin, in the Third International.

Formerly, during the meetings of the Party branch, I only listened to the discussion; I had a vague belief that all were logical, and could not differentiate as to who were right and who were wrong. But from then on, I also plunged into the debates and discussed with fervour. Though I was still lacking French words to express all my thoughts, I smashed the allegations attacking Lenin and the Third International with no less vigour. My only argument was: "If you do not condemn colonialism, if you do not side with the colonial people, what kind of revolution are you waging?"

. . .

At first, patriotism, not yet communism, led me to have confidence in Lenin, in the Third International. Step by step, along the struggle, by studying Marxism-Leninism parallel with participation in practical activities, I gradually came upon the fact that only socialism and communism can liberate the oppressed nations and the working people throughout the world from slavery.

STUDY QUESTIONS

1. What did Ho make of the inner divisions among socialists? How did these divisions affect the interests of the Vietnamese, as he saw them?
2. In what respects did Ho see Lenin as a liberator of all "colonized" peoples? Was he justified in this conclusion?

14.2 *THE UNIVERSAL DECLARATION OF HUMAN RIGHTS*, DECEMBER 10, 1948

At the end of the Second World War, the great powers created the United Nations, an international organization designed to foster peaceful relations among states. The delegates to the United Nations agreed to devise a set of individual rights to be respected throughout the world. The Canadian legal scholar John Peters Humphrey drafted a document for review by the UN committee chaired by Eleanor Roosevelt, the widow of the United States' wartime president and a strong advocate for human rights. After much negotiation, the UN General Assembly voted to adopt the Universal Declaration of Human Rights on December 10, 1948 during its meeting in Paris. No member state voted against the Declaration, although eight—the Soviet Union and its surrounding communist-led countries—abstained.

THE GENERAL ASSEMBLY PROCLAIMS

This Universal Declaration of Human Rights as a common standard of achievement for all peoples and all nations, to the end that every individual and every organ of society, keeping this Declaration constantly in mind, shall strive by teaching and education to promote respect for these rights and freedoms and by progressive measures, national and international, to secure their universal and effective recognition and observance, both among the peoples of Member States themselves and among peoples of territories under their jurisdiction.

Article 1

All human beings are born free and equal in dignity and rights. They are endowed with reason and conscience and should act toward one another in a spirit of brotherhood.

Article 2

Everyone is entitled to all the rights and freedoms set forth in this Declaration, without distinction of any kind, such as race, color, sex, language, religion, political or other opinion, national or social origin, property, birth or other status.

Furthermore, no distinction shall be made on the basis of the political, jurisdictional or international status of the country or territory to which a person belongs, whether it be independent, trust, non-self-governing or under any other limitation of sovereignty.

Article 3

Everyone has the right to life, liberty and security of person.

Article 4

No one shall be held in slavery or servitude; slavery and the slave trade shall be prohibited in all their forms.

Article 5

No one shall be subjected to torture or to cruel, inhuman or degrading treatment or punishment.

Article 6

Everyone has the right to recognition everywhere as a person before the law.

Article 7

All are equal before the law and are entitled without any discrimination to equal protection of the law. All are entitled to equal protection against any discrimination in violation of this Declaration and against any incitement to such discrimination.

Article 8

Everyone has the right to an effective remedy by the competent national tribunals for acts violating the fundamental rights granted him by the constitution or by law.

Article 9

No one shall be subjected to arbitrary arrest, detention or exile.

Article 10

Everyone is entitled in full equality to a fair and public hearing by an independent and impartial tribunal, in the determination of his rights and obligations and of any criminal charge against him.

Article 11

1) Everyone charged with a penal offense has the right to be presumed innocent until proved guilty according to law in a public trial at which he has had all the guarantees necessary for his defense.
2) No one shall be held guilty of any penal offense on account of any act or omission which did not constitute a penal offense, under national or international law, at the time when it was committed. Nor shall a heavier penalty be imposed than the one that was applicable at the time the penal offense was committed.

Article 12

No one shall be subjected to arbitrary interference with his privacy, family, home or correspondence, nor to attacks upon his honor and reputation. Everyone has the right to the protection of the law against such interference or attacks.

Article 13

1) Everyone has the right to freedom of movement and residence within the borders of each State.
2) Everyone has the right to leave any country, including his own, and to return to his country.

Article 14

1) Everyone has the right to seek and to enjoy in other countries asylum from persecution.
2) This right may not be invoked in the case of prosecutions genuinely arising from non-political crimes or from acts contrary to the purposes and principles of the United Nations.

Article 15

1) Everyone has the right to a nationality.
2) No one shall be arbitrarily deprived of his nationality nor denied the right to change his nationality.

Article 16

1) Men and women of full age, without any limitation due to race, nationality or religion, have the right to marry and to found a family. They are entitled to equal rights as to marriage, during marriage and at its dissolution.
2) Marriage shall be entered into only with the free and full consent of the intending spouses.
3) The family is the natural and fundamental group unit of society and is entitled to protection by society and the State.

Article 17

1) Everyone has the right to own property alone as well as in association with others.
2) No one shall be arbitrarily deprived of his property.

Article 18

Everyone has the right to freedom of thought, conscience and religion; this right includes freedom to change his religion or belief, and freedom, either alone or in community with others and in public and private, to manifest his religion or belief in teaching, practice, worship and observance.

Article 19

Everyone has the right to freedom of opinion and expression; this right includes freedom to hold opinions without interference and to seek, receive and impart information and ideas through any media and regardless of frontiers.

Article 20

1) Everyone has the right to freedom of peaceful assembly and association.
2) No one may be compelled to belong to an association.

Article 21

1) Everyone has the right to take part in the government of his country, directly or through freely chosen representatives.
2) Everyone has the right of equal access to public service in his country.
3) The will of the people shall be the basis of the authority of government; this will shall be expressed in periodic and genuine elections which shall be by universal and equal suffrage and shall be held by secret vote or by equivalent free voting procedures.

Article 22

Everyone, as a member of society, has the right to social security and is entitled to realization, through national effort and international co-operation and in accordance with the organization and resources of each State, of the economic, social and cultural rights indispensable for his dignity and the free development of his personality.

Article 23

1) Everyone has the right to work, to free choice of employment, to just and favorable conditions of work and to protection against unemployment.
2) Everyone, without any discrimination, has the right to equal pay for equal work.
3) Everyone who works has the right to just and favorable remuneration ensuring for himself and his family an existence worthy of human dignity, and supplemented, if necessary, by other means of social protection.
4) Everyone has the right to form and to join trade unions for the protection of his interests.

Article 24

Everyone has the right to rest and leisure, including reasonable limitation of working hours and periodic holidays with pay.

Article 25

1) Everyone has the right to a standard of living adequate for the health and well-being of himself and of his family, including food, clothing, housing and medical care and necessary social services, and the right to security in the event of unemployment, sickness, disability, widowhood, old age or other lack of livelihood in circumstances beyond his control.
2) Motherhood and childhood are entitled to special care and assistance. All children, whether born in or out of wedlock, shall enjoy the same social protection.

Article 26

1) Everyone has the right to education. Education shall be free, at least in the elementary and fundamental stages. Elementary education shall be compulsory. Technical and professional education shall be made generally available and higher education shall be equally accessible to all on the basis of merit.
2) Education shall be directed to the full development of the human personality and to the strengthening of respect for human rights and fundamental freedoms. It shall promote understanding, tolerance and friendship among all nations, racial or religious groups, and shall further the activities of the United Nations for the maintenance of peace.
3) Parents have a prior right to choose the kind of education that shall be given to their children.

Article 27

1) Everyone has the right freely to participate in the cultural life of the community, to enjoy the arts and to share in scientific advancement and its benefits.
2) Everyone has the right to the protection of the moral and material interests resulting from any scientific, literary or artistic production of which he is the author.

Article 28

Everyone is entitled to a social and international order in which the rights and freedoms set forth in this Declaration can be fully realized.

Article 29

1) Everyone has duties to the community in which alone the free and full development of his personality is possible.

2) In the exercise of his rights and freedoms, everyone shall be subject only to such limitations as are determined by law solely for the purpose of securing due recognition and respect for the rights and freedoms of others and of meeting the just requirements of morality, public order and the general welfare in a democratic society.

3) These rights and freedoms may in no case be exercised contrary to the purposes and principles of the United Nations.

Article 30
Nothing in this Declaration may be interpreted as implying for any State, group or person any right to engage in any activity or to perform any act aimed at the destruction of any of the rights and freedoms set forth herein.

STUDY QUESTIONS

1. What, according to the UDHR, would be the practical benefits of guaranteeing human rights for the entire human family?
2. How likely were these goals to be applied, in global society, in 1948? Which articles remained to be fulfilled at that point—and perhaps even today?

14.3 SIR WILLIAM BEVERIDGE, *SOCIAL INSURANCE AND ALLIED SERVICES*, NOVEMBER 20, 1942

The postwar period was an era of growing equality, a time when wealth and incomes were more evenly distributed than at any other point in modern history, except perhaps during the two world wars. Because rapid growth fostered equality, labor unions in many countries—France was a notable exception—only infrequently resorted to strikes and were largely content with modest increases in pay.

In several countries, there was an explicit tie between wage restraint and government-financed or subsidized social benefits, as workers agreed to sacrifice some wage gains in exchange for contributions by their employers to social welfare funds. Britain's National Health Service, created in 1948, was a case in point, as it provided free, tax-financed healthcare to everyone. The call for a national health service had been outlined during the depths of the war in what was known as the Beveridge Report, written by the economist and centrist politician William Beveridge. Beveridge's report foreshadowed what would become Britain's postwar welfare state and provided its rationale, namely that the British people had made great sacrifices to preserve their country's democracy and were entitled not just to political rights but also to the right of economic well-being.

From Sir William Beveridge, *Social Insurance and Allied Services: A Report* (London: His Majesty's Stationery Office, 1942), http://news.bbc.co.uk/2/shared/bsp/hi/pdfs/19_07_05_beveridge.pdf.

2. The schemes of social insurance and allied services which the Interdepartmental Committee have been called on to survey have grown piecemeal. Apart from the Poor Law, which dates from the time of Elizabeth, the schemes surveyed are the product of the last 45 years beginning with the Workmen's Compensation Act, 1897. That Act, applying in the first instance to a limited number of occupations, was made general in 1906. Compulsory health insurance began in 1912. Unemployment insurance began for a few industries in 1912 and was made general in 1920. The first Pensions Act, giving non-contributory pensions subject to a means test at the age of 70, was passed in 1908. In 1925 came the Act which started contributory pensions for old age, for widows and for orphans. Unemployment insurance, after a troubled history, was put on a fresh basis by the Unemployment Act of 1934, which set up at the same time a new national service of Unemployment Assistance. Meantime, the local machinery for relief of destitution, after having been exhaustively examined by the Royal Commission of 1905–1909, has been changed both by the new treatment of unemployment and in many other ways, including a transfer of the responsibilities of the Boards of Guardians to Local Authorities. Separate provision for special types of disability—such as blindness—has been made from time to time. Together with this growth of social insurance and impinging on it at many points have gone developments of medical treatment, particularly in hospitals and other institutions; developments of services devoted to the welfare of children, in school and before it; and a vast growth of voluntary provision for death and other contingencies, made by persons of the insured classes through Industrial Life Offices, Friendly Societies and Trade Unions.

3. In all this change and development, each problem has been dealt with separately, with little or no reference to allied problems. The first task of the Committee has been to attempt for the first time a comprehensive survey of the whole field of social insurance and allied services, to show just what provision is now made and how it is made for many different forms of need. The results of this survey are set out in Appendix 15 describing social insurance and the allied services as they exist today in Britain. The picture presented is impressive in two ways. First, it shows that provision for most of the many varieties of need through interruption of earnings and other causes that may arise in modern industrial communities has already been made in Britain on a scale not surpassed and hardly rivalled in any other country of the world. In one respect only of the first importance, namely limitation of medical service, both in the range of treatment which is provided as of right and in respect of the classes of persons for whom it is provided, does Britain's achievement fall seriously short of what has been accomplished elsewhere: it falls short also in its provision for cash benefit for maternity and funerals and through the defects of its system for workmen's compensation. In all other fields British provision for security, in adequacy of amount and in comprehensiveness, will stand comparison with that of any other country; few countries will stand comparison with Britain. Second, social insurance and the allied services, as they exist today, are conducted by a complex of disconnected administrative organs, proceeding on different principles, doing invaluable service but at a cost in money and trouble and anomalous treatment of identical problems for which there is no justification. In a system of social security better on the whole than can be found in almost any other country there are serious deficiencies which call for remedy. . . .

6. In proceeding from this first comprehensive survey of social insurance to the next task—of making recommendations—three guiding principles may be laid down at the outset.

7. The first principle is that any proposals for the future, while they should use to the full the experience gathered in the past, should not be restricted by consideration of sectional interests established in the obtaining of that experience. Now, when the war is abolishing landmarks of every kind, is the opportunity for using experience in a clear field. A revolutionary moment in

the world's history is a time for revolutions, not for patching.

8. The second principle is that organisation of social insurance should be treated as one part only of a comprehensive policy of social progress. Social insurance fully developed may provide income security; it is an attack upon Want. But Want is one only of five giants on the road of reconstruction and in some ways the easiest to attack. The others are Disease, Ignorance, Squalor and Idleness.

9. The third principle is that social security must be achieved by co-operation between the State and the individual. The State should offer security for service and contribution. The State in organising security should not stifle incentive, opportunity, responsibility; in establishing a national minimum, it should leave room and encouragement for voluntary action by each individual to provide more than that minimum for himself and his family.

10. The Plan for Social Security set out in this Report is built upon these principles. It uses experience but is not tied by experience. It is put forward as a limited contribution to a wider social policy, though as something that could be achieved now without waiting for the whole of that policy. It is, first and foremost, a plan of insurance—of giving in return for contributions benefits up to subsistence level, as of right and without means test, so that individuals may build freely upon it.

STUDY QUESTIONS

1. Why does the Beveridge Report refer to Britain's past attempts at poor relief in this context?
2. Which one of these "principles" do you think was the most significant in the proper establishment of a national healthcare system?

14.4 THE TREATY OF ROME, ESTABLISHING THE EUROPEAN ECONOMIC COMMUNITY, MARCH 25, 1957

In postwar Western Europe, trade and economic output could grow substantially because neighboring economies complemented rather than mirrored each other, making regular and systematic economic cooperation possible. The European Coal and Steel Community—France, West Germany, Italy, and the Benelux nations—was created in 1951, and the European Common Market, formally known as the European Economic Community (EEC) and including the same countries, was established in 1957 with the Treaty of Rome. The six parties to the Treaty pledged to gradually abolish their tariff barriers and establish a free-trade zone.

Although it took until 1969 to implement these plans, even the gradual reduction of impediments to trade created huge economic benefits, raising the national incomes of member states, on

From http://europa.eu/law/decision-making/treaties/index_en.htm.

average, eight percent above what they would have been without the EEC. The majority of members saw the EEC as a stepping-stone to greater European integration and political unity.

PART TWO

FOUNDATIONS OF THE COMMUNITY

Title I Free Movement of Goods

ARTICLE 9 1. The Community shall be based upon a customs union which shall cover all trade in goods and which shall involve the prohibition between Member States of customs duties on imports and exports and of all charges having equivalent effect, and the adoption of a common customs tariff in their relations with third countries.

The provisions of Chapter 1, Section 1, and of Chapter 2 of this Title shall apply to products originating in Member States and to products coming from third countries which are in free circulation in Member States.

ARTICLE 10 1. Products coming from a third country shall be considered to be in free circulation in a Member State if the import formalities have been complied with and any customs duties or charges having equivalent effect which are payable have been levied in that Member State, and if they have not benefited from a total or partial drawback of such duties or charges.

2. The Commission shall, before the end of the first year after the entry into force of this Treaty, determine the methods of administrative co-operation to be adopted for the purpose of applying Article 9(2), taking into account the need to reduce as much as possible formalities imposed on trade. Before the end of the first year after the entry into force of this Treaty, the Commission shall lay down the provisions applicable, as regards trade between Member States, to goods originating in another Member State in whose manufacture products have been used on which the exporting Member State has not levied the appropriate customs duties or charges having equivalent effect or which have benefited from a total or partial drawback of such duties or charges. In adopting

these provisions, the Commission shall take into account the rules for the elimination of customs duties within the Community and for the progressive application of the common customs tariff.

ARTICLE 11 Member States shall take all appropriate measures to enable Governments to carry out, within the periods of time laid down, the obligations with regard to customs duties which devolve upon them pursuant to this Treaty.

CHAPTER 1 THE CUSTOMS UNION SECTION

1 Elimination of Customs Duties Between Member States

ARTICLE 12 Member States shall refrain from introducing between themselves any new customs duties on imports or exports or any charges having equivalent effect, and from increasing those which they already apply in their trade with each other.

ARTICLE 13 1. Customs duties on imports in force between Member States shall be progressively abolished by them during the transitional period in accordance with Articles 14 and 15.

2. Charges having an effect equivalent to customs duties on imports, in force between Member States, shall be progressively abolished by them during the transitional period. The Commission shall determine by means of directives the timetable for such abolition. It shall be guided by the rules contained in Article 14(2) and (3) and by the directives issued by the Council pursuant to Article 14(2).

ARTICLE 14 1. For each product, the basic duty to which the successive reductions shall be applied shall be the duty applied on 1 January 1957.

2. The timetable for the reductions shall be determined as follows: (a) during the first stage, the first reduction shall be made one year after the

date when this Treaty enters into force; the second reduction, eighteen months later; the third reduction, at the end of the fourth year after the date when this Treaty enters into force; (b) during the second stage, a reduction shall be made eighteen months after that stage begins; a second reduction, eighteen months after the preceding one; a third reduction, one year later; (c) any remaining reductions shall be made during the third stage; the Council shall, acting by a qualified majority on a proposal from the Commission, determine the timetable therefor by means of directives.

3. At the time of the first reduction, Member States shall introduce between themselves a duty on each product equal to the basic duty minus 10 percent. At the time of each subsequent reduction, each Member State shall reduce its customs duties as a whole in such manner as to lower by 10 percent its total customs receipts as defined in paragraph 4 and to reduce the duty on each product by at least 5 percent of the basic duty. In the case, however, of products on which the duty is still in excess of 30 percent, each reduction must be at least 10 percent of the basic duty.

4. The total customs receipts of each Member State, as referred to in paragraph 3, shall be calculated by multiplying the value of its imports from other Member States during 1956 by the basic duties.

5. Any special problems raised in applying paragraphs 1 to 4 shall be settled by directives issued by the Council acting by a qualified majority on a proposal from the Commission.

6. Member States shall report to the Commission on the manner in which effect has been given to the preceding rules for the reduction of duties. They shall endeavour to ensure that the reduction made in the duties on each product shall amount: at the end of the first stage, to at least 25 percent of the basic duty; at the end of the second stage, to at least 50 percent of the basic duty. If the Commission finds that there is a risk that the objectives laid down in Article 13, and the percentages laid down in this paragraph, cannot be attained, it shall make all appropriate recommendations to Member States.

7. The provisions of this Article may be amended by the Council, acting unanimously on a proposal from the Commission and after consulting the Assembly [European Parliament].

ARTICLE 15 1. Irrespective of the provisions of Article 14, any Member State may, in the course of the transitional period, suspend in whole or in part the collection of duties applied by it to products imported from other Member States. It shall inform the other member States and the Commission thereof.

2. The Member States declare their readiness to reduce customs duties against the other Member States more rapidly than is provided for in Article 14 if their general economic situation and the situation of the economic sector concerned so permit. To this end, the Commission shall make recommendations to the Member States concerned.

ARTICLE 16 Member States shall abolish between themselves customs duties on exports and charges having equivalent effect by the end of the first stage at the latest.

ARTICLE 17 1. The provisions of Articles 9 to 15(1) shall also apply to customs duties of a fiscal nature. Such duties shall not, however, be taken into consideration for the purpose of calculating either total customs receipts or the reduction of customs duties as a whole as referred to in Article 14(3) and (4). Such duties shall, at each reduction, be lowered by not less than 10 percent of the basic duty. Member States may reduce such duties more rapidly than is provided for in Article 14.

2. Member States shall, before the end of the first year after the entry into force of this Treaty, inform the Commission of their customs duties of a fiscal nature.

3. Member States shall retain the right to substitute for these duties an internal tax which complies with the provisions of Article 95.

4. If the Commission finds that substitution for any customs duty of a fiscal nature meets with serious difficulties in a Member State, it shall authorise that State to retain the duty on condition that it shall abolish it not later than six years after the entry into force of this Treaty.

STUDY QUESTIONS

1. Why were "customs duties" important to the establishment of the EEC? What did they promise for the future?
2. Does the treaty imply that the individual countries would retain their sovereignty in economic decision-making? Why or why not?

14.5 SIMONE DE BEAUVOIR, *THE SECOND SEX*, 1949

Simone de Beauvoir (1908–1986) was a French philosopher and social critic who published *The Second Sex* just after the Second World War ended. She had spent the war years with Albert Camus and her longtime companion Jean-Paul Sartre, among others, working with the French resistance against Nazi occupation. In her book she analyzed the roles women have played in Western history with particular attention to marriage. She and Sartre rejected marriage, maintaining it was an outdated bourgeois concept that bound people together by law instead of by constant choice. De Beauvoir noted that although women had advanced to take on new responsibilities, they still did not enjoy real equality with men. *The Second Sex* is one of the most important European works that explores the subordination of women. As the struggle for equality grew more militant in the 1960s and 1970s, de Beauvoir remained a powerful voice calling for women's liberation.

This balanced couple is not a utopia; such couples exist sometimes even within marriage, more often outside of it; some are united by a great sexual love that leaves them free in their friendships and occupations; others are linked by a friendship that does not hamper their sexual freedom; more rarely there are still others who are both lovers and friends but without seeking in each other their exclusive reason for living. Many nuances are possible in the relations of a man and a woman: in companionship, pleasure, confidence, tenderness, complicity, and love, they can be for each other the most fruitful source of joy, richness, and strength offered to a human being. It is not the individuals who are responsible for the failure of marriage: it is . . . the institution that is perverted at its base. Declaring that a man and a woman who do not even choose each other must meet each other's needs in all respects, at once, for their whole life, is a monstrosity that necessarily gives rise to hypocrisy, hostility, and unhappiness.

The traditional form of marriage is changing: but it still constitutes an oppression that both spouses feel in different ways. Considering the abstract rights they enjoy, they are almost equals; they choose each other more freely than before, they can separate much more easily, especially in America, where divorce is commonplace; there is less difference in age and culture between the spouses than previously;

the husband more easily acknowledges the autonomy his wife claims; they might even share housework equally: they have the same leisure interests: camping, bicycling, swimming, and so on. She does not spend her days waiting for her spouse's return: she practices sports, she belongs to associations and clubs, she has outside occupations, sometimes she even has a little job that brings her some money. Many young couples give the impression of perfect equality. But as long as the man has economic responsibility for the couple, it is just an illusion. He is the one who determines the conjugal domicile according to the demands of his job: she follows him from the provinces to Paris, from Paris to the provinces, the colonies, abroad; the standard of living is fixed according to his income; the rhythm of the days, the weeks, and the year is organized on the basis of his occupations; relations and friendships most often depend on his profession. Being more positively integrated than his wife into society, he leads the couple in intellectual, political, and moral areas. Divorce is only an abstract possibility for the wife, if she does not have the means to earn her own living: while alimony in America is a heavy burden for the husband, in France the lot of the wife and mother abandoned with a derisory pension is scandalous. But the deep inequality stems from the fact that the husband finds concrete accomplishment in work or action while for the wife in her role as wife, freedom has only a negative form: the situation of American girls, among others, recalls that of the emancipated girls of the Roman decadence. We saw that they had the choice between two types of behavior: some perpetuated the style of life and the virtues of their grandmothers; others spent their time in futile activity; likewise, many American women remain "housewives" in conformity with the traditional model; the others mostly whittle away their energy and time. In France, even if the husband has all the goodwill in the world, the burdens of the home do not weigh on him anymore once the young wife is a mother.

It is a commonplace to say that in modern households, and especially in the United States, the wife has reduced the husband to slavery. The fact is not new. Since the Greeks, males have complained of Xanthippe's tyranny; what is true is that the wife intervenes in areas that previously were forbidden to

her; I know, for example, of students' wives who contribute to the success of their man with frenetic determination; they organize their schedules, their diet, they watch over their work; they cut out all distractions, and almost keep them under lock and key. It is also true that man is more defenseless than previously against this despotism; he recognizes his wife's abstract rights, and he understands that she can concretize them only through him: it is at his own expense that he will compensate for the powerlessness and the sterility the wife is condemned to; to realize an apparent equality in their association, he has to give her more because he possesses more. But precisely because she receives, takes, and demands, she is the poorer. The dialectic of the master and slave has its most concrete application here: in oppressing, one becomes oppressed. Males are in chains by their very sovereignty; it is because they alone earn money that the wife demands checks, because men alone practice a profession that the wife demands that they succeed, because they alone embody transcendence that the wife wants to steal it from them by taking over their projects and successes. And inversely, the tyranny wielded by the woman only manifests her dependence: she knows the success of the couple, its future, its happiness, and its justification, resides in the hands of the other; if she bitterly seeks to subjugate him to her will, it is because she is alienated in him. She makes a weapon of her weakness; but the fact is she is weak. Conjugal slavery is ordinary and irritating for the husband; but it is deeper for the wife; the wife who keeps her husband near her for hours out of boredom irritates him and weighs on him; but in the end, he can do without her more easily than she him; if he leaves her, it is she whose life will be ruined. The big difference is that for the wife, dependence is interiorized; she is a slave even when she conducts herself with apparent freedom, while the husband is essentially autonomous and enchained from the outside. If he has the impression he is the victim, it is because the burdens he bears are more obvious: the wife feeds on him like a parasite; but a parasite is not a triumphant master. In reality, just as biologically males and females are never victims of each other but all together of the species, the spouses together submit to the oppression of an institution they have not created. If it is said *men* oppress *women*, the husband reacts indignantly; he feels oppressed: he is; but in fact, it is the masculine code, the society developed by males and in their interest, that has defined the feminine condition in a form that is now for both sexes a source of distress.

The situation has to be changed in their common interest by prohibiting marriage as a "career" for the woman. Men who declare themselves antifeminist with the excuse that "women are already annoying enough as it is" are not very logical: it is precisely because marriage makes them "praying mantises," "bloodsuckers," and "poison" that marriage has to be changed and, as a consequence, the feminine condition in general. Woman weighs so heavily on man because she is forbidden to rely on herself; he will free himself by freeing her, that is, by giving her something *to do* in this world.

There are young women who are already trying to win this positive freedom; but seldom do they persevere in their studies or their jobs for they know the interests of their work will most often be sacrificed to their husband's career; their salary will only "help out" at home; they hesitate to commit themselves to undertakings that do not pull them away from enslavement. Those who do have a serious profession will not draw the same social advantages as men: lawyers' wives, for example, are entitled to a pension on their husbands' death; women lawyers are prohibited from paying a corresponding pension to their husbands in case of death. This shows that the woman who works cannot keep the couple at the same level as the man. There are women who find real independence in their profession; but many discover that work "outside" only represents another source of fatigue within the framework of marriage. Moreover and most often, the birth of a child forces them to confine themselves to their role of matron; it is still very difficult to reconcile work and motherhood.

STUDY QUESTIONS

1. What bothered de Beauvoir about the institution of marriage? What did it offer men in society in comparison with women?
2. What new opportunities were available to women in mid-twentieth-century Europe? What remained beyond their grasp?

14.6 HUNGARIAN GOVERNMENT PROTEST AND NIKITA KHRUSHCHEV'S RECOLLECTIONS, NOVEMBER 2–3, 1956

In Hungary, after a series of demonstrations in 1955, student leaders boldly established an independent, noncommunist organization that advocated for economic reforms, democratic elections, and free speech. Revolution was in the air as student demonstrations grew larger and more militant and workers joined the fray. In an effort to calm the situation, the Hungarian Party, with reluctant Soviet backing, decided to return to power the highly popular Imre Nagy (1896–1958), the former communist party leader who had been ousted two years earlier. Once in office, Nagy

From Csaba Békés, Malcolm Byrne, and János M. Rainer, *The 1956 Hungarian Revolution: A History in Documents* (Budapest: Central European University Press, 2002), pp. 343–345 and 355.

From https://www.pofis.sk/en/catalog/products/postage-stamp-2018-art-ladislav-bielik-a-man-with-a-bare-chest.

publicly acknowledged the legitimacy of the people's grievances and declared Hungary "free, democratic, and independent."

To the Soviets, this declaration turned the Hungarian rebellion into an impermissible "counterrevolution," and the Kremlin sent in an army to put it down. Hungarians fought valiantly, if futilely, and nearly 3,000 died in the effort to assert their independence. The victorious Russians replaced Nagy with the compliant János Kádár (1912–1989), who immediately nullified his predecessor's reforms and jailed more than 35,000 people. Some 200,000 Hungarians fled the country, many to the United States and Canada. These documents illustrate some of the complexities of this dramatic series of events.

The Chairman of the Council of Ministers, in his role as Acting Foreign Minister of the Hungarian People's Republic, informs the Budapest Embassy of the Union of Soviet Socialist Republics of the following, and requests [the Embassy] to forward the [information] included in this note immediately to its government:

On October 26, 1956, the Hungarian government requested the government of the Soviet Union to undertake immediate negotiations in connection with the withdrawal of Soviet troops stationed in Hungary on the basis of the Warsaw Treaty, and stated its desire to settle this question through negotiations. With reference to the October 30, 1956 declaration of the government of the Soviet Union approving the Hungarian government's initiative, as well as to the response to this declaration given and published by the government of the Hungarian People's Republic, and [with reference] to the statement of his excellency the Soviet ambassador in Budapest given on his visit to the chairman of the Council of Ministers of the Hungarian People's Republic on November 1, 1956, the Hungarian government announces the following:

Unfortunately, despite the above-mentioned consultations between the two governments, further Soviet units crossed the Hungarian border between October 31 and November 1, 1956. The Hungarian government exerted all efforts in its power to achieve the withdrawal of the troops, but these attempts proved to be in vain. Moreover, the Soviet troops continued their advance and some units surrounded Budapest. As a consequence of this, the Hungarian government denounced the Warsaw Treaty on November 1, 1956.

Nevertheless, the government of the Hungarian People's Republic has repeatedly declared its desire to maintain to the utmost [its] friendly relationship with the Soviet Union in the future, as well. This relationship should be based on the principles of complete equality, sovereignty, and non-interference in one another's affairs, as well as on respect for the neutrality that was declared by the government of the Hungarian People's Republic on November 1, 1956.

For the sake of this, the government of the Hungarian People's Republic proposes to start immediate negotiations, on the basis of the above-mentioned principles, between the government delegations from the Hungarian People's Republic and the Union of Soviet Socialist Republics concerning the execution of the secession from the Warsaw Pact, with special regard to the immediate withdrawing of Soviet troops stationed in Hungary. The Hungarian government proposes Warsaw as the location of these negotiations. Members of the Hungarian government delegation are:

Géza Losonczy, minister of state, head of delegation
József Kővágó,
András Márton,
Ferenc Farkas and
Vilmos Zentai.

The Chairman of the Council of Ministers, in his role as Acting Foreign Minister, takes the opportunity to assure the Union of Soviet Socialist Republics of his high esteem.

Quotation from Nikita Khrushchev's memoirs, published in 1998, as translated by Svetlana Savranskaya:

We reached the Soviet capital only in the second half of the day [November 3, 1956], closer to the evening. Members of the CPSU [Communist Party of the Soviet Union] CC [Central Committee] Presidium gathered immediately, and we went to the Kremlin straight from the airport. We reported on the results of the fraternal negotiations together with Malenkov. Molotov had already spoken about the conversation at the border [with the PZPR (Polish United Workers' Party, communist Poland's ruling party) delegation]. We confirmed that the majority was in favor of the new Hungarian government in consultation with Kádár and Münnich. Molotov [the Soviet foreign minister] spoke sharply against Kádár . . . He used an insulting expression referring to Kádár (however, at the moment, Kádár was not present in person). Molotov justified his position by pointing out that Kádár continued to see himself as a member of the leadership together with [Imre] Nagy, however now, having spent two days in Moscow while Malenkov [a high communist party official] and I were away, he began to express anxiety and tried to return to Budapest. Yes, I understood Molotov's position: how can one propose a person who sees himself as a member of the leadership against which we are preparing to strike? He would have to lead the struggle against the acting leadership. Molotov insisted: "I am voting for Münnich." . . . I said: "Let us invite both of them." They were escorted in. We immediately told them frankly that the counterrevolution had begun in Hungary, and that we had to use troops against it. That it was the only opportunity to return to normalcy and to suppress the rebellion, which was raging in Budapest. I was watching Kádár intently. He was listening silently. Then came his turn to speak: "Yes," he agreed, "you are right, in order to stabilize the situation, we need your assistance now." . . . Münnich also expressed his support for actions involving the assistance of Soviet troops. Both Kádár and Münnich expressed their confidence that the Hungarian people in general would support the suppression of the counterrevolution. We started forming the government. It was done mostly by Kádár and Münnich—they knew the people.

STUDY QUESTIONS

1. How did the Hungarian government attempt to persuade the Soviets to turn back their invasion force? Were they likely to have been successful in the effort?
2. What constraints did Khrushchev face, and how did he meet the challenges facing him?

14.7 VISUAL SOURCE: SLOVAK COMMEMORATIVE STAMP, 2018, BASED ON LADISLAV BIELIK, *THE BARE-CHESTED MAN IN FRONT OF THE OCCUPIER'S TANK*, BRATISLAVA, 1968

In 1948, Czechoslovakia vowed loyalty to the Soviet Union and declined aid from the Marshall Plan, as Stalin had required them to do. But this was not enough for the Soviet dictator, who ousted the Czech leaders in favor of even more compliant men. Twenty years later, persistent repression and a stagnant Czech economy sparked a series of demonstrations against Czech party leaders who refused to reform. In response, officials of the Czech communist party deposed the sitting leader in favor Alexander Dubček, a reformer who brought hope to disgruntled students and intellectuals eager for change. Fearful that Dubček's attempt to liberalize restrictions on free speech would inspire other rebellions across Eastern Europe, the leader of the USSR, Leonid Brezhnev, sent the Soviet army to Prague, arrested Dubček, and crushed the resulting uprisings across the country.

In 1968, Ladislav Bielik (1939–1984) took a photo destined to become an iconic representation of the Czechoslovak rebellions of that year and later the inspiration for the postage stamp pictured here. Bielik was covering events in Bratislava, a city in south-central Czechoslovakia, now the capital of Slovakia, when revolts against the Soviets began. His photograph shows protestor Emil Gallo opening his shirt in front of a Soviet tank, highlighting his vulnerability as a civilian. In the background is Comenius University, indicating that many of the protestors were students. Bielik's photograph documents the frustration felt by millions of people living in Warsaw Pact countries forced to remain subservient to the Soviet Union. The postage stamp issued by the Slovak government on the fiftieth anniversary of the uprising celebrates the bravery of both Gallo and Bielik. By zooming in tightly on Bielik's image, crowding out a fuller view of the tank and soldiers patrolling nearby, the stamp personalizes the struggle of one man against a repressive regime. Consider the audience for the stamp and how it would be used (or preserved) as an object that memorializes the 1968 uprising.

FIGURE 14.7 Slovak Commemorative Stamp

STUDY QUESTIONS

1. What does Bielik's photograph reveal about events in Czechoslovakia in 1968?
2. Why would the Slovak government choose this image for a postage stamp in 2018? What does the stamp reveal about how contemporary Slovaks remember the Communist era?

USING PARALLELISM
TO SIMPLIFY COMPLEX IDEAS

With parallelism, "equal" thoughts are expressed in "equal" grammar:

"I came, I saw, I conquered" (parallel)

"I came, I was seeing, conquering was what I achieved" (non-parallel, or faulty parallelism)

Parallelism works through repetition. As we read, each grammatical structure lingers in memory for a moment. When the next structure is the same, we read it more quickly. Repeated structures function as a form of practice too, so we better remember what we have read.

Repetition may make ideas easier to *believe* as well, thanks to the "familiarity effect." Our brains are wired to equate the familiar with the true, so new content expressed in the same grammar may be more persuasive because it feels more familiar and thus more true.

Easier to read, *easier to remember*, and *easier to believe*: this sequence is an example of parallelism. "Equal" thoughts expressed in "equal" grammar.

Parallelism happens between sentences as well as within them:

After the Suez debacle, each country drew a major conclusion. <u>The British realized</u> that they would have to defer to the United States. <u>The Israelis realized</u> that only the United States could offer the support they needed. And <u>the French realized</u> that the Americans could not be trusted.

Faulty parallelism:

<u>The British realized</u> that they would have to defer to the United States. <u>The Israelis realized</u> that only the United States could offer the support they needed. And the untrustworthiness of America <u>was the message received by the French</u>.

EXERCISE: USE PARALLELISM TO REVISE SENTENCES

Instructions

Use parallelism to revise the sentences below.

---

1. The Marshall Plan reduced deficits, improved worker benefits, and intra-European trade was also facilitated.
REVISED:

---

2. Dubček was arrested, his reforms were annulled, the Communists removed pro-reform party members, and activist students were dismissed from the universities.
REVISED:

---

3. Some Eastern European countries hoped to introduce market incentives. Others focused on freer speech and cultural expression. Ending the Communist Party's monopoly of power was the goal for still others.
REVISED:

4. Of the 24 men tried at Nuremberg, 12 received death sentences, three were acquitted, and the court sent the rest to prison.
REVISED:

5. In Kenya, British forces used the torturing of prisoners, capital punishment, and prison camps to suppress the Mau Mau Revolt.
REVISED:

USING PARALLELISM TO OMIT WORDS

Parallelism allows you to omit words:

> *By the end of the war, Russia's industry and agriculture were shattered, its lines of transportation <u>were</u> pummeled, <u>and</u> its population <u>was</u> decimated.*
> *By the end of the war, Russia's industry and agriculture were shattered, its lines of transportation pummeled, its population decimated.*

Omitting words can speed the pace of your prose while repeating words slows the pace so the point sinks in. Both options have their uses. Full repetition—repeating words you could just as easily omit—is the grammatical equivalent of underlining or boldfacing.

EXERCISE: USE PARALLELISM TO OMIT WORDS

Instructions

Revise the sentences below using parallelism and omitting a word or words from the second instance of the parallel structure. In the first exercise, the words to be omitted are underlined.

6. Between 1950 and 1952, Austrian exports increased by 89 percent, <u>and</u> German exports <u>increased</u> by 87.
REVISED:

7. Laws against "obscenity" were liberalized, and censorship of the theater was abolished.
REVISED:

You will find suggested answers to the exercises in the back of this book. For more Writing History exercises, as well as study resources for this chapter, visit oup.com/us/berenson.

CHAPTER 15

ECONOMIC DILEMMAS, EUROPEAN UNITY, AND THE COLLAPSE OF COMMUNISM, 1970–2010

15.1 MIKHAIL GORBACHEV, *PERESTROIKA: NEW THINKING FOR OUR COUNTRY AND THE WORLD*, 1987

Two years after becoming first secretary of the Soviet Politburo in 1985, Mikhail Gorbachev (1931–) launched his two trademark economic and political programs: *perestroika* ("restructuring") and *glasnost* ("openness"). Under *perestroika*, Gorbachev, hoping to revitalize communism, restructured and partially dismantled the command economy that had dominated the USSR since the 1930s. While *perestroika* did not work out as intended, *glasnost*, which permitted frank commentary and the exposure of incompetence and cover-ups by Soviet leadership, led to more wideranging consequences for the USSR, which ultimately collapsed in 1991. Four years earlier, Gorbachev had summarized his approaches to domestic and international politics, especially Cold War conflicts with the United States and the need for arms control, in *Perestroika: New Thinking for Our Country and the World*, a book he wrote specifically for a Western audience.

WHO NEEDS THE ARMS RACE AND WHY?

Pondering the question of what stands in the way of good Soviet-American relations, one arrives at the conclusion that, for the most part, it is the arms race. I am not going to describe its history. Let me just note once again that at almost all its stages the Soviet Union has been the party catching up. By the beginning of the seventies we had reached approximate military-strategic parity, but on a level that is really frightening. Both the Soviet Union and the United States now have the capacity to destroy each other many times over.

It would seem logical, in the face of a strategic stalemate, to halt the arms race and get down to disarmament. But the reality is different. Armories already overflowing continue to be filled with sophisticated new types of weapons, and new areas of military technology are being developed. The US sets the tone in this dangerous, if not fatal pursuit.

I shall not disclose any secret if I tell you that the Soviet Union is doing all that is necessary to maintain up-to-date and reliable defenses. This is our duty to our own people and our allies. At the same time I wish to say quite definitely that this is not our choice. It has been imposed upon us.

All kinds of doubts are being spread among Americans about Soviet intentions in the field of disarmament. But history shows that we can keep the word we gave and that we honor the obligations assumed. Unfortunately, this cannot be said of the United States. The administration is conditioning public opinion, intimidating it with a Soviet threat, and does so with particular stubbornness when a new military budget has to be passed through Congress. We have to ask ourselves why all this is being done and what aim the US pursues.

It is crystal clear that in the world we live in, the world of nuclear weapons, any attempt to use them to solve Soviet-American problems would spell suicide. This is a fact. I do not think that US politicians are unaware of it. Moreover, a truly paradoxical situation has now developed. Even if one country engages in a steady arms buildup while the other does nothing, the side that arms itself will all the same gain nothing. The weak side may simply explode all its nuclear charges, even on its own territory, and that would mean suicide for it and a slow death for the enemy. This is why any striving for military superiority means chasing one's own tail. It can't be used in real politics.

Nor is the US in any hurry to part with another illusion. I mean its immoral intention to bleed the Soviet Union white economically, to prevent us from carrying out our plans of construction by dragging us ever deeper into the quagmire of the arms race.

. . .

We sincerely advise Americans: try to get rid of such an approach to our country. Hopes of using any advantages in technology or advanced equipment so as to gain superiority over our country are futile. To act on the assumption that the Soviet Union is in a "hopeless position" and that it is necessary just to press it harder to squeeze out everything the US wants is to err profoundly. Nothing will come of these plans. In real politics there can be no wishful thinking. If the Soviet Union, when it was much weaker than now, was in a position to meet all the challenges that it faced, then indeed only a blind person would be unable to see that our capacity to maintain strong defenses and simultaneously resolve social and other tasks has enormously increased.

I shall repeat that as far as the United States foreign policy is concerned, it is based on at least two delusions. The first is the belief that the economic system of the Soviet Union is about to crumble and that the USSR will not succeed in restructuring. The second is calculated on Western superiority in equipment and technology and, eventually, in the military field. These illusions nourish a policy geared toward exhausting socialism through the arms race, so as to dictate terms later. Such is the scheme; it is naïve.

Current Western policies aren't responsible enough, and lack the new mode of thinking. I am outspoken about this. If we don't stop now and start practical disarmament, we may all find ourselves on the edge of a precipice. Today, as never before, the Soviet Union and the United States need responsible policies. Both countries have their political, social and economic problems: a vast field for activities. Meanwhile, many brain trusts work at strategic plans and juggle millions of lives. Their recommendations boil down to this: the Soviet Union is the most horrible threat for the United States and the world. I repeat: it is high time this caveman mentality was given up. Of course, many political leaders and diplomats have engaged in just such policies based on just such a mentality for decades. But their time is past. A new outlook is necessary in a nuclear age. The United States and the Soviet Union need it most in their bilateral relations.

We are realists. So we take into consideration the fact that in a foreign policy all countries, even the smallest, have their own interests. It is high time great powers realized that they can no longer reshape the world according to their own patterns. That era has receded or, at least, is receding into the past.

STUDY QUESTIONS

1. Why does Gorbachev describe American foreign policy as being dictated by "illusions" and "delusions"? Was he being disingenuous or hypocritical in this assertion?
2. In what ways was Gorbachev advocating a global position on the problems of the world? Was he also guided by "delusions" in this advocacy?

15.2 JAMES A. CASON AND RICHARD F. POST, THE "CARNATION REVOLUTION" IN PORTUGAL, APRIL–DECEMBER 1974

Between 1932 and 1970, Portugal was governed by the autocratic António Salazar (1889–1970), who kept his country in a backward, impoverished state. While Portugal's largely illiterate peasant population mostly accepted the status quo, Salazar also counted on the support of Spain's authoritarian leader Francisco Franco and on that of the US government. The Americans feared Soviet incursions into Western Europe and considered anti-communists like the Spanish and Portuguese strongmen preferable to their communist counterparts.

A 1961 rebellion in Portugal's African colonies—Angola, Mozambique, São Tomé, and Guinea-Bissau—led the Portuguese army to spend fully half of its defense budget in Africa. By the mid-1970s young conscripts were increasingly unwilling to fight futile wars to hold together the remnants of Portugal's sixteenth-century empire. Finally, in April 1974, army officers calling themselves the Armed Forces Movement (MFA) ousted Salazar's successor, Marcello Caetano (1906–1980) and created a provisional government dedicated to democratization, decolonization, and economic change.

Unusually for army officers, the MFA supported Portugal's now-legalized Communist Party, which sought to nationalize banks and major industries and redistribute land from large proprietors to peasants. But the program proved unpopular in most of the country and led to Portugal's first democratic election. The largest vote-getter was Mário Soares's moderate socialist party, which shepherded the country from dictatorship to democracy. The following document features the recollections of two American diplomats of this remarkable moment in European history, one who was serving as the Political Officer (James A. Cason) and the other who was acting as the Deputy Chief of Mission at the US Embassy in Lisbon (Richard F. Post).

JAMES A. CASON: Portugal in 1974 was a quiet place, with no hints of the revolution to come. There was really no political opposition, as Portugal was led by a dictator, Marcello Caetano. Being new to political work, I was given the safe job of domestic political analysis, and began making my contacts and

American Diplomats Recall the "Carnation Revolution" in Portugal, April–December 1974/adst.org
http://adst.org/2015/04/the-carnation-revolution-a-peaceful-coup-in-portugal/?fdx_switcher=mobile.

did a lot of biographic reporting. And I was given the task as well of watching the colonies from there, Guinea-Bissau, Angola, Mozambique. We had a whole rotation out of all the experienced officers.

Politically, things were routine, quiet until one day in May 1974 as I was taking my morning train from Oeiras, down the coast, where I lived; I remember the crowd on the train was uncharacteristically very quiet.

As we approached the downtown station, I looked up and saw this whole line of tanks along the train track with troops with guns out on the top. I thought perhaps the troops were on maneuvers or something.

We were caught flat-footed and had no inkling that the revolution was coming. As I disembarked at the Central Station I heard the crack of rifle fire—chuchuchuchuchu. I said, "Uh-oh," alerted the embassy and took a cab there right away.

The revolution was underway.

It was a fascinating time to be in Portugal, particularly since my job analyzing the domestic politics now suddenly became very interesting. Young army captains and majors and officers from the other services who had been stationed in the colonies made the revolution. Within a few days, rebelling troops had taken over the country. The elite fled, including the Espirito Santo Silva family [founders of the Banco Espirito Santo], and many of the bankers and regime supporters. The whole state security apparatus was rolled up; hundreds were arrested and others fled.

None of us knew who these young officers were, what they wanted and their ideological orientation. They were complete unknowns, to the diplomatic community at least. They planned their revolution in secrecy while in Angola, Guinea Bissau and Mozambique. They snookered the whole government, taking over in a lightning blow with very few casualties . . .

The revolution scared our government. Was Portugal going communist? Would it fall into the Soviet orbit? The uncertainty was a *big* deal for Kissinger and our President. Some observers gasped that, Oh my God, the Communists have taken over a European country! That's because some of the officers appeared and spoke like Maoists, they really were far left. The head of the military, General Antonio de Spínola, supported the revolution but was a moderate.

Soon it was evident that there were tensions between the junior officers and their seniors. The extremist spokesman was Otelo Nuno Saraiva de Carvalho, who we thought was a Communist and who became our nemesis.

Anyway, Kissinger didn't like the reporting that was coming out from the Ambassador that basically said this is not a Communist uprising but a nationalist one, which stemmed from frustrations with African policy.

Portugal was a very conservative society and was not interested in communist ideology. I reported that. People were fed up. They wanted to accelerate the decolonization process and end a dictatorship that had lasted for 40-something years and only benefited the entrenched elite. And so I reported that this is not a communist wave.

The revolution took place the 2[5]th of April.

On May Day 100,000 Communists passed by the embassy chanting ["The people united can't be defeated!"] Where did they come from? A couple of days later [then Secretary General of the Socialist Party] Mario Soares came in with 100,000 in his rally. He'd come in from Brussels, and was the Socialist leader. And then several conservative parties popped up. All these parties had been banned under Caetano.

RICHARD F. POST: To me it was a very satisfactory kind of coup to have. Because on the night of the coup, the new Junta of National Salvation was introduced to the Portuguese public on radio and television. In the five-man junta, two were close friends of mine; one was [Francisco da] Costa Gomes, Chief of Staff of the army. He had been the Commander of the forces in Angola when I was Consul General. He was probably my best contact when he was there.

. . .

Of course the reason for it was the majors and captains who carried out the coup were basically apolitical types. The Portuguese army was not the kind of place that attracted very many of the left side of the ideology camp and it was a disciplined army. So of course they go to their top generals. And Costa Gomez was one of them. Spínola was another. This was the authority structure that they were accustomed to. Even though their own ideological druthers might be somewhat different, they were basically apolitical.

Then we had this other problem of trying to persuade Washington that these were not communists. "Write Portugal off. It's finished." We were arguing that these guys are apolitical. The one thing that they know about the United States is that we supported the last government. Therefore they had to be somewhat suspicious of us.

. . .

On December 11th of 1974—I remember it because it was my birthday—we got a telegram: "You may inform the President that we are going to provide aid."

The Foreign Minister was then Mario Soares, [later] President, with whom I had had a lot of dealings. The Ambassador and I got to the President to inform him of this aid package but not to Soares.

However, that was okay because I was going to a dinner party at the French ambassador's house where Mario Soares was to be the guest of honor.

. . .

I had extensive conversations with a couple of them. People I did not know beforehand, but that I got to know after the coup. And we maintained pretty good relations with this revolutionary council.

There was then the question of elections. Of course the people who were about to write Portugal off assumed that there never really would be free and fair elections, but that these army officers would skew things in favor of the Communists and they would win.

They went ahead and did hold elections and the Communists did not win. They did not win more than 20 percent of the vote. It was the Socialists, people at the center and the right that came up with the big majority. That was a clear indication that the people of Portugal were people who wanted to stick with democracy in the West and all the rest of it.

STUDY QUESTIONS

1. Why was the American government unprepared for the position of the Portuguese military?
2. Why did American foreign policy leaders finally agree to support the revolution in Portugal?

15.3 THE HELSINKI ACCORDS, 1975

The Helsinki Accords (1975) recognized the territorial integrity of Eastern Europe's communist countries and bound the 35 Eastern and Western signatories to a policy of détente. But buried within the Accords was a set of principles outlining not just the rights of states but the rights of individuals living within those states. The Accords affirmed "human rights and fundamental freedoms" and obliged all 35 signatories to "promote and encourage the effective exercise of civil, political, economic, social, cultural and other rights and freedoms." These clauses, which diplomats had intended as mere cosmetic boilerplate, proved to be political dynamite. Suddenly, a variety of groups sprang up in the Soviet Union and Eastern Europe demanding that their countries live up to the accords their leaders had signed.

From http://www.osce.org/mc/39501?download=true.

THE FINAL ACT OF THE CONFERENCE ON SECURITY AND COOPERATION IN EUROPE, AUG. 1, 1975, 14 I.L.M. 1292 (HELSINKI DECLARATION)

The Conference on Security and Co-operation in Europe, which opened at Helsinki on 3 July 1973 and continued at Geneva from 18 September 1973 to 21 July 1975, was concluded at Helsinki on 1 August 1975 by the High Representatives of Austria, Belgium, Bulgaria, Canada, Cyprus, Czechoslovakia, Denmark, Finland, France, the German Democratic Republic, the Federal Republic of Germany, Greece, the Holy See, Hungary, Iceland, Ireland, Italy, Liechtenstein, Luxembourg, Malta, Monaco, the Netherlands, Norway, Poland, Portugal, Romania, San Marino, Spain, Sweden, Switzerland, Turkey, the Union of Soviet Socialist Republics, the United Kingdom, the United States of America and Yugoslavia.

During the opening and closing stages of the Conference the participants were addressed by the Secretary-General of the United Nations as their guest of honour. The Director-General of UNESCO and the Executive Secretary of the United Nations Economic Commission for Europe addressed the Conference during its second stage.

During the meetings of the second stage of the Conference, contributions were received, and statements heard, from the following non-participating Mediterranean States on various agenda items: the Democratic and Popular Republic of Algeria, the Arab Republic of Egypt, Israel, the Kingdom of Morocco, the Syrian Arab Republic, Tunisia.

Motivated by the political will, in the interest of peoples, to improve and intensify their relations and to contribute in Europe to peace, security, justice and cooperation as well as to rapprochement among themselves and with the other States of the world,

Determined, in consequence, to give full effect to the results of the Conference and to assure, among their States and throughout Europe, the benefits deriving from those results and thus to broaden, deepen and make continuing and lasting the process of détente,

The High Representatives of the participating States have solemnly adopted the following:

Questions Relating to Security in Europe

The States participating in the Conference on Security and Co-operation in Europe,

Reaffirming their objective of promoting better relations among themselves and ensuring conditions in which their people can live in true and lasting peace free from any threat to or attempt against their security;

Convinced of the need to exert efforts to make détente both a continuing and an increasingly viable and comprehensive process, universal in scope, and that the implementation of the results of the Conference on Security and Cooperation in Europe will be a major contribution to this process;

Considering that solidarity among peoples, as well as the common purpose of the participating States in achieving the aims as set forth by the Conference on Security and Cooperation in Europe, should lead to the development of better and closer relations among them in all fields and thus to overcoming the confrontation stemming from the character of their past relations, and to better mutual understanding;

Mindful of their common history and recognizing that the existence of elements common to their traditions and values can assist them in developing their relations, and desiring to search, fully taking into account the individuality and diversity of their positions and views, for possibilities of joining their efforts with a view to overcoming distrust and increasing confidence, solving the problems that separate them and cooperating in the interest of mankind;

Recognizing the indivisibility of security in Europe as well as their common interest in the development of cooperation throughout Europe and among selves and expressing their intention to pursue efforts accordingly;

Recognizing the close link between peace and security in Europe and in the world as a whole and conscious of the need for each of them to make its contribution to the strengthening of world peace and security and to the promotion of fundamental rights, economic and social progress and well-being for all peoples;

Have adopted the following:

1.(A) Declaration on Principles Guiding Relations Between Participating States

The participating States,

Reaffirming their commitment to peace, security and justice and the continuing development of friendly relations and co-operation;

Recognizing that this commitment, which reflects the interest and aspirations of peoples, constitutes for each participating State a present and future responsibility, heightened by experience of the past;

Reaffirming, in conformity with their membership in the United Nations and in accordance with the purposes and principles of the United Nations, their full and active support for the United Nations and for the enhancement of its role and effectiveness in strengthening international peace, security and justice, and in promoting the solution of international problems, as well as the development of friendly relations and cooperation among States;

Expressing their common adherence to the principles which are set forth below and are in conformity with the Charter of the United Nations, as well as their common will to act, in the application of these principles, in conformity with the purposes and principles of the Charter of the United Nations;

Declare their determination to respect and put into practice, each of them in its relations with all other participating States, irrespective of their political, economic or social systems as well as of their size, geographical location or level of economic development, the following principles, which all are of primary significance, guiding their mutual relations:

I. Sovereign Equality, Respect for the Rights Inherent in Sovereignty

The participating States will respect each other's sovereign equality and individuality as well as all the rights inherent in and encompassed by its sovereignty, including in particular the right of every State to juridical equality, to territorial integrity and to freedom and political independence. They will also respect each other's right freely to choose and develop its political, social, economic and cultural systems as well as its right to determine its laws and regulations.

Within the framework of international law, all the participating States have equal rights and duties. They will respect each other's right to define and conduct as it wishes its relations with other States in accordance with international law and in the spirit of the present Declaration. They consider that their frontiers can be changed, in accordance with international law, by peaceful means and by agreement. They also have the right to belong or not to belong to international organizations, to be or not to be a party to bilateral or multilateral treaties including the right to be or not to be a party to treaties of alliance; they also have the right to neutrality . . .

VII. Respect for Human Rights and Fundamental Freedoms, Including The Freedom of Thought, Conscience, Religion or Belief

The participating States will respect human rights and fundamental freedoms, including the freedom of thought, conscience, religion or belief, for all without distinction as to race, sex, language or religion.

They will promote and encourage the effective exercise of civil, political, economic, social, cultural and other rights and freedoms all of which derive from the inherent dignity of the human person and are essential for his free and full development.

Within this framework the participating States will recognize and respect the freedom of the individual to profess and practice, alone or in community with others, religion or belief acting in accordance with the dictates of his own conscience.

The participating States on whose territory national minorities exist will respect the right of persons belonging to such minorities to equality before the law, will afford them the full opportunity for the actual enjoyment of human rights and fundamental freedoms and will, in this manner, protect their legitimate interests in this sphere.

The participating States recognize the universal significance of human rights and fundamental freedoms, respect for which is an essential factor for the peace, justice and well-being necessary to ensure the development of friendly relations and co-operation among themselves as among all States.

They will constantly respect these rights and freedoms in their mutual relations and will endeavour jointly and separately, including in co-operation with the United Nations, to promote universal and effective respect for them.

They confirm the right of the individual to know and act upon his rights and duties in this field.

In the field of human rights and fundamental freedoms, the participating States will act in conformity with the purposes and principles of the Charter of the United Nations and with the Universal Declaration of Human Rights. They will also fulfil their obligations as set forth in the international declarations and agreements in this field, including inter alia the International Covenants on Human Rights, by which they may be bound.

VIII. Equal Rights and Self-Determination of Peoples

The participating States will respect the equal rights of peoples and their right to self-determination, acting at all times in conformity with the purposes and principles of the Charter of the United Nations and with the relevant norms of international law, including those relating to territorial integrity of States.

By virtue of the principle of equal rights and self-determination of peoples, all peoples always have the right, in full freedom, to determine, when and as they wish, their internal and external political status, without external interference, and to pursue as they wish their political, economic, social and cultural development.

The participating States reaffirm the universal significance of respect for and effective exercise of equal rights and self-determination of peoples for the development of friendly relations among themselves as among all States; they also recall the importance of the elimination of any form of violation of this principle.

STUDY QUESTIONS

1. How did the signatories of the Helsinki Accords believe they could achieve "collective security"? Was this a reasonable goal for Europe in the Cold War, even during a time of détente?
2. What did the diplomats at Helsinki believe was the connection between security and human rights? Was this connection a valid one?

15.4 MARGARET THATCHER, "THE LADY'S NOT FOR TURNING" SPEECH, OCTOBER 10, 1980

Margaret Roberts Thatcher (1925–2013) served three terms as Britain's prime minister. Before going into politics Thatcher studied chemistry at Oxford University, where she was the president of the student Conservative Association. In her mid-twenties, she trained as a tax lawyer and ran unsuccessfully for Parliament; then, in 1959, she won a seat in Parliament, which she held for decades.

From Margaret Thatcher Foundation, *Speech to Conservative Party Conference*, Thatcher Archive: CCOPR 735/80, https://www. margaretthatcher.org/document/104431. Reproduced with permission of the estate of Lady Thatcher.

After serving as education minister, Thatcher became the leader of the Conservative Party, the first woman to head a Western political party, and then prime minister in May 1979. At the time, Britain suffered from high inflation and unemployment as a series of strikes gripped the nation. The excerpts here come from an October 1980 speech Thatcher gave to her fellow Conservatives in which she outlined her approach to solving the domestic and foreign crises facing Britain. Her line "the lady's not for turning" became famous as it typified her approach to leadership. In response to the strong image she projected and her refusal to yield, a Soviet Army newspaper dubbed her the "Iron Lady," a nickname that stuck. Consider which problems she prioritized early in her first term and what solutions she offered. Also note how she saw the Soviet Union and its role in Europe after the passage of the Helsinki Accords.

There are many things to be done to set this nation on the road to recovery, and I do not mean economic recovery alone, but a new independence of spirit and zest for achievement.

It is sometimes said that because of our past, we, as a people, expect too much and set our sights too high. That is not the way I see it. Rather it seems to me that throughout my life in politics our ambitions have steadily shrunk. Our response to disappointment has not been to lengthen our stride but to shorten the distance to be covered. But with confidence in ourselves and in our future, what a nation we could be!

In its first 17 months, this government have laid the foundations for recovery. We have undertaken a heavy load of legislation, a load we do not intend to repeat because we do not share the socialist fantasy that achievement is measured by the number of laws you pass. But there was a formidable barricade of obstacles that we had to sweep aside. . . . Prosperity comes not from grand conferences of economists but by countless acts of personal self-confidence and self-reliance.

. . .

The left continues to refer with relish to the death of capitalism. Well, if this is the death of capitalism, I must say that it is quite a way to go.

But all this will avail us little unless we achieve our prime economic objective—the defeat of inflation. Inflation destroys nations and societies as surely as invading armies do. Inflation is the parent of unemployment. It is the unseen robber of those who have saved. No policy which puts at risk the defeat of inflation—however great its short-term

attraction—can be right. Our policy for the defeat of inflation is, in fact, traditional. . . .

But some people talk as if control of the money supply was a revolutionary policy. Yet it was an essential condition for the recovery of much of continental Europe. Those countries knew what was required for economic stability. Previously, they had lived through rampant inflation; they knew that it led to suitcase money, massive unemployment and the breakdown of society itself. They determined never to go that way again.

Today, after many years of monetary self-discipline, they have stable, prosperous economies better able than ours to withstand the buffeting of world recession. So at international conferences to discuss economic affairs, many of my fellow heads of government find our policies not strange, unusual or revolutionary, but normal, sound and honest. And that is what they are. Their only question is: "Has Britain the courage and resolve to sustain the discipline for long enough to break through to success?"

Yes, Mr. Chairman, we have, and we shall. This government are determined to stay with the policy and see it through to its conclusion. That is what marks this administration as one of the truly radical ministries of postwar Britain. Inflation is falling and should continue to fall.

Meanwhile, we are not heedless of the hardships and worries that accompany the conquest of inflation. Foremost among these is unemployment. Today our country has more than 2 million unemployed.

. . . Let me make it clear beyond doubt. I am profoundly concerned about unemployment. Human dignity and self-respect are undermined when men and women are condemned to idleness. The waste of a country's most precious assets—the talent and energy of its people—makes it the bounden duty of government to seek a real and lasting cure.

If I could press a button and genuinely solve the unemployment problem, do you think that I would not press that button this instant? Does anyone imagine that there is the smallest political gain in letting this unemployment continue, or that there is some obscure economic religion which demands this unemployment as part of its ritual? This government are pursuing the only policy which gives any hope of bringing our people back to real and lasting employment. . . .

I know that there is another real worry affecting many of our people. Although they accept that our policies are right, they feel deeply that the burden of carrying them out is falling much more heavily on the private than on the public sector. They say that the public sector is enjoying advantages but the private sector is taking the knocks and at the same time maintaining those in the public sector with better pay and pensions than they enjoy.

I must tell you that I share this concern and understand the resentment. That is why I and my colleagues say that to add to public spending takes away the very money and resources that industry needs to stay in business, let alone to expand. Higher public spending, far from curing unemployment, can be the very vehicle that loses jobs and causes bankruptcies in trade and commerce. That is why we warned local authorities that since rates are frequently the biggest tax that industry now faces, increases in them can cripple local businesses. Councils must, therefore, learn to cut costs in the same way that companies have to.

. . .

Of course, our vision and our aims go far beyond the complex arguments of economics, but unless we get the economy right we shall deny our people the opportunity to share that vision and to see beyond the narrow horizons of economic necessity. Without a healthy economy we cannot have a healthy society. Without a healthy society the economy will not stay healthy for long.

But it is not the state that creates a healthy society. When the state grows too powerful, people feel that

they count for less and less. The state drains society, not only of its wealth but of initiative, of energy, the will to improve and innovate as well as to preserve what is best. Our aim is to let people feel that they count for more and more. If we cannot trust the deepest instincts of our people, we should not be in politics at all. Some aspects of our present society really do offend those instincts.

Decent people do want to do a proper job at work, not to be restrained or intimidated from giving value for money. They believe that honesty should be respected, not derided. They see crime and violence as a threat, not just to society but to their own orderly way of life. They want to be allowed to bring up their children in these beliefs, without the fear that their efforts will be daily frustrated in the name of progress or free expression. Indeed, that is what family life is all about.

There is not a generation gap in a happy and united family. People yearn to be able to rely on some generally accepted standards. Without them you have not got a society at all, you have purposeless anarchy. A healthy society is not created by its institutions, either. Great schools and universities do not make a great nation any more than great armies do. Only a great nation can create and involve great institutions—of learning, of healing, of scientific advance. And a great nation is the voluntary creation of its people—a people composed of men and women whose pride in themselves is founded on the knowledge of what they can give to a community of which they in turn can be proud.

If our people feel that they are part of a great nation and they are prepared to will the means to keep it great, a great nation we shall be, and shall remain. So, what can stop us from achieving this? What then stands in our way? The prospect of another winter of discontent? I suppose it might. But I prefer to believe that certain lessons have been learned from experience, that we are coming, slowly, painfully, to an autumn of understanding. And I hope that it will be followed by a winter of common sense. If it is not, we shall not be diverted from our course.

To those waiting with bated breath for that favourite media catchphrase, the "U" turn, I have only one thing to say. "You turn if you want to. The lady's not for turning." I say that not only to you but to our friends overseas and also to those who are not our friends.

In foreign affairs we have pursued our national interest robustly while remaining alive to the needs and interests of others. Long before we came into office, and therefore long before the invasion of Afghanistan, I was pointing to the threat from the east. I was accused of scaremongering. But events have more than justified my words. Soviet Marxism is ideologically, politically and morally bankrupt. But militarily the Soviet Union is a powerful and growing threat.

Yet it was Mr. Kosygin who said, "No peace loving country, no person of integrity, should remain indifferent when an aggressor holds human life and world opinion in insolent contempt." We agree. The British government are not indifferent to the occupation of Afghanistan. We shall not allow it to be forgotten. Unless and until the Soviet troops are withdrawn, other nations are bound to wonder which of them may be next. Of course there are those who say that by speaking out we are complicating east-west relations, that we are endangering detente. But the real danger would lie in keeping silent. Detente is indivisible and it is a two-way process.

The Soviet Union cannot conduct wars by proxy in south-east Asia and Africa, foment trouble in the Middle East and Caribbean and invade neighbouring countries and still expect to conduct business as usual. Unless detente is pursued by both sides it can be pursued by neither, and it is a delusion to suppose otherwise. That is the message we shall be delivering loud and clear at the meeting of the European security conference in Madrid in the weeks immediately ahead.

But we shall also be reminding the other parties in Madrid that the Helsinki accord was supposed to promote the freer movement of people and ideas. The Soviet government's response so far has been a campaign of repression worse than any since Stalin's day. It had been hoped that Helsinki would open gates across Europe. In fact, the guards today are better armed and the walls are no lower. But behind those walls the human spirit is unvanquished. . . .

In Europe we have shown that it is possible to combine a vigorous defence of our own interests with a deep commitment to the idea and to the ideals of the community.

. . .

The British government intend to stand by both these great institutions: the community and NATO. We will not betray them. The restoration of Britain's place in the world and of the west's confidence in its own destiny are two aspects of the same process. No doubt there will be unexpected twists in the road, but with wisdom and resolution we can reach our goal. I believe we will show the wisdom and you may be certain that we will show the resolution.

In his warm-hearted and generous speech, Peter Thorneycroft said that when people are called upon to lead great nations, they must look into the hearts and minds of the people whom they seek to govern. I would add that those who seek to govern must, in turn, be willing to allow their hearts and minds to lie open to the people.

This afternoon I have tried to set before you some of my most deeply held convictions and beliefs. This party, which I am privileged to serve, and this government, which I am proud to lead, are engaged in the massive task of restoring confidence and stability to our people.

I have always known that that task was vital. . . . So let us resist the blandishments of the faint hearts; let us ignore the howls and threats of the extremists; let us stand together and do our duty, and we shall not fail.

STUDY QUESTIONS

1. What did Thatcher mean in saying, "the lady's not for turning"? What promises was she making to her fellow Conservatives and to the wider British population?

2. What problems did the previous Labour ministry cause that Thatcher felt her administration could correct?

15.5 LECH WALESA, *THE STRUGGLE AND THE TRIUMPH*, 1991

When the heavily indebted government of Communist Poland raised the price of meat on July 1, 1980, a massive wave of strikes engulfed the country. In response, the electrician Lech Walesa (1943–) and a few other activists announced the creation of a new national trade union called Solidarity. The union spread like wildfire and, by the end of the year, registered more than 10 million members in a country of 35 million people. Solidarity's huge size and overwhelming popularity left the government little choice but to make it an official, independent organization, with Walesa as its president. Shortly afterward, however, the Polish leader General Wojciech Jaruzelski, under pressure from the USSR, placed Poland under martial law, imprisoned Walesa and other Solidarity leaders, and banned the union.

Released from prison in November 1982, Walesa received the Nobel Peace Prize (1983) and became a shadow leader waiting in the wings. The wait was not long. When, in 1987, Jaruzelski again tried to reduce Poland's indebtedness by raising prices for consumer items 80 percent, Walesa stepped in to lead the opposition. Poland's Communist government—and the entire Eastern Bloc—unraveled in 1989, and Walesa became the country's president in 1990.

In his memoirs, excerpted below, Walesa cast his mind back to both his personal experiences and to his very public life in the years preceding the book's publication.

It all became increasingly unbearable for the adults. The year 1987 reinforced that feeling. General Jaruzelski's government was grinding to a halt, and I was talking to dozens of political figures and giving countless interviews in an attempt to convince the government that some kind of compromise with its opposition—Solidarity and all the other opposition groups—was the only recourse. My wife's patience was sorely tested.

Our day began when the alarm clock went off at 5:15 a.m., when I had to get up and go to work. I rarely felt I had had any sleep. I would say a brief prayer: "God, grant me a peaceful, uneventful day and grant me a little time to spend with Danka and with the children. Give me strength and a sense of purpose. I am a union leader, a politician, an activist, a husband, a father, a Nobel laureate, a citizen of Gdansk, a worker at the shipyards, and I don't know

what else. Help me also to remain myself." While I washed, shaved, and dressed, Danka made my lunch and breakfast, which I would take with me. I didn't have time to eat and didn't want to be late (I was late only once and remember it to this day). The kids were still asleep, of course; even little Brygidka didn't get up until around six o'clock. It was always in the morning, when everyone was still in bed, that I would realize that even this apartment had become too small.

There were always three cars waiting for me in front of the house: my special group. I was afforded at least as much protection as the Party's first secretary. Sometimes the Security Service agents would be snoozing, so I'd knock on the car windows. The trip to the shipyards wasn't long, maybe three and a half miles. The tram was usually jam-packed. . . .

For part of the trip, the tram ran along a wall of concrete pillars the color of which constantly changed.

From Lech Walesa, *The Struggle and the Triumph: An Autobiography*, translated by Franklin Philip (New York: Arcade, 1992), pp. 17–20.

Painters hired by the government couldn't manage to cover over the graffiti scrawled there each night by members of the Solidarity underground (mostly high school students). Until martial law was declared, the walls carried messages and demands large enough for all to see. "TELEVISION TELLS LIES," read one slogan. But there were also specific messages, such as "WATCH IT! THE CAR WITH LICENSE PLATE #XXXX BELONGS TO THE SECURITY SERVICE." Some graffiti demanded freedom for Leszek Moczulski of the Confederation for an Independent Poland (KPN), who had prematurely and unpardonably proclaimed Poland's independence; we had not managed to get him out of prison even when our union ranks had swelled to ten million. In 1987, people scrawled, "SOLIDARITY LIVES!" on the walls.

. . .

If I took the tram to work, I always had to empty my pockets on the docks of the shipyards because by the time I got there all sorts of messages were crammed into them—requests for secret meetings or for medicine, warnings, sometimes even threats.

I returned to work after prison just before May 1, 1983, in order to repair the electric forklifts; their connectors, sometimes even their wheels, had been torn off. Once martial law was declared, the workers stopped caring about the equipment and let it fall apart. In the early days, during breaks, I would go to the canteen. People would sit next to me in order to get into discussions; we were always surrounded by agents with tape recorders and cameras. But those seen with me would later be summoned to the management offices for a "conversation" with the Militia, so I thought it better to hold my conferences outside the shipyards. Religious services were always useful for this, and I was invited to them by workers, students and professors, and intellectuals.

What, you might ask, was a Nobel Prize winner doing at the shipyards? The fact that I went on working there seemed to surprise everyone. Yes, I no doubt could have found a better job practically anywhere. I could have been employed as a sexton at Father Jankowski's church and earned more. But I wanted and needed continuity, even if it meant working in this technological dinosaur of a factory, and repairing equipment much of which dated from before World War II.

STUDY QUESTIONS

1. How did Walesa's political stance affect his daily life in Gdansk?
2. In the late 1980s, did the Polish government already know that its days were numbered?

15.6 ZLATA FILIPOVIĆ, *ZLATA'S DIARY*, 1992

In 1993, amid the brutal war that pitted two former Yugoslav republics—Serbia and Bosnia—against each other, an 11-year-old girl name Zlata Flilpović published a searing diary that chronicled the profound human costs of the conflict. The book became an international bestseller and awakened people in Western Europe and the United States to the horrors of the Balkan wars and the "ethnic cleansing" they produced. These wars had resulted from the efforts of Slobodan Milošević (1941–2006), a former Communist Party boss who became president of Serbia in 1989, to expand the borders of Serbia into the parts of Croatia and Bosnia that contained sizable Serb populations. In the process, the Serbian forces tried to expel all non-Serbs from these regions. These expulsions came to be known as "ethnic cleansing" and resulted in the death and displacement of large numbers of people. In these diary entries, Flilpović graphically describes the murderous shelling of the Bosnian capital Sarajevo, a multiethnic city in which Serbs, Croats, and Bosnian Muslim had, until 1991, lived in relative peace.

APRIL 12, 1992
DEAR MIMMY,

The new sections of town—Dobrinja, Mojmilo, Vojnicko Polje—are being badly shelled. Everything is being destroyed, burned, the people are in shelters. Here in the middle of town, where we live, it's different. It's quiet. People go out. It was a nice warm spring day today. We went out too. Vaso Miskin Street was full of people, children. It looked like a peace march. People came out to be together, they don't want war. They want to live and enjoy themselves the way they used to. That's only natural, isn't it? Who likes or wants war, when it's the worst thing in the world?

I keep thinking about the march I joined today. It's bigger and stronger than war. That's why it will win. The people must be the ones to win, not the war, because war has nothing to do with humanity. War is something inhuman.

MAY 2, 1992
DEAR MIMMY,

Today was truly, absolutely the worst day ever in Sarajevo. The shooting started around noon. Mommy and I moved into the hall. Daddy was in his office, under our flat, at the time. We told him on the interphone to run quickly to the downstairs lobby where we'd meet him. We brought Cicko [Zlata's canary] with us. The gunfire was getting worse, and we couldn't get over the wall to the Bobars, so we ran down to our own cellar.

The cellar is ugly, dark, and smelly. Mommy, who's terrified of mice, had two fears to cope with. The three of us were in the same corner as the other day. We listened to the pounding shells, the shooting, the thundering noise overhead. We even heard planes. At one moment, I realized that this awful cellar was the only place that could save our lives.

Suddenly, it started to look almost warm and nice. It was the only way we could defend ourselves against all this terrible shooting. We heard glass shattering in our street. Horrible. I put my fingers in my ears to block out the terrible sounds. I was worried about Cicko. We had left him behind in the lobby. Would he catch cold there? Would something hit him? I was terribly hungry and thirsty. We had left our half-cooked lunch in the kitchen.

When the shooting died down a bit, Daddy ran over to our flat and brought us back some sandwiches. He said he could smell something burning and that the phones weren't working. He brought our TV set down to the cellar. That's when we learned that the main post office (near us) was on fire and that they had kidnapped our president . . . I saw the post office in flames. A terrible sight. The firefighters battled with the raging fire. Daddy took a few photos of the post office being devoured by the flames. . . . The whole flat smelled of the burning fire. God, and I used to pass by there every day. It has just been done up. It was huge and beautiful, and now it was being swallowed up by the flames. It was disappearing . . . A terrible day. This has been the worst, most awful day in my eleven-year-old life. I hope it will be the only one. Mommy and Daddy are very edgy. I have to go to bed.

MAY 7, 1992
DEAR MIMMY,

I was almost positive the war would stop, but today . . . Today a shell fell on the park in front of my house, the park where I used to play with my girlfriends. A lot of people were hurt. From what I hear Jaca, Jaca's mother, Selma, Nina, our neighbor Dado, and who knows how many other people who happened to be there were wounded. Dado, Jaca, and her mother have come home from the hospital; Selma lost a kidney, but I don't know how she is, because she's still in the hospital. AND NINA IS DEAD. A piece of shrapnel lodged in her brain and she died. She was such a sweet, nice girl. We went to kindergarten together, and we used to play together in the park. Is it possible I'll never see Nina again? Nina, an innocent eleven-year-old little girl—the victim of a stupid war. I feel sad. I cry and wonder why. She didn't do anything. A disgusting war has destroyed a young child's life. Nina, I'll always remember you as a wonderful little girl.

MAY 27, 1992

DEAR MIMMY,

SLAUGHTER! MASSACRE! HORROR! CRIME! BLOOD! SCREAMS! TEARS! DESPAIR!

That's what Vaso Miskin Street looks like today. Two shells exploded in the street and one in the market. Mommy was nearby at the time. She ran to Grandma's and Grandad's. Daddy and I were beside ourselves because she hadn't come home. I saw some of it on TV but I still can't believe what I actually saw. It's unbelievable. I've got a lump in my throat and a knot in my tummy. HORRIBLE. They're taking the wounded to the hospital. It's a madhouse. We kept going to the window hoping to see Mommy, but she wasn't back. They released a list of the dead and wounded. Daddy and I were tearing our hair out. We didn't know what had happened to her. Was she alive? At 16:00, Daddy decided to go and check the hospital. He got dressed, and I got ready to go to the Bobars', so as not to stay at home alone. I looked out the window one more time and . . . I SAW MOMMY RUNNING ACROSS THE BRIDGE. As she came into the house she started shaking and crying. Through her tears she told us how she had seen dismembered bodies. All the neighbors came because they had been afraid for her. Thank God, Mommy is with us. Thank God.

A HORRIBLE DAY. UNFORGETTABLE.

STUDY QUESTIONS

1. How did Zlata Flilpović understand the events going on around her—what fears dominated her diary entries?
2. What aspects of ethnic cleansing were beyond her comprehension?

15.7 VISUAL SOURCE: BERLIN WALL FRAGMENT, UNITED NATIONS, 2002

On November 9, 1989, the Berlin Wall fell. East Germany's communist regime had erected the barricade twenty-eight years earlier to block immigration to West Germany. Over the years, the wall had divided the two Germanys, serving as both a literal and a symbolic barrier. Crowds began to dismantle the wall that evening, and, by the end of 1990, it was completely demolished.

From https://www.un.org/ungifts/content/trophy-civil-rights-berlin-wall-fragment.

In 2002 the government of united Germany presented Kofi Anan (1938–2018), the secretary-general of the United Nations, with a three-slab section of the wall that had originally stood in Potzdamer Platz. Anan placed the slab in the garden of the UN Headquarters in New York. At the ceremony marking the UN's receipt of the Cold War artefact, Anan observed that the Berlin Wall "expressed, in a uniquely horrible way, the propensity of human beings to erect walls and borders, and then glare across them, hearts filled with hate, minds full of fear and distrust, all the while numb to the notion that there might be a better way." Anan commented on the painted image, the "Trophy of Civil Rights" (added by the French artist Thierry Noir after the wall had fallen), affirming "the lesson that divisions in the human community are not so insurmountable as we feared; that gaps of misunderstanding and material well-being can be bridged; and that we can, like the couple depicted here, join hands and unite for a better world."

FIGURE 15.7   Berlin Wall Fragment

STUDY QUESTIONS

1. What was the newly united Germany trying to convey by giving this fragment of the Berlin Wall to the United Nations?
2. What does the image drawn on the wall reveal about how Europeans remembered the wall that divided Berlin?

USING COORDINATION AND SUBORDINATION TO FIND AND FIX COMMON PUNCTUATION MISTAKES

Students are often told to use a comma to signal a pause. *Comma equals pause* is a good rule of thumb, but it neglects the basic principle underlying most of the punctuation choices writers make: commas, periods, semicolons, colons, and dashes are inserted according to the grammar of the sentence. More specifically, the rules that govern punctuation are determined by the rules that govern *coordination* and *subordination*.

STANDARD MISTAKES INVOLVING COORDINATION: RUN-ON SENTENCES AND COMMA SPLICES

Run-ons and comma splices, two of the most common mistakes involving coordination,[1] happen when independent clauses (or sentences)[2] are joined without the proper punctuation.

Take the following two sentences:

SENTENCE 1: One of Gorbachev's grandfathers was briefly deported to Siberia in the 1930s.
SENTENCE 2: The other was arrested during the Great Terror.

A *run-on sentence* joins sentences without any punctuation:

One of Gorbachev's grandfathers was briefly deported to Siberia in the 1930s the other was arrested during the Great Terror.

A *comma splice* joins sentences with a comma:

One of Gorbachev's grandfathers was briefly deported to Siberia in the 1930s, the other was arrested during the Great Terror.

There are three ways to join sentences correctly without creating run-on sentences or comma splices:

SEMICOLON OR DASH:[3] One of Gorbachev's grandfathers was briefly deported to Siberia in the 1930s; the other was arrested during the Great Terror.

---

1 The other common mistake involving coordination is faulty parallelism, covered in Chapter 13.

2 We covered independent and subordinate (or dependent) clauses in Chapter 2. An independent clause has a subject and a verb; it can stand on its own as a complete sentence.

3 Colons may also be used to join sentences when the second sentence explains or illustrates the first. For example: "Devalued currency made raw materials and imports more expensive: nonfuel commodities went up by 70 percent and food by 100 percent."

One of Gorbachev's grandfathers was briefly deported to Siberia in the 1930s—the other was arrested during the Great Terror.

COMMA AND COORDINATING CONJUNCTION: One of Gorbachev's grandfathers was briefly deported to Siberia in the 1930s, **and** the other was arrested during the Great Terror.

SEMICOLON, TRANSITIONAL WORD, COMMA: One of Gorbachev's grandfathers was briefly deported to Siberia in the 1930s; **moreover,** the other was arrested during the Great Terror.

EXERCISE: CORRECT RUN-ON SENTENCES AND COMMA SPLICES

Instructions

Find and correct the punctuation mistakes in the following sentences.

1. On December 28, 1989, the new parliament voted to create a "market economy," a month later the Communist Party ceased to exist.
   REVISED: _____

   _____

2. Germany's political reunification was relatively easy, its economic reunification proved far more difficult.
   REVISED:_____

   _____

3. The USSR's economy had to be modernized, it needed a new "openness"—*glasnost* in Russian—to innovative ideas.
   REVISED:_____

   _____

SENTENCE FRAGMENTS

A *sentence fragment* is a subordinate (or dependent) clause punctuated as a sentence:

INCORRECT: Devalued currency made raw materials and imports more expensive. Which meant that prices inflated: nonfuel commodities went up by 70 percent and food by 100 percent.

CORRECT: Devalued currency made raw materials and imports more expensive, which meant that prices inflated: nonfuel commodities went up by 70 percent and food by 100 percent.

EXERCISE: CORRECT SENTENCE FRAGMENTS

Instructions

Find and correct the punctuation mistakes in the following sentences.

4. The great virtue of the Bretton Woods system was that it allowed for both stability and flexibility. Stability in that importers and exporters would know the value of their country's currency; and flexibility in that countries could readily adjust their exchange rates.

REVISED:_____

_____

5. Cardinal Karol Wojtyla's crowning as Jean Paul II in October 1978 marked an extraordinarily important moment for Poland. Because unlike other communist countries, it had retained its religious, Catholic identity.

REVISED:_____

_____

DANGLING MODIFIERS

A *modifier* is a word, phrase, or clause that adds information to another word, phrase, or clause. In the bullets that follow, the modifier is underlined:

- the *Polish* pope
- the pope *from Poland*
- the pope *who was from Poland*
- *hailing from Poland*, the pope

The fourth example—"*hailing from Poland*"—is a clause with a verb (*hailing*) but no subject. Readers expect to find its subject—"the pope"—immediately adjacent, in the independent—or main—clause of the sentence:

Hailing from Poland, **the pope** was a religious traditionalist.

If the subject does not appear immediately after a subject-less subordinate clause, you have written a dangler, which your reader may experience as confusing or awkward or both:

Hailing from Poland, religious traditions were important to the pope. (*It wasn't "religious traditions" that hailed from Poland. It was the pope.*)

This dangler is especially misleading:

Returning to Poland in June 1979, millions of his countrymen and women came out to greet him.

The structure of this sentence implies that millions of countrymen and women returned to Poland, when in fact it was Pope John Paul II who returned, as this revision makes clear:

Returning to Poland in June 1979, [CLAUSE WITHOUT A SUBJECT] **Pope John Paul II** [SUBJECT] was greeted by millions of his countrymen and women.

The other way to fix a dangler is to place the subject inside the subordinate clause:

When Pope John Paul II [SUBJECT] **returned** [VERB] **to Poland in June 1979,** [SUBORDINATE CLAUSE] millions of his countrymen and women came out to greet him. [INDEPENDENT CLAUSE]

EXERCISE: ELIMINATE DANGLING MODIFIERS

Instructions

Revise the following sentences, eliminating the dangling modifiers.

---

6. Denouncing the protesters from the balcony of his party headquarters, the crowd heckled and booed. [NOTE: the person doing the denouncing was Nicolae Ceausescu, General Secretary of the Romanian Communist Party.]
REVISED:_____

_____

---

7. Once in office, even greater resources would flow to Kuchma's backers.
REVISED:_____

SUBTLE DANGLERS

Strictly speaking, dangling modifiers are not grammatical mistakes;[4] they are stylistic mistakes. Danglers are so universal they can be hard to see, especially in subtle cases:

Having conquered inflation, Thatcher's next move was to privatize England's large state-owned sector. (*It wasn't Thatcher's next move that conquered inflation. It was Thatcher. But so many writers use this construction now that we have no trouble understanding it.*)

REVISION: Having conquered inflation, Thatcher moved to privatize England's large state-owned sector of the economy.

After graduating in 1955, it was time for Gorbachev to begin his career. (*"It" didn't graduate; Gorbachev did. But readers easily understand this sentence.*)

REVISION: After graduating in 1955, Gorbachev began his career.

REVISION: After he graduated in 1955, Gorbachev began his career.

Detailing the crimes of Stalinism, there seemed to be a new beginning for communists of Gorbachev's generation. (*Who or what detailed the crimes of Stalinism?*)

REVISION: **Detailing the crimes of Stalinism,** Khrushchev's speech seemed to be a new beginning for communists of Gorbachev's generation.

---

4 "Strictly speaking" isn't a dangler because its subject—whoever is doing the speaking—is no one in particular and doesn't need to be named. Any number of participles fall into this category: concerning, considering, excluding, given, granted, regarding, and so on.

Many readers would not pick up on these danglers, but given that some do, it is a good idea to avoid them in formal prose.

EXERCISE: ELIMINATE SUBTLE DANGLERS

Instructions

Revise the following sentences, eliminating the dangling modifiers.

---

8. Having kept his people in penury, there was not a lot of support for Ceausescu.
REVISED:_____

_____

---

9. Calling themselves the State Emergency Committee, their measures included placing Gorbachev under house arrest, declaring martial law, and sending tanks to Moscow as if it were Prague in 1968.
REVISED:_____

_____

You will find suggested answers to the exercises in the back of this book. For more Writing History exercises, as well as study resources for this chapter, visit oup.com/us/berenson.

EPILOGUE

EUROPE IN THE TWENTY-FIRST CENTURY

EP.1 AYAAN HIRSI ALI, *INFIDEL*, 2007

When she was 22 years old, a Somali woman named Ayaan Hirsi Ali (1969–) was sent to Canada to marry a cousin she had met just once. To reach her destination, Hirsi Ali was to fly to Frankfurt, Germany and then on to Canada. But after completing the first leg of her journey, she decided to escape. She made her way to the Netherlands, where she received political asylum and took up residence in Ede, a small industrial town where several thousand Muslim immigrants already lived and worked. A local couple taught Hirsi Ali to speak Dutch and eventually took her into their home. She earned a master's degree in political science at the State University of Leiden and got involved in politics.

Hirsi Ali became an advocate for Muslim immigrant women in Europe, who often found themselves treated no better than in their native lands. Hirsi Ali faulted a certain left-wing "multiculturalism" for tolerating, even excusing, the mistreatment of women on what she considered the fallacious grounds of cultural difference—the idea that Westerners have no right to judge those whose cultures differ from theirs. For Hirsi Ali, mistreatment was mistreatment, and "culture" was no excuse.

In criticizing both "intolerance" and Dutch "tolerance," Hirsi Ali made a great many enemies. After a tumultuous time in the Netherlands, she moved to the United States and became a citizen in 2013.

CHAPTER 14 LEAVING GOD

I was becoming integrated into student society, and that society was nowhere near as predictable or as sedate as my circle in Ede. Geeske and my other friends in Leiden were either agnostics or atheists. Elroy, Marco's best friend, was homosexual.

For example, Marco's friend Giovanni and his girlfriend, Mirjam, broke up after Giovanni went to

Israel to do biology research for three months. In his absence, Mirjam fell in love with Olivier, one of Giovanni's friends. When Giovanni returned, he was upset—they had been together for years—but there was no honor killing, not even a hint of violence. Mirjam had a perfect right to fall in love with someone else. Even her mother thought so, though she'd adored Giovanni. I was fascinated by this vision of a completely different moral system.

In May 1998, there were elections. Now that I was Dutch, I could vote. I gave it a lot of thought. Actually to have the ability to choose the government of Holland—it felt like a momentous responsibility. I voted, like most of my friends, for Wim Kok from the Labor Party, a social democrat. My heart was on the left. I chose Kok because of his fairness and honesty, because he promised jobs and I believed him; he had experience, and I liked his track record. Although I was a political science student working as a translator, it had not occurred to me yet to analyze any party's stance on immigration and integration. I was not yet questioning the government's role in why immigrants were so overrepresented in crime statistics, unemployment, and other social problems.

In January 2000, the political commentator Paul Scheffer published an article, "The Multicultural Drama," in the NRC *Handelsblad,* a well-respected evening newspaper. It instantly became the talk of Holland. Everybody had an opinion about it. Scheffer said a new ethnic underclass of immigrants had formed, and it was much too insular, rejecting the values that knit together Dutch society and creating new, damaging social divisions. There wasn't enough insistence on immigrants adapting; teachers even questioned the relevance of teaching immigrant children Dutch history, and a whole generation of these children were being written off under a pretence of tolerance. Scheffer said there was no place in Holland for a culture that rejected the separation of church and state and denied rights to women and homosexuals. He foresaw social unrest.

At the time, I pooh-poohed Scheffer's concerns. To me, it seemed that the Dutch lived in an absolute paradise and tended to call any small problem a crisis. I thought of Holland in the 1990s as a country living through an Embarrassment of Riches, like its

Golden Age in the 1600s. It was a trim little country, where everybody was always nice. The economy was booming. Trains arrived on time, although markedly less so since they had been privatized. Politics were collegial and even friendly. There were women and homosexuals in the cabinet, and everyone respected them enormously. I didn't believe the country could really have problems. To me, the words Scheffer used—crisis, social upheaval—seemed just newspaper chatter. . . .

In the spring of 2000 my father, by then almost blind from cataracts, managed to get a visa to go to Germany for an operation on his eyes, for which I gladly helped him pay. I visited him in Düsseldorf, driving all the way in my Peugeot 206 with Mirjam. Marco and Ellen joined us a day later. Marco wanted badly to meet my father, and we agreed that Ellen and he should pretend to be a couple because I wasn't ready to discuss with my father the fact that I was living in sin. Not yet.

Abeh embraced me. He looked much older, but he smelled exactly the same. It felt deeply good to be enfolded by him again. At first we just talked about general things: what I was studying, politics. All my father wanted to talk about was Somalia, the great state Somalia could one day become. And he clearly said he wanted an Islamic government, a rule by Allah's laws. Any system of politics devised by man was bound to go wrong.

I took the opposite stance. I surprised myself: I spoke sharply. I said Divine Law wouldn't be fair to everyone who wasn't Muslim. Even within Islam, not everyone thought the same way. Who would make the law? I told my father, "The rule of clerics is totalitarian. It means people can't choose. Humanity is varied, and we should celebrate that instead of suppressing it."

My father just said, "We must all work hard to convert everyone to Islam." He disappointed me with this simple-minded logic and his depressing lack of realism.

My father had decided to arrange for my divorce. I didn't feel the slightest bit married: Osman Moussa was just a vague memory for me. But to my father, it was vital. He told me that he shouldn't have obliged me to marry against my will. I should be free to choose the husband I wanted. I think he wanted to think of himself as someone who accorded freedom; there was still a democrat buried inside him, after all.

Abeh told me he was sad to see changes in me. He said I was becoming too worldly, not spiritual enough. He said, "I won't ask you to wear a headscarf, but please, grow your hair." I told him I would, and I have. When he asked me if I still prayed, I said of course I did. In some sense this was still true. I had all sorts of un-Muslim ideas, and yet, in those days, I did still think of myself as being, in some larger, more important way, a believer.

STUDY QUESTIONS

1. What did Hirsi Ali see as the connection between women's rights and the demands of her religious tradition?
2. Did the integration of ethnic minorities in the Netherlands necessarily conflict with the Dutch tradition of religious "tolerance"?

EP. 2 VLADIMIR PUTIN, *ADDRESS TO THE DUMA CONCERNING THE ANNEXATION OF CRIMEA,* MARCH 19, 2014

In March 2014, Vladimir Putin, the former KGB officer who has dominated Russian political life since the late 1990s, delivered this remarkable oration after annexing the Crimea region from the government of Ukraine. The annexation took place after a protest movement drove the pro-Russian president of Ukraine out of office and as tensions between ethnic Ukrainians and ethnic Russians inside Ukraine became violent. Putin feared that Ukraine, a strategically located country that had been part of the defunct Soviet Union, would escape Russian control and ally with the West. In this speech, Putin justified his country's move against a former "Soviet Socialist Republic" by appealing to both recent and distant history—and, perhaps, signaled further intentions for the future.

Dear friends, we have gathered here today in connection with an issue that is of vital, historic significance to all of us. A referendum was held in Crimea on March 16 in full compliance with democratic procedures and international norms.

More than 82 percent of the electorate took part in the vote. Over 96 percent of them spoke out in favour of reuniting with Russia. These numbers speak for themselves.

To understand the reason behind such a choice it is enough to know the history of Crimea and what Russia and Crimea have always meant for each other.

Everything in Crimea speaks of our shared history and pride. This is the location of ancient Khersones, where Prince Vladimir was baptised. His spiritual feat of adopting Orthodoxy predetermined the overall basis of the culture, civilisation and human values that unite the peoples of Russia,

From http://rt.com/politics/official-word/vladimir-putin-crimea-address-658/.

Ukraine and Belarus. The graves of Russian soldiers whose bravery brought Crimea into the Russian empire are also in Crimea. This is also Sevastopol—a legendary city with an outstanding history, a fortress that serves as the birthplace of Russia's Black Sea Fleet. Crimea is Balaklava and Kerch, Malakhov Kurgan and Sapun Ridge. Each one of these places is dear to our hearts, symbolising Russian military glory and outstanding valour.

Crimea is a unique blend of different peoples' cultures and traditions. This makes it similar to Russia as a whole, where not a single ethnic group has been lost over the centuries. Russians and Ukrainians, Crimean Tatars and people of other ethnic groups have lived side by side in Crimea, retaining their own identity, traditions, languages and faith.

In people's hearts and minds, Crimea has always been an inseparable part of Russia. This firm conviction is based on truth and justice and was passed from generation to generation, over time, under any circumstances, despite all the dramatic changes our country went through during the entire 20th century.

After the revolution, the Bolsheviks, for a number of reasons—may God judge them—added large sections of the historical South of Russia to the Republic of Ukraine. This was done with no consideration for the ethnic make-up of the population, and today these areas form the southeast of Ukraine. Then, in 1954, a decision was made to transfer Crimean Region to Ukraine, along with Sevastopol, despite the fact that it was a city of union subordination. This was the personal initiative of the Communist Party head Nikita Khrushchev. What stood behind this decision of his—a desire to win the support of the Ukrainian political establishment or to atone for the mass repressions of the 1930's in Ukraine—is for historians to figure out.

What matters now is that this decision was made in clear violation of the constitutional norms that were in place even then. The decision was made behind the scenes. Naturally, in a totalitarian state nobody bothered to ask the citizens of Crimea and Sevastopol. They were faced with the fact. People, of course, wondered why all of a sudden Crimea became part of Ukraine. But on the whole—and we must state

this clearly, we all know it—this decision was treated as a formality of sorts because the territory was transferred within the boundaries of a single state. Back then, it was impossible to imagine that Ukraine and Russia may split up and become two separate states. However, this has happened.

Unfortunately, what seemed impossible became a reality. The USSR fell apart. Things developed so swiftly that few people realised how truly dramatic those events and their consequences would be. Many people both in Russia and in Ukraine, as well as in other republics hoped that the Commonwealth of Independent States that was created at the time would become the new common form of statehood. They were told that there would be a single currency, a single economic space, joint armed forces; however, all this remained empty promises, while the big country was gone. It was only when Crimea ended up as part of a different country that Russia realised that it was not simply robbed, it was plundered.

At the same time, we have to admit that by launching the sovereignty parade Russia itself aided in the collapse of the Soviet Union. And as this collapse was legalised, everyone forgot about Crimea and Sevastopol—the main base of the Black Sea Fleet. Millions of people went to bed in one country and awoke in different ones, overnight becoming ethnic minorities in former Union republics, while the Russian nation became one of the biggest, if not the biggest ethnic group in the world to be divided by borders.

Now, many years later, I heard residents of Crimea say that back in 1991 they were handed over like a sack of potatoes. . . .

Like a mirror, the situation in Ukraine reflects what is going on and what has been happening in the world over the past several decades. After the dissolution of bipolarity on the planet, we no longer have stability. Key international institutions are not getting any stronger; on the contrary, in many cases, they are sadly degrading. Our western partners, led by the United States of America, prefer not to be guided by international law in their practical policies, but by the rule of the gun. They have come to believe in their exclusivity and exceptionalism, that they can decide the destinies of the world, that only they can ever be right. They act as they please: here and there, they use force against sovereign states, building coalitions based on the principle *"If you are not with us, you are against us."* To make this aggression look legitimate, they force the necessary resolutions from international organisations, and if for some reason this does not work, they simply ignore the UN Security Council and the UN overall.

This happened in Yugoslavia; we remember 1999 very well. It was hard to believe, even seeing it with my own eyes, that at the end of the 20th century, one of Europe's capitals, Belgrade, was under missile attack for several weeks, and then came the real intervention. Was there a UN Security Council resolution on this matter, allowing for these actions? Nothing of the sort. And then, they hit Afghanistan, Iraq, and frankly violated the UN Security Council resolution on Libya, when instead of imposing the so-called no-fly zone over it they started bombing it too.

Let me say one other thing too. Millions of Russians and Russian-speaking people live in Ukraine and will continue to do so. Russia will always defend their interests using political, diplomatic and legal means. But it should be above all in Ukraine's own interest to ensure that these people's rights and interests are fully protected. This is the guarantee of Ukraine's state stability and territorial integrity.

We want to be friends with Ukraine and we want Ukraine to be a strong, sovereign and self-sufficient country. Ukraine is one of our biggest partners after all. We have many joint projects and I believe in their success no matter what the current difficulties. Most importantly, we want peace and harmony to reign in Ukraine, and we are ready to work together with other countries to do everything possible to facilitate and support this. But as I said, only Ukraine's own people can put their own house in order.

STUDY QUESTIONS

1. In what specific ways, and for what purpose, did Putin appeal to the historical past?
2. What does he believe will be the consequences of the end of "bipolarity" in global politics— and of the belief in American "exceptionalism" demonstrated by US military action since 1999?

EP. 3 MATT ZUVELA, "MERKEL STAYS THE COURSE IN GERMAN REFUGEE DEBATE," NOVEMBER 25, 2015

In September 2015, Chancellor Angela Merkel of Germany (1954–, chancellor since 2005) announced her government's decision to admit a large number of refugees from the ongoing civil war in Syria, which has killed an estimated 470,000 people since it broke out in 2011. Merkel has reacted several times to criticism, both within and outside Germany, of her policy on refugees. In this article, the journalist Matt Zuvela covers a speech she gave to the German Budestag on the subject of refugees on November 25, 2015. Toward the end of Merkel's speech, she expresses solidarity with France after it suffered a deadly terrorist attacks on November 13.

From DW.com News, https://p.dw.com/p/1HCBu.

German Chancellor Merkel has called for indirect efforts to stem the flow of migrants to Germany. Calls from within her own ranks to set an upper limit on asylum seekers are still not part of her plan.

An audibly hoarse Merkel addressed the German Bundestag on Wednesday in a speech that touched on Germany's policy regarding the continuing stream of refugees to Germany and other European countries. Despite the sore throat, her message regarding Germany's refugee policy remained clear: "We can do it."

She called for the European Union to follow through on plans for "hotspots" in countries on the bloc's external borders such as Greece where many refugees seeking asylum first enter the EU. The hotspots would enable more efficient processing and further resettlement or deportation of refugees, but Merkel cautioned that a country like Greece needs to know the willingness of its European partners to take on refugees before it implements such measures.

"Only when the inner-European solidarity has been secured would [a country like Greece] pursue building these hotspots," Merkel said.

In addition, Merkel said Turkey was a "key partner" for reducing the number of refugees coming to the EU's borders. Noting that Turkey had already taken on 2 million refugees from Syria and other bordering countries, Merkel said helping Turkey deal with the refugee crisis there would provide relief for the European Union.

Merkel is under fire for her "open-door" stance toward refugees, which critics say has led to even more refugees seeking asylum in Europe and Germany in particular.

Günther Oettinger, the EU's Commissioner for Digital Economy and Society, said in an interview with the Handelsblatt on Wednesday that Germany's asylum laws "work like a magnet on the refugees."

Germany's family minister Manuela Schwesig of Merkel's coalition partner Social Democrats said Germany could not continue to accept refugees at the same rate as in the last few months and that a "breather" would be beneficial.

SETTING PRIORITY

Over the weekend, the German political divide on the issue was clearly on display at the party conference of Merkel's right-wing coalition partners, the Christian Social Union (CSU). Normally seen as the sister party to Merkel's Christian Democratic Union (CDU), CSU leader and Bavarian State Premier Horst Seehofer was openly at odds with Merkel on the stage they shared at the conference, calling for an upper limit to the number of refugees Germany was willing to accept.

French Prime Minister Manuel Valls made a similar call for limiting the number of refugees the entire EU accepts in an interview with several European papers on Wednesday.

While Merkel made no specific reference of an upper limit in her speech to the Bundestag on Wednesday, many of her remarks dealt with other, indirect ways that would reduce the number of refugees coming to Germany. This included the hotspots and efforts to help Turkey, but she also highlighted the success of a stricter policy regarding Balkan asylum seekers, who are now more or less sent directly back to the country they came from when they apply for asylum in Germany.

"We expect that those who are denied asylum after the normal civil procedures leave the country so those who need our protection get it," Merkel said.

Later, she said "it makes a difference if we are talking about 30,000 people or 800,000. Then we have to decide: 'who needs our protection, and who must leave our country?'"

In addition to opposition from the CSU, Merkel is being criticized by opposition parties in the Bundestag. Anton Hofreiter of the opposition Greens Party said that while Merkel called for accelerated integration of refugees, she was not backing this with appropriate funding, preferring instead to strictly pursue a balanced budget.

"That's a budget with no courage, no heart, and no plan," Hofreiter said following Merkel's speech, adding that if the German economy was doing as well as Merkel described, it should not be a problem to take a few risks.

"Do something instead of just talking," Hofreiter said.

"UNITED" WITH FRANCE

Merkel also addressed her impending visit to Paris to meet with French President Francois Hollande on Wednesday evening.

Hollande has spent much of his time since the November 13 terror attacks in Paris meeting with world leaders on ways to ramp up joint efforts to destroy the so-called "Islamic State," which claimed responsibility for the Paris attacks.

"I will address a question with François Hollande that affects us both," she said, "the spirit of this discussion will surely be that we act together with our friends, and when additional measures are needed, we won't rule that out from the beginning."

Following last week's terror attack at a hotel in Mali, German Defense Minister Ursula von der Leyen announced on Wednesday that up to 650 German Bundeswehr soldiers would join a French-led peacekeeping mission in the country.

STUDY QUESTIONS

1. How and why did Merkel connect the plight of Syrian refugees to the project of European unity?
2. How did Merkel respond to her critics' efforts to connect the refugees with potential terrorist threats?

EP. 4 BORIS JOHNSON, LETTER TO EUROPEAN COUNCIL PRESIDENT DONALD TUSK, OCTOBER 19, 2019

Newly appointed as prime minister of Britain in July 2019, Boris Johnson (1964–) faced considerable headwinds during his first months in office. Having taken the reins after his Conservative predecessor Theresa May stepped down, Johnson intended to broker a quick British exit (Brexit) from the European Union. But, like May, Johnson faced opposition even from within his own Conservative party. As he shows in this letter to European Council President Donald Tusk (1957–), a deadlock in Parliament prevented Britain from meeting deadlines set by the EU for negotiating a smooth withdrawal. To overcome the stalemate, Johnson called for new parliamentary elections to be held in December 2019, having secured pledges from every one of the 635 candidates running as Conservatives that they would vote for Johnson's Brexit plan. The results gave a huge majority to Johnson's Conservative Party, and Brexit became a reality in the new year.

10 Downing Street
London SW1A 2AA
The Prime Minister
19 October 2019

Dear Donald

It was good to see you again at the European Council this week where we agreed [on] the historic new deal to permit the orderly withdrawal of the United Kingdom from the European Union on 31 October. I am deeply grateful to you, President Juncker and to all my fellow European leaders for the statesmanship and statecraft which enabled us to achieve this historic milestone. I should also register my appreciation for Michel Barnier and his team for

From https://www.gov.uk/government/publications/prime-ministers-letter-to-president-donald-tusk-19-october-2019.

their imagination and diplomacy as we concluded the negotiations.

When I spoke in Parliament this morning, I noted the corrosive impact of the long delay in delivering the mandate of the British people from the 2016 referendum. I made clear that, while I believe passionately that both the UK and the EU will benefit from our decision to withdraw and develop a new relationship, that relationship will be founded on our deep respect and affection for our shared culture, civilisation, values and interests. We will remain the EU's closest partner and friend. The deal we approved at last week's European Council is a good deal for the whole of the UK and the whole of the EU.

Regrettably, Parliament missed the opportunity to inject momentum into the ratification process for the new Withdrawal Agreement. The UK Permanent Representative will therefore submit the request mandated by the EU (Withdrawal) (No.2) Act 2019 later today. It is, of course, for the European Council to decide when to consider this request and whether to grant it. In view of the unique circumstances, while I regret causing my fellow leaders to devote more of their time and energy to a question I had hoped we had resolved last week, I recognise that you may need to convene a European Council. If it would be helpful to you, I would of course be happy to attend the start of any A50 Council so that I could answer properly any question on the position of HM Government and progress in the ratification process at that time.

Meanwhile, although I would have preferred a different result today, the Government will press ahead with ratification and introduce the necessary legislation early next week. I remain confident that we will complete that process by 31 October. Indeed, many of those who voted against the Government today have indicated their support for the new deal and for ratifying it without delay. I know that I can count on your support and that of our fellow leaders to move the deal forward, and I very much hope therefore that on the EU side also, the process can be completed to allow the agreement to enter into force, as the European Council Conclusions mandated.

While it is open to the European Council to accede to the request mandated by Parliament or to offer an alternative extension period, I have made clear since becoming Prime Minister, and made clear to Parliament again today, my view, and the Government's position, that a further extension would damage the interests of the UK and our EU partners, and the relationship between us. We must bring this process to a conclusion so that we can move to the next phase and build our new relationship on the foundations of our long history as neighbours and friends in this continent our people's share. I am passionately committed to that endeavour.

I am copying this letter to Presidents Juncker and Sassoli, and to members of the European Council.

Yours sincerely

Boris Johnson

STUDY QUESTIONS

1. How does Johnson account for Britain's failure to meet deadlines set up by the European Union?
2. According to this letter, what kind of post-Brexit relationship does Johnson envision between the EU and Britain?

EP. 5 MARY ROBINSON FOUNDATION-CLIMATE JUSTICE, *PRINCIPLES OF CLIMATE JUSTICE*, 2019

Mary Bourke Robinson (1944–) is a renowned Irish lawyer, politician, and diplomat who has served as Ireland's first woman president (1990–1997), as the United Nations' High Commissioner for Human Rights, and as chancellor of Trinity College Dublin, her alma mater. As High Commissioner, she visited China and Kosovo to monitor their citizens' human rights, and she undertook efforts to stem racism and xenophobia throughout the world. She has held leadership roles in numerous organizations, such as Oxfam, a charitable organization focusing on global poverty, and has received major awards, including the US Presidential Medal of Freedom and the Ambassador of Conscience award from Amnesty International.

In 2010, she founded the Mary Robinson Foundation-Climate Justice, a research and policy group devoted to promoting climate justice, human rights, and women's empowerment. After nine years, the foundation scaled back its operations, in part because it had achieved its benchmarks and also, as Robinson reported, due to "the changing landscape of climate policy and the shift in focus from international negotiations to multi-stakeholder coalitions." This excerpt, from the foundation's final report, spells out principles of climate justice.

RESPECT AND PROTECT HUMAN RIGHTS

The international rights framework provides a reservoir for the supply of legal imperatives with which to frame morally appropriate responses to climate change, rooted in equality and justice.

the idea of human rights point societies towards internationally agreed values around which common action can be negotiated and then acted upon. Human rights yardsticks deliver valuable minimal thresholds, legally defined, about which there is widespread consensus. the guarantee of basic rights rooted in respect for the dignity of the person which is at the core of this approach makes it an indispensable foundation for action on climate justice.

SUPPORT THE RIGHT TO DEVELOPMENT

The vast gulf in resources between rich and poor, evident in the gap between countries in the North and south and also within many countries (both North and south) is the deepest injustice of our age. this failure of resource-fairness makes it impossible for billions of humans to lead decent lives, the sort of life- opportunities that a commitment to true equality should make an absolute essential.

Climate change both highlights and exacerbates this gulf in equality. It also provides the world with an opportunity. Climate change highlights our true interdependence and must lead to a new and respectful paradigm of sustainable development, based on the urgent need to scale up and transfer green technologies and to support low carbon climate resilient strategies for the poorest so that they become part of the combined effort in mitigation and adaptation.

SHARE BENEFITS AND BURDENS EQUITABLY

The benefits and burdens associated with climate change and its resolution must be fairly allocated.

this involves acceptance of common but differentiated responsibilities and respective capabilities in relation to reduction of greenhouse gas emissions. those who have most responsibility for greenhouse gas emissions and most capacity to act must cut emissions first.

In addition, those who have benefited and still benefit from emissions in the form of on-going economic development and increased wealth, mainly in industrialised countries, have an ethical obligation to share benefits with those who are today suffering from the effects of these emissions, mainly vulnerable people in developing countries. people in low income countries must have access to opportunities to adapt to the impacts of climate change and embrace local carbon development to avoid future environmental damage.

ENSURE THAT DECISIONS ON CLIMATE CHANGE ARE PARTICIPATORY, TRANSPARENT AND ACCOUNTABLE

The opportunity to participate in decision-making processes which are fair, accountable, open and corruption-free is essential to the growth of a culture of climate justice. the voices of the most vulnerable to climate change must be heard and acted upon. a basic of good international practice is the requirement for transparency in decision-making and accountability for decisions that are made. It must be possible to ensure that policy developments and policy implementation in this field are seen to be informed by an understanding of the needs of low income countries in relation to climate justice and that these needs are adequately understood and addressed.

Decisions on policies with regard to climate change taken in a range of fora from the UNFCCC to trade, human rights, business, investment and development must be implemented in a way that is transparent and accountable: poverty can never be an alibi for government failure in this sphere.

HIGHLIGHT GENDER EQUALITY AND EQUITY

The gender dimension of climate change and in turn climate justice, must be highlighted. The impacts of climate changes are different for women and men, with women likely to bear the greater burden in situations of poverty.

Women's voices must be heard and their priorities supported as part of climate justice. In many countries and cultures, women are at the forefront of living with the reality of the injustices caused by climate change. They are critically aware of the importance of climate justice in contributing to the right to development being recognised and can play a vital role as agents of change within their communities.

HARNESS THE TRANSFORMATIVE POWER OF EDUCATION FOR CLIMATE STEWARDSHIP

The transformative power of education underpins other principles, making their successful adoption more likely and inculcating into cultures a deeper awareness of human rights and climate justice than is presently to be found. To achieve climate stabilisation will necessitate radical changes in lifestyle and behaviour and education has the power to equip future generations with the skills and knowledge they will need to thrive and survive.

As well as being a fundamental human right which is already well developed in the international framework of rights referred to above, education is indispensable to the just society. It draws those in receipt of it towards a fuller understanding of the world about them, deepening their awareness both of themselves and of those around them. Done well, it invites reflection on ethics and justice that make the well-educated also good citizens, both of their home state and (in these global times) of the world as well.

Delivered in an effective multi-disciplinary school, college or university environmental education can increase consciousness of climate change, producing new insights not only at the scientific but also at the sociological and political level. Education is also achievable outside the formal system, through public and, increasingly, virtual (i.e. web-based) activity. the learning required to see climate change in justice terms cannot be done at the schools and university alone: it is a life-long responsibility and therefore a commitment.

USE EFFECTIVE PARTNERSHIPS TO SECURE CLIMATE JUSTICE

The principle of partnership points in the direction of solutions to climate change that are integrated both within states and across state boundaries.

Climate justice requires effective action on a global scale which in turn requires a pooling of resources and a sharing of skills across the world. the nation state may remain the basic building block of the international system but without openness to coalitions of states and corporate interests and elements within civil society as well, the risk is that the whole house produced by these blocks will be rendered uninhabitable. Openness to partnership is a vital aspect of any coherent approach to climate change and in the name of climate justice, this must also involve partnership with those most affected by climate change and least able adequately to deal with it—the poor and under-resourced.

These principles are rooted in the frameworks of international and regional human rights law and do not require the breaking of any new ground on the part of those who ought, in the name of climate justice, to be willing to take them on.

STUDY QUESTIONS

1. How and why does the Mary Robinson Foundation link the issue of climate stewardship with that of gender equality?
2. How does this statement compare with the principles laid out in the 1948 United Nations Declaration of Human Rights?

DOUBLE FOCUS

Although the two sentences below contain the same words, the effect is different:

Hirsi Ali's parents enrolled her in an elite Muslim girls' school where instruction was entirely in English.

Hirsi Ali's parents enrolled her in an elite Muslim girls' school—a school where instruction was entirely in English.

As we've seen, readers expect the most important material in a sentence to appear at the end (sentence end focus). Thus the first sentence in the pair above leaves the impression that the school's use of English is what matters—while the second sentence suggests that the school's decision *not* to use Arabic, the sacred language of Islam, is equally important.

The second sentence achieves this effect via double focus. Instead of just one stress position the sentence has two, one at the end of each clause:

Hirsi Ali's parents enrolled her in an elite Muslim girls' school—a school where instruction was entirely in English.

To create double focus, writers 1) repeat content from the end of the first clause in the beginning of the second clause and 2) separate the second clause from the first by means of a dash or comma, or sometimes a colon. The punctuation creates a natural pause; the repetition turns the stressed information at the end of the first clause into "old," *un*stressed information at the beginning of the second.

ANOTHER EXAMPLE

Alter the sentence below to add emphasis to "ethnic Russians."

At least 10 percent of Russians are Muslim or of Muslim heritage. Russian Muslims tend to live in ethnic enclaves surrounded by ethnic Russians who persistently dominate them.

With double focus:

At least 10 percent of Russians are Muslim or of Muslim heritage—Russian Muslims who tend to live in ethnic enclaves surrounded by ethnic Russians, a population that persistently dominates them.

(In this case "a population" was used as a synonym for "ethnic Russians.")

EXERCISES

Revise each of the sentences below to create double focus.

---

1. Add emphasis to "a movie."
Together, Hirsi Ali and Theo van Gogh made a movie that they intended as a merciless critique of the violence against women they both saw as embedded in Muslim culture.

---

2. Add emphasis to "two-year-long war."
The result was a murderous two-year-long war in which Islamic radicals increasingly took over the Chechen resistance to Russian rule.

---

3. Add emphasis to "other acts of terror."
Beyond these horrific attacks, Europe has seen numerous other acts of terror that have nothing to do with Islam or are carried out in opposition to it.

4. Add emphasis to "bleak suburban ghettos."
All too many Muslim immigrants are confined to bleak suburban ghettos where children languish in subpar schools that fail to prepare them for university study or productive careers.

5. Add emphasis to "subpar schools."
All too many Muslim immigrants are confined to bleak suburban ghettos where children languish in subpar schools that fail to prepare them for university study or productive careers.

6. Add emphasis to "a right-wing extremist."
The mass murder of 77 Norwegians in 2011 was the work of a right-wing extremist who denounced Muslim immigrants, Marxism, political correctness, and people of color.

7. Add emphasis to "a Growth and Stability Pact."
In addition, the EU required all countries adopting the euro to sign a Growth and Stability Pact that imposed stringent limits on budget deficits, inflation, and national debt.

8. Add emphasis to "the growing service sector."
Some European workers never found new employment and others were forced to take positions in the growing service sector where pay tended to be considerably lower and jobs less permanent than in the old manufacturing concerns.

9. Add emphasis to "intensely pro-European parties."
The big winners in the elections were intensely pro-European parties that nonetheless advocated major reforms within the European Union.

10. Add emphasis to "massive victory."
The balloting gave Johnson and the Conservatives a massive victory and a huge majority in Parliament.

You will find suggested answers to the exercises in the back of this book. For more Writing History exercises, as well as study resources for this chapter, visit oup.com/us/berenson.

SUGGESTED ANSWERS TO WRITING HISTORY EXERCISES

CHAPTER 1

1. 2, 3, 1, 4—"Here I stand; I can do no other." (From page 8)
2. 3, 2, 1, 4, 5 *or* 3, 1, 2, 4, 5—Like essentially everyone in sixteenth-century Europe, Hans Luther believed in God and Jesus and he could not help but admire those who devoted their lives to serving the Lord. *Or* Hans Luther believed in God and Jesus, like essentially everyone in sixteenth-century Europe, and he could not help but admire those who devoted their lives to serving the Lord.

NOTE: Placing the dependent clause at the end of the sentence changes its meaning:

Hans Luther believed in God and Jesus, and he could not help but admire those who devoted their lives to serving the Lord, like essentially everyone in sixteenth-century Europe.

In this version, the phrase "everyone in sixteenth-century Europe" refers to people who devote their lives to serving the Lord, making it sound as if everyone in sixteenth century-Europe was a monk. (From page 3)

3. 7, 2, 9, 6, 5, 1, 3, 8, 4—Jesuit generals deliberately sent their top soldiers into the middle of religious civil wars and to places like Ireland, where they worked to shore up the Catholic population. (From page 33)
4. The era's warfare was expensive and logistically complex, and to finance and organize it required expanded bureaucracies and centralized governments. (From page 45)

5. The era's warfare was expensive and logistically complex; to finance and organize it required expanded bureaucracies and centralized governments. (From page 45)
6. Calvin wrote relatively little, but he spoke a great deal. (From page 17)
7. Calvin wrote relatively little but spoke a great deal. (From page 17)
8. Calvin composed his sermons in bed and delivered them without notes; Luther depended on ink and paper. (From page 17)
9. Luther shaved his head, donned jet-black robes, and moved into a "cell" barely large enough for a bed.
10. Becoming a monk required a vow of poverty and the surrender of all worldly possessions.

NOTE: Sentences 8 and 9 were drawn from Chapter 1, and in context they end with the more important information. (From page 3)

CHAPTER 2

1. 1, 3, 2, 4, 5 (From page 54)
2. 2, 5, 8, 7, 1, 3, 6, 4 (From page 61)
3. 2, 6, 4, 8, 9, 1, 7, 3, 5 (From page 72)
4. 8, 7, 4, 1, 3, 5, 2, 6 (From page 81)
5. 3, 6, 4, 1, 2, 5 (From page 54)
6. Roxelana demonstrated that women's ability to participate in the affairs of state was beneficial to the Ottoman Empire.
7. Ottoman rulers ceased to marry because they did not want to elevate another family to an elite status.

8. Because they did not want to elevate another family to an elite status, Ottoman rulers ceased to marry.

9. All empires contained a variety of different peoples, although no empire matched the diversity of the Ottomans.

10. No empire matched the diversity of the Ottomans, although all empires contained a variety of different peoples.

11. Although France and Spain stood apart as mortal enemies during much of the period from 1500 to 1700, their political systems had much in common.

12. Although they were brought into the sultan's harem as slaves, the mothers of royal sons sometimes became powerful figures.

13. Hernando Cortés was a conqueror who claimed territory in Mexico in April 1519.

14. In 1494, the pope announced the Treaty of Tordesillas, which purported to divide the New World between Portugal and Spain.

15. The influx of silver from the New World produced a Europe-wide price inflation that impoverished the Spanish people, who were already suffering from highly regressive taxation.

16. A.

17. A.

18. B.

19. B.

20. A.

CHAPTER 3

1.
   a. The Thirty Years' War was the deadliest war in seventeenth-century Europe, resulting in the loss of two million soldiers, mostly German, and of another three million noncombatants, also mostly German.

   b. **The Thirty Years' War was the deadliest war in seventeenth-century Europe because it mobilized an unprecedented number of soldiers, coincided with dramatic climate change, caused massive damage to crops and housing, and stoked murderous religious passions.**

   c. The Thirty Years' War was the deadliest war in seventeenth-century Europe.

2.
   a. **The experience of the Fronde convinced Louis XIV to establish control over France's leading nobles, the only group with the potential to dilute his power, by luring them to Versailles and making them dependent on him.**

   b. Louis XIV established control over France's leading nobles, the only group with the potential to dilute his power, by luring them to Versailles and making them dependent on him.

   c. The Fronde convinced Louis XIV to establish control over France's leading nobles, the only group with the potential to dilute his power.

3.
   a. Throughout the seventeenth century, many rulers shored up their powers by oppressing peasants and currying the favor of nobles.

   b. **Throughout the seventeenth century, peasants suffered the most of all social groups because they worked harder for less compensation, had to pay higher taxes and serve in the military, and, in some cases, were treated as virtual slaves.**

   c. Throughout the seventeenth century, peasants rose up in rebellion, avoided military service, and refused to pay their taxes.

4.
   a. Louis XIV went to war with Spain, the Netherlands, the German States, and England, culminating in the War of Spanish Succession, which involved numerous European countries and also the Caribbean Islands and parts of India and North America.

   b. Louis XIV went to war so often that he undermined his own power and also the power of France.

   c. **Had Louis XIV gone to war less often—or not at all—his reign would have been more successful than was actually the case, because constant warfare left his treasury depleted and his rival powers, especially England and the Netherlands, relatively strong.**

5.
   a. The English Revolution was both a religious and political contest, pitting Anglicans against Puritans and the monarchy against parliament.

   b. **While the English Revolution was partly a political struggle, pitting the monarchy against parliament, it was more fundamentally a religious one, the result of a deep schism within English Protestantism.**

c. The English Revolution led to the execution of a king, the rise of a dictator, and the invasion of Ireland.

CHAPTER 4

1. Because the Scottish Enlightenment did not reject religion while the French Enlightenment generally did, the French Enlightenment was more radical than the Scottish Enlightenment.
2. Hobbes' pessimistic view of human nature convinced him of the need for absolutist government, whereas the Scottish Enlightenment's more optimistic views opened the way to political liberty.
3. Changes in thought in the seventeenth century did not amount to a "scientific revolution" because they occurred gradually and because new forms of thought and practice often co-existed with older ones.
4. Galileo epitomized the new scientific methods of the seventeenth century, especially empiricism and experimentation, which sought to understand the natural world through direct human observation; he thereby challenged existing religious and philosophical dogmas, which were based on unverified beliefs.
5. Because the most prominent philosophers of the eighteenth century focused on reason, religion, and what it meant to be a human being, they made a major departure from existing forms of explanation and understanding.
6. While Smith is well known for his arguments in favor of the division of labor, what often remains unacknowledged is the extent to which his ideas about sympathy made him sensitive to the negative aspects of this phenomenon.
7. Although female Enlightenment thinkers did not gain as much recognition as their male counterparts, they nonetheless contributed to the movement in important ways, many of them managing to have their works published, others hosting salons and deciding whom to invite and what to discuss.
8. Enlightenment thinkers such as Mandeville, the Scottish philosophers, and Kant challenged organized religion in different ways, but no one was more critical of it than Voltaire, because he denounced most aspects of religious practice and belief.

CHAPTER 5

1. **X** The French Revolution resulted from four profound crises that the government was unable to resolve—a financial crisis, political crisis, legitimacy crisis, and an economic crisis.

    1. The French Revolution resulted from a financial crisis the government was unable to resolve. **(SUPPORTING IDEA)**
    2. The French Revolution resulted from a political crisis the government was unable to resolve. **(SUPPORTING IDEA)**
    3. The French Revolution resulted from a legitimacy crisis the government was unable to resolve. **(SUPPORTING IDEA)**
    4. The French Revolution resulted from an economic crisis the government was unable to resolve. **(SUPPORTING IDEA)**
    (From pages 196–202)

2. **X** Together, the bankruptcy of the treasury and the organized expression of public opinion precipitated the fall of the monarchy, and neither would have done so alone. **(THESIS)**

    1. The collapse of the monarchy was precipitated, in part, by the bankruptcy of the treasury. **(SUPPORTING IDEA)**
    2. The collapse of the monarchy was also precipitated, in part, by the organized expression of public opinion. **(SUPPORTING IDEA)**
    3. The collapse of the monarchy would not have taken place if only one had occurred. **(SUPPORTING IDEA)**
    (From pages 196–198)

3. **X** Both slaves and free people of color in Haiti came to believe that Haiti's social and economic system was incompatible with the ideals of the French Revolution, although each group had reasons of its own for understanding the revolution in this way. **(THESIS)**

    1. Slaves in Haiti came to believe that Haiti's social and economic system was incompatible with the ideals of the French Revolution. **(SUPPORTING IDEA)**
    2. Free people of color in Haiti came to believe that Haiti's social and economic system was

incompatible with the ideals of the French Revolution. **(SUPPORTING IDEA)**

3. Slaves and free people had different reasons for coming to believe that Haiti's social and economic system was incompatible with the ideals of the French Revolution. **(SUPPORTING IDEA)**

(From pages 191–196)

CHAPTER 6

1. B: Education opened opportunities. (From page 271)
2. B: The English advantage came from their sheep, which had far more land to graze on. (From page 246)
3. A: The manufacturers' insatiable demand transformed the economy of the American South. (From page 257)
4. A: The stoves resulted in a skyrocketing demand for coal. (From page 252)
5. B: By the mid-century, most tailors were employed by sizable workshops. (From pages 259–264)
6. B: The Acts forbade banding together for the purpose of striking for higher wages or better working conditions. (From page 281)

CHAPTER 7

1. **End-to-beginning** Metternich had hoped to end the age of **revolution** once and for all. But the Revolution and its Napoleonic aftermath remained very much alive in the minds of kings and statesmen, poets and painters, and ordinary members of the increasingly active middle and working classes. (From pages 293–295)
2. **End-to-beginning** Louis XVIII adopted a series of repressive measures, which became even more severe when his brother, **Charles X**, assumed the throne. Charles tightened censorship and infuriated the middle classes by paying former émigrés some 26 million francs in compensation for their confiscated lands
3. **Beginning-to-beginning** For **Metternich** any constitution, no matter how weak, opened the door to revolution. He quickly moved to undermine Bavaria's new system. (From page 313)
4. $_1$In Western Europe, **liberalism** emerged in the wake of Britain and France's revolutions of the seventeenth and eighteenth centuries. $_2$**Liberalism** responded to the perceived dangers of absolutism, revolutionary dictatorship, and popular democracy. $_3$**Liberals** thus wanted not only to guarantee individual rights—speech, assembly, and religious worship, among others—but to protect private property from potential encroachment by the state.

5. (From pages 300–301)
   it Refers to the new regime
   it Refers to the Charter
   (From page 315)
6. One of George Sand's greatest loves was the militant republican lawyer Michel de Bourges, who introduced her to France's leading republican and socialist activists. Under **their influence**, she wrote the novel *Spiridion*.
7. In 1844, the weavers rebelled, threatening the region's wealthiest merchants and demanding higher pay. When the protests turned violent, the government called in military force. Protests **such as these** erupted regularly throughout continental Europe as severe economic difficulties created what contemporaries called the "hungry forties."

CHAPTER 8

1. 4, 3, 2, 1 (From page 340)
2. 2, 1, 4, 3 (From page 345)
3. 3, 5, 1, 2, 4 (From page 357)

CHAPTER 9

1. 2, 1, 6, 4, 5, 3 (From page 400)
2. 2, 4, 1, 3 *or* 4, 3, 1, 2 (From page 396)
3. 3, 2, 1 (From page 403)
4. Before 1880, only Britain and France possessed colonies of any significance; the old empires of Spain and Portugal had declined almost to nothing. And even Britain and France did not devote much attention to empire, with the great exceptions of India, crucial for British trade and political prestige, and Algeria, which France claimed in 1830 and struggled for fifty years to subdue. True, Britain possessed a large "informal" empire of countries it dominated economically, but it did not seek to govern them. And although Canada, Australia, and New Zealand still belonged to Britain's "formal" empire, these countries had become largely independent by the late nineteenth century. As for

France, it controlled some dots of territory in West Africa, Southeast Asia, and the Caribbean but encouraged settlement only in Algeria, whose European population came mostly from Spain, Italy, Greece, and Malta rather than France. (From page 400)

5. France's cacophony of political voices revealed considerably more social equality than existed in many of its European neighbors. In Great Britain, just 2,184 landowners, with an average of 5,000 acres each, possessed fully half of the country's property. In France, 50,000 owners, averaging 250 acres each, together held only one-quarter of their country's land. The rest belonged to smallholding peasants, who remained France's largest social group, despite substantial migration to cities and towns. (From page 396)

CHAPTER 10

Paragraph order: 1, 3, 2, 5, 4, 7, 6

1. In "Thoughts for the Times on War and Death" (1915), Freud maintains that the common attitude of shock and disillusionment over the brutality and bloodshed of World War I reveals the public's ignorance about human nature. Freud argues that "civilized" Europeans have always been capable of terrible violence, since violence is inherent to human beings. Joseph Conrad largely shares Freud's view, while Ernest Renan and Erich Maria Remarque differ from both of them in maintaining that it is the state or other forces external to individuals that move them to act violently.

2. Addressing the public shock over the brutality of World War I, Freud writes, "our mortification and our painful disillusionment over the uncivilized behavior of our fellow-citizens of the world during this war were unjustified," based as they were on "an illusion to which we had given way" (Freud, 5–6). This "illusion" is the idea that the advanced state of civilization in Europe cured people of their natural capacity for violence. In fact, Freud says, society has merely "forced its members into . . . an unceasing suppression of instinct." During wartime, those instincts are no longer suppressed, resulting in the extreme violence of the war (Freud, 5).

3. Even before 1914, Conrad anticipated Freud's beliefs about the violence inherent to human beings. In *Heart of Darkness* (1899), Conrad portrays the unspeakable acts of brutality that "civilized" European imperialists committed against the native peoples of Africa's Congo region. Colonialism, declares Marlow, the book's protagonist, is "just robbery with violence, aggravated murder on a great scale, and men going at it blind" (Conrad, 7). Throughout his novel, Conrad suggests that individuals who behaved peacefully in Europe readily turned to violence in Africa, where there was no civilization to suppress their instincts.

4. Like Conrad, Ernest Renan anticipated Freud with regard to the European capacity for violence. In "What Is a Nation" (1882), Renan maintains that even within Europe itself, nations and peoples have throughout history been extraordinarily violent and bloodthirsty. The St. Bartholomew's Day massacre (1572), for example, left some 5,000 French Protestants dead. Events such as this are so terrible, Renan writes, that people must forget them in order to coexist as members of the same nation (Renan, 145). It is no surprise, then, that by the time World War I erupted, the European populace had forgotten the atrocious violence of the past.

5. Had he lived long enough to witness the First World War, Renan would have recognized, as Freud and Conrad did, that the violence of World War I was not unprecedented. Where Renan differs from Freud and Conrad is in his beliefs about the origins of this violence. Renan thinks it comes from sources external to individuals, especially religion and the state, and not from their own inherent inclinations, as Freud and Conrad believe.

6. At certain times, the state, in particular, encourages people to be merciless and violent, as the novelist Erich Maria Remarque underscores. In Remarque's *All Quiet on the Western Front* (1929), a young German soldier named Paul declares that the state has made him into a killing machine. Speaking of the enemy, Paul remarks, "a word of command has made these silent figures our enemies" (Remarque, 193–194). Here, the motivation to kill comes not from the individual himself, but from a command given by an authority figure representing the state. Unlike Freud, Remarque suggests that the individual has no inherent desire to kill.

7. Although World War I turned the world upside-down and horrified those who lived through it, there were thinkers and writers who saw the Great War as just

another expression of the brutality that had long been a part of "civilized" European culture. These writers differed, however, in their views of the sources of this violence—whether it came from within the individual or without. Less than twenty-five years after the end of the War, another bloody conflict would take the lives of an estimated sixty million people and revive this debate. Was violence innate to human beings or the result of living under governments that regularly called for violence to achieve their ends?

CHAPTER 11

The NEP did not allow the Soviet Union to industrialize quickly:

*   Russia needed high investment to build heavy industry like steel, automobiles, coal, electricity, and chemicals (1921–1928)
*   NEP's peasant-based market economy did not produce enough money to support industrialization (1921–1928):
*   Mediocre consumer-goods sector did not produce enough consumer products to buy, so peasants hoarded grain or produced less grain in the first place and ate more of their yield (1921–1928)
*   Breaking up large estates created "millions of mostly tiny plots" so there were no economies of scale in agriculture—many peasants could not produce larger crops even if they wanted to (1921–1928)
*   Russia could not attract significant foreign investment (1921–1928)
*   According to Stalin, peasants were the problem because they were unwilling or unable to sell enough grain (1927)
*   Stalin was disillusioned with NEP because it did not industrialize country fast enough (1927)

The NEP produced political repression:
*   Suppression of sailors' rebellion at Kronstadt naval base (March 1921)
*   The more free and open the economic system became, the more Russia's leaders clamped down politically (1921–1928)
*   Lenin expanded the secret police—(1921–1928)
*   Purge of Mensheviks (1922)
*   All parties were banned, except for the Bolsheviks (by 1923)

*   Organized religion was abolished (by 1923)
*   Democratic centralism—Bolshevik leaders agreed not to disagree in public—always presented completely unified front to the Russian people (circa 1923)

The NEP allowed Stalin to seize control of the Communist Party and turn the Soviet Union into an authoritarian state:

*   Stalin was appointed General Secretary of the Communist Party (1922)
*   As General Secretary, Stalin controlled bureaucratic appointments, so he appointed only people loyal to him (1922–1929)
*   Power struggle to succeed Lenin (1924–1929)
*   Bukharin, Trotsky, and Stalin fought for control of the Communist Party (1924–1929)
*   Trotsky expelled from the Party (1927) and banished from country after Bukharin and Stalin join forces against him. Trotsky assassinated in Mexico City in 1940.
*   Bukharin could not appeal to the Russian people for support because he believed in democratic centralism—he believed in a monolithic, authoritarian Communist Party
*   Bukharin expelled from Politburo (1929) (sentenced to death in "show trial" in 1938)
*   Communist officials probably agreed with Stalin more than Bukharin (1924–1929)
*   Stalin's first step once he gained full control: collectivization of Russian peasantry (beginning in 1927)
*   Stalin: "liquidation of the kulaks as a class" (1929)
*   "Terror famine" (1932–1933)

X On the whole, the NEP was a failure because it did not allow the Soviet Union to industrialize quickly, it produced political repression, and it allowed Stalin to seize control of the Communist Party and turn the Soviet Union into an authoritarian state. **(THESIS)**

*   The NEP did not allow the Soviet Union to industrialize quickly.
*   The NEP produced political repression.
*   The NEP allowed Stalin to seize control of the Communist Party and turn the Soviet Union into an authoritarian state.

NOTE: This paper would probably open with a paragraph conceding that the NEP was successful to a degree. And, in a conclusion, it might make the following points:

Real wages for other workers dropped by 50% across Russia (1928–1933). One writer has called the Soviet period from 1928 to 1933 "the culmination of the most precipitous peacetime decline in living standards known in recorded history." (From pages 515–520)

CHAPTER 12

NOTE: The punctuation used to set off supplemental noun phrases is mostly a matter of style. Dates, however, should be enclosed within parentheses.

1. By 1924, the German National People's Party (DNVP) had garnered 20 percent of the vote and stood as the country's second largest party after the SPD.

   Or:
   By 1924, the DNVP (the German National People's Party) had garnered 20 percent of the vote and stood as the country's second largest party after the SPD. (From page 546)

2. Members of traditionally monarchist social groups—teachers, professors, and administrators—did little to instill respect for democracy.

   Or:
   Teachers, professors, and administrators—members of traditionally monarchist social groups—did little to instill respect for democracy. (From page 546)

3. Nationalism, the ideology that glorified the nation, lay at the core of fascist belief.

   Or:
   The ideology that glorified the nation—nationalism—lay at the core of fascist belief. (From page 542)

4. Leni Riefenstahl, a talented dancer, actress, and filmmaker, is best known for her lyrical propaganda film, *Triumph of the Will* (1934).

   Or:
   A talented dancer, actress, and filmmaker, Leni Riefenstahl is best known for her lyrical propaganda film, *Triumph of the Will* (1934). (From page 529)

5. In Hitler's mind, the Final Solution—the genocide of the Jews—was already taking shape.

   Or:
   In Hitler's mind, the genocide of the Jews—the Final Solution—was already taking shape. (From page 569)

6. By the mid-1920s, *Il Duce* ("leader") had created an absolutist dictatorship built on political terror and mass propaganda. (From page 541)

7. In 1932, Riefenstahl read Hitler's book, *Mein Kampf*. (From page 530)

8. Kristallnacht ("Night of the Broken Glass") took a devastating toll. (From page 568)

9. In Hungary, where a fascist-style movement surfaced immediately after the war, the country's lack of democratic institutions prevented the fascists from taking control.

   Or:
   In Hungary, where a fascist-style movement surfaced immediately after the war, the lack of democratic institutions prevented the fascists from taking control. (From page 536)

10. The Nazi regime was the most extreme to emerge in Europe (outside of the Soviet Union), but Germany was far from alone in its rejection of liberalism and democracy. (From page 533)

CHAPTER 13

1. It was only after Mussolini's alliance with Nazi Germany in the late 1930s that Italian officials began to enact anti-Semitic laws. (From page 575)

2. What made this war especially dangerous for European civilians was the fact that the Germans decided to destroy or displace entire populations. (From page 579)

3. Despite these harsh conditions, most French men and women were relieved by the settlement with the Nazis. (From page 593)

4. The surviving officers were systematically murdered by Stalin's secret police.
   Or:
   It was Stalin's secret police who systematically murdered the surviving officers. (From page 591)

5. It was the Allied bombing of German cities that really brought the war effort home to the Reich's population.

   Or:
   What really brought the war effort home to the Reich's population was the Allied bombing of German cities.
   Or:
   The war effort was really brought home to the Reich's population by the Allied bombing of German cities. (From page 610)

CHAPTER 14

1. The Marshall Plan reduced deficits, improved worker benefits, and facilitated intra-European trade. (From page 642)
2. Dubček was arrested, his reforms annulled, pro-reform party members removed, and activist students dismissed from the universities. (From page 674)
3. Some Eastern European countries hoped to introduce market incentives. Others focused on freer speech and cultural expression. Still others wanted to end their communist party's monopoly of power. (From page 665)
4. Of the 24 men tried at Nuremberg, 12 received death sentences, three were acquitted, and the rest were sent to prison for terms varying from ten years to life. (From page 636)
5. In Kenya, British forces used torture, capital punishment, and prison camps to suppress the Mau Mau Revolt. (From page 658)
6. Between 1950 and 1952, Austrian exports increased by 89 percent, German exports by 87 percent. (From page 642)
7. Laws against "obscenity" were liberalized, and censorship of the theater abolished.

   Or:

   Laws against "obscenity" were liberalized, censorship of the theater abolished. (From page 669)

CHAPTER 15

1. On December 28, 1989, the new parliament voted to create a "market economy"; a month later the Communist Party ceased to exist.

   Or:

   On December 28, 1989, the new parliament voted to create a "market economy," and a month later the Communist Party ceased to exist. (From page 705)

2. Germany's political reunification was relatively easy; its economic reunification proved far more difficult.

   Or:

   Germany's political reunification was relatively easy, but its economic reunification proved far more difficult. (From page 719)

3. The USSR's economy had to be modernized; it needed a new "openness"—*glasnost* in Russian—to innovative ideas. (From page 682)

4. The great virtue of the Bretton Woods system was that it allowed for both stability and flexibility: stability in that importers and exporters would know the value of their country's currency; and flexibility in that countries could readily adjust their exchange rates.

   Or:

   The great virtue of the Bretton Woods system was that it allowed for both stability and flexibility—stability in that importers and exporters would know the value of their country's currency; and flexibility in that countries could readily adjust their exchange rates. (From page 684)

5. Cardinal Karol Wojtyla's crowning as Jean Paul II in October 1978 marked an extraordinarily important moment for Poland, because unlike other communist countries, it had retained its religious, Catholic identity. (From page 700)

6. Denouncing the protesters from the balcony of his party headquarters, Ceausescu was heckled and booed.
   Or:
   When Ceausescu denounced the protesters from the balcony of his party headquarters, the crowd heckled and booed. (From page 707)

7. Once in office, Kuchma channeled even greater resources to his backers.

   Or:

   Once Kuchma was in office, even greater resources would flow to his backers. (From page 723)

8. Having kept his people in penury, Ceausescu also ordered his ruthless secret police to crush even the mildest dissent. (From page 707)

9. Calling themselves the State Emergency Committee (SEC), they placed Gorbachev under house arrest, declared martial law, and sent tanks to Moscow as if it were Prague in 1968. (From page 713)

EPILOGUE

1. Add emphasis to "a movie."
   Together, Hirsi Ali and Theo van Gogh made a movie—a movie they intended as a merciless critique of the violence against women they both saw as embedded in Muslim culture.
2. Add emphasis to "two-year-long war."

The result was a murderous two-year-long war, a war in which Islamic radicals increasingly took over the Chechen resistance to Russian rule.

3. Add emphasis to "other acts of terror."
Beyond these horrific attacks, Europe has seen numerous other acts of terror, acts that have nothing to do with Islam or are carried out in opposition to it.

4. Add emphasis to "bleak suburban ghettos."
All too many Muslim immigrants are confined to bleak suburban ghettos—ghettos where children languish in subpar schools that fail to prepare them for university study or productive careers.

5. Add emphasis to "subpar schools."
All too many Muslim immigrants are confined to bleak suburban ghettos where children languish in subpar schools—schools that fail to prepare them for university study or productive careers.

6. Add emphasis to "a right-wing extremist."
The mass murder of seventy-seven Norwegians in 2011 was the work of a right-wing extremist, an individual who denounced Muslim immigrants, Marxism, political correctness, and people of color.

7. Add emphasis to "a Growth and Stability Pact."
In addition, the EU required all countries adopting the euro to sign a Growth and Stability Pact: an agreement that imposed stringent limits on budget deficits, inflation, and national debt.

8. Add emphasis to "the growing service sector."
Some European workers never found new employment and others were forced to take positions in the growing service sector—a sector where pay tended to be considerably lower and jobs less permanent than in the old manufacturing concerns.

9. Add emphasis to "intensely pro-European parties."
The big winners in the elections were intensely pro-European parties—parties that nonetheless advocated major reforms within the European Union.

10. Add emphasis to "massive victory."
The balloting gave Johnson and the Conservatives a massive victory—a victory that produced a huge majority in Parliament.